CAMBRIDGE GREEK AND LATIN CLASSICS

CICERO

DE RE PVBLICA

SELECTIONS

EDITED BY

JAMES E. G. ZETZEL

Professor of Classics,
Columbia University in the City of New York

PUBLISHED BY THE PRESS SYNDICATE OF THE UNIVERSITY OF CAMBRIDGE
The Pitt Building, Trumpington Street, Cambridge CB2 1RP, United Kingdom

CAMBRIDGE UNIVERSITY PRESS
The Edinburgh Building, Cambridge CB2 2RU, UK http://www.cup.cam.ac.uk
40 West 20th Street, New York, NY 10011–4211, USA http://www.cup.org
10 Stamford Road, Oakleigh, Melbourne 3166, Australia

First published 1995
Reprinted 1998

A catalogue record for this book is available from the British Library

Library of Congress cataloguing in publication data

Cicero, Marcus Tullius.
[De re publica]
De re publica/Cicero: edited by James E. G. Zetzel.
p. cm. – (Cambridge Greek and Latin Classics)
Includes bibliographical references and indexes.
ISBN 0 521 34465 4 (hardback) – ISBN 0 521 34896 x (paperback)
1. Political science – Early works to 1800.
2. State, The – Early works to 1800.
I. Title. II. Series.
PA6296.D8 1995
320.1 – dc20 94–12714 CIP

ISBN 0 521 34465 4 hardback
ISBN 0 521 34896 x paperback

Transferred to digital printing 2002

For Rosemary and David Coffin

animae, quales neque candidiores
terra tulit neque quis me sit deuinctior alter

CONTENTS

PREFACE

It is many years since there has been a commentary in English on any part of *De re publica* other than the *Somnium Scipionis*; there has never been a complete commentary in English. This edition will not fill that gap; but I hope that it will make accessible to students most of the surviving text of a book which, when complete, was one of the genuinely original works of ancient political and moral philosophy, and a text of great power and beauty as well. The format and goals of this series have made it necessary to abridge the text: I have included almost all of books 1 and 2 and the *Somnium*, but I have omitted, with regret, the discussion of eclipses and orreries in book 1, the surviving portions of the end of book 2, and the debate on justice in book 3, in addition to the scattered fragments of books 4 and 5. Had I included these passages, some more important or more comprehensible section would have had to be left out. The unfamiliarity of the text to most English-speaking students and the absence of any substantial tradition of exegesis in any language has led me to do more in the way of explanation and paraphrase than might otherwise be necessary. In general, I have tried to explain the argument and language; to adduce Ciceronian parallels for thought and diction; and to offer limited parallels and sources from other texts, both historical and philosophical. There is no apparatus, and I have kept discussion of textual problems to a minimum; there is also little here about the insoluble problems of early Roman history or about the reconstruction of lost sources. References to the immense secondary literature are relatively sparse: I have tried particularly to include works in English (unfortunately few), works too recent to have been included in Schmidt's 1973 bibliography, and studies of whatever date that have helped me most. The interpretation offered in the Introduction is necessarily brief and dogmatic; I have made another attempt to explain *De re publica* in its historical context in *Pegasus* for 1994, and I hope to publish a fuller analysis elsewhere.

This edition has taken longer to produce than I had originally hoped, and my obligations have only increased with time. I was originally encouraged to undertake it by the late Elizabeth Rawson, who has done more than anyone else in recent times to shape our understanding of Cicero. I am most grateful to the editors of this series for inviting me to edit *De re publica*, and for their forbearance, advice, and editorial acumen: Professor Kenney has emended every page of my commentary (the text of Cicero also, if less frequently). Pauline Hire and Glennis Foote of Cambridge University Press have also made numerous suggestions and improvements. For financial support, I am indebted to the National Endowment for the Humanities for a fellowship during which I wrote much of the first draft, and to Columbia University for the sabbatical and research leaves during which the edition was completed. Over the past seven years my students, both undergraduate and graduate, have used and made suggestions on portions of the commentary; in particular, I have profited from the ideas of David Clark, Riccardo di Giuseppe, Jerise Fogel, and G. Fredric Franko. Elizabeth Stambler read an early draft of the introduction, and Susanna Zetzel has read or heard more versions of it than either of us can remember; she also introduced me to the modern theory of republicanism and to the writings of this country's most Ciceronian statesman, John Adams. Good friends have read and improved all or most of this edition: David Coffin, Elaine Fantham, Erich Gruen, Robert Kaster, Peter White, and Peter Wiseman. All remaining errors and perverse interpretations are, needless to say, my own.

A book designed for students is an appropriate place to thank one's own teachers. I was fortunate enough as an undergraduate to study *De oratore* and *De re publica* with Glen Bowersock and Herbert Bloch respectively. David Coffin, Cilley Professor of Greek Emeritus at Phillips Exeter Academy, first introduced me to Cicero and to Latin grammar; I am relieved that he found slightly less to correct in this edition than he did in my papers long ago. Much of what I learned from all these teachers has made its way into this commentary, I hope without damaging alterations; to all of them I owe much. Above all, the friendship of David and Rosemary Coffin for more than thirty years has meant more to me than I can say, and certainly more than the dedication of this book could possibly convey.

Elizabethtown, NY J. E. G. Z.
July 4, 1994

ABBREVIATIONS AND REFERENCES

ANRW (edd.) H. Temporini–W. Haase, *Aufstieg und Niedergang der römischen Welt.* Berlin–New York 1972– .

*CAH*² *Cambridge Ancient History.* 2nd edn Cambridge 1970– .

FGH (ed.) F. Jacoby, *Die Fragmente der griechischen Historiker.* Berlin–Leiden 1923– .

FIRA (edd.) S. Riccobono *et al.*, *Fontes iuris romani anteiustiniani.* 2nd edn Florence 1940–3.

GLK (ed.) H. Keil, *Grammatici Latini.* Leipzig 1857–70, repr. 1961.

HRR (ed.) H. Peter, *Historicorum romanorum reliquiae*, Vol. 1 2nd edn Leipzig 1914.

H–S J. B. Hofmann–A. Szantyr, *Lateinische Syntax und Stilistik.* Munich 1965.

ILLRP (ed.) A. Degrassi, *Inscriptiones latinae liberae rei publicae.* 2nd edn Florence 1965.

K–S R. Kühner–C. Stegmann, *Ausführliche Grammatik der lateinischen Sprache.* 4. Auflage ed. A. Thierfelder. Darmstadt 1962.

LSJ H. G. Liddell, R. Scott, H. Stuart-Jones, *A Greek–English Lexicon*, 9th edn. Oxford 1940

MRR T. R. S. Broughton, *The Magistrates of the Roman Republic.* New York 1951, 1960; Atlanta 1986.

N–W F. Neue–C. Wagener, *Formenlehre der lateinischen Sprache.* 3. Auflage. Leipzig–Berlin 1892–1905.

OLD (ed.) P. G. W. Glare, *Oxford Latin Dictionary.* Oxford 1982.

ORF (ed.) H. Malcovati, *Oratorum romanorum fragmenta liberae rei publicae.* 4th edn Turin 1976.

RE (edd.) G. Wissowa *et al.*, *Paulys Real-Enzyklopädie der classischen Altertumswissenschaft.* Stuttgart 1894–1979.

SH (edd.) H. Lloyd-Jones and P. Parsons, *Supplementum Hellenisticum.* Berlin 1983.

SVF (ed.) H. von Arnim, *Stoicorum ueterum fragmenta.* Leipzig 1903–24.

TLL *Thesaurus Linguae Latinae.* Munich 1900– .

Abbreviations of classical authors and texts follow *OLD* and LSJ; it should be noted that *R.* and *Lg.* refer to Plato's *Republic* and *Laws*, while *Rep.* and *Leg.* refer to Cicero's equivalent works.

Cross-references within any one book give chapter and sentence numbers only; in case of possible ambiguity, a section sign (§) is used. For ease of reference, all republican dates and the spelling of all proper names of Roman magistrates conform to those given in *MRR*.

INTRODUCTION

1. CONTEXT

When Cicero looked back in 44 on the impressive series of philosophical treatises that he had composed during the preceding decade, he differentiated between the works written after the Civil War and *De re publica*, which he said he had written *cum gubernacula rei publicae tenebamus*.[1] In the years from 54 to 51 when he was writing it, however, the helm of the ship of state seemed far from his grasp. At the end of October 54, he wrote to Atticus that 'there is no Republic any longer to give me joy and solace'; two months later, he wrote in a similar vein to his brother Quintus.[2] C.'s despair at the quality of public life at Rome began nearly a decade earlier. The moment of his greatest public triumph came on 5 December 63, when he was hailed as *pater patriae* and escorted home by grateful citizens of all classes after the execution of the Catilinarian conspirators; but less than a month after that, one of the new tribunes (Metellus Nepos) prohibited the customary speech of a retiring consul on the grounds that C. had put citizens to death without a trial.[3] Over the next few years, dissension between senatorial and equestrian interests, and between followers of Pompey and the optimate oligarchy, disrupted the civic consensus of 63 which C. had shaped and led; he found himself unappreciated by Pompey, scorned by the optimates for his *nouitas*, and attacked by *populares* (above all, P. Clodius Pulcher) for violating the rights of citizens. His

[1] *Div.* 2.3. Text and discussion of all the Ciceronian evidence for the composition of *Rep.* in Heck 17–21; for the background to *Rep.* cf. also Pfligersdorffer 7–11. The account given here is summary; for details of C.'s life between 63 and 51, the most useful modern accounts are those of Gelzer 105–218; Rawson (1975) 89–145; and T. Mitchell 63–203. For the historical background, cf. Wiseman in *CAH*² IX 327–423.

[2] *Att.* 4.18.2 (cf. 4.20.2); *Q. fr.* 3.7.2. Translations of Cicero's correspondence are from D. R. Shackleton Bailey, *Cicero's letters to Atticus* (Cambridge 1965–8 = Harmondsworth 1978) and *Cicero's letters to his friends* (Harmondsworth 1978 = Atlanta 1988). The complaint was not new: during the turmoil of Caesar's consulate in 59 he had complained to both Quintus and Atticus of the death of the Republic (*Q. fr.* 1.2.15, *Att.* 2.25.2).

[3] Cf. 1.7.1n.

exaggerated sense of his own importance and of the strength of his support left him increasingly vulnerable as the coalition of Pompey, Caesar, and Crassus known as the First Triumvirate took shape at the end of 60, and through the violent and frightening events of Caesar's consulate in 59. His lack of strong political connections and the hatred of Clodius (who became tribune at the end of 59) led to his exile in early March of 58; he was banished for having put citizens to death without trial, and his property was confiscated.

Although after his return from exile in September 57 C. attempted to reassert himself and to play a significant political role, he found little encouragement or support. He felt betrayed by the optimates and by Pompey; he was appalled at the short-sightedness and intransigence of Cato and his allies; he had a vivid sense of the precariousness of his own position as politics became increasingly polarized and violent. In March 56 C. delivered *Pro Sestio*, an elaborate defence of his own career and the traditional constitution; but shortly thereafter he gave in to the domination of the dynasts. For the next five years, although he remained active in the courts, he largely withdrew from public affairs. With the exception of a few speeches (notably *Pro Milone* of 52) he cooperated with the dynasts, defended their supporters, and abstained from active politics. Between 56 and 51, he wrote two major poems (now lost), one on his own deeds and one on Caesar's; he also wrote his two most elaborate and original theoretical works, the three books of *De oratore* (completed by November 55), and the six books of *Rep.*[4] The three years which C. took for *Rep.* are longer than the time taken to compose the entire collection of philosophic works written under Caesar's dictatorship: a treatise *de optimo statu ciuitatis et de optimo ciue*, as he described it to Quintus, was C.'s political testament, and a work dear to his heart.[5] *Rep.* was made public at the time of C.'s reluctant departure in the spring of 51 to assume the governorship of

[4] For *De temporibus suis* and the epic on Caesar, cf. Soubiran 33–41, 51–4. During this period C. also wrote much, if not all, of *De legibus*, which was however never published during his lifetime and was probably never completed. For the most thorough analysis of the chronological problem, see Schmidt (1969) with the comments of Rawson (1991) 125–9; for its implications for the interpretation of *Rep.*, see below, pp. 27–8.

[5] *Q. fr.* 3.5.1. C. judged himself against the standard of the ideal statesman he described in book 6; cf. *Att.* 7.3.2.

Cilicia;[6] the care and effort that went into its composition reflect his devotion to the collapsing institutions of republican Rome.

2. COMPOSITION, SETTING, FORM

For his first dialogue, *De oratore*, C. chose a dramatic setting in his own lifetime, with speakers whom he had met and heard. It takes place in the autumn of 91 B.C.E. on the eve of the outbreak of the Social War; the protagonist is the orator Crassus, one of the leading conservatives in the politics of the time.[7] In approaching the composition of *Rep.*, C. chose a similar scene a generation earlier: Scipio Aemilianus and his friends, conversing early in 129 B.C.E., during the crisis over the legal powers of the Gracchan land commission. Within a few months of beginning work, however, C. reconsidered his plan. In October 54, C. wrote to his brother, his friend Sallustius (not the historian) had listened to a reading of the draft of the first two books of *Rep.* and had objected to the choice of setting.[8] C., Sallustius said, was an eminent statesman, and should speak on public affairs in his own voice, not through other characters; he should not imitate the dialogues of the Platonist Heraclides of Pontus, which were set in a distant and fictitious past and in which the author took no part,[9] but should follow Aristotle, who was the major speaker in his own dialogues.[10] The setting in the distant past, according to Sallustius, made *Rep.* seem fictional. Sallustius' criticisms made sense (*Q. Fr.* 3.5.2):

> This shook me, all the more so as I was debarred from touching upon the greatest upheavals in our community because they took place after the lifetimes of the interlocutors. In point of fact that was my object at the time, to avoid giving offence in any quarter if I came into contact with our own period. Now, while avoiding

[6] *Fam.* 8.1.4 (Caelius to C.) *tui politici libri omnibus uigent.*

[7] For Crassus' influence on C., cf. Rawson (1991) 16–33.

[8] *Q. fr.* 3.5.1–2.

[9] Cf. Schmidt (1969) 27–8, against the interpretation of Wehrli on Heraclides fr. 24.

[10] The works of Aristotle that C. knew were the 'exoteric' works, including the lost dialogue *Politicus*; cf. *Att.* 4.16.3, where he refers to the prefaces of these works. He almost certainly did not know the *Politics* or the *Nicomachean Ethics* directly.

> this, I shall speak myself in conversation with you; none the less I shall send you what I had begun when I return to Rome. I think that you will appreciate that it cost me some heartburning to give up those two books.

The letter is not entirely clear, but the change described here probably resulted in the form that we have: a dialogue set in the past, in order to avoid offending contemporaries, but with prefaces addressed to C.'s brother Quintus (to whom the dialogue is dedicated), in which he could touch on more immediate concerns than the dramatic setting of the dialogue would permit. What emerges is – to use the terms C. himself employs in this letter – a combination of Heraclides and Aristotle: the colour given by the evocation of great men of the past, and the credibility given by the weight of the author's own voice.

Why did C. give *Rep.* a dramatic date more than twenty years before his own birth? 'To avoid giving offence in any quarter' is his own explanation; and the offence he feared was political.[11] After his confrontation with Caesar and Pompey in 56, he had no interest in raising their hackles by an honest discussion of the problems of his own time; and if he did not mean to be honest, there was little point in writing about public life at all. But the choice of a distant setting had positive merits as well as the defensive value of self-protection: in particular, it was a means to evoke the model uppermost in Cicero's mind, the dialogues of Plato.

[11] Schmidt (1969) 33–41 interprets the letter differently; in particular, he suggests that the offence C. wanted to avoid by the historical setting was the omission of the names of friends to whom he was indebted, but the parallel passages he cites are not germane. The main difficulty in interpretation lies in the sentence (3.5.2) *nunc et id uitabo et loquar ipse tecum et tamen illa quae institueram ad te, si Romam uenero, mittam.* The most plausible meaning is (1) 'I will avoid offence' (i.e. by setting the dialogue in the past); (2) 'I will speak to you in my own voice' (i.e. in the prefaces of the dialogue); and (3) 'I will still send my first draft to you' (even though I am going to have to alter it to accommodate the new style of preface). Schmidt understands (1) and (2) to mean 'I will avoid offending friends by addressing you alone' (because, since a brother is a special case, there will be no cause for offence at the omission), and thus that C., at the time of the letter, was planning to revise *Rep.* to be a two-person conversation set in the present. That such a work would be far less compelling than the extant dialogue does not need demonstration, and it is hard to imagine C. entertaining it for long enough to write this letter. A third interpretation of (2), 'I will talk it over with you' is not possible, as Quintus was in Gaul.

The dialogues that C. created in *De orat.* and *Rep.* were something new in Latin literature. The jurisconsult M. Brutus seems to have written his *responsa* in the form of a conversation with his son, and Varro's *Menippean Satires*, some in dialogue form, were probably written before C.'s dialogues. But in essence, the Ciceronian dialogue is an original creation: it is largely Platonic in inspiration, with the addition of prefaces in his own voice after the model of Aristotle's dialogues.[12] The closeness with which C. studied Plato is revealed by *Att.* 4.16.3, in which C. says that the character of Scaevola in *De orat.* was drawn from Cephalus in the *Republic*: just as in that work the old man only takes part in the first book and then withdraws, so too C. felt that the aged Scaevola should not take part in a long conversation on technical rhetoric. In *Rep.* as in *De orat.*, the Platonic model influences setting as well as content: just as in most of the dialogues the dramatic date is well before Plato's own maturity and the protagonist is Socrates, who was long dead at the time of writing, so too C. sought to recreate portions of his own intellectual ancestry. In C.'s third Platonic dialogue, *De legibus*, the situation is very different: that work (whenever it was written) has a contemporary setting and C. is his own protagonist, just as in Plato's *Laws* the principal speaker is not Socrates, but the anonymous Athenian (generally understood to be Plato himself). C. shaped his own two political dialogues to emphasize the parallels with Plato's works; and as the ostensible purpose of *Leg.* was to make suggestions about law and government in C.'s own time, a past setting would have been as inconsistent with his subject as with his model.

Rep. is set in the past for many reasons: it was politically expedient to do so, and it was a function of its literary model. More than that, the choice of setting is an important ingredient in C.'s argument. In both *De orat.* and *Rep.* the dialogue takes place just before the sudden and unexpected death of its protagonist; each is presented as if it were the last tranquil moment before Rome took a decisive downward turn, and each reports the inspired last words of a great statesman. The conversation of Scipio and his friends is the vehicle for C.'s argument, but it is also an illustration of the ideal behaviour of Roman senators.

[12] On C.'s dialogues and their background, cf. Hirzel I 433–93 and Zoll 25–72; Schütrumpf provides detailed study of C.'s use of Plato in *De orat.*

Similarly, the transmission of knowledge and experience from one generation to the next is simultaneously extolled and displayed.[13] Scipio has learned from the previous generation – Cato, Manilius, and the dream-vision of his grandfather – the proper conduct of public life; and the reader of *Rep.* sees him transmit what he has learned to Scaevola and Fannius, Tubero and Rutilius. The setting of *Rep.* is meant to give a background for the setting of *De orat.* and the education of C. himself, and the links between the two works are important: Q. Mucius Scaevola the Augur, present in *Rep.* as the son-in-law of Laelius and as a representative of the younger generation, was the father-in-law of Crassus and the senior participant in the conversation of *De orat.* in 91; P. Rutilius, one of the other junior members of the cast of *Rep.* and C.'s alleged source for the conversation, was the uncle of C. Cotta, one of the junior members of *De orat.* and C.'s alleged source for that dialogue.[14] The chain of connection with the great statesmen of earlier days was important to C. in providing a pedigree, however fictional, for his own ideas. That the two dialogues present the final thoughts of Crassus and Scipio as delivered to their younger protégés is meant to offer a retroactive aetiology for C.'s own work in writing them: he offers his own considered reflections to the next generation in the guise of reporting the similar words of his own heroes to their successors. The dramatic setting is not the frame: it is part of the picture.

The conversation of *Rep.* takes place at a precisely defined place and time that readers were expected to recognize and appreciate. The participants gather on the estate of Scipio just outside Rome, during the *Feriae Latinae* early in 129 B.C.E., four years after the tumultuous tribunate of Tiberius Gracchus.[15] Gracchus, acting with the advice and support of senior members of the Senate, including the *princeps senatus* Appius Claudius Pulcher (Gracchus' father-in-law, cos. 143)

[13] The presence of two generations is seen as a Platonic trait by Zoll 63.

[14] C. returned in 44 to the same milieu for *De senectute*, a conversation between the elder Cato, Scipio, and Laelius in 150, and *De amicitia*, a conversation between Laelius and his sons-in-law Fannius and Scaevola shortly after Scipio's death in 129.

[15] The most important modern account of Tiberius Gracchus remains that of Earl (1963); cf. also Badian (1972), Bernstein, and Stockton 23–94. Astin (1967) 190–226 examines Gracchus' tribunate in the context of Scipio's life.

and the brothers P. Mucius Scaevola (cos. 133) and P. Licinius Crassus Dives Mucianus (to become pontifex maximus in 132, cos. 131), had promulgated a law for the distribution of *ager publicus* to landless citizens under the supervision of an agrarian commission with considerable judicial powers. A majority of the Senate had opposed this proposal; the tribune M. Octavius, who had attempted to veto Gracchus' legislation, had been removed from office; the law had been passed and Gracchus had financed it through a law devoting the estate of Attalus III of Pergamum, bequeathed to Rome in that year, to the purposes of the agrarian law; and, in seeking re-election to the tribunate, Gracchus had been killed in rioting by a mob led by the pontifex maximus, P. Cornelius Scipio Nasica Serapio. The strong divisions aroused by the agrarian law, by the tactics of Tiberius and his allies, and by the violent death of a sacrosanct tribune of the *plebs*, had long-lasting repercussions: for C. as for other conservatives, the tribunate of Gracchus was a terrible illustration of popular rule gone wild, a sign of the failure of the traditional aristocratic constitution of Rome.

During the year of Gracchus' tribunate, Scipio was absent from Rome in Spain, commanding the final siege, surrender, and destruction of Numantia. His position on the substantive issues of the agrarian law is not clear, but Gracchus, although Scipio's first cousin and his brother-in-law,[16] was his political opponent, the son-in-law of his greatest rival, Appius Claudius. Scipio Nasica, the leader of the mob against Gracchus, was also Scipio's cousin. In 131, the tribune Carbo asked Scipio in a public gathering his opinion of Gracchus' death and Scipio's response, though guarded, is not sympathetic to Gracchus: *si is occupandae rei publicae animum habuisset, iure caesum uideri.*[17] The result of both the Gracchan legislation and its aftermath was a great loss of popularity for Scipio, a man who had built his career on popular, rather than senatorial, support; in the last year or so of his life he emerged as the leader of senatorial opposition to the Gracchan law.[18]

[16] Gracchus' mother Cornelia was the daughter of the elder Scipio Africanus, Scipio's grandfather by adoption; his sister Sempronia was Scipio's wife.

[17] For the various versions of Scipio's comments on the death of Gracchus, cf. Astin (1967) 263–6.

[18] For Scipio's last years, cf. Astin (1967) 227–41; in general, Astin's interpretation of Scipio is followed here.

Although the agrarian law was popular among Roman citizens, it created considerable unhappiness among the non-citizen inhabitants of Italy, particularly because they were subject, in their view unfairly, to the judicial powers of the land commission. Early in 129, at Scipio's urging, the Senate transferred the judicial powers of the commission to the consul Sempronius Tuditanus until the complaints of the Italians could be considered. Scipio apparently intended to propose passage of a law permanently to weaken or end the judicial powers of the commission, but before anything could be done, he died unexpectedly in his sleep. It seems probable that his death was natural, but C. in *Rep.* (6.12.4) implies that he was murdered.[19]

It is during the disturbances (*hoc praesertim motu rei publicae*, 1.14.3) surrounding Scipio's proposal to suspend the judicial powers of the land commission that the conversation of *Rep.* takes place.[20] The question of the treatment of Rome's allies by the Gracchans is important within the dialogue, as it was in 129: Laelius in 1.31.4 refers to the disturbance of the allies and the violation of treaties, and at 3.41 he repeats the charge that the Gracchans have neglected the rights and treaties of the allies; in the *Somnium Scipionis* the dream-figure of the elder Africanus places the allies and Latins at the climax of a list of those who look to Scipio as a leader (6.12.3). Laelius, in fact, made the mistreatment of the allies by the Gracchans the final sign of the deterioration of Rome from *ius* to *uis*, and thus a portent of its ultimate decay and demise. It may also be significant that C., in his revision of *Rep.*, changed the dramatic date from the *Feriae nouendiales*, which took place to expiate an unknown portent in 129, to the *Feriae Latinae*, which commemorated the treaty between Rome and the Latins.[21]

[19] On Scipio's death, cf. Astin (1967) 241. The evidence for a natural death is found in a corrupt fragment (22 *ORF*) of Laelius' funeral oration for Scipio, on which see Badian (1964) 249 and (1971) 1–3.

[20] The *Feriae Latinae* have no fixed date, and the date of Scipio's death is unknown; it is thus impossible to determine exactly what chronology C. had in mind. Scipio died just after the passage of the *senatus consultum* on the judicial powers of the agrarian commission, and the dramatic date of *Rep.* must be earlier than that.

[21] The *Feriae nouendiales* were normally connected to the portent of a rain of stones (cf. Wissowa 301–2) and thus may have had nothing to do with the portent of the double sun discussed in 1.15ff. (although C. may have thought that they did); Pohlenz 78 believes they were related. On the connection

There are nine participants in the dialogue: four young men, four older men, and the protagonist, Scipio.

P. Cornelius Scipio Aemilianus Africanus (*RE* Cornelius 335), consul in 147 and 134, censor in 142, the destroyer of Carthage in 146 and of Numantia in 133, was the son of L. Aemilius Paullus, who defeated the Macedonians at Pydna in 168; he was adopted by P. Cornelius Scipio, the son of the great Africanus. Born probably in 185, he was one of the dominant public figures of the second century, renowned equally for his political and military skills and for his cultural attainments. His natural father appropriated the library of the Macedonian kings for his use; he was taught by the historian Polybius, who left a memorable record of conversation with Scipio as a youth (31.23–30), and he was later friendly with the Stoic philosopher Panaetius. Among his Latin literary associates were the satirist Lucilius and the comic poet Terence. Scipio is by far the most prominent speaker in the surviving portions of *Rep.*: it is he who is asked by Laelius (1.33.3) to speak about the *optimus status ciuitatis*, and who consequently delivers lengthy speeches about the theory of constitutions and the development of the Roman constitution in books 1 and 2 respectively; he apparently summarized and extended the argument about justice in book 3; and it is his dream which concludes the work.[22]

C. Laelius (*RE* Laelius 3), given the cognomen Sapiens for his wisdom and judgment, was consul in 140; he was Scipio's elder and his closest friend throughout his life; his father had been equally close to Africanus. In 132 he played an active role in the *quaestio* set up to prosecute the supporters of Tiberius Gracchus. In the opening portions of *Rep.*, Laelius' scepticism about the worth of astronomical discussion turns the conversation to political theory; throughout the first two books, he is Scipio's principal interlocutor; and in book 3, he delivers

of the *Latinae* with the treaty, see Macrob. *Sat.* 1.16.16–17, D. H. 6.95.2–3; also Scullard 111–15. The first version (described in *Att.* 4.16.2 and *Q. fr.* 3.5.1) reveals three other differences from the extant text: Sp. Mummius is not listed as a speaker; there were to be nine books, not six; and there were to be prefaces in each book, not alternate books.

22 For Scipio's life and career, see Astin (1967). For the sake of clarity, in this edition 'Scipio' refers to Scipio Aemilianus, while 'Africanus' refers to his grandfather, the conqueror of Hannibal.

the (unfortunately very fragmentary) argument that a state cannot survive without justice.

L. Furius Philus (*RE* Furius 78), consul in 136, is frequently grouped with Scipio and Laelius in the ancient sources (see below, pp. 12–13). As consul he was in charge of the inquiry into the treaty made by the consul C. Hostilius Mancinus and the Numantines in 138 (and negotiated by Mancinus' quaestor, Ti. Gracchus), resulting in the repudiation of the treaty and the surrender of Mancinus to the Numantines. His major contribution in the extant portions of *Rep.* is in book 3, where he reluctantly delivers a version of Carneades' argument that a state cannot exist without injustice.

M'. Manilius (*RE* Manilius 12), consul in 149 and one of the great jurists of his age, is the representative in *Rep.* of the generation before Scipio, who was his subordinate in 149 at the opening of the Third Punic War (6.9.1).[23] He apparently spoke in book 5, but he says very little in the extant portions of the text.

Sp. Mummius (*RE* Mummius 13) never reached the consulate. His brother Lucius, the destroyer of Corinth, was Scipio's colleague in the censorship of 142, during which the two had serious disagreements; Spurius himself, with L. Caecilius Metellus Calvus, took part with Scipio in the embassy to the eastern Mediterranean in 140–139 on which the philosopher Panaetius also accompanied Scipio.[24] C. (*Brut.* 94) reports that he was a Stoic, and also that he sent witty verse letters to his friends when he was at Corinth with his brother (*Att.* 13.6.4). He says almost nothing in the extant portions of the text, but was apparently a representative of anti-democratic views (cf. 3.46–8).

Q. Aelius Tubero (*RE* Aelius 155), the son of Scipio's sister Aemilia, held the tribunate at an uncertain date before 129. He was a serious Stoic, to whom Panaetius and his pupil Hecaton dedicated works, and he attempted to apply his philosophy to the study of law.[25] His impractical rigidity (ridiculed by C. at *Mur.* 75–6) caused him to

[23] Manilius was certainly over 60 in 129; according to *Rep.* 3.17, he was already speaking in public (albeit as an *adulescens*) before the passage of the lex Voconia in 169. For his writings (*monumenta* and *actiones*), cf. Schanz–Hosius I 239; Schulz 90, 92.

[24] For the embassy, see Astin (1967) 127 with further references.

[25] A collection of testimonia in Schanz–Hosius I 222.

fail as a candidate for the praetorship.[26] He says little in the extant text; he is the first to arrive at Scipio's villa, and raises the question of the portent of the double sun (1.15.1).

P. Rutilius Rufus (*RE* Rutilius 34), consul in 105, was only in his late 20s at the dramatic date of the dialogue. A protégé of Scipio and military tribune under him at Numantia, he was a pupil of Panaetius and renowned for his Stoic rectitude. He was (almost certainly unjustly) convicted of extortion in the 90s and went into exile in Smyrna, in the province which he had allegedly wronged,[27] and where C. visited him and supposedly heard from him about the conversation reported in *Rep.* (1.13.2), nearly fifty years after the event. His autobiography may have been one of C.'s genuine sources for the historical circumstances.[28] He does not speak in the extant portions of the dialogue.

Q. Mucius Q.f. Scaevola (*RE* Mucius 21), consul in 117, known as Scaevola Augur to distinguish him from his homonymous younger cousin, Scaevola Pontifex. The son-in-law of Laelius and father-in-law of L. Crassus, he was a renowned jurist, whom C. himself knew late in Scaevola's life. He is one of the participants in the conversation of book I of *De orat.* In the extant portion of *Rep.* he speaks only one sentence (1.33.1).

C. Fannius M.f. (*RE* Fannius 7), consul in 122, also a son-in-law of Laelius. Like Laelius and Ti. Gracchus, he served under Scipio at Carthage in 147–146.[29] C.'s statement at *Am.* 25 that Fannius was not present for the conversation of *Rep.* must be taken as an error, but in fact he does not speak in the extant portions of the work, and it is

[26] On the chronology of his career, cf. Sumner (1973) 70–1.

[27] In *De orat.* 1.230, he is described as having defended himself as if he were in Plato's *Republic.* On the circumstances of his trial, see Badian (1956) and Bauman 382–400; sources listed by Alexander 49.

[28] For his autobiography and historical writings (fragments in *HRR*), cf. Schanz–Hosius I 208–9. Fr. 3 refers to the philosophers' embassy of 155; cf. also 1.17.4n.

[29] C. himself was confused about the distinction between the Fannii, two homonymous cousins (one M.f., the other C.f.), one of whom was a historian (cf. *Brut.* 99, 101; *Att.* 12.5.3), and much is still uncertain; for brief discussion with further references, cf. *MRR* III 89–90.

possible, as Mai thought, that he left after the first day's conversation.[30]

The setting of *Rep.* is itself a work of careful scholarship, but its historical accuracy may well be questioned. As far as the content of the conversation is concerned, there is no reason to believe that anything said in *Rep.* is an accurate reflection of anything ever said by any of the participants: the conversation with Sallustius reported in *Q. Fr.* 3.5 makes it clear that the fiction was recognized by contemporaries. We do know, however, that C. took great pains to make the settings of his dialogues true to history: he did not group figures who were not actually associated with one another, and he attempted (with notorious lack of success in the *Academica*) to ascribe to his characters views that were not inconsistent with their actual opinions, knowledge, and interests. Scipio, Laelius, and the rest were leaders of the state, and they were engaged at the dramatic date of the dialogue in concerted action against the Gracchans, focusing specifically on the issue of the treatment of the Italians; that much is completely accurate. The philosophically inclined Tubero is made to raise the scientific question that begins the dialogue; Laelius is as practical and learned as he apparently was in real life; Scipio's account of Roman history makes use of Polybius, as the real Scipio might have done. But that they ever engaged in a learned discussion of political theory and Roman institutions in the fashion of a Platonic dialogue – and that they did so on the last holiday before Scipio's death – is very unlikely.

The significance of the group of figures gathered in *Rep.* is a more difficult question. C.'s dialogues have long been used as evidence for the reconstruction of second-century intellectual history, in particular for a 'Scipionic Circle' which was the centre of diffusion for enlightened Greek ideas, composed of men who were patrons of letters as well as models of *humanitas* and *urbanitas*. That idea has been generally discredited. Scipio, Laelius, and Furius Philus are frequently linked with one another for their shared cultural interests, and in particular for their connection with Terence; but there were other patrons of letters, and there is no evidence for a coherent cultural programme on the part of Scipio and his friends, much less that they

30 On the question of Fannius' presence, see Heck 35–6 with references.

were the sole oasis of Hellenic civilization in the desert of Roman culture.[31]

Indeed, it is in the portrait of Scipio and his friends as models of humane and decent behaviour and as advocates of strict constitutionality that C.'s portrait is most inaccurate. Scipio himself was a proud and ambitious aristocrat, who seems to have been notably harsh in meting out judgments and punishments. More important, his career was marked by extreme legal irregularities in both his elections to the consulate, and Astin is surely right to argue that it is the career of Scipio himself, who 'had created a situation of exceptional and extreme factional hostility in which popular appeal was a key factor', which made possible the actions, and the disaster, of Tiberius Gracchus' tribunate.[32] For C. to make him the advocate of constitutionalism and adherence to the *mos maiorum* may reflect the political position of his last year, but does not do justice to his career as a *popularis* and his repeated violations of customary procedure. The portrait of Scipio and his friends drawn by C. is both moving and compelling, but it is an ideal vision of the Roman past, not the truth.

3. ARGUMENT, STRUCTURE, SOURCES

(*a*) *The two* Republics

The title and the preface of *Rep.* draw attention to C.'s use of Plato's *Republic*.[33] Similarities between the two are evident: each concerns the relationship between citizen and state; each discusses the nature of justice; each offers a theory of constitutions; each contains an elaborate discussion of education; and each concludes with a vision of an afterlife designed to reaffirm the ideals set out in the work itself.[34] A few

[31] On the 'Scipionic Circle' cf. Astin (1967) 294–306 and Zetzel (1972); full bibliography in Schmidt (1973) 287–9. Rawson (1991) 80–101 discusses the shared interest of Scipio, Laelius and Furius Philus in religious matters. The connection with Terence is rightly questioned by Gruen (1992) 197–202.

[32] Astin (1967) 226.

[33] In fr. 1b Ziegler, C. described himself as Plato's *comes*.

[34] For clear summaries of the major similarities between C. and Plato, cf. Pohlenz, How, and Sharples; bibliography in Schmidt (1973) 309–10. The fullest comparison is that of Pöschl, but much of his argument is unconvincing.

passages of *Rep.* are directly based on *R.*: at 1.66–8, C. translates a section of *R.* 8; part of Philus' speech in book 3 denying the possibility of just government draws on Glaucon's speech in *R.* 2 (3.27 from 2.359–62); and in the introduction to the *Somnium Scipionis* (6.3–4) there seems to have been an explicit reference to the Myth of Er in *R.* 10.[35] There are also frequent reminiscences of the style of Platonic dialogue: the arrival of the interlocutors at 1.14–18, the Socratic conversation at 1.56–63, the silence that follows the end of Scipio's speech at 2.64.[36]

Although *R.* is a constant presence in *Rep.*, it serves more as foil than as model; as Sharples rightly says: 'Cicero's *Republic* is, in a sense, Plato's turned inside out.'[37] Both C. in the introduction (1.2–3) and the characters in the dialogue draw attention to the shortcomings of Plato's work: that it is inconsistent with human behaviour; that its educational theories are abhorrent; and above all that it is not based on the real life of states (cf. 2.3.2, 22.2, 51.1). The emphasis of the two works, moreover, is quite different: Plato begins from justice in the individual soul, uses the analogy of the state to identify and define it, and returns at the end to the rewards of individual virtue. C. on the other hand is concerned with states and political virtue; the discussion of justice (book 3) is subordinated to the discussion of government, and the justice with which he is concerned is primarily that of states, not individuals. While Plato's justice is based on the internal relationship of the parts of the soul or the state, C.'s is also an aspect of the external relationships of individuals or nations. As Pohlenz saw, the difference in the dramatic settings of the two works is emblematic of C.'s revision of Plato: *R.* takes place in the house of a foreigner during the festival of

[35] Cf. *Rep.* 6.3–7. The Epicurean Colotes had criticized the improbability of Er's death and return to life twelve days later, and C. made a point of distinguishing Scipio's dream from Er's vision. It is probable that C. had Scipio himself remark on the difference between the two, just as at *De orat.* 1.28 Scaevola draws attention to the imitation of Plato's *Phaedrus* in which he is a character.

[36] There are also a great many allusions to or borrowings from other Platonic (and pseudo-Platonic) works; C. translates from *Phaedrus* at 6.27–8, and also makes use of *Apology*, *Crito*, *Phaedo*, *Phaedrus*, *Gorgias*, *Politicus*, *Timaeus*, *Laws*, *First Alcibiades*, and *Axiochus*; for references, see General Index. Boyancé (1970) 222–300 studies a number of specific problems.

[37] Sharples 30.

the Thracian goddess Bendis, and concludes with the mystical vision of the Pamphylian Er, all emblematic of the universal application of Plato's ideas; *Rep.* presents a conversation of Roman aristocrats in Scipio's villa during the *Feriae Latinae*, and concerns Roman government and Roman history.[38]

The most extended imitation of Plato, the *Somnium*, reveals the differences most clearly. Plato's Myth of Er is meant to be the final proof that justice is better than injustice for the individual: it concerns the journey of the soul in the afterlife, describing punishment and rewards for earthly actions and the choice of a future earthly existence. The *Somnium* is occasioned by Laelius' complaint that Scipio Nasica (who had led the mob which murdered Tiberius Gracchus) had received no public statues to honour his actions; Scipio replies that true virtue needs more substantial and lasting rewards than statues and triumphal garlands.[39] He then narrates the dream, the purpose of which in context is to show that public service is a divinely sanctioned and divinely rewarded activity; the afterlife and the nature of the soul are subordinated to the proof of the importance of civic life in the here and now. The Myth of Er, moreover, refers only metaphorically to the physical structure of the universe in which we live, which Plato describes as a set of whorls revolving around the spindle of Necessity; for C. in the *Somnium*, geography and astronomy are crucial, demonstrating at once the literal centrality of the earth – and therefore of its governance – in the order of the universe, and the triviality of human glory in comparison with the celestial glory of the world to come. The Myth of Er and the *Somnium* provide transcendent summations of the concerns of the works which they conclude; nevertheless, the ideals which they represent are antithetical. Aside from C.'s allusions and borrowings from *R.*, what the two works have most in common is a shared concern with justice and moral behaviour; but Plato is interested in individual morality, while for Cicero the justice of an individual has no meaning apart from the state to which he belongs.

In addition to his importance as a literary model, however, Plato for C. stands at one pole of a set of antitheses that runs through *Rep.*,

[38] Pohlenz 77.

[39] *Rep.* 6.8 *illa diuina uirtus non statuas plumbo inhaerentes nec triumphos arescentibus laureis, sed stabiliora quaedam et uiridiora praemiorum genera desiderat.*

between the Greek, theoretical, and abstract on the one hand, and the Roman, historical, and practical on the other. In the preface to book 1, this polarity takes the form of the contrast between the active and the speculative life (1.2.1); in the opening of book 2, between Cato's *Origines* and Plato's ***Republic***. Scipio, like Crassus in *De orat.* (and C. himself), represents a synthesis of the two extremes: an experienced statesman, who is knowledgeable about both Greek political theory and Roman history, and is therefore capable both of theoretical analysis of the Roman constitution and of taking action on the basis of his knowledge and experience.[40]

The antithesis between theory and history, between the general and the particular, informs the entire structure of ***Rep***. The dialogue takes place over three days, and the work accordingly falls into three pairs of books, in each of which a theoretical analysis is followed by a more historical one. The stages of the discussion are marked by prefaces in C.'s own voice, introducing books 1, 3, and 5. In book 1, C. offers a general introduction to the subject of the work, including justifications of political activity and of C.'s own writing of the dialogue, followed by a description of the dramatic setting. In book 3, he appears to have used the mind–body dichotomy as the starting-point for a discussion of the importance of human reason in the development of society and institutions, praising above all else the art of politics and the practical manifestation of that art in the great figures of Roman statesmen of the past, particularly the protagonists of the dialogue. In the one surviving excerpt from the preface of book 5, after quoting Ennius' famous verse *moribus antiquis res stat Romana uirisque* (156 Sk.) he describes and laments Rome's decline from the grandeur of an earlier day.

The direction of the prefaces – moving from governmental institutions and history in book 1, through the moral and psychological underpinnings of society in book 3, to the relationships between individual character and civic health in book 5 – accords with the direction of ***Rep***. as a whole. The first two books concern the cycle of constitutions and the general theory of the mixed constitution (book 1), balanced by an account of the particular development of Roman government in terms of this theory (book 2). In the central portion of the dialogue, a pair of antithetical speeches on the possibility of justice

[40] Cf. 1.36.2n.

in government (based on the famous speeches of Carneades in 155)[41] leads to recapitulation of the discussion of constitutions in book 1, arguing for the necessity of a moral basis for all legitimate government (book 3); this general analysis, in turn, seems to have been balanced by a concrete discussion of Roman education and the inculcation of moral values in early Roman society (book 4). The final pair of books dealt first with the general qualities desirable in the true statesman, the *rector rei publicae* who is capable of guiding the state when needed (book 5), then with the particular behaviour of the Roman statesman at times of crisis, especially the Gracchan crisis (book 6); this leads, at the end of the whole work, to the *Somnium Scipionis*, providing a description of the posthumous rewards awaiting the true statesman. The separation between theoretical and empirical analysis, however, is not complete; and since the ideal statesman combines both abstract knowledge and practical experience, one should not expect it to be. The loss of most of the last four books makes it impossible to reconstruct C.'s procedure, but it appears that as his topic became ever more precisely focused in the second half of the work on the role of the individual statesman, the context in which the qualities of the statesman are seen expands from Rome to the entire cosmos.

(*b*) *The theory of constitutions*

The starting-point for the argument of *Rep.* is Laelius' question (1.33.3) about the best form of state, *optimus status ciuitatis*, to which Scipio gives a long and involved response. After an extremely compressed definition of the *res publica* (1.39), a brief discussion of the origins of society (40–1), and the introduction of the three simple forms of good government (monarchy, aristocracy, and democracy, 42), Scipio describes in summary form the drawbacks of each and their common tendency to degenerate to the corresponding bad form

[41] The sceptic Carneades was head of the Academy in 155; together with the Stoic Diogenes and the Peripatetic Critolaus he was sent to represent Athens before the Roman Senate, and while in Rome delivered a pair of speeches in which he first argued in favour of the necessity of justice, and then argued against it (cf. Long 104–6). In Cicero's version of the speeches in book 3, the argument against justice delivered by Philus is refuted by Laelius' speech in favour of justice; for analysis of the two, cf. Ferrary (1974) and (1977).

(tyranny, oligarchy, and ochlocracy respectively, 43–4). He then discusses the various permutations among the six types, expressing his preference for a form of government that is a mixture of the three primary forms (45). At this point, Laelius interrupts to ask which of the three simple forms Scipio prefers (46); the response comes in the form of speeches delivered from the point of view of a democrat (47–50) and an aristocrat (51–3). Laelius then repeats his question; Scipio expresses a preference for monarchy (54–5), and after further prodding conducts a Socratic discussion with Laelius demonstrating, on the basis of a series of analogical arguments, the superiority of the rule of one man to all other forms of government (56–61). The contrast between kingship and tyranny (62–4) leads back to the instability and cycle of the simple constitutions, including an extended translation from *Republic* 8 (65–8), and, finally, to a renewed verdict in favour of the mixed constitution (69).

The theory of constitutions underlying Scipio's speech bears a strong resemblance to that set out by the second-century Greek historian Polybius (who was in fact a friend of Scipio; see p. 9 above) in book 6 of his *Histories*. Furthermore, both C. and Polybius were clearly drawing on a Peripatetic source in which the same basic scheme was deployed: the three simple constitutions, their degenerate equivalents, the fundamental instability of them all and the permutations among them, and the superiority and greater stability of a mixed constitution combining elements of all three. The idea of the mixed constitution goes back to Plato, but it was elaborated in the generation after Aristotle by his pupils; and C. had certainly read works on political theory by both Dicaearchus and Theophrastus as well as being deeply indebted to Polybius himself.[42] And yet, there are striking differences between C.'s version of the mixed constitution and that of Polybius, whose theory involved a fixed cycle of simple constitutions, progressing from primitive monarchy to kingship to tyranny to aristocracy to oligarchy to democracy to ochlocracy and back to primordial chaos.

[42] For C.'s familiarity with Dicaearchus and Theophrastus, cf. *Att.* 2.9.2, 12.4, 16.3. On C.'s Peripatetic sources, cf. among earlier studies Solmsen, and Pöschl 10–39; among recent ones Frede. Further bibliography in Schmidt (1973) 297–9 and Suerbaum (1978) 69–71. On the theory of the mixed constitution in general and C.'s use of Polybius in particular, cf. von Fritz, Cole (1964), and Walbank 130–56.

Instead, Scipio states both that any one of the three primary forms may be the original constitution of a state, and that virtually any order of succession is possible.[43] He also believes (and in book 2 illustrates from Roman history) that the transformation from a good to a bad form of any of the simple constitutions can occur through a change of character in the same rulers, rather than necessarily involving a change of personnel. Furthermore, C. rejects Polybius' belief that the origin of society was to be found in human weakness rather than natural sociability, and he locates the strength of the mixed constitution not in a system of checks and balances but in the appropriate exercise of different capacities by the different elements of society.[44] Finally, C. does not employ, at least in book 1, the biological analogies traditional in Peripatetic theory and in Polybius: there is no discussion of the birth, growth, and decline of constitutions, merely a description of them.[45]

In his account of the theory of constitutions, in other words, C. appears to treat his sources with as much liberty as he treats Plato; and even disregarding the question of sources, Scipio's account is puzzling. Why, for instance, does Scipio state a preference for monarchy over the other simple forms of constitution? Why are the arguments for democracy and aristocracy presented in the words of their advocates, in closely parallel speeches almost certainly drawn from a Peripatetic source, while Scipio himself presents the argument for monarchy? Why is the argument for monarchy conducted in terms so different from those for democracy and aristocracy?[46] The approval expressed by Scipio for monarchy is so elaborate, and that for the mixed constitution so perfunctory, that one can only question Scipio's (or C.'s) faith in the theory presented; but in a work in which pure theory is rejected, that is scarcely surprising.

The difficulties of the speech begin, in fact, with the definition of *res*

[43] On this, cf. Sharples 36–9.

[44] Cf. Cole (1964) 466–7.

[45] For biological imagery cf. Walbank 142–4. It should be noted that biological analogies are employed in book 2, which also derives from Polybius; cf. 2.3.2n.

[46] These questions have been raised in a great many studies of *Rep.*; the most careful analyses remain those of Solmsen, and Pöschl cited in n.42. The missing speech on monarchy has been the subject of heated debate; cf. 1.50n.

publica. As Scipio suggests, it is a provisional definition, and the true meaning of the definition of the *populus* as *coetus multitudinis iuris consensu et utilitatis communione sociatus* is not in fact settled until the higher meaning of justice seen in terms of natural law is explained at the end of book 3.[47] A major function of the debate between democracy and aristocracy which follows is, however, if not to give a single meaning to the crucial terms of the definition, at least to explore the competing claims of various parties to control the language of political debate, the meanings in particular of *populus*, *libertas*, and *aequabilitas*.[48]

For the democrats (1.47–50), *res populi* to be meaningful can only be taken in its strongest sense, not merely as popular sovereignty but as popular rule. The state in which the *populus* controls legislation, courts, and foreign affairs is the only true republic: *hanc unam rite rem publicam, id est rem populi, appellari putant* (1.48.3). Equality, too, must be taken in the strong sense of equal access to political power, *par . . . condicio ciuium* and *iura . . . paria* (1.49.2–3). But both Scipio, in his previous summary of the qualities of the three types, and the aristocrats in their speech of rebuttal, reject these meanings of the terms; they reject *aequabilitas* as *iniqua* (1.43.1, 53.1–2), preferring instead the recognition of natural *dignitas* under the banner of *aequitas*, proportional rather than arithmetical equality. From this point of view, the *populus* is not the entire body of citizens, but the masses; liberty consists in passive rather than active rights; justice consists in proportional rather than equal distribution of power and distinctions.

In the terms in which this debate is set, there is little need for advocates of monarchy to have a role. From the point of view of a democrat (and even in Scipio's summary in 1.43.1), both kings and aristocrats suppress liberty; from that of an aristocrat, neither monarchy nor democracy recognizes an equitable distribution of power and rights. The argument in favour of monarchy is totally different, and emphasizes the problems of administration rather than the problem of rights. That argument is a minor element in the first half of Scipio's speech: it appears in his own comments on administrative structures and their weaknesses in 1.42, 44–5, and the argument

47 Cf. 1.39.1n.

48 For the meaning of terms, cf. on 1.42.6, 43.1, 50.1. The semantic arguments may explain some of the peculiar linguistic turns of these speeches; cf. esp. on 1.49.2, 50.3, 51.4, 51.5.

that even democracies need to delegate authority plays a part in the aristocratic critique of democracy (1.51.2, 53.1). But in Scipio's argument in favour of monarchy, practical concerns are paramount: *imperium, quod quidem nisi unum sit esse nullum potest* (1.60.5).

The argument for monarchy does not involve a claim to control the political catchwords of justice, liberty, and equality. Instead, Scipio offers a set of arguments in favour of the actual universality and priority of a single strong executive. The order of Scipio's arguments is significant. Starting from the kingship of Jupiter and the universal belief in a single ruler of the universe, Scipio turns to the historical priority of monarchy at Rome (56–8). At that point, the basis of the argument changes from *testes* to *argumenta* (59) – that is to say, from arguments about kingship itself to arguments in favour of unitary control based on the workings of the mind (59–60) and of the household (61). In the final portion of the discussion, he turns back from analogical reasoning to the political sphere once more. On the one hand, he introduces the problem of the degeneration of monarchy to tyranny; on the other, he uses the example of the Roman dictatorship to sever executive authority in general from monarchy in particular.[49] The final paragraph, on the virtues of Romulus and the later decay of the monarchy into tyranny (64), leads back to the cycle of constitutions and the translation of Plato's description of ochlocracy in *Republic* 8.

The two halves of the discussion of simple constitutions, then, have not only different structures but different goals. The arguments for democracy and aristocracy concern the virtues of government, the true meanings of equality and liberty, and the best ways to embody them in a state. The argument for monarchy concerns not the virtues of government but its necessities: the need for a single locus of executive authority and the problems of the apportionment of power. Neither half of the argument is exclusively directed toward one of these goals: the first half deals briefly with administration, the second with justice and injustice; but the overall difference of emphasis is clear. So too is the relationship of the two halves of the speech to the remainder of *Rep.*: the discussion of *libertas*, *aequabilitas*, and the meanings of *res populi* and *iuris consensus* is resumed in the second half of book 3, where the

[49] 1.63; cf. Büchner 68–77.

definition of *res publica* is refined and altered in the light of the debate on justice, and where it is shown that the degenerate constitutional forms, which do not respect justice, have no claim to be called *res publicae* at all in the absence of *iuris consensus*. So too, the *prima causa coeundi* of 1.39.1 is taken up again at 4.3. The argument for monarchy has two functions: on the one hand, the references to Romulus and Tarquinius Superbus point ahead to the account of Roman history in book 2; on the other, the discussion of executive authority was presumably elaborated and refined in the discussion of the *rector* in books 5 and 6. Scipio's speech on the mixed constitution, while never abandoning the traditional framework of constitutional theory, uses it to discuss the far more general issues of rights and obligations, of authority and power.

(*c*) *History and theory*

The influence of Polybius extends beyond the constitutional theory of book 1. In the sixth book of his *Histories*, Polybius paused from his narrative of the Second Punic War to give an account of Roman government and social organization in which he tried to explain the success and stability of Rome. In this account, he included not only a description of the cycle of constitutions and of the ideal mixed constitution (exemplified, for him, by Sparta and Rome), but a history of the development of Roman government up to the fall of the Decemvirate, and a detailed analysis of the Roman constitution as he knew it in terms of the mixed constitution. After a description of Roman military organization, he returned at the end of the book to a comparison between Roman and Carthaginian government. The similarity between the opening parts of book 6 and the structure of the first two books of *Rep.* has long been apparent: in particular, the juxtaposition of the theory of constitutions and the 'archaeology' matches the arrangement of *Rep.* 1.38 – 2.63.[50]

In the historical account of book 2, what C. most clearly derives from Polybius is the chronological framework (for which he cites Polybius explicitly at 2.27.4) and the belief that Rome attained its

[50] For the relationship of *Rep.* 2 to Polybius' 'archaeology', cf. Pöschl 40–107, von Fritz 123–54, Walbank on Polybius 6.11a and Ferrary (1984).

mixed constitution with the Valerio-Horatian laws of 449.[51] C.'s version of the growth of the Roman constitution is, however, considerably more complicated. While Polybius almost certainly used his rigid scheme of the succession of simple constitutions in describing the history of Rome, C. takes great pains to emphasize elements of mixture in Rome from the very beginning: Polybius compared the Lycurgan constitution at Sparta (the best Greek government, in the view of the Peripatetics) to the constitution of the middle Republic, but C. compared it to the regime of Romulus (2.15.1). C. repeatedly emphasizes aristocratic and democratic elements in the monarchy, and he seems to attribute the fall of both monarchy and aristocracy (in the Decemvirate) to their failure to recognize the need for due mixture in the constitution. Furthermore, C. tempers Polybius' insistence on the natural progress (κατὰ φύσιν) of the cycle by emphasizing instead the role of *consilium* and the *prudentia* of individual statesmen in shaping the development of Rome. There is a *natura rerum publicarum* and an *iter naturale* of political development, but it is the task of the statesman to anticipate such developments and to direct them (cf. 2.30, 45, 57.1). Thus, at the very beginning of Roman history, Romulus knew enough to co-opt the support of *optimus quisque* in creating a proto-senate and Numa voluntarily asked the people to confer *imperium* on him (2.15.1, 25.2); the founder of the Republic, L. Iunius Brutus, recognized *in conseruanda ciuium libertate esse priuatum neminem* (2.46.2); the consuls of 449 are described as *hominum concordiae causa sapienter popularium* (2.54.1). Just as the bad behaviour of individuals (Superbus, Appius Claudius) can lead to political upheaval, so the *ratio* of the great statesman can avoid it and lead the state on a proper course.

Not enough of Polybius' 'archaeology' survives to permit thorough comparison, but it seems likely that here as elsewhere C. maintained his independence from any 'source': although he admired Polybius' history, and readily borrowed his chronology, he distrusted the theory in which it was embedded. Just as Plato's scheme for reconstructing human society paid no attention to human nature, so Polybius' attempt to fit Roman history into the Procrustean bed of a fixed

[51] Polybius was not C.'s only historical source; he certainly used Cato's *Origines* and knew other works, including those of Licinius Macer and Cornelius Nepos. For C.'s historical knowledge and methods, cf. Rawson (1991) 58–79 (63–6 on *Rep.*); for a survey of cited sources, cf. Krarup (1956) 182–4.

pattern of constitutional development paid no attention to the untidiness of human affairs. C.'s account not only criticized the idea that the simple constitutions ever existed in pure form in Rome, he rejected the rigid dogmatism that elevated constitutional form over individual action.[52]

Throughout *Rep.*, forms of government matter far less than the men who shape them. The two-fold description of the subject of *Rep.* which C. gave to Quintus, *de optimo statu ciuitatis et de optimo ciue* (*Q. fr.* 3.5.1), is in fact an important element in the structure of *Rep.*, overriding the division into three days. The first half of the work largely concerns government as a whole (although, as discussed above, individuals play a large part even there): in book 1, constitutions; in book 2, Roman history; and in book 3, the debate over whether any government can be just. The second half is far more concerned with individuals: the educational and social institutions that produce good citizens in book 4; the general characteristics of the *rector* in book 5; and the particular behaviour of the statesman in crisis in book 6.

The central concern of *Rep.* is not the detailed examination of constitutional forms, but the interrelationship between social institutions (including government) and the individuals who both preserve and are produced by them. At the end of Scipio's account of Roman history in book 2, Tubero objects to what Scipio has said on the grounds that he has given a panegyric of Rome rather than an exposition of constitutional theory based on the example of Rome (as he had said that he would in 1.70), and that he had not explained *qua disciplina quibus moribus aut legibus constituere uel conseruare possimus* (2.64). The topic of *leges* is taken up in book 3; book 4 concerns the *disciplina* and *mores* which can lead to the preservation of states, and of Rome in particular. C. praised the educational and social institutions of early Rome as a means of rearing virtuous citizens; he attacked Plato's views of education, property, and the family. Law and education, the topics of the central books of *Rep.*, are the middle terms between the state and its members: by establishing good laws and a good education, the state forms citizens who will in turn reinforce the institutions which have shaped them. That point is made explicit in the preface to book 5. In

[52] C.'s use of Polybius and Plato in book 2 is the subject of Ferrary (1984), perhaps the best introduction to the problem of C.'s sources.

deploring the decline of Rome from its early glory, C. argues that without the *mores* of old the great men of early Rome would not have existed, nor, without the great men, would the ancient *mores* have prevailed: 'Ancestral custom itself provided outstanding men, and great men confirmed ancient custom and the institutions of our ancestors' (5.1). Good customs and good men are mutually interdependent; a good constitution is not enough, unless it produces individuals who are willing to serve and preserve it.

(*d*) *The best citizen*

The preface to *Rep.* describes public life as the closest approach of human beings to the divine; *Rep.* ends with the dream-exhortation of Africanus to the same effect: the soul of the man who has been concerned with the safety of his country will return more rapidly to its celestial home. The divinity of the human soul, the importance of contemplation both of the physical heavens and of the universal order which they manifest, the existence of transcendent and immutable moral standards to which earthly governments and individual humans must conform – all these are central to *Rep.*, and are the beliefs which show C. to be more a Platonist than the explicit comments on Plato in *Rep.* would lead one to expect.[53]

The universe itself and the divine ideals embodied in it frame and shape the argument of *Rep.* The topic appears in the opening discussion of the dialogue, concerning the prodigy of the double sun: when Laelius objects to a discussion of such irrelevant matters, Philus replies,

[53] The question of C.'s philosophical sources is difficult. Few now would say that *Rep.* was derived from a single philosophical source, be it Panaetius, Posidonius, or Antiochus of Ascalon, all of whom have been made the virtual authors of all or part of it. C. was widely read in Greek philosophy, particularly on political and ethical subjects; when he describes the subject of *Rep.* as *locus magnus philosophiaeque proprius a Platone, Aristotele, Theophrasto totaque Peripateticorum familia tractatus uberrime* (*Div.* 2.3), there is no reason to believe that he had not read them all. C. himself claimed to be a moderate Academic in the mould of his teacher Philo of Larisa; it is also likely that he was influenced by the syncretistic views of Antiochus of Ascalon, who believed that the ethical ideas of the older Academy, the Peripatetics and the Stoics were compatible with one another – which may explain C.'s willingness to mix Stoic, Platonic and Peripatetic ideas in *Rep.* On the influence of Antiochus, see now Barnes.

in Stoic terms, by arguing that the entire universe is our home; and, more practically, that the knowledge of astronomy is actually useful (1.21–2). In this he is supported by Scipio, who then delivers a speech (1.26–9) on the importance of philosophical knowledge in general: that it imparts a proper perspective on the unimportance of human affairs; that it releases men from petty concerns about their own well-being; and that, above all, philosophical learning is the defining characteristic of human beings.

The cosmos plays an important role within the argument of *Rep.* as well. In his demonstration of the superiority of kingship, Scipio uses the analogy of the single ruler of the universe; at the end of book 2, in using analogies from nature, Scipio introduces the model of musical harmony, and may well have made the *rector* the counterpart in the state to the Demiurge of Plato's *Timaeus* in the universe.[54] The crucial passage, however, is Laelius' speech on justice in book 3, in which he asserts the universality of natural law, which he equates with right reason. Both individual and universe are ruled by the divine principle of right reason; each is eternal; the nature of each is congruent with natural law. And it is only through the extension of the law of the universe to the behaviour of states (which are not natural beings and therefore have no soul to be the repository of natural law) that those states can be preserved. The conclusion of Laelius' speech is deeply pessimistic: the improper actions of Gracchus and his trampling on the rights of citizens, allies, and Latins will lead to the death of Rome: 'I am worried about our descendants, and about the immortality of the Republic: it could have been eternal, if we lived by ancestral institutions and customs' (3.41). At the end of the book, the recognition of a transcendental standard of justice leads to a revision of the definition of *res publica* offered at 1.39: only a state that is just has any right to be considered a state at all.[55]

The statesman and the universe, in both its physical and moral aspects, come together at last in the *Somnium*. From the contemplation of the cosmos in the opening dialogue of book 1, Scipio and his

[54] Cf. Ferrary (1984) 97–8.

[55] It should be emphasized that the high ideals of Roman statesmanship upheld in *Rep.* are very clearly only ideals. Laelius' speech places the immortality of Rome in a contrary-to-fact condition, and Scipio, the prospective saviour of Rome in the *Somnium*, died before accomplishing his goals.

fellow-statesmen become literally a part of the cosmos; the support of just government on earth is rewarded by eternal happiness in the universe governed by its own *rector*; the pettiness of human aspirations to earthly glory is transformed, through the order of the world, to participation in the glory of the whole. C.'s argument in the preface, defining *uirtus* as moral action and public service as the highest form of moral action, receives its confirmation in the final words of Africanus in the dream.

Ancient philosophy classified politics as a branch of ethics; modern experience does not. It is scarcely surprising that a text on public affairs by a politician should be interpreted as a practical work: in this century *Rep.* has been interpreted as an anticipation of the principate or a plea for Pompey to become dictator;[56] as a call for an extra-constitutional charismatic leader;[57] or most recently, as a blueprint for the restoration of the conservative Roman constitution of the middle Republic.[58] Such pragmatic interpretations are mistaken for a number

[56] This interpretation of the *rector* is most closely associated with the names of R. Reitzenstein and E. Meyer; their views were rebutted by Heinze 141–59 (originally published 1924); How 36–42 and Meister (1939) 57–73 provide useful summary and criticism of the controversy. There are several useful surveys of the issues: Lepore 9–19 has a lucid exposition of the strands of modern scholarship and their origins in Mommsen's attacks on Cicero; Schmidt (1973) 323–32 provides a guide to the vast bibliography; and Krarup (1956) 197–205 (English summary) provides a straightforward exposition of the evidence.

[57] Most explicit in Reitzenstein's reply to Heinze (362): 'Das Wort [sc. *princeps*] aber sollte nur den "Führer" und die "Führernatur" bezeichnen, die auch wir jetzt für die Regeneration unsres Volkes ersehnen.' The pervasiveness of such ideas in Pöschl (for 'political and national renewal', cf. p.9) diminishes considerably the value of his book. For bibliography on Nazi use of *Rep.*, cf. Suerbaum (1978) 80–1; the blatant misuse of *Rep.* by Pöschl and others presumably inspired Syme's description of *Rep.* as 'a book about which too much has been written' (*Roman Revolution* (Oxford, 1939) 144 n.1). The question of the *princeps* has indeed been discussed too much; Rawson (1975) 152 understood it best: 'Had Machiavelli known the *De Republica* ... he would have seen here something like his own doctrine of the *riordinatore*.'

[58] This is the interpretation of Girardet (1983), a much more detailed – and therefore less plausible – version of Schmidt's beliefs (cf. Schmidt (1973) 320–3). In so far as the pragmatic interpretations are directed against overly mystical or idealizing readings, they are valuable, and have been supported by

of reasons: some overestimate the importance of the constitutional theory of book 1, forgetting that it was a much smaller part of *Rep.* complete than it is of the fragment we possess; some rely on reading *Rep.* and *Leg.* as companion texts, even though *Leg.* was not issued with *Rep.* and was probably never completed;[59] and all require that *Rep.* be read as if it were a political pamphlet, not an elaborate and carefully composed philosophical dialogue. Cicero's subject is ethics, and the concern of pragmatic critics is power; the two are not the same thing.

At the same time, however, *Rep.* reflects the political world in which it was written. C.'s *rector* is not Pompey, but he cannot be understood without remembering the rise of dominant individuals who acted outside the framework of the constitution. *Rep.* is not a battle-plan for the forces of reaction, but C. was indeed appalled by the decay of Roman institutions from the virtuous Republic of an earlier generation. *Rep.* reflects C.'s genuine belief in a traditional structure of authority dominated by the *auctoritas* of the Senate, guaranteeing social stability and ruled by respect for property and status; he believed that the individual *auctoritas* of pre-eminent members of the ruling class should direct both the policies of the state and the behaviour of its citizens.[60]

many scholars for many years; but the strong form of the pragmatic interpretation as adopted by Schmidt and Girardet is untenable.

[59] It is indicative of the weakness of such arguments that Schmidt's massive study (1969) of the date of *Leg.* devotes only four pages (of 290) to the question of completion. *Leg.* is now incomplete; there is no mention of it in the list of C.'s writings at *Div.* 2.1–4; there is no detectable allusion to it anywhere in C.'s correspondence. Even if what we have of *Leg.* was largely written in the late 50s, as Schmidt argues, it is improbable that C. expected his readers to interpret the theory of *Rep.* in the light of the legislative details of *Leg.*, a work which was certainly not issued at the same time, even if it may have been completed (then or later). Schmidt (1973) 290 also advances an argument on the relationship of the drafts of *Rep.* and *Leg.*: that C. kept the first two books of the nine-draft version (changing only the holiday on which the conversation took place) in the final text, reduced the remaining (unwritten) seven to four by cutting out material, and then used the excised material (with the contemporary setting that Sallustius recommended for *Rep.*) to write *Leg.* This is unlikely for many reasons: not least are that the chronology of C.'s letters shows that he never even started a draft with a contemporary setting; that the law-code of *Leg.* has no conceivable place in *Rep.*; and that *Leg.* in any case had at least five books, not just the three now extant.

[60] For clear recent summaries of C.'s political ideas (not just in *Rep.*) cf. Wood 90–142 and T. Mitchell 9–62; for *Rep.* in particular, cf. How and the

There can be little doubt that C. would have been overjoyed if the good old days had returned, but for him that would involve not so much the reform of institutions as the reform of individual attitudes about government, morality, and civic responsibility. Ultimately the subject of *Rep.*, like that of its Platonic model, is broadly ethical, not narrowly political. And like the later theorists of classical republicanism in the Renaissance and after, C. believed that there is a direct relationship between the virtuous conduct of citizens and the successful governance of states.[61] That belief went out of fashion shortly before the palimpsest of *Rep.* was discovered; perhaps it deserves to be revived.

4. STYLE

The most striking feature of the style of *Rep.* is its range of styles.[62] There are conversational interludes, philosophical argumentation, historical narrative, and the high rhetorical style of the prefaces and a few set speeches, including Scipio's praise of philosophy at 1.26–9 and the whole *Somnium*. Hence there is a range of discourse from the colloquial to the elevated, and a range of diction to match. Stylistic variation in C. is not confined to the dialogues; the orations too move from the plain to the ornate, from narrative to exclamation. All C.'s public writings have certain broad stylistic tendencies in common: a concern with purity of diction, particularly the avoidance of un-

fuller treatment in Lepore. That C. in *Rep.* is not presenting a political programme is not surprising, as that was not in the nature of Roman public life. Earl (1967) 17 rightly observes: 'At Rome, politics dealt with individuals and factions, not political parties, with personalities, not programmes'; he offers (11–43) a clear exposition of Roman political morality and behaviour in the Republic.

[61] So especially Montesquieu, *Spirit of the Laws*, book 5. On the theory of classical republicanism, see above all J. G. A. Pocock, *The Machiavellian moment* (Princeton, 1975); for the separation of virtue from government in the 1780s in America, cf. G. Wood, *The creation of the American republic, 1776–1787* (New York, 1972) 606–15.

[62] For a general treatment of C.'s style, cf. von Albrecht, *RE* Suppl. XIII 1237–1347; earlier works of value include Lebreton, Laurand, and Laughton. No special study has been made of the style of the dialogues; for particular aspects, cf. Fantham (1972) 137–75 on imagery in *De orat.*, Bréguet (1964) on archaism in *Rep.*, and von Albrecht (1989) 102–11 on *Rep.* 6.25–6.

familiar or inappropriate words;[63] great regularity of morphology and syntax; and constant attention to the structure and rhythm of sentences.[64] That is true no less of *Rep.* than of C.'s orations.

There are, however, differences between *Rep.* (and other dialogues) and C.'s orations. In terms of diction, one of the most noticeable mannerisms in the dialogues is C.'s taste for the prefix *per-* (cf. 1.9.1n.), at home in urbane conversation. Archaisms are more prevalent in *Rep.* than in any other work of C., perhaps reflecting his desire to recreate the historical milieu of Scipio and his friends. Whatever the reason, of the seven archaisms listed at *De orat.* 3.152–3 as making a speech *grandior et antiquior*, four appear in *Rep.*[65] Archaic colour appears in a number of ways: in the use of words no longer current (e.g. *opitulari* 1.10.4; *erus* 1.64.3; *accire* 2.25.1; *penes* 2.62.2); in the use of words in an obsolete sense (e.g. *quando* for *cum* 6.27.1; *propter* for *prope* 1.17.2; *tempestas* for *tempus* 2.11.2; *templum* as an augural term 6.24.3); in the use of archaic forms (*reapse* 1.2.1; gerundives in *-undus* rather than *-endus* 2.27.2, 44.1; passive infinitive in *-ier* 2.59.1; *ferme* for *fere* 1.65.2 and elsewhere; genitive and dative *plebei* 2.63.1); and in the use of archaic word-types such as *soliuagus* (1.39.2), *alienigena* (2.25.1), and *stellifer* (6.18.3).[66] Closely related to archaism are two other features of the style of *Rep.*, the use of quotations from archaic poetry, notably from Ennius, and the use of the highly conservative language of the law, such as *exceptio ... extra quam si* (1.10.1), the play on the language of *uindicatio* at 1.27.2, or on *quaerere* and *respondere* at 1.30.2, and the use of future imperatives (most frequently found in legal texts) at solemn moments. As Bréguet points out, the archaic tone is concentrated in passages of importance and solemnity, or which refer to the early

[63] C. in general follows the advice of his contemporary Caesar (cited by Gellius 1.10.4): *ut tamquam scopulum, sic fugias inauditum atque insolens uerbum.*

[64] C. was particularly attentive to the rhythm of the ends of clauses or sentences (clausulae), generally based on spondaic (– –), trochaic (– ⏑), or cretic (– ⏑ –) elements. Little will be said in this edition about prose rhythm or about sound patterns in general: C.'s concern with them is so pervasive that it needs no demonstration. On the difficult and technical subject of prose rhythm, cf. Habinek; a good introductory account in Wilkinson 135–64.

[65] *tempestas* for *tempus* (2.11.2); *proles* (2.40.1, 6.23.1); *effari* (5.1); *nuncupare* (2.14, 6.16.1).

[66] For archaisms in *Rep.* see esp. Bréguet (1964) and von Albrecht, *RE* Suppl. XIII 1255–7, 1298.

history of Rome itself; the same passages are often marked also by the use of alliteration, another characteristic of archaic style. At the other end of the spectrum is C.'s use of colloquialism to create the impression of lively conversation, as in the opening dialogue or the Socratic debate between Scipio and Laelius at 1.56–62. The use of *tam mane* at 1.14.2 is colloquial; so too *quo Ioue* at 1.56.2, *ain* (1.19.4), initial *uero* (1.58.2), *ualde* (1.58.3), and the imperative *cedo* (1.58.7). Syntactically, the conversation is marked by the frequent elliptical expressions of real speech.

In general, the style of *Rep.* is marked by relative simplicity of syntax: long sentences are generally paratactic; there is relatively little use of ablative absolute constructions; relative clauses are frequent. The style of the dialogues has been justly compared with C.'s own descriptions of epideictic rather than forensic style, particularly in the use of extended metaphors as a mode of argument.[67] Important analogies of this sort include the ship of state (e.g. 1.11.1; cf. 1.1.3n.), cultural influence described in terms of a river (2.34.2) and philosophical self-possession in terms of legal ownership (1.27.2), and biological growth used to describe the progress of a state or society (2.3.2 etc.). Another feature that deserves notice is the extensive use of antithesis: C. uses *non ... sed* more than thirty times in the first two books. This kind of amplification is used in order to give clarity and concreteness to the ideas presented; the same is true of the extensive use of pleonasm (cf. 2.15.1n.) and of repetition, of demonstratives, and of logical particles (*nam, enim, igitur, autem*).[68]

An illustration of some of these stylistic mannerisms can be found in C.'s discussion of *uirtus* in the preface (1.2.1):

> Nec uero habere uirtutem satis est quasi artem aliquam nisi utare; etsi ars quidem cum ea non utare scientia tamen ipsa teneri potest, uirtus in usu sui tota posita est; usus autem eius est maximus ciuitatis gubernatio, et earum ipsarum rerum quas isti in angulis personant reapse non oratione perfectio.

Adversative elements (*cum ea non utare* ~ *scientia tamen ... potest*; *reapse non oratione*); logical particles and conjunctions to make the reasoning clear (*etsi, cum, tamen, autem*); the use of demonstratives, particularly *is*;

[67] Fantham (1972) 137–40.
[68] On these features cf. von Albrecht 103–10.

and above all repetition (*uirtutem . . . uirtus*; *utare . . . utare . . . usu . . . usus*; *artem . . . ars*) make the progress of the argument clear. The same sentence, however, contains other stylistic elements that have nothing to do with clarity of logic: an allusion to Plato (*quas . . . personant*); the repeated *per-*; the archaism *reapse*; and the use of abstract nouns, two of which (*gubernatio*, *perfectio*) are not attested before C.

Within a few lines of this somewhat austere argument, however, the style changes abruptly (1.2.3):

> unde enim pietas, aut a quibus religio? unde ius aut gentium aut hoc ipsum ciuile quod dicitur? unde iustitia fides aequitas? unde pudor continentia fuga turpi<tu>dinis appetentia laudis et honestatis? unde in laboribus et periculis fortitudo?

The set of rhetorical questions is intended to show that moral virtues derive not from philosophers but from statesmen. The first one balances two elements, varying between *unde* and *a quibus*; the second has one noun (*ius*) with two modifiers; the third has three elements in asyndeton. C. shapes the list through the anaphora of *unde*, but within that framework there is considerable variety, both in the order and type of expressions (unmodified nouns, genitive, adjective, prepositional phrase). There is considerable pleonasm (one might say redundancy), but other than the anaphora there is no verbal repetition of significant terms at all, and the effect is created by accumulation rather than by logic.

One final stylistic type deserves to be mentioned, and that is the extensive use of parataxis and parenthesis, particularly in the historical narrative of book 2. Thus at 2.16.2, Scipio summarizes the achievements of Romulus:

> nam et ipse, quod principium rei publicae fuit, urbem condidit auspicato, et omnibus publicis rebus instituendis, qui sibi <ad>essent in auspiciis ex singulis tribubus singulos cooptauit augures, et habuit plebem in clientelas patrum discriptam (quod quantae fuerit utilitati post uidero), multaeque dictione ouium et boum (quod tunc erat res in pecore et locorum possessionibus, ex quo pecuniosi et locupletes uocabantur), non ui et suppliciis coercebat.

The backbone of the sentence consists of four main verbs linked paratactically: *condidit ... et ... cooptauit ... et habuit ... -que ... coercebat*; C. uses similar parataxis to list the accomplishments of each king. Within this framework, moreover, there is a set of parenthetical clauses (*quod ... fuit*; *qui ... in auspiciis*; *quod... uidero*; *quod ... uocabantur*). These four clauses are not parallel: the first is a simple description of the founding of the city; the second is a relative clause of purpose; the third is Scipio's authorial cross-reference; and the fourth is an antiquarian digression. Nevertheless, they all have a similar effect: they break up the flow of the narrative, they draw attention to the speaker's voice, and they imitate the choppy pattern of speech. Elsewhere (e.g. 2.14), a similar effect is created by the use of anacoluthon in long narrative sentences.

5. TEXT

Rep. existed complete in late antiquity, but no copy of it is known to have survived later than the seventh century. Our knowledge of the text comes from several different sources:

1. Vaticanus Latinus 5757 (P) is a seventh-century manuscript of Augustine's commentary on the Psalms; on 23 December 1819 Angelo Mai (who had arrived in Rome as Prefect of the Vatican Library only six weeks earlier) reported to Pope Pius VII his discovery of *Rep.* as the erased lower script under the text of Augustine. The text of *Rep.* (of the late fourth or early fifth century) is written in uncial letters in two columns to the page; each page contains on average 305 letters, or between 6 and 7 lines of this edition. Most of what is printed in this edition of *Rep.* is preserved in P, which contains roughly two-thirds of book 1, slightly more than half of book 2, a sixth of book 3, and only five leaves of the last half of the work. P was written by a remarkably careless scribe, and corrected by a relatively responsible one (p), whose evidence is of value at least equal to that of P. A full photographic facsimile of P was published by G. Mercati in 1934.[69]

[69] Facsimile: G. Mercati, *M. Tulli Ciceronis De re publica libri e codice rescripto Vaticano Latino 5757 phototypice expressi* (Vatican, 1934); Mai's letter about his discovery of *Rep.* is printed on pp. 226–8 of Mercati's *Prolegomena*. The principal information about P is in Ziegler's preface; cf. also Clark 124–38. On the corrector cf. also Taylor, and Krarup (1963). Reviews of textual matters since

2. The *Somnium Scipionis* has a completely separate tradition: it was the beneficiary of a Neoplatonic commentary by Macrobius in the fifth century, and was preserved thereafter in conjunction with Macrobius' work. The evidence of this tradition is twofold: the text of the *Somnium* itself and the extensive quotations from it embedded in the commentary. A great many manuscripts survive, many of which (including some earlier than the twelfth century) have never been examined carefully. There are, however, too few significant variant readings in the *Somnium* to permit reconstruction of the history of the text.[70]

3. Before the discovery of P, the principal source for *Rep.* was quotations in later authors. These are many, and are primarily from two types of writer. On the one hand, a great many short phrases and sentences are cited by the grammarians, particularly Nonius Marcellus, for particular locutions; on the other hand, large quotations and paraphrases are found in the church fathers, particularly Augustine, who used *Rep.* as one of his principal foils in *City of God*.[71]

The present edition relies largely on Ziegler's reports of P; on Ziegler and Ronconi for the *Somnium* (the collation of several previously unused MSS offered nothing new of any interest); and on Heck with consultation of critical editions of the texts in question for the fragments. Several broad changes have been made from Ziegler's edition: sentence numbers have been added for ease of reference; orthography has been regularized (in general, names to the form used in *MRR*, words to the spelling of lemmata in *OLD*); and punctuation, which is not based on any evidence in P, has been altered in the interest of clarity. The text given here differs from Ziegler's in the following passages (omitting changes of orthography and minor changes of punctuation); all significant variants are discussed in the commentary.

Ziegler in Schmidt (1973) 271–84 and E. Heck, *Gnomon* 55 (1983) 486–93 (review of Bréguet) and *Gnomon* 60 (1988) 684–91 (review of Büchner).

[70] On the transmission of the *Somnium* and the Commentary, cf. Barker-Benfield 224–32.

[71] Text and discussion of the fragments in Heck; for a new fragment, cf. Behr. For Augustine's use of *Rep.* cf. also Hagendahl 112–31, 540–53.

	Ziegler	*Zetzel*
1.2.2	discripta	descripta
1.3.2	ille,	ille
1.4.1	re publica	<in> re publica
1.5.1	adflixerat,	adflixerat.
1.5.2	deficiunt.	deficiunt,
1.25.3	<et> CCC	CCC
1.30.6	<id> ualent	<ualent, id> ualent
1.31.4	locupletibus	[locupletibus]
1.37.2	nobis	hominibus
1.42.5	aliud <ut> alio	aliud alio
1.43.1	habet	habeat
1.44.4	<uirorum illorum>	<illorum>
1.45.1	factiosa	factionis,
1.51.2	ciuitatium	ciuium
1.51.2	praeesse	praeessent
1.56.4	dicimus	didicimus
1.58.7	num Scipio	num
1.59.5	[in]felicem	infelicem
1.61.4	quid? domi	quid domi?
1.64.1	dura	diu
1.64.3	appellant	appellabant
1.67.1	omnis	omni
1.71.2	habemus	habeamus
2.10.2	mari	<a> mari
2.20.1	*us	<Stesichor>us
2.36.3	MDCCC	M ac CC
2.39.2	neque	<ut> neque
2.40.1	asse	aere
2.40.4	cornicinibus	liticinibus cornicinibus
2.42.1	sexaginta	<quinque et> sexaginta
2.42.3	sit	est

2.51.1	perpolito	† peripeateto †
2.57.1	consecutus	consecutum
2.58.2	illi quos	quos illi
2.63.1	plebiscito	plebei scito
6.9.1	M.' Manilio consuli	hoc Manilio consule
6.9.2	recreor ipso	ipso recreor
6.11.3	hereditarium a nobis	a nobis hereditarium
6.17.2	huic	cui
6.17.5	eam iam	iam
6.18.1	quis hic	quid? hic
6.18.1	[quis]	quis
6.20.4	incolunt	incolant
6.28.1	se ipsum moueat	a se ipso moueatur

M. TVLLI CICERONIS

DE RE PVBLICA LIBRI

LIBER I

[1]... <im>petu liberauissent, nec C. Duilius A. Atilius L. **1**
Metellus terrore Carthaginis, non duo Scipiones oriens incen-
dium belli Punici secundi sanguine suo restinxissent, nec id
excitatum maioribus copiis aut Q. Maximus eneruauisset, aut
M. Marcellus contudisset, aut a portis huius urbis auolsum P.
Africanus compulisset intra hostium moenia. M. uero Catoni 2
homini ignoto et nouo, quo omnes qui isdem rebus studemus
quasi exemplari ad industriam uirtutemque ducimur, certe
licuit Tusculi se in otio delectare, salubri et propinquo loco. sed 3
homo demens ut isti putant, cum cogeret eum necessitas nulla,
in his undis et tempestatibus ad summam senectutem maluit
iactari, quam in illa tranquillitate atque otio iucundissime
uiuere. omitto innumerabiles uiros, quorum singuli saluti huic 4
ciuitati fuerunt, et qui sunt <haud> procul ab aetatis huius
memoria; commemorare eos desino, ne quis se aut suorum
aliquem praetermissum queratur. unum hoc definio, tantam 5
esse necessitatem uirtutis generi hominum a natura tantumque
amorem ad communem salutem defendendam datum, ut ea uis
omnia blandimenta uoluptatis otique uicerit.

[2] Nec uero habere uirtutem satis est quasi artem aliquam **2**
nisi utare; etsi ars quidem cum ea non utare scientia tamen ipsa
teneri potest, uirtus in usu sui tota posita est; usus autem eius est
maximus ciuitatis gubernatio, et earum ipsarum rerum quas isti
in angulis personant reapse non oratione perfectio. nihil enim 2
dicitur a philosophis, quod quidem recte honesteque dicatur,
quod <non> ab iis partum confirmatumque sit, a quibus ciuitatibus iura descripta sunt. unde enim pietas, aut a quibus 3
religio? unde ius aut gentium aut hoc ipsum ciuile quod dicitur?
unde iustitia fides aequitas? unde pudor continentia fuga
turpi<tu>dinis appetentia laudis et honestatis? unde in labori-
bus et periculis fortitudo? nempe ab iis qui haec disciplinis 4
informata alia moribus confirmarunt, sanxerunt autem alia
legibus. quin etiam Xenocraten ferunt, nobilem in primis **3**

philosophum, cum quaereretur ex eo quid assequerentur eius
discipuli, respondisse ut id sua sponte facerent quod cogerentur
2 facere legibus. ergo ille ciuis qui id cogit omnes imperio legum-
que poena quod uix paucis persuadere oratione philosophi
possunt, etiam iis qui illa disputant ipsis est praeferendus
3 doctoribus. quae est enim istorum oratio tam exquisita quae sit
anteponenda bene constitutae ciuitati publico iure et moribus?
4 equidem quem ad modum 'urbes magnas atque imperiosas,' ut
appellat Ennius, uiculis et castellis praeferendas puto, sic eos
qui his urbibus consilio atque auctoritate praesunt, iis qui
omnis negotii publici expertes sint longe duco sapientia ipsa
5 esse anteponendos. et quoniam maxime rapimur ad opes aug-
endas generis humani, studemusque nostris consiliis et labori-
bus tutiorem et opulentiorem uitam hominum reddere, et ad
hanc uoluptatem ipsius naturae stimulis incitamur, teneamus
eum cursum qui semper fuit optimi cuiusque, neque ea signa
audiamus quae receptui canunt, ut eos etiam reuocent qui iam
processerint.

4 [3] His rationibus tam certis tamque illustribus opponuntur
ab iis qui contra disputant primum labores qui sint <in> re
publica defendenda sustinendi, leue sane impedimentum uigi-
lanti et industrio, neque solum in tantis rebus sed etiam in
mediocribus uel studiis uel officiis uel uero etiam negotiis con-
2 temnendum. adiunguntur pericula uitae, turpisque ab his
formido mortis fortibus uiris opponitur, quibus magis id
miserum uideri solet, natura se consumi et senectute, quam sibi
dari tempus ut possint eam uitam, quae tamen esset reddenda
3 naturae, pro patria potissimum reddere. illo uero se loco copiosos et disertos putant, cum calamitates clarissimorum uirorum
5 iniuriasque iis ab ingratis impositas ciuibus colligunt. hinc enim
illa et apud Graecos exempla, Miltiadem uictorem domitorem-
que Persarum, nondum sanatis uolneribus iis quae corpore
aduerso in clarissima uictoria accepisset, uitam ex hostium telis
seruatam in ciuium uinclis profudisse, et Themistoclem patria

quam liberauisset pulsum atque proterritum, non in Graeciae
portus per se seruatos sed in barbariae sinus confugisse quam
adflixerat. nec uero leuitatis Atheniensium crudelitatisque in 2
amplissimos ciues exempla deficiunt, quae nata et frequentata
apud illos etiam in grauissumam ciuitatem nostram dicunt
redundasse. nam uel exilium Camilli uel offensio commemora- **6**
tur Ahalae uel inuidia Nasicae uel expulsio Laenatis uel Opimi
damnatio uel fuga Metelli uel acerbissima C. Mari clades . . .
principum caedes, uel eorum multorum pestes quae paulo post
secutae sunt. nec uero iam meo nomine abstinent, et credo quia 2
nostro consilio ac periculo sese in illa uita atque otio conserua-
tos putant, grauius etiam de nobis queruntur et amantius. sed 3
haud facile dixerim, cur cum ipsi discendi aut uisendi causa
maria tramittant *

deest folium unum

[4]* saluam esse consulatu abiens in contione populo **7**
Romano idem iurante iurassem, facile iniuriarum omnium
compensarem curam et molestiam. quamquam nostri casus 2
plus honoris habuerunt quam laboris, neque tantum molestiae
quantum gloriae, maioremque laetitiam ex desiderio bonorum
percepimus quam ex laetitia improborum dolorem. sed si aliter 3
ut dixi accidisset, qui possem queri, cum mihi nihil improuiso
nec grauius quam expectauissem pro tantis meis factis eue-
nisset? is enim fueram, cui cum liceret aut maiores ex otio 4
fructus capere quam ceteris propter uariam suauitatem studi-
orum in quibus a pueritia uixeram, aut si quid accideret acerb-
ius uniuersis, non praecipuam sed parem cum ceteris fortunae
condicionem subire, non dubitauerim me grauissimis tempestatibus ac paene fulminibus ipsis obuium ferre conseruandorum
ciuium causa, meisque propriis periculis parere commune reliquis otium. neque enim hac nos patria lege genuit aut educauit, **8**
ut nulla quasi alimenta exspectaret a nobis, ac tantummodo
nostris ipsa commodis seruiens tutum perfugium otio nostro
suppeditaret et tranquillum ad quietem locum, sed ut plurimas

et maximas nostri animi ingenii consilii partes ipsa sibi ad
utilitatem suam pigneraretur, tantumque nobis in nostrum
priuatum usum quantum ipsi superesse posset remitteret.

9 [5] Iam illa perfugia quae sumunt sibi ad excusationem quo
facilius otio perfruantur certe minime sunt audienda, cum ita
dicunt accedere ad rem publicam plerumque homines nulla re
bona dignos, cum quibus comparari sordidum, confligere
autem multitudine praesertim incitata miserum et periculosum
2 sit. quam ob rem neque sapientis esse accipere habenas cum
insanos atque indomitos impetus uolgi cohibere non possit,
neque liberi cum impuris atque immanibus aduersariis decertantem uel contumeliarum uerbera subire uel expectare sapi-
3 enti non ferendas iniurias: proinde quasi bonis et fortibus et
magno animo praeditis ulla sit ad rem publicam adeundi causa
iustior, quam ne pareant improbis neue ab isdem lacerari rem
publicam patiantur, cum ipsi auxilium ferre si cupiant non
queant.

10 [6] Illa autem exceptio cui probari tandem potest, quod
negant sapientem suscepturum ullam rei publicae partem,
2 extra quam si eum tempus et necessitas coegerit? quasi uero
maior cuiquam necessitas accidere possit quam accidit nobis; in
3 qua quid facere potuissem, nisi tum consul fuissem? consul
autem esse qui potui, nisi eum uitae cursum tenuissem a pueritia, per quem equestri loco natus peruenirem ad honorem
4 amplissimum? non igitur potestas est ex tempore aut cum uelis
opitulandi rei publicae, quamuis ea prematur periculis, nisi eo
11 loco sis ut tibi id facere liceat. maximeque hoc in hominum
doctorum oratione mihi mirum uideri solet, quod qui tranquillo mari gubernare se negent posse, quod nec didicerint nec
umquam scire curauerint, iidem ad gubernacula se accessuros
2 profiteantur excitatis maximis fluctibus. isti enim palam dicere
atque in eo multum etiam gloriari solent, se de rationibus
rerum publicarum aut constituendarum aut tuendarum nihil
nec didicisse umquam nec docere, earumque rerum scientiam
non doctis hominibus ac sapientibus sed in illo genere exercita-

tis concedendam putant. quare qui conuenit polliceri operam 3
suam rei publicae tum denique si necessitate cogantur, cum,
quod est multo procliuius, nulla necessitate premente rem
publicam regere nesciant? equidem, ut uerum esset sua uolun- 4
tate sapientem descendere ad rationes ciuitatis non solere, sin
autem temporibus cogeretur tum id munus denique non recusare, tamen arbitrarer hanc rerum ciuilium minime neglegen-
dam scientiam sapienti propterea quod omnia essent ei praepa-
randa, quibus nesciret an aliquando uti necesse esset.

[7] Haec plurimis a me uerbis dicta sunt ob eam causam, **12**
quod his libris erat instituta et suscepta mihi de re publica
disputatio; quae ne frustra haberetur, dubitationem ad rem
publicam adeundi in primis debui tollere. ac tamen si qui sunt 2
qui philosophorum auctoritate moueantur, dent operam parumper atque audiant eos quorum summa est auctoritas apud
doctissimos homines et gloria; quos ego existimo, etiamsi qui
ipsi rem publicam non gesserint, tamen quoniam de re publica
multa quaesierint et scripserint, functos esse aliquo rei publicae
munere. eos uero septem quos Graeci sapientes nominauerunt, 3
omnes paene uideo in media re publica esse uersatos. neque 4
enim est ulla res in qua propius ad deorum numen uirtus
accedat humana, quam ciuitates aut condere nouas aut conseruare iam conditas.

[8] Quibus de rebus, quoniam nobis contigit ut idem et in **13**
gerenda re publica aliquid essemus memoria dignum consecuti,
et in explicandis rationibus rerum ciuilium quandam facultatem, non modo usu sed etiam studio discendi et docendi <. . .>
essemus auctores, cum superiores alii fuissent in disputationibus
perpoliti, quorum res gestae nullae inuenirentur, alii in gerendo
probabiles, in disserendo rudes. nec uero nostra quaedam est 2
instituenda noua et a nobis inuenta ratio, sed unius aetatis
clarissimorum ac sapientissimorum nostrae ciuitatis uirorum
disputatio repetenda memoria est, quae mihi tibique quondam
adulescentulo est a P. Rutilio Rufo, Smyrnae cum simul
essemus complures dies, exposita, in qua nihil fere quod magno

opere ad rationes omnium <harum> rerum pertineret praetermissum puto.

14 [9] Nam cum P. Africanus hic Paulli filius feriis Latinis
Tuditano consule et Aquilio constituisset in hortis esse, familia-
rissimique eius ad eum frequenter per eos dies uentitaturos se
esse dixissent, Latinis ipsis mane ad eum primus sororis filius
2 uenit Q. Tubero. quem cum comiter Scipio appellauisset libenterque uidisset, 'quid tu' inquit 'tam mane, Tubero? dabant
enim hae feriae tibi opportunam sane facultatem ad explicandas tuas litteras.'

3 Tum ille: 'mihi uero omne tempus est ad meos libros
uacuum; numquam enim sunt illi occupati. te autem permag-
num est nancisci otiosum, hoc praesertim motu rei publicae.'

4 Tum Scipio: 'atqui nactus es, sed mehercule otiosiorem opera
quam animo.'

5 Et ille: 'at uero animum quoque relaxes oportet; sumus enim
multi ut constituimus parati, si tuo commodo fieri potest, abuti
tecum hoc otio.'

6 'Libente me uero, ut aliquid aliquando de doctrinae studiis
admoneamur.'

15 [10] Tum ille: 'uisne igitur, quoniam et me quodam modo
inuitas et tui spem das, hoc primum, Africane, uideamus, ante
quam ueniunt alii, quidnam sit de isto altero sole quod nunti-
2 atum est in senatu? neque enim pauci neque leues sunt qui se
duo soles uidisse dicant, ut non tam fides non habenda quam
ratio quaerenda sit.'

3 Hic Scipio: 'quam uellem Panaetium nostrum nobiscum
haberemus! qui cum cetera tum haec caelestia uel studiosissime
4 solet quaerere. sed ego, Tubero, – nam tecum aperte quod
sentio loquar – non nimis assentior in omni isto genere nostro
illi familiari, qui quae uix coniectura qualia sint possumus
suspicari, sic affirmat ut oculis ea cernere uideatur aut tractare
5 plane manu. quo etiam sapientiorem Socratem soleo iudicare,
qui omnem eius modi curam deposuerit, eaque quae de natura

quaererentur aut maiora quam hominum ratio consequi possit
aut nihil omnino ad uitam hominum attinere dixerit.'

Dein Tubero: 'nescio, Africane, cur ita memoriae proditum **16**
sit, Socratem omnem istam disputationem reiecisse, et tantum
de uita et de moribus solitum esse quaerere. quem enim auc- 2
torem de illo locupletiorem Platone laudare possumus? cuius in
libris multis locis ita loquitur Socrates, ut etiam cum de
moribus de uirtutibus denique de re publica disputet, numeros
tamen et geometriam et harmoniam studeat Pythagorae more
coniungere.'

Tum Scipio: 'sunt ista ut dicis; sed audisse te credo, Tubero, 3
Platonem Socrate mortuo primum in Aegyptum discendi
causa, post in Italiam et in Siciliam contendisse ut Pythagorae
inuenta perdisceret, eumque et cum Archyta Tarentino et cum
Timaeo Locro multum fuisse, et Philolai commentarios esse
nanctum, cumque eo tempore in his locis Pythagorae nomen
uigeret, illum se et hominibus Pythagoreis et studiis illis dedisse.
itaque cum Socratem unice dilexisset, eique omnia tribuere 4
uoluisset, leporem Socraticum subtilitatemque sermonis cum
obscuritate Pythagorae et cum illa plurimarum artium grauitate contexuit.'

[11] Haec Scipio cum dixisset, L. Furium repente uenientem **17**
aspexit, eumque ut salutauit, amicissime apprehendit et in lecto
suo collocauit. et cum simul P. Rutilius uenisset, qui est nobis 2
huius sermonis auctor, eum quoque ut salutauit, propter
Tuberonem iussit adsidere.

Tum Furius: 'quid uos agitis? num sermonem uestrum 3
aliquem diremit noster interuentus?'

'Minime uero,' Africanus. 'soles enim tu haec studiose in- 4
uestigare quae sunt in hoc genere de quo instituerat paulo ante
Tubero quaerere; Rutilius quidem noster etiam sub ipsis Numantiae moenibus solebat mecum interdum eius modi aliquid
conquirere.'

'Quae res tandem inciderat?' inquit Philus. 5

6 Tum ille: 'de solibus istis duobus; de quo studeo, Phile, ex te audire quid sentias.'

18 [12] Dixerat hoc ille, cum puer nuntiauit uenire ad eum
2 Laelium domoque iam exisse. tum Scipio calceis et uestimentis
sumptis e cubiculo est egressus, et cum paululum inambu-
lauisset in porticu, Laelium aduenientem salutauit et eos qui
una uenerant, Spurium Mummium quem in primis diligebat et
C. Fannium et Q. Scaeuolam generos Laeli, doctos adulescentes iam aetate quaestorios; quos cum omnes salutauisset, con-
3 uertit se in porticu et coniecit in medium Laelium. fuit enim
hoc in amicitia quasi quoddam ius inter illos, ut militiae
propter eximiam belli gloriam Africanum ut deum coleret
Laelius, domi uicissim Laelium, quod aetate antecedebat,
4 obseruaret in parentis loco Scipio. dein cum essent perpauca
inter se uno aut altero spatio collocuti, Scipionique eorum
aduentus periucundus et pergratus fuisset, placitum est ut in
aprico maxime pratuli loco, quod erat hibernum tempus anni,
5 considerent. quod cum facere uellent, interuenit uir prudens
omnibusque illis et iucundus et carus, M'. Manilius, qui a
Scipione ceterisque amicissime consalutatus adsedit proximus
Laelio.

19 [13] Tum Philus: 'non mihi uidetur' inquit 'quod hi uenerunt alius nobis sermo esse quaerendus, sed agendum accuratius et dicendum dignum aliquid horum auribus.'

2 Hic Laelius: 'quid tandem agebatis, aut cui sermoni nos interuenimus?'

3 'Quaesierat ex me Scipio quidnam sentirem de hoc quod duo soles uisos esse constaret.'

4 'Ain uero, Phile? iam explorata nobis sunt ea quae ad domos nostras quaeque ad rem publicam pertinent, siquidem quid agatur in caelo quaerimus?'

5 Et ille: 'an tu ad domos nostras non censes pertinere scire quid agatur et quid fiat domi? quae non ea est quam parietes nostri cingunt, sed mundus hic totus, quod domicilium quamque patriam di nobis communem secum dederunt, cum

praesertim si haec ignoremus, multa nobis et magna ignoranda
sint. ac me quidem, ut hercule etiam te ipsum, Laeli, omnesque 6
auidos sapientiae, cognitio ipsa rerum consideratioque
delectat.'

Tum Laelius: 'non impedio, praesertim quoniam feriati **20**
sumus; sed possumus audire aliquid an serius uenimus?'

'Nihil est adhuc disputatum, et quoniam est integrum, liben- 2
ter tibi, Laeli, ut de eo disseras equidem concessero.'

'Immo uero te audiamus, nisi forte Manilius interdictum 3
aliquod inter duos soles putat esse componendum, ut ita caelum
possideant ut uterque possiderit.'

Tum Manilius: 'pergisne eam, Laeli, artem illudere, in qua 4
primum excellis ipse, deinde sine qua scire nemo potest quid sit
suum, quid alienum? sed ista mox; nunc audiamus Philum,
quem uideo maioribus iam de rebus quam me aut quam P.
Mucium consuli.'

[*sections* 21–24 *omitted*]

[16] 'Atque eius modi quiddam etiam bello illo maximo, quod **25**
Athenienses et Lacedaemonii summa inter se contentione ges-
serunt, Pericles ille et auctoritate et eloquentia et consilio
princeps ciuitatis suae, cum obscurato sole tenebrae factae
essent repente Atheniensiumque animos summus timor occu-
pauisset, docuisse ciues suos dicitur, id quod ipse ab Anaxagora
cuius auditor fuerat acceperat, certo illud tempore fieri et
necessario, cum tota se luna sub orbem solis subiecisset; itaque
etsi non omni intermenstruo, tamen id fieri non posse nisi
intermenstruo tempore. quod cum disputando rationibusque 2
docuisset, populum liberauit metu; erat enim tum haec noua et
incognita ratio, solem lunae oppositu solere deficere, quod
Thaletem Milesium primum uidisse dicunt. id autem postea ne 3
nostrum quidem Ennium fugit; qui ut scribit, anno quinquagesimo CCC fere post Romam conditam

Nonis Iunis soli luna obstitit et nox.

4 atque hac in re tanta inest ratio atque sollertia, ut ex hoc die
quem apud Ennium et in maximis annalibus consignatum
uidemus superiores solis defectiones reputatae sint usque ad
illam quae Nonis Quinctilibus fuit regnante Romulo; quibus
quidem Romulum tenebris etiamsi natura ad humanum
exitum abripuit, uirtus tamen in caelum dicitur sustulisse.'

26 [17] Tum Tubero: 'uidesne, Africane, quod paulo ante secus
tibi uidebatur, doc *

deest folium unum

2 *'lis, quae uideant ceteri. quid porro aut praeclarum putet in
rebus humanis, qui haec deorum regna perspexerit, aut diuturnum, qui cognouerit quid sit aeternum, aut gloriosum, qui
uiderit quam parua sit terra, primum uniuersa, deinde ea pars
eius quam homines incolant, quamque nos in exigua eius parte
affixi, plurimis ignotissimi gentibus, speremus tamen nostrum
27 nomen uolitare et uagari latissime? agros uero et aedificia et
pecudes et immensum argenti pondus atque auri qui bona nec
putare nec appellare soleat, quod earum rerum uideatur ei leuis
fructus, exiguus usus, incertus dominatus, saepe etiam taeterrimorum hominum immensa possessio, quam est hic fortunatus
2 putandus! cui soli uere liceat omnia non Quiritium sed sapi-
entium iure pro suis uindicare, nec ciuili nexo sed communi
lege naturae, quae uetat ullam rem esse cuiusquam, nisi eius
qui tractare et uti sciat; qui imperia consulatusque nostros in
necessariis, non in expetendis rebus, muneris fungendi gratia
subeundos, non praemiorum aut gloriae causa appetendos
putet; qui denique, ut Africanum auum meum scribit Cato
solitum esse dicere, possit idem de se praedicare, numquam se
plus agere quam nihil cum ageret, numquam minus solum esse
28 quam cum solus esset. quis enim putare uere potest, plus egisse
Dionysium tum cum omnia moliendo eripuerit ciuibus suis
libertatem, quam eius ciuem Archimedem cum istam ipsam
sphaeram, nihil cum agere uideretur, de qua modo dicebatur,
2 effecerit? quis autem non magis solos esse, qui in foro turbaque
quicum colloqui libeat non habeant, quam qui nullo arbitro uel

secum ipsi loquantur, uel quasi doctissimorum hominum in
concilio adsint, cum eorum inuentis scriptisque se oblectent?
quis uero diuitiorem quemquam putet quam eum cui nihil desit 3
quod quidem natura desideret, aut potentiorem quam illum
qui omnia quae expetat consequatur, aut beatiorem quam qui
sit omni perturbatione animi liberatus, aut firmiore fortuna
quam qui ea possideat quae secum ut aiunt uel e naufragio
possit efferre? quod autem imperium, qui magistratus, quod 4
regnum potest esse praestantius quam despicientem omnia
humana et inferiora sapientia ducentem nihil umquam nisi
sempiternum et diuinum animo uolutare? cui persuasum sit 5
appellari ceteros homines, esse solos eos qui essent politi propriis
humanitatis artibus? ut mihi Platonis illud, seu quis dixit alius, **29**
perelegans esse uideatur. quem cum ex alto ignotas ad terras 2
tempestas et in desertum litus detulisset, timentibus ceteris
propter ignorationem locorum, animaduertisse dicunt in arena
geometricas formas quasdam esse descriptas; quas ut uidisset,
exclamauisse ut bono essent animo: uidere enim se hominum
uestigia; quae uidelicet non ex agri consitura quam cernebat,
sed ex doctrinae indiciis interpretabatur. quam ob rem, 3
Tubero, semper mihi et doctrina et eruditi homines et tua ista
studia placuerunt.'

[18] Tum Laelius: 'non audeo quidem' inquit 'ad ista, **30**
Scipio, dicere, neque tam te aut Philum aut Manilium *

deest folium unum

* in ipsius paterno genere fuit noster ille amicus, dignus huic ad 2
imitandum,

Egregie cordatus homo, catus Aelius Sextus,

qui "egregie cordatus" et "catus" fuit et ab Ennio dictus est, non quod ea quaerebat quae numquam inueniret, sed quod ea respondebat quae eos qui quaesissent et cura et negotio soluerent, cuique contra Gali studia disputanti in ore semper erat ille de Iphigenia Achilles:

3 Astrologorum signa in caelo quid sit obseruationis?
cum Capra aut Nepa aut exoritur nomen aliquod beluarum,
quod est ante pedes nemo spectat, caeli scrutantur plagas.

4 atque idem (multum enim illum audiebam et libenter) Zethum
illum Pacuui nimis inimicum doctrinae esse dicebat: magis eum
delectabat Neoptolemus Ennii, qui se ait philosophari uelle, sed
5 paucis; nam omnino haud placere. quodsi studia Graecorum
uos tanto opere delectant, sunt alia liberiora et transfusa latius,
quae uel ad usum uitae uel etiam ad ipsam rem publicam
6 conferre possumus. istae quidem artes, si modo aliquid <ualent,
id> ualent, ut paulum acuant et tamquam irritent ingenia
puerorum, quo facilius possint maiora discere.'

31 [19] Tum Tubero: 'non dissentio a te, Laeli, sed quaero quae
tu esse maiora intellegas.'

2 'Dicam mehercule et contemnar a te fortasse, cum tu ista
caelestia de Scipione quaesieris, ego autem haec quae uidentur
3 ante oculos esse magis putem quaerenda. quid enim mihi L.
Paulli nepos, hoc auunculo, nobilissima in familia atque in hac
tam clara re publica natus, quaerit quo modo duo soles uisi sint,
non quaerit cur in una re publica duo senatus et duo paene iam
4 populi sint? nam ut uidetis mors Tiberii Gracchi et iam ante
tota illius ratio tribunatus diuisit populum unum in duas
partes; obtrectatores autem et inuidi Scipionis, initiis factis a P.
Crasso et Appio Claudio, tenent nihilo minus illis mortuis
senatus alteram partem, dissidentem a uobis auctore Metello et
P. Mucio, neque hunc qui unus potest, concitatis sociis et
nomine Latino, foederibus uiolatis, triumuiris seditiosissimis
aliquid cotidie noui molientibus, bonis uiris [locupletibus] per-
32 turbatis, his tam periculosis rebus subuenire patiuntur. quam
ob rem si me audietis, adulescentes, solem alterum ne metueritis: aut enim nullus esse potest, aut sit sane ut uisus est, modo ne
sit molestus, aut scire istarum rerum nihil, aut etiamsi maxime
sciemus, nec meliores ob eam scientiam nec beatiores esse
2 possumus. senatum uero et populum ut unum habeamus et fieri

potest, et permolestum est nisi fit, et secus esse scimus, et uidemus si id effectum sit et melius nos esse uicturos et beatius.'

[20] Tum Mucius: 'quid esse igitur censes, Laeli, discendum **33**
nobis ut istud efficere possimus ipsum quod postulas?'

'Eas artes quae efficiant ut usui ciuitati simus; id enim esse 2
praeclarissimum sapientiae munus maximumque uirtutis uel documentum uel officium puto. quam ob rem ut hae feriae 3
nobis ad utilissimos rei publicae sermones potissimum conferantur, Scipionem rogemus ut explicet quem existimet esse optimum statum ciuitatis; deinde alia quaeremus, quibus cognitis spero nos ad haec ipsa uia peruenturos, earumque rerum rationem quae nunc instant explicaturos.'

[21] Cum id et Philus et Manilius et Mummius admodum **34**
approba<uissent>*

deest folium unum

*'non solum ob eam causam fieri uolui quod erat aequum de 2
re publica potissimum principem rei publicae dicere, sed etiam quod memineram persaepe te cum Panaetio disserere solitum coram Polybio, duobus Graecis uel peritissimis rerum ciuilium, multaque colligere ac docere, optimum longe statum ciuitatis esse eum quem maiores nostri nobis reliquissent. qua in dispu- 3
tatione quoniam tu paratior es, feceris – ut etiam pro his dicam – si de re publica quid sentias explicaris, nobis gratum omnibus.'

[22] Tum ille: 'non possum equidem dicere me ulla in cogi- **35**
tatione acrius aut diligentius solere uersari, quam in ista ipsa quae mihi, Laeli, a te proponitur. etenim cum in suo quemque 2
opere artificem, qui quidem excellat, nihil aliud cogitare meditari curare uideam nisi quo sit in illo genere melior, ego cum mihi sit unum opus hoc a parentibus maioribusque meis relictum, procuratio atque administratio rei publicae, non me inertiorem esse confitear quam opificem quemquam, si minus in maxima arte quam illi in minimis operae consumpserim? sed **36**
neque iis contentus sum quae de ista consultatione scripta nobis summi ex Graecia sapientissimique homines reliquerunt, neque

2 ea quae mihi uidentur anteferre illis audeo. quam ob rem peto a
uobis ut me sic audiatis: neque ut omnino expertem Graecarum
rerum, neque ut eas nostris in hoc praesertim genere ante-
ponentem, sed ut unum e togatis patris diligentia non illiber-
aliter institutum studioque discendi a pueritia incensum, usu
tamen et domesticis praeceptis multo magis eruditum quam
litteris.'

37 [23] Hic Philus: 'non hercule,' inquit 'Scipio, dubito, quin
tibi ingenio praestiterit nemo, usuque idem in re publica rerum
maximarum facile omnis uiceris; quibus autem studiis semper
2 fueris tenemus. quam ob rem si, ut dicis, animum quoque
contulisti in istam rationem et quasi artem, habeo maximam
gratiam Laelio; spero enim multo uberiora fore quae a te
dicentur quam illa quae a Graecis hominibus scripta sunt
omnia.'

3 Tum ille: 'permagnam tu quidem expectationem, quod onus
est ei qui magnis de rebus dicturus est grauissimum, imponis
orationi meae.'

4 Et Philus: 'quamuis sit magna, tamen eam uinces ut soles;
neque enim est periculum ne te de re publica disserentem
deficiat oratio.'

38 [24] Hic Scipio: 'faciam quod uultis ut potero, et ingrediar in
disputationem ea lege, qua credo omnibus in rebus disserendis
utendum esse si errorem uelis tollere, ut eius rei de qua quaer-
etur si nomen quod sit conueniat, explicetur quid declaretur eo
nomine; quod si conuenerit, tum demum decebit ingredi in
sermonem; numquam enim quale sit illud de quo disputabitur
2 intellegi poterit, nisi quod sit fuerit intellectum prius. quare
quoniam de re publica quaerimus, hoc primum uideamus quid
sit id ipsum quod quaerimus.'

3 Cum approbauisset Laelius, 'nec uero' inquit Africanus 'ita
disseram de re tam illustri tamque nota, ut ad illa elementa
reuoluar quibus uti docti homines his in rebus solent, ut a prima
congressione maris et feminae, deinde a progenie et cognatione
ordiar, uerbisque quid sit et quot modis quidque dicatur defi-

niam saepius; apud prudentes enim homines et in maxima re
publica summa cum gloria belli domique uersatos cum loquar,
non committam ut sit illustrior illa ipsa res de qua disputem
quam oratio mea. nec enim hoc suscepi ut tamquam magister 4
persequerer omnia, neque hoc polliceor me effecturum ut ne
qua particula in hoc sermone praetermissa sit.'

Tum Laelius: 'ego uero istud ipsum genus orationis quod 5
polliceris expecto.'

[25] 'Est igitur' inquit Africanus 'res publica res populi, **39**
populus autem non omnis hominum coetus quoquo modo congregatus, sed coetus multitudinis iuris consensu et utilitatis
communione sociatus. eius autem prima causa coeundi est non 2
tam imbecillitas quam naturalis quaedam hominum quasi congregatio; non est enim singulare nec soliuagum genus hoc, sed
ita generatum ut ne in omnium quidem rerum affluen<tia>*

deest folium unum

[26] * '<quae>dam quasi semina, neque reliquarum uirtu- **41**
tum nec ipsius rei publicae reperiatur ulla institutio. hi coetus 2
igitur hac de qua exposui causa instituti, sedem primum certo
loco domiciliorum causa constituerunt; quam cum locis
manuque saepsissent, eius modi coniunctionem tectorum
oppidum uel urbem appellauerunt, delubris distinctam spatiis-
que communibus. omnis ergo populus, qui est talis coetus 3
multitudinis qualem exposui, omnis ciuitas, quae est constitutio
populi, omnis res publica, quae ut dixi populi res est, consilio
quodam regenda est, ut diuturna sit. id autem consilium 4
primum semper ad eam causam referendum est quae causa
genuit ciuitatem. deinde aut uni tribuendum est, aut delectis **42**
quibusdam, aut suscipiendum est multitudini atque omnibus. 2
quare cum penes unum est omnium summa rerum, regem illum
unum uocamus, et regnum eius rei publicae statum. cum autem 3
est penes delectos, tum illa ciuitas optimatium arbitrio regi
dicitur. illa autem est ciuitas popularis (sic enim appellant) in 4
qua in populo sunt omnia. atque horum trium generum 5
quoduis, si teneat illud uinculum quod primum homines inter

se rei publicae societate deuinxit, non perfectum illud quidem
neque mea sententia optimum, sed tolerabile tamen, et aliud
6 alio possit esse praestantius. nam rex aequus ac sapiens, uel
delecti ac principes ciues, uel ipse populus, quamquam id est
minime probandum, tamen nullis interiectis iniquitatibus aut
cupiditatibus posse uidetur aliquo esse non incerto statu.

43 [27] 'Sed et in regnis nimis expertes sunt ceteri communis
iuris et consilii, et in optimatium dominatu uix particeps libertatis potest esse multitudo, cum omni consilio communi ac
potestate careat, et cum omnia per populum geruntur quamuis
iustum atque moderatum, tamen ipsa aequabilitas est iniqua,
2 cum habeat nullos gradus dignitatis. itaque si Cyrus ille Perses
iustissimus fuit sapientissimusque rex, tamen mihi populi res (ea
enim est ut dixi antea publica) non maxime expetenda fuisse
illa uidetur, cum regeretur unius nutu ac †modo†; si Massilienses nostri clientes per delectos et principes ciues summa
iustitia reguntur, inest tamen in ea condicione populi similitudo
quaedam seruitutis; si Athenienses quibusdam temporibus
sublato Areopago nihil nisi populi scitis ac decretis agebant,
quoniam distinctos gradus non habebant, non tenebat ornatum
suum ciuitas.

44 [28] 'Atque hoc loquor de tribus his generibus rerum publicarum non turbatis atque permixtis, sed suum statum tenenti-
2 bus. quae genera primum sunt in iis singula uitiis quae ante
dixi, deinde habent perniciosa alia uitia: nullum est enim genus
illarum rerum publicarum, quod non habeat iter ad finitimum
3 quoddam malum praeceps ac lubricum. nam illi regi, ut eum
potissimum nominem, tolerabili aut si uoltis etiam amabili
Cyro subest ad immutandi animi licentiam crudelissimus ille
Phalaris, cuius in similitudinem dominatus unius procliui cursu
4 et facile delabitur. illi autem Massiliensium paucorum et principum administrationi ciuitatis finitimus est qui fuit quodam
tempore apud Athenienses triginta <illorum> consensus et
5 factio. iam Atheniensium populi potestatem omnium rerum

ipsi, ne alios requiramus, ad furorem multitudinis licentiamque conuersam pesti*

deest folium unum

[29] *'taeterrimus, et ex hac uel optimatium uel factionis, **45**
tyrannica illa uel regia uel etiam persaepe popularis, itemque
ex ea genus aliquod efflorescere ex illis quae ante dixi solet,
mirique sunt orbes et quasi circuitus in rebus publicis commutationum et uicissitudinum. quos cum cognosse sapientis est, 2
tum uero prospicere impendentes, in gubernanda re publica
moderantem cursum atque in sua potestate retinentem, magni
cuiusdam ciuis et diuini paene est uiri. itaque quartum 3
quoddam genus rei publicae maxime probandum esse sentio,
quod est ex his quae prima dixi moderatum et permixtum
tribus.'

[30] Hic Laelius: 'scio tibi ita placere, Africane: saepe enim **46**
ex te audiui; sed tamen, nisi molestum est, ex tribus istis modis
rerum publicarum uelim scire quod optimum iudices. nam uel 2
profuerit aliquid ad cog'*

deest folium unum

[31] *'et talis est quaeque res publica, qualis eius aut natura **47**
aut uoluntas qui illam regit. itaque nulla alia in ciuitate, nisi in 2
qua populi potestas summa est, ullum domicilium libertas
habet; qua quidem certe nihil potest esse dulcius, et quae si
aequa non est ne libertas quidem est. qui autem aequa potest 3
esse, omitto dicere in regno, ubi ne obscura quidem est aut
dubia seruitus, sed in istis ciuitatibus in quibus uerbo sunt liberi
omnes? ferunt enim suffragia, mandant imperia magistratus, 4
ambiuntur, rogantur, sed ea dant [magis] quae etiamsi nolint
danda sint, et quae ipsi non habent unde alii petunt: sunt enim
expertes imperii, consilii publici, iudicii delectorum iudicum,
quae familiarum uetustatibus aut pecuniis ponderantur. in 5
libero autem populo, ut Rhodis, ut Athenis, nemo est ciuium
qui*

deest folium unum

48 [32] *'<po>pulo aliquis unus pluresue diuitiores opulentioresque extitissent, tum ex eorum fastidio et superbia nata esse
commemorant, cedentibus ignauis et imbecillis et arrogantiae
2 diuitum succumbentibus. si uero ius suum populi teneant,
negant quicquam esse praestantius, liberius, beatius; quippe
qui domini sint legum, iudiciorum, belli, pacis, foederum,
3 capitis unius cuiusque, pecuniae. hanc unam rite rem publi-
4 cam, id est rem populi, appellari putant. itaque et a regum et a
patrum dominatione solere in libertatem rem populi uindicari,
non ex liberis populis reges requiri aut potestatem atque opes
49 optimatium. et uero negant oportere indomiti populi uitio
genus hoc totum liberi populi repudiari: concordi populo et
omnia referente ad incolumitatem et ad libertatem suam nihil
esse immutabilius, nihil firmius; facillimam autem in ea re
publica esse posse concordiam, in qua idem conducat omnibus;
ex utilitatis uarietatibus, cum aliis aliud expediat, nasci dis-
cordias; itaque cum patres rerum potirentur, numquam consti-
tisse ciuitatis statum; multo iam id in regnis minus, quorum, ut
2 ait Ennius, "nulla [regni] sancta societas nec fides est." quare
cum lex sit ciuilis societatis uinculum, ius autem legis aequale,
quo iure societas ciuium teneri potest, cum par non sit condicio
3 ciuium? si enim pecunias aequari non placet, si ingenia
omnium paria esse non possunt, iura certe paria debent esse
4 eorum inter se qui sunt ciues in eadem re publica. quid est enim
ciuitas nisi iuris societas ciuium?*

deest folium unum

50 [33] *'ceteras uero res publicas ne appellandas quidem
2 putant iis nominibus quibus illae sese appellari uelint. cur enim
regem appellem Iouis optimi nomine hominem dominandi
cupidum aut imperii singularis, populo oppresso dominantem,
3 non tyrannum potius? tam enim esse clemens tyrannus quam
rex importunus potest, ut hoc populorum intersit utrum comi
domino an aspero seruiant; quin seruiant quidem fieri non
4 potest. quo autem modo assequi poterat Lacedaemo illa tum,
cum praestare putabatur disciplina rei publicae, ut bonis uter-

etur iustisque regibus, cum esset habendus rex quicumque
genere regio natus esset? nam optimates quidem quis ferat, qui 5
non populi concessu sed suis comitiis hoc sibi nomen arrogauer-
unt? qui enim iudicatur iste optimus? doctrina, artibus, studiis, 6
audio: quando*

desunt folia duo

[34] *'si fortuito id faciet, tam cito euertetur quam nauis, si e **51**
uectoribus sorte ductus ad gubernacula accesserit. quodsi liber 2
populus deliget quibus se committat (deligetque si modo saluus
esse uult optimum quemque), certe in optimorum consiliis
posita est ciuium salus, praesertim cum hoc natura tulerit, non
solum ut summi uirtute et animo praeessent imbecillioribus, sed
ut hi etiam parere summis uelint. uerum hunc optimum statum 3
prauis hominum opinionibus euersum esse dicunt, qui ignor-
atione uirtutis, quae cum in paucis est tum a paucis iudicatur et
cernitur, opulentos homines et copiosos, tum genere nobili
natos esse optimos putant. hoc errore uulgi cum rem publicam 4
opes paucorum, non uirtutes tenere coeperunt, nomen illi principes optimatium mordicus tenent, re autem carent eo nomine.
nam diuitiae nomen opes uacuae consilio et uiuendi atque aliis 5
imperandi modo dedecoris plenae sunt et insolentis superbiae,
nec ulla deformior species est ciuitatis quam illa in qua opulen-
tissimi optimi putantur. uirtute uero gubernante rem publi- **52**
cam, quid potest esse praeclarius? cum is qui imperat aliis seruit 2
ipse nulli cupiditati, cum quas ad res ciues instituit et uocat, eas
omnes complexus est ipse, nec leges imponit populo quibus ipse
non pareat, sed suam uitam ut legem praefert suis ciuibus. qui si 3
unus satis omnia consequi posset, nihil opus esset pluribus; si
uniuersi uidere optimum et in eo consentire possent, nemo
delectos principes quaereret. difficultas ineundi consilii rem a 4
rege ad plures, error et temeritas populorum a multitudine ad
paucos transtulit. sic inter <in>firmitatem unius temeritatem- 5
que multorum medium optimates possederunt locum, quo nihil
potest esse moderatius; quibus rem publicam tuentibus beatissi-
mos esse populos necesse est, uacuos omni cura et cogitatione,

aliis permisso otio suo quibus id tuendum est neque committen-
53 dum ut sua commoda populus neglegi a principibus putet. nam
aequabilitas quidem iuris, quam amplexantur liberi populi,
neque seruari potest – ipsi enim populi, quamuis soluti effrena-
tique sint, praecipue multis multa tribuunt, et est in ipsis
magnus dilectus hominum et dignitatum – eaque quae appella-
2 tur aequabilitas iniquissima est. cum enim par habetur honos
summis et infimis, qui sint in omni populo necesse est, ipsa
aequitas iniquissima est; quod in iis ciuitatibus quae ab optimis
3 reguntur accidere non potest. haec fere, Laeli, et quaedam
eiusdem generis ab iis qui eam formam rei publicae maxime
laudant disputari solent.'

54 [35] Tum Laelius: 'quid tu,' inquit 'Scipio? e tribus istis quod
maxime probas?'

2 'Recte quaeris quod maxime e tribus, quoniam eorum
nullum ipsum per se separatim probo, anteponoque singulis
3 illud quod conflatum fuerit ex omnibus. sed si unum ac simplex
p<ro>bandum <sit>, regium <pro>bem .... pri .... in .... f
.... hoc loco appellatur, occurrit nomen quasi patrium regis,
ut ex se natis ita consulentis suis ciuibus et eos con<s>eruantis
stu<dio>sius quam ..... entis .... tem .... us .... tibus ....
55 uos sustentari unius optimi et summi uiri diligentia. adsunt
optimates, qui se melius hoc idem facere profiteantur plusque
fore dicant in pluribus consilii quam in uno, et eandem tamen
2 aequitatem et fidem. ecce autem maxima uoce clamat populus
neque se uni neque paucis uelle parere; libertate ne feris
quidem quicquam esse dulcius; hac omnes carere, siue regi siue
3 optimatibus seruiant. ita caritate nos capiunt reges, consilio
optimates, libertate populi, ut in comparando difficile ad
eligendum sit quid maxime uelis.'

4 'Credo' inquit 'sed expediri quae restant uix poterunt, si hoc
incohatum reliqueris.'

56 [36] 'Imitemur ergo Aratum, qui magnis de rebus dicere
exordiens a Ioue incipiendum putat.'

2 'Quo Ioue? aut quid habet illius carminis simile haec oratio?'

'Tantum' inquit 'ut rite ab eo dicendi principia capiamus, 3
quem unum omnium deorum et hominum regem esse omnes
docti indoctique [expoliri] consentiunt.'

'Quid?' inquit Laelius.

Et ille: 'quid censes nisi quod est ante oculos? siue haec ad 4
utilitatem uitae constituta sunt a principibus rerum publicarum, ut rex putaretur unus esse in caelo qui nutu, ut ait Homerus, totum Olympum conuerteret, idemque et rex et pater haberetur omnium, magna auctoritas est multique testes – siquidem omnes multos appellari placet – ita consensisse gentes decretis uidelicet principum, nihil esse rege melius, quoniam deos omnes censent unius regi numine; siue haec in errore imperitorum posita esse et fabularum similia didicimus, audiamus communes quasi doctores eruditorum hominum, qui tamquam oculis illa uiderunt quae nos uix audiendo cognoscimus.'

'Quinam' inquit Laelius 'isti sunt?' 5

Et ille: 'qui natura omnium rerum peruestiganda senserunt omnem hunc mundum mente*

desunt folia duo

[37] *'sed si uis, Laeli, dabo tibi testes nec nimis antiquos nec **58**
ullo modo barbaros.'

'Istos' inquit 'uolo.'

'Videsne igitur minus quadringentorum annorum esse hanc 2
urbem ut sine regibus sit?'

'Vero minus.'

'Quid ergo? haec quadringentorum annorum aetas ut urbis 3
et ciuitatis num ualde longa est?'

'Ista uero' inquit 'adulta uix.'

'Ergo his annis quadringentis Romae rex erat?' 4

'Et superbus quidem.'

'Quid supra?' 5

'Iustissimus, et deinceps retro usque ad Romulum, qui ab hoc tempore anno sescentesimo rex erat.'

'Ergo ne iste quidem peruetus?' 6

'Minime, ac prope senescente iam Graecia.'

7 'Cedo, num barbarorum Romulus rex fuit?'

'Si ut Graeci dicunt omnes aut Graios esse aut barbaros, uereor ne barbarorum rex fuerit; sin id nomen moribus dandum est, non linguis, non Graecos minus barbaros quam Romanos puto.'

8 Et Scipio: 'atqui ad hoc de quo agitur non quaerimus gentem, ingenia quaerimus. si enim et prudentes homines et non ueteres reges habere uoluerunt, utor neque perantiquis neque inhumanis ac feris testibus.'

59 [38] Tum Laelius: 'uideo te, Scipio, testimoniis satis instructum, sed apud me, ut apud bonum iudicem, argumenta plus quam testes ualent.'

2 Tum Scipio: 'utere igitur argumento, Laeli, tute ipse sensus tui.'

'Cuius' inquit ille 'sensus?'

3 'Si quando, si forte tibi uisus es irasci alicui.'

'Ego uero saepius quam uellem.'

4 'Quid? tum cum tu es iratus, permittis illi iracundiae dominatum animi tui?'

5 'Non mehercule' inquit 'sed imitor Archytam illum Tarentinum, qui cum ad uillam uenisset et omnia aliter offendisset ac iusserat, "a te infelicem" inquit uilico, "quem necassem iam uerberibus, nisi iratus essem."'

60 'Optime' inquit Scipio. 'ergo Archytas iracundiam uidelicet dissidentem a ratione seditionem quandam animi esse iure ducebat, atque eam consilio sedari uolebat; adde auaritiam, adde imperii, adde gloriae cupiditatem, adde libidines, et illud uides: si in animis hominum regale imperium sit, unius fore dominatum, consilii scilicet (ea est enim animi pars optima); consilio autem dominante nullum esse libidinibus, nullum irae, nullum temeritati locum.'

'Sic' inquit 'est.'

2 'Probas igitur animum ita affectum?'

'Nihil uero' inquit 'magis.'

'Ergo non probares, si consilio pulso libidines, quae sunt 3
innumerabiles, iracundiaeue tenerent omnia?'

'Ego uero nihil isto animo, nihil ita animato homine miserius ducerem.'

'Sub regno igitur tibi esse placet omnes animi partes, et eas 4
regi consilio?'

'Mihi uero sic placet.'

'Cur igitur dubitas quid de re publica sentias? in qua si in 5
plures translata res sit, intellegi iam licet nullum fore quod praesit imperium, quod quidem nisi unum sit esse nullum potest.'

[39] Tum Laelius: 'quid quaeso interest inter unum et plures, **61**
si iustitia est in pluribus?'

Et Scipio: 'quoniam testibus meis intellexi, Laeli, te non 2
ualde moueri, non desinam te uti teste, ut hoc quod dico probem.'

'Me?' inquit ille 'quonam modo?'

'Quia animum aduerti nuper, cum essemus in Formiano, te 3
familiae ualde interdicere, ut uni dicto audiens esset.'

'Quippe uilico.'

'Quid domi? pluresne praesunt negotiis tuis?' 4

'Immo uero unus' inquit.

'Quid? totam domum num quis alter praeter te regit?' 5

'Minime uero.'

'Quin tu igitur concedis <it>idem in re publica singulorum 6
dominatus, si modo iusti sint, esse optimos?'

'Adducor' inquit 'et propemodum assentior.'

[40] Et Scipio: 'tum magis assentiare, Laeli, si (ut omittam **62**
similitudines, uni gubernatori, uni medico, si digni modo sint iis artibus, rectius esse alteri nauem committere, aegrum alteri quam multis) ad maiora peruenero.'

'Quaenam ista sunt?'

'Quid? tu non uides unius importunitate et superbia Tar- 2
quinii nomen huic populo in odium uenisse regium?'

'Video uero' inquit.

3 'Ergo etiam illud uides, de quo progrediente oratione plura
me dicturum puto, Tarquinio exacto mira quadam exultasse
populum insolentia libertatis: tum exacti in exilium innocentes,
tum bona direpta multorum, tum annui consules, tum demissi
populo fasces, tum prouocationes omnium rerum, tum secessiones plebis, tum prorsus ita acta pleraque ut in populo essent
omnia.'

4 'Est' inquit 'ut dicis.'

63 'Est uero' inquit Scipio 'in pace et otio (licet enim lasciuire,
2 dum nihil metuas) ut in naui ac saepe etiam in morbo leui. sed
ut ille qui nauigat, cum subito mare coepit horrescere, et ille
aeger ingrauescente morbo, unius opem implorat, sic noster
populus in pace et domi imperat et ipsis magistratibus,
minatur, recusat, appellat, prouocat, in bello sic paret ut regi;
3 ualet enim salus plus quam libido. grauioribus uero bellis etiam
sine collega omne imperium nostri penes singulos esse uoluer-
4 unt, quorum ipsum nomen uim suae potestatis indicat. nam
dictator quidem ab eo appellatur quia dicitur, sed in nostris
libris uides eum, Laeli, magistrum populi appellari.'

5 'Video' inquit.

6 Et Scipio: 'sapienter igitur illi uete<res>*

deest folium unum

64 [41] *'iusto quidem rege cum est populus orbatus, "pectora"
diu "tenet desiderium," sicut ait Ennius, post optimi regis
obitum:

2 simul inter
sese sic memorant: "o Romule, Romule die,
qualem te patriae custodem di genuerunt!
o pater, o genitor, o sanguen dis oriundum!"

3 non eros nec dominos appellabant eos quibus iuste paruerunt,
denique ne reges quidem, sed patriae custodes, sed patres, sed
deos, nec sine causa. quid enim adiungunt?

"tu produxisti nos intra luminis oras."

uitam honorem decus sibi datum esse iustitia regis existima- 4
bant. mansisset eadem uoluntas in eorum posteris, si regum 5
similitudo permansisset; sed uides unius iniustitia concidisse
genus illud totum rei publicae.'

'Video uero' inquit 'et studeo cursus istos mutationum non 6
magis in nostra quam in omni re publica noscere.'

[42] Et Scipio: 'est omnino, cum de illo genere rei publicae **65**
quod maxime probo quae sentio dixero, accuratius mihi dicendum de commutationibus rerum publicarum, etsi minime facile
eas in ea re publica futuras puto. sed huius regiae prima et 2
certissima est illa mutatio: cum rex iniustus esse coepit, perit
illud ilico genus, et est idem ille tyrannus, deterrimum genus et
finitimum optimo; quem si optimates oppresserunt, quod ferme
euenit, habet statum res publica de tribus secundarium; est
enim quasi regium, id est patrium consilium populo bene con-
sulentium principum. sin per se populus interfecit aut eiecit 3
tyrannum, est moderatior, quoad sentit et sapit, et sua re gesta
laetatur, tuerique uult per se constitutam rem publicam. sin 4
quando aut regi iusto uim populus attulit regnoue eum spo-
liauit aut etiam, id quod euenit saepius, optimatium sanguinem
gustauit ac totam rem publicam substrauit libidini suae, caue
putes aut[em] mare ullum aut flammam esse tantam quam non
facilius sit sedare quam effrenatam insolentia multitudinem.
tum fit illud quod apud Platonem est luculente dictum, si modo 5
id exprimere Latine potuero; difficile factu est, sed conabor
tamen.

[43] '"Cum" enim inquit "inexplebiles populi fauces exa- **66**
ruerunt libertatis siti, malisque usus ille ministris non modice
temperatam sed nimis meracam libertatem sitiens hausit, tum
magistratus et principes, nisi ualde lenes et remissi sint et large
sibi libertatem ministrent, insequitur insimulat arguit, prae-
potentes reges tyrannos uocat." puto enim tibi haec esse nota.' 2

'Vero mihi' inquit ille 'notissima.' 3

'Ergo illa sequuntur: "eos qui pareant principibus agitari ab **67**
eo populo et seruos uoluntarios appellari; eos autem qui in

magistratu priuatorum similes esse uelint, eosque priuatos qui
efficiant ne quid inter priuatum et magistratum differat,
<ef>ferunt laudibus, [et] mactant honoribus, ut necesse sit in
eius modi re publica plena libertatis esse omnia, ut et priuata
domus omni uacet dominatione, et hoc malum usque ad bestias
perueniat, denique ut pater filium metuat, filius patrem neglegat, absit omnis pudor, ut plane liberi sint, nihil intersit ciuis sit
an peregrinus, magister ut discipulos metuat et iis blandiatur,
spernantque discipuli magistros, adulescentes ut senum sibi
pondus assumant, senes autem ad ludum adulescentium
2 descendant, ne sint iis odiosi et graues. ex quo fit ut etiam serui
se liberius gerant, uxores eodem iure sint quo uiri, inque tanta
libertate canes etiam et equi, aselli denique libere [sint] sic
3 incurrant ut iis de uia decedendum sit. ergo ex hac infinita"
inquit "licentia haec summa cogitur, ut ita fastidiosae molles-
que mentes euadant ciuium, ut si minima uis adhibeatur
imperii, irascantur et perferre nequeant; ex quo leges quoque
incipiunt neglegere, ut plane sine ullo domino sint."'

68 [44] Tum Laelius: 'prorsus' inquit 'expressa sunt a te quae
dicta sunt ab illo.'

2 'Atque ut iam ad sermonis mei auctorem reuertar, ex hac
nimia licentia, quam illi solam libertatem putant, ait ille ut ex
3 stirpe quadam existere et quasi nasci tyrannum. nam ut ex
nimia potentia principum oritur interitus principum, sic hunc
4 nimis liberum populum libertas ipsa seruitute afficit. sic omnia
nimia, cum uel in tempestate uel in agris uel in corporibus
laetiora fuerunt, in contraria fere conuertuntur, maximeque
<id> in rebus publicis euenit, nimiaque illa libertas et populis et
5 priuatis in nimiam seruitutem cadit. itaque ex hac maxima
libertate tyrannus gignitur et illa iniustissima et durissima ser-
6 uitus. ex hoc enim populo indomito uel potius immani deligitur
aliqui plerumque dux contra illos principes afflictos iam et
depulsos loco, audax, impurus, consectans proterue bene saepe
7 de re publica meritos, populo gratificans et aliena et sua. cui
quia priuato sunt oppositi timores, dantur imperia et ea con-

tinuantur; praesidiis etiam, ut Athenis Pisistratus, saepiuntur;
postremo, a quibus producti sunt, existunt eorum ipsorum
tyranni. quos si boni oppresserunt, ut saepe fit, recreatur 8
ciuitas; sin audaces, fit illa factio, genus aliud tyrannorum,
eademque oritur etiam ex illo saepe optimatium praeclaro
statu, cum ipsos principes aliqua prauitas de uia deflexit. sic 9
tamquam pilam rapiunt inter se rei publicae statum tyranni ab
regibus, ab iis autem principes aut populi, a quibus aut fac-
tiones aut tyranni, nec diutius umquam tenetur idem rei publicae modus.

[45] 'Quod ita cum sit, <ex> tribus primis generibus longe **69**
praestat mea sententia regium, regio autem ipsi praestabit id
quod erit aequatum et temperatum ex tribus primis rerum
publicarum modis. placet enim esse quiddam in re publica 2
praestans et regale, esse aliud auctoritati principum impertitum
ac tributum, esse quasdam res seruatas iudicio uoluntatique
multitudinis. haec constitutio primum habet aequabilitatem 3
quandam [magnam], qua carere diutius uix possunt liberi,
deinde firmitudinem, quod et illa prima facile in contraria uitia
conuertuntur, ut exsistat ex rege dominus, ex optimatibus
factio, ex populo turba et confusio, quodque ipsa genera generibus saepe commutantur nouis. hoc in hac iuncta moderateque 4
permixta constitutione rei publicae non ferme sine magnis
principum uitiis euenit. non est enim causa conuersionis, ubi in 5
suo quisque est gradu firmiter collocatus, et non subest quo
praecipitet ac decidat.

[46] 'Sed uereor, Laeli uosque homines amicissimi ac pru- **70**
dentissimi, ne si diutius in hoc genere uerser, quasi praecipientis
cuiusdam et docentis et non uobiscum simul considerantis esse
uideatur oratio mea. quam ob rem ingrediar in ea quae nota 2
sunt omnibus, quaesita autem a nobis iam diu. sic enim 3
decerno, sic sentio, sic affirmo, nullam omnium rerum publicarum aut constitutione aut discriptione aut disciplina confer-
endam esse cum ea, quam patres nostri nobis acceptam iam
inde a maioribus reliquerunt. quam si placet, quoniam ea quae 4

tenebatis ipsi etiam ex me audire uoluistis, simul et qualis sit et
optimam esse ostendam, expositaque ad exemplum nostra re
publica, accommodabo ad eam si potero omnem illam
orationem quae est mihi habenda de optimo ciuitatis statu.
quod si tenere et consequi potuero, cumulate munus hoc, cui
me Laelius praeposuit, ut opinio mea fert effecero.'

71 [47] Tum Laelius: 'tuum uero,' inquit 'Scipio, ac tuum
2 quidem unius. quis enim te potius aut de maiorum dixerit
institutis, cum sis clarissimis ipse maioribus? aut de optimo statu
ciuitatis? quem si habeamus, etsi ne nunc quidem, tum uero,
quis te possit esse florentior? aut de consiliis in posterum prouidendis, cum tu duobus huius urbis terroribus depulsis in
omne tempus prospexeris?'

LIBER II

1 [1] *<cupidi>tate audiendi, ingressus est sic loqui Scipio:
'Catonis hoc senis est, quem ut scitis unice dilexi maximeque
sum admiratus, cuique uel patris utriusque iudicio uel etiam
meo studio me totum ab adulescentia dedidi, cuius me
2 numquam satiare potuit oratio: tantus erat in homine usus rei
publicae, quam et domi et militiae cum optime tum etiam
diutissime gesserat, et modus in dicendo, et grauitate mixtus
lepos, et summum uel discendi studium uel docendi, et orationi
2 uita admodum congruens. is dicere solebat ob hanc causam
praestare nostrae ciuitatis statum ceteris ciuitatibus, quod in
illis singuli fuissent fere quorum suam quisque rem publicam
constituisset legibus atque institutis suis, ut Cretum Minos,
Lacedaemoniorum Lycurgus, Atheniensium, quae persaepe
commutata esset, tum Theseus tum Draco tum Solo tum
Clisthenes tum multi alii, postremo exsanguem iam et iacentem
doctus uir Phalereus sustentasset Demetrius, nostra autem res
publica non unius esset ingenio sed multorum, nec una hominis
2 uita sed aliquot constituta saeculis et aetatibus. nam neque
ullum ingenium tantum exstitisse dicebat, ut quem res nulla

fugeret quisquam aliquando fuisset, neque cuncta ingenia
collata in unum tantum posse uno tempore prouidere, ut omnia
complecterentur sine rerum usu ac uetustate. quam ob rem, ut **3**
ille solebat, ita nunc mea repetet oratio populi Romani originem; libenter enim etiam uerbo utor Catonis. facilius autem 2
quod est propositum consequar, si nostram rem publicam uobis
et nascentem et crescentem et adultam et iam firmam atque
robustam ostendero, quam si mihi aliquam, ut apud Platonem
Socrates, ipse finxero.'

[2] Hoc cum omnes adprobauissent, 'quod habemus' inquit **4**
'institutae rei publicae tam clarum ac tam omnibus notum
exordium quam huius urbis condendae principium profectum a
Romulo? qui patre Marte natus (concedamus enim famae 2
hominum, praesertim non inueteratae solum sed etiam sapienter a maioribus proditae, bene meriti de rebus communibus
ut genere etiam putarentur, non solum ingenio esse diuino) – is 3
igitur ut natus sit, cum Remo fratre dicitur ab Amulio rege
Albano ob labefactandi regni timorem ad Tiberim exponi
iussus esse; quo in loco cum esset siluestris beluae sustentatus
uberibus, pastoresque eum sustulissent et in agresti cultu
laboreque aluissent, perhibetur ut adoleuerit et corporis
uiribus et animi ferocitate tantum ceteris praestitisse ut omnes
qui tum eos agros ubi hodie est haec urbs incolebant, aequo
animo illi libenterque parerent. quorum copiis cum se ducem 4
praebuisset, ut [et]iam a fabulis ad facta ueniamus, oppressisse
Longam Albam, ualidam urbem et potentem temporibus illis,
Amuliumque regem interemisse fertur. [3] qua gloria parta **5**
urbem auspicato condere et firmare dicitur primum cogitauisse
rem publicam.

'Vrbi autem locum, quod est ei qui diuturnam rem publicam 2
serere conatur diligentissime prouidendum, incredibili oppor-
tunitate delegit. neque enim ad mare admouit, quod ei fuit illa 3
manu copiisque facillimum, ut in agrum Rutulorum Aboriginumue procederet aut in ostio Tiberino, quem in locum multis
post annis rex Ancus coloniam deduxit, urbem ipse conderet,

sed hoc uir excellenti prouidentia sensit ac uidit, non esse
opportunissimos situs maritimos urbibus eis quae ad spem diuturnitatis conderentur atque imperii, primum quod essent
urbes maritimae non solum multis periculis oppositae sed etiam
6 caecis. nam terra continens aduentus hostium non modo
expectatos sed etiam repentinos multis indiciis et quasi fragore
quodam et sonitu ipso ante denuntiat, neque uero quisquam
potest hostis aduolare terra quin eum non modo <ad>esse sed
2 etiam quis et unde sit scire possimus. maritimus uero ille et
naualis hostis ante adesse potest quam quisquam uenturum esse
suspicari queat, nec uero cum uenit prae se fert aut qui sit aut
unde ueniat aut etiam quid uelit, denique ne nota quidem ulla,
pacatus an hostis sit, discerni ac iudicari potest.

7 [4] 'Est autem maritimis urbibus etiam quaedam corruptela
2 ac mutatio morum. admiscentur enim nouis sermonibus ac
disciplinis, et importantur non merces solum aduenticiae sed
etiam mores, ut nihil possit in patriis institutis manere inte-
3 grum. iam qui incolunt eas urbes non haerent in suis sedibus,
sed uolucri semper spe et cogitatione rapiuntur a domo longius,
atque etiam cum manent corpore, animo tamen exulant et
4 uagantur. nec uero ulla res magis labefactatam diu et Carthaginem et Corinthum peruertit aliquando, quam hic error ac
dissipatio ciuium, quod mercandi cupiditate et nauigandi et
8 agrorum et armorum cultum reliquerant. multa etiam ad luxu-
riam inuitamenta perniciosa ciuitatibus suppeditantur mari,
quae uel capiuntur uel importantur; atque habet etiam amoe-
nitas ipsa uel sumptuosas uel desidiosas illecebras multas cupi-
2 ditatum. et quod de Corintho dixi, id haud scio an liceat de
cuncta Graecia uerissime dicere; nam et ipsa Peloponnesus fere
tota in mari est, nec praeter Phliasios ulli sunt quorum agri non
contingant mare, et extra Peloponnesum Aenianes et Doris et
3 Dolopes soli absunt a mari. quid dicam insulas Graeciae? quae
fluctibus cinctae natant paene ipsae simul cum ciuitatum insti-
9 tutis et moribus. atque haec quidem ut supra dixi ueteris sunt
2 Graeciae. coloniarum uero quae est deducta a Graiis in Asiam

Thracam Italiam Siciliam Africam praeter unam Magnesiam,
quam unda non alluat? ita barbarorum agris quasi attexta 3
quaedam uidetur ora esse Graeciae; nam e barbaris quidem
ipsis nulli erant antea maritimi praeter Etruscos et Poenos,
alteri mercandi causa, latrocinandi alteri. quae causa perspicua 4
est malorum commutationumque Graeciae propter ea uitia
maritimarum urbium quae ante paulo perbreuiter attigi. sed 5
tamen in his uitiis inest illa magna commoditas, et quod ubique
genitum est ut ad eam urbem quam incolas possit adnare, et
rursus ut id quod agri efferant sui, quascumque uelint in terras
portare possint ac mittere.

[5] 'Qui potuit igitur diuinius et utilitates complecti mariti- **10**
mas Romulus et uitia uitare, quam quod urbem perennis amnis
et aequabilis et in mare late influentis posuit in ripa? quo posset 2
urbs et accipere a mari quo egeret et reddere quo redundaret,
eodemque ut flumine res ad uictum cultumque maxime necessarias non solum <a> mari absorberet, sed etiam inuectas
acciperet ex terra, ut mihi iam tum diuinasse ille uideatur hanc
urbem sedem aliquando et domum summo esse imperio praebi-
turam; nam hanc rerum tantam potentiam non ferme facilius
alia ulla in parte Italiae posita urbs tenere potuisset.

[6] 'Vrbis autem ipsius natiua praesidia quis est tam neg- **11**
legens qui non habeat animo notata planeque cognita? cuius is 2
est tractus ductusque muri cum Romuli tum etiam reliquorum
regum sapientia definitus ex omni parte arduis praeruptisque
montibus, ut unus aditus, qui esset inter Esquilinum Quiri-
nalemque montem, maximo aggere obiecto fossa cingeretur
uastissima, atque ut ita munita arx circuitu arduo et quasi
circumciso saxo niteretur, ut etiam in illa tempestate horribili
Gallici aduentus incolumis atque intacta permanserit. locum- 3
que delegit et fontibus abundantem et in regione pestilenti
salubrem; colles enim sunt, qui cum perflantur ipsi tum afferunt
umbram uallibus.

[7] 'Atque haec quidem perceleriter confecit; nam et urbem **12**
constituit, quam e suo nomine Romam iussit nominari, et ad

firmandam nouam ciuitatem nouum quoddam et subagreste
consilium, sed ad muniendas opes regni ac populi sui magni
hominis et iam tum longe prouidentis secutus est, cum Sabinas
honesto ortas loco uirgines, quae Romam ludorum gratia
uenissent quos tum primum anniuersarios in circo facere insti-
tuisset Consualibus, rapi iussit easque in familiarum amplissi-
13 marum matrimoniis collocauit. qua ex causa cum bellum
Romanis Sabini intulissent proeliique certamen uarium atque
anceps fuisset, cum T. Tatio rege Sabinorum foedus icit, matronis ipsis quae raptae erant orantibus; quo foedere et Sabinos in
ciuitatem asciuit sacris communicatis, et regnum suum cum
illorum rege sociauit.

14 [8] 'Post interitum autem Tatii cum ad eum dominatus
omnis reccidisset, quamquam cum Tatio in regium consilium
delegerat principes (qui appellati sunt propter caritatem
patres), populumque et suo et Tati nomine et Lucumonis, qui
Romuli socius in Sabino proelio occiderat, in tribus tres curiasque triginta discripserat (quas curias earum nominibus nuncupauit quae ex Sabinis uirgines raptae postea fuerant oratrices
pacis et foederis) – sed quamquam ea Tatio sic erant discripta
uiuo, tamen eo interfecto multo etiam magis Romulus patrum
auctoritate consilioque regnauit.

15 [9] 'Quo facto primum uidit iudicauitque idem quod Spartae
Lycurgus paulo ante uiderat, singulari imperio et potestate
regia tum melius gubernari et regi ciuitates, si esset optimi
2 cuiusque ad illam uim dominationis adiuncta auctoritas. itaque
hoc consilio et quasi senatu fultus et munitus, et bella cum
finitimis felicissime multa gessit et, cum ipse nihil ex praeda
16 domum suam reportaret, locupletare ciues non destitit. tum, id
quod retinemus hodie magna cum salute rei publicae, auspiciis
2 plurimum obsecutus est Romulus. nam et ipse, quod principium rei publicae fuit, urbem condidit auspicato, et omnibus
publicis rebus instituendis, qui sibi <ad>essent in auspiciis ex
singulis tribubus singulos cooptauit augures, et habuit plebem
in clientelas patrum discriptam (quod quantae fuerit utilitati

post uidero), multaeque dictione ouium et boum (quod tunc
erat res in pecore et locorum possessionibus, ex quo pecuniosi et
locupletes uocabantur), non ui et suppliciis coercebat.

[10] 'Ac Romulus, cum septem et triginta regnauisset annos, **17**
et haec egregia duo firmamenta rei publicae peperisset, auspi-
cia et senatum, tantum est consecutus, ut cum subito sole
obscurato non comparuisset, deorum in numero collocatus
putaretur; quam opinionem nemo umquam mortalis assequi
potuit sine eximia uirtutis gloria. atque hoc eo magis est in **18**
Romulo admirandum, quod ceteri qui dii ex hominibus facti
esse dicuntur, minus eruditis hominum saeculis fuerunt, ut
fingendi procliuis esset ratio, cum imperiti facile ad credendum
impellerentur, Romuli autem aetatem minus his sescentis annis
iam inueteratis litteris atque doctrinis omnique illo antiquo ex
inculta hominum uita errore sublato fuisse cernimus. nam si, id 2
quod Graecorum inuestigatur annalibus, Roma condita est
secundo anno olympiadis septimae, in id saeculum Romuli
cecidit aetas, cum iam plena Graecia poetarum et musicorum
esset, minorque fabulis nisi de ueteribus rebus haberetur fides.
nam centum et octo annis postquam Lycurgus leges scribere 3
instituit, prima posita est olympias, quam quidam nominis
errore ab eodem Lycurgo constitutam putant; Homerum
autem qui minimum dicunt Lycurgi aetati triginta annis ante-
ponunt fere. ex quo intellegi potest permultis annis ante **19**
Homerum fuisse quam Romulum, ut iam doctis hominibus ac
temporibus ipsis eruditis ad fingendum uix quicquam esset loci.
antiquitas enim recepit fabulas fictas etiam non numquam 2
incondite, haec aetas autem iam exculta praesertim eludens
omne quod fieri non potest respuit *

* '<Stesichor>us nepos eius, ut dixerunt quidam, ex filia. quo **20** 2
uero ille mortuus, eodem est anno natus Simonides olympiade
sexta et quinquagesima, quo facilius intellegi possit tum de
Romuli [iam] immortalitate creditum, cum iam inueterata uita
hominum ac tractata esset et cognita. sed profecto tanta fuit in 3
eo uis ingenii atque uirtutis, ut id de Romulo Proculo Iulio

homini agresti crederetur, quod multis iam ante saeclis nullo
alio de mortali homines credidissent; qui impulsu patrum, quo
illi a se inuidiam interitus Romuli pellerent, in contione dixisse
fertur, a se uisum esse in eo colle Romulum qui nunc Quirinalis
uocatur; eum sibi mandasse ut populum rogaret, ut sibi eo in
colle delubrum fieret; se deum esse et Quirinum uocari.

21 [11] 'Videtisne igitur unius uiri consilio non solum ortum
nouum populum, neque ut in cunabulis uagientem relictum,
sed adultum iam et paene puberem?'

2 Tum Laelius: 'nos uero uidemus, et te quidem ingressum
ratione ad disputandum noua, quae nusquam est in Graecorum
3 libris. nam princeps ille, quo nemo in scribendo praestantior
fuit, aream sibi sumpsit, in qua ciuitatem exstrueret arbitratu
suo, praeclaram ille quidem fortasse, sed a uita hominum
22 abhorrentem et a moribus; reliqui disseruerunt sine ullo certo
exemplari formaque rei publicae de generibus et de rationibus
2 ciuitatum. tu mihi uideris utrumque facturus: es enim ita
ingressus ut quae ipse reperias tribuere aliis malis quam, ut facit
apud Platonem Socrates, ipse fingere, et illa de urbis situ
reuoces ad rationem quae a Romulo casu aut necessitate facta
sunt, et disputes non uaganti oratione sed defixa in una re
3 publica. quare perge ut instituisti; prospicere enim iam uideor
te reliquos reges persequente quasi perfectam rem publicam.'

23 [12] 'Ergo' inquit Scipio 'cum ille Romuli senatus, qui con-
stabat ex optimatibus, quibus ipse rex tantum tribuisset ut eos
patres uellet nominari patriciosque eorum liberos, temptaret
post Romuli excessum ut ipse regeret sine rege rem publicam,
populus id non tulit, desiderioque Romuli postea regem flagi-
tare non destitit; cum prudenter illi principes nouam et inaudi-
tam ceteris gentibus interregni ineundi rationem excogitauer-
unt, ut quoad certus rex declaratus esset, nec sine rege ciuitas
nec diuturno rege esset uno, nec committeretur ut quisquam
inueterata potestate aut ad deponendum imperium tardior
24 esset aut ad obtinendum munitior. quo quidem tempore nouus
ille populus uidit tamen id quod fugit Lacedaemonium Lycur-

gum, qui regem non deligendum duxit, si modo hoc in Lycurgi potestate potuit esse, sed habendum, qualiscumque is foret, qui modo esset Herculi stirpe generatus; nostri illi etiam tum agrestes uiderunt uirtutem et sapientiam regalem, non progeniem quaeri oportere.

[13] 'Quibus cum esse praestantem Numam Pompilium fama **25**
ferret, praetermissis suis ciuibus regem alienigenam patribus
auctoribus sibi ipse populus asciuit, eumque ad regnandum
Sabinum hominem Romam Curibus acciuit. qui ut huc uenit, 2
quamquam populus curiatis eum comitiis regem esse iusserat,
tamen ipse de suo imperio curiatam legem tulit, hominesque
Romanos instituto Romuli bellicis studiis ut uidit incensos,
existimauit eos paulum ab illa consuetudine esse reuocandos.

[14] 'Ac primum agros quos bello Romulus ceperat diuisit **26**
uiritim ciuibus, docuitque sine depopulatione atque praeda
posse eos colendis agris abundare commodis omnibus, amorem-
que eis otii et pacis iniecit, quibus facillime iustitia et fides
conualescit, et quorum patrocinio maxime cultus agrorum perceptioque frugum defenditur. idemque Pompilius et auspiciis 2
maioribus inuentis ad pristinum numerum duo augures
addidit, et sacris e principum numero pontifices quinque
praefecit, et animos propositis legibus his quas in monumentis
habemus ardentes consuetudine et cupiditate bellandi relig-
ionum caerimoniis mitigauit, adiunxitque praeterea flamines
Salios uirginesque Vestales, omnesque partes religionis statuit
sanctissime. sacrorum autem ipsorum diligentiam difficilem, **27**
apparatum perfacilem esse uoluit; nam quae perdiscenda
quaeque obseruanda essent, multa constituit, sed ea sine
impensa. sic religionibus colendis operam addidit, sumptum 2
remouit, idemque mercatus ludos omnesque conueniundi
causas et celebritates inuenit. quibus rebus institutis ad human- 3
itatem atque mansuetudinem reuocauit animos hominum
studiis bellandi iam immanes ac feros. sic ille cum undequadra- 4
ginta annos summa in pace concordiaque regnauisset (sequ-
amur enim potissimum Polybium nostrum, quo nemo fuit in

exquirendis temporibus diligentior), excessit e uita, duabus praeclarissimis ad diuturnitatem rei publicae rebus confirmatis, religione atque clementia.'

28 [15] Quae cum Scipio dixisset, 'uerene' inquit Manilius 'hoc
memoriae proditum est, Africane, regem istum Numam Pytha-
2 gorae ipsius discipulum aut certe Pythagoreum fuisse? saepe
enim hoc de maioribus natu audiuimus, et ita intellegimus
uulgo existimari; neque uero satis id annalium publicorum
auctoritate declaratum uidemus.'

3 Tum Scipio: 'falsum est enim, Manili,' inquit 'id totum,
4 neque solum fictum sed etiam imperite absurdeque fictum. ea
sunt enim demum non ferenda mendacia, quae non solum ficta
5 esse sed ne fieri quidem potuisse cernimus. nam quartum iam
annum regnante Lucio Tarquinio Superbo Sybarim et Cro-
tonem et in eas Italiae partes Pythagoras uenisse reperitur:
olympias enim secunda et sexagesima eadem Superbi regni
29 initium et Pythagorae declarat aduentum. ex quo intellegi
regiis annis dinumeratis potest anno fere centesimo et quad-
ragesimo post mortem Numae primum Italiam Pythagoram
attigisse; neque hoc inter eos qui diligentissime persecuti sunt
temporum annales ulla est umquam in dubitatione uersatum.'

2 'Di immortales' inquit Manilius 'quantus iste est hominum et
quam inueteratus error! ac tamen facile patior non esse nos
transmarinis nec importatis artibus eruditos, sed genuinis dom-
esticisque uirtutibus.'

30 [16] 'Atqui multo id facilius cognosces,' inquit Africanus 'si progredientem rem publicam atque in optimum statum naturali quodam itinere et cursu uenientem uideris; quin hoc ipso sapientiam maiorum statues esse laudandam, quod multa intelleges etiam aliunde sumpta meliora apud nos multo esse facta quam ibi fuissent unde huc translata essent atque ubi primum exstitissent, intellegesque non fortuito populum Romanum sed consilio et disciplina confirmatum esse, nec tamen aduersante fortuna.

31 [17] 'Mortuo rege Pompilio Tullum Hostilium populus

regem interrege rogante comitiis curiatis creauit, isque de
imperio suo exemplo Pompili populum consuluit curiatim.
cuius excellens in re militari gloria magnaeque exstiterunt res 2
bellicae, fecitque idem et saepsit de manubiis comitium et
curiam, constituitque ius quo bella indicerentur, quod per se
iustissime inuentum sanxit fetiali religione, ut omne bellum
quod denuntiatum indictumque non esset, id iniustum esse
atque impium iudicaretur. et ut aduertatis animum quam 3
sapienter iam reges hoc nostri uiderint, tribuenda quaedam esse
populo – multa enim de eo genere dicenda sunt – , ne insignibus
quidem regiis Tullus nisi iussu populi est ausus uti. nam ut sibi 4
duodecim lictores cum fascibus anteire liceret' *

deest folium unum

[18] * '<neque> enim serpit sed uolat in optimum statum **33**
instituto tuo sermone res publica.'

'post eum Numae Pompili nepos ex filia rex a populo est 2
Ancus Marcius constitutus, itemque de imperio suo legem curiatam tulit. qui cum Latinos bello deuicisset, asciuit eos in 3
ciuitatem, atque idem Auentinum et Caelium montem adiunxit
urbi, quosque agros ceperat diuisit, et siluas maritimas omnes
publicauit quas ceperat, et ad ostium Tiberis urbem condidit
colonisque firmauit. atque ita cum tres et uiginti regnauisset 4
annos est mortuus.'

Tum Laelius: 'laudandus etiam iste rex; sed obscura est 5
historia Romana, siquidem istius regis matrem habemus, ignoramus patrem.'

'Ita est' inquit; 'sed temporum illorum tantum fere regum 6
illustrata sunt nomina.

[19] 'Sed hoc loco primum uidetur insitiua quadam disci- **34**
plina doctior facta esse ciuitas. influxit enim non tenuis quidam 2
e Graecia riuulus in hanc urbem, sed abundantissimus amnis
illarum disciplinarum et artium. fuisse enim quendam ferunt 3
Demaratum Corinthium, et honore et auctoritate et fortunis
facile ciuitatis suae principem; qui cum Corinthiorum tyrannum Cypselum ferre non potuisset, fugisse cum magna pecunia

dicitur ac se contulisse Tarquinios, in urbem Etruriae florentiss-
4 imam. cumque audiret dominationem Cypseli confirmari,
defugit patriam uir liber ac fortis, et ascitus est ciuis a Tarquin-
5 iensibus atque in ea ciuitate domicilium et sedes collocauit. ubi
cum de matre familias Tarquiniensi duo filios procreauisset,
omnibus eos artibus ad Graecorum disciplinam eru*

deest folium unum

35 [20] *'facile in ciuitatem receptus esset, propter humanitatem atque doctrinam Anco regi familiaris est factus usque eo
ut consiliorum omnium particeps et socius paene regni putare-
2 tur. erat in eo praeterea summa comitas, summa in omnes ciues
3 opis, auxilii, defensionis, largiendi etiam benignitas. itaque
mortuo Marcio cunctis populi suffragiis rex est creatus L.
Tarquinius; sic enim suum nomen ex Graeco nomine inflexerat,
ut in omni genere huius populi consuetudinem uideretur imi-
4 tatus. isque ut de suo imperio legem tulit, principio duplicauit
illum pristinum patrum numerum, et antiquos patres maiorum
gentium appellauit, quos priores sententiam rogabat, a se
36 ascitos minorum. deinde equitatum ad hunc morem constituit
qui usque adhuc est retentus, nec potuit Titiensium et Rham-
nensium et Lucerum mutare cum cuperet nomina, quod auctor
2 ei summa augur gloria Attus Nauius non erat. atque etiam
Corinthios uideo publicis equis assignandis et alendis orborum
3 et uiduarum tributis fuisse quondam diligentes. sed tamen
prioribus equitum partibus secundis additis M ac CC fecit
4 equites numerumque duplicauit. postea bello subegit Aequo-
rum magnam gentem et ferocem et rebus populi Romani
imminentem, idemque Sabinos cum a moenibus urbis reppu-
5 lisset, equitatu fudit belloque deuicit. atque eundem primum
ludos maximos, qui Romani dicti sunt, fecisse accepimus,
aedemque in Capitolio Ioui optimo maximo bello Sabino in
ipsa pugna uouisse faciendam, mortuumque esse cum duodequadraginta regnauisset annos.'

37 [21] Tum Laelius: 'nunc fit illud Catonis certius, nec temporis unius nec hominis esse constitutionem <nostrae> rei publi-

cae; perspicuum est enim, quanta in singulos reges rerum
bonarum et utilium fiat accessio. sed sequitur is qui mihi 2
uidetur ex omnibus in re publica uidisse plurimum.'

'Ita est' inquit Scipio. 'nam post eum Seruius Tullius primus 3
iniussu populi regnauisse traditur, quem ferunt ex serua
Tarquiniensi natum, cum esset ex quodam regis cliente concep-
tus. qui cum famulorum <in> numero educatus ad epulas regis 4
assisteret, non latuit scintilla ingenii quae iam tum elucebat in
puero: sic erat in omni uel officio uel sermone sollers. itaque 5
Tarquinius, qui admodum paruos tum haberet liberos, sic
Seruium diligebat, ut is eius uulgo haberetur filius, atque eum
summo studio omnibus iis artibus quas ipse didicerat ad exquisitissimam consuetudinem Graecorum erudiit. sed cum **38**
Tarquinius insidiis Anci filiorum interisset, Seruiusque ut ante
dixi regnare coepisset, non iussu sed uoluntate atque concessu
ciuium, quod cum Tarquinius ex uulnere aeger fuisse et uiuere
falso diceretur, ille regio ornatu ius dixisset obaeratosque
pecunia sua liberauisset, multaque comitate usus iussu Tarquinii se ius dicere probauisset, non commisit se patribus, sed
Tarquinio sepulto populum de se ipse consuluit, iussusque
regnare legem de imperio suo curiatam tulit. et primum 2
Etruscorum iniurias bello est ultus; ex quo cum ma*

deest folium unum

[22] *'duodeuiginti censu maximo. deinde equitum magno **39**
numero ex omni populi summa separato, reliquum populum
distribuit in quinque classes, senioresque a iunioribus diuisit,
easque ita disparauit ut suffragia non in multitudinis sed in
locupletium potestate essent, curauitque, quod semper in re
publica tenendum est, ne plurimum ualeant plurimi. quae 2
discriptio si esset ignota uobis, explicaretur a me; nunc
rationem uidetis esse talem, ut equitum centuriae cum sex
suffragiis et prima classis, addita centuria quae ad summum
usum urbis fabris tignariis est data, LXXXVIIII centurias
habeat; quibus e centum quattuor centuriis – tot enim reliquae
sunt – octo solae si accesserunt, confecta est uis populi uniuersa,

reliquaque multo maior multitudo sex et nonaginta centuriarum <ut> neque excluderetur suffragiis, ne superbum esset,
40 nec ualeret nimis, ne esset periculosum. in quo etiam uerbis ac
nominibus ipsis fuit diligens: qui cum locupletes assiduos
appellasset ab aere dando, eos qui aut non plus mille quingentos aeris aut omnino nihil in suum censum praeter caput attu-
lissent, proletarios nominauit, ut ex iis quasi proles, id est quasi
2 progenies ciuitatis, expectari uideretur. illarum autem sex et
nonaginta centuriarum in una centuria tum quidem plures
3 censebantur quam paene in prima classe tota. ita nec prohibe-
batur quisquam iure suffragii, et is ualebat in suffragio plurimum cuius plurimum intererat esse in optimo statu ciuitatem.
4 quin etiam accensis uelatis liticinibus cornicinibus proletariis *

desunt folia duo

42 [23] *‘<quinque et> sexaginta annis antiquior, quod erat
XXXVIIII ante primam olympiadem condita, et antiquissi-
2 mus ille Lycurgus eadem uidit fere. itaque ista aequabilitas
atque hoc triplex rerum publicarum genus uidetur mihi
3 commune nobis cum illis populis fuisse. sed quod proprium est
in nostra re publica, quo nihil possit esse praeclarius, id perse-
quar si potero subtilius; quod erit eius modi, nihil ut tale ulla in
4 re publica reperiatur. haec enim quae adhuc exposui ita mixta
fuerunt et in hac ciuitate et in Lacedaemoniorum et in Cartha-
43 giniensium ut temperata nullo fuerint modo. nam in qua re
publica est unus aliquis perpetua potestate, praesertim regia,
quamuis in ea sit et senatus, ut tum fuit Romae cum erant reges,
ut Spartae Lycurgi legibus, et ut sit aliquod etiam populi ius, ut
fuit apud nostros reges, tamen illud excellit regium nomen,
neque potest eius modi res publica non regnum et esse et uocari.
2 ea autem forma ciuitatis mutabilis maxime est hanc ob causam,
quod unius uitio praecipitata in perniciosissimam partem
3 facillime decidit. nam ipsum regale genus ciuitatis non modo
non est reprehendendum, sed haud scio an reliquis simplicibus
longe anteponendum (si ullum probarem simplex rei publicae
4 genus), sed ita quoad statum suum retineat. is est autem status,

ut unius perpetua potestate et iustitia uniusque sapientia
regatur salus et aequabilitas et otium ciuium. desunt omnino ei 5
populo multa qui sub rege est, in primisque libertas, quae non
in eo est ut iusto utamur domino, sed ut nul<lo>*

deest folium unum

[24] *'ferebant. etenim illi iniusto domino atque acerbo **44**
aliquamdiu in rebus gerundis prospere fortuna comitata est.
nam et omne Latium bello deuicit, et Suessam Pometiam 2
urbem opulentam refertamque cepit, et maxima auri argenti-
que praeda locupletatus uotum patris Capitolii aedificatione
persoluit, et colonias deduxit, et institutis eorum a quibus ortus
erat dona magnifica quasi libamenta praedarum Delphos ad
Apollinem misit.

[25] 'Hic ille iam uertetur orbis, cuius naturalem motum **45**
atque circuitum a primo discite agnoscere. id enim est caput 2
ciuilis prudentiae, in qua omnis haec nostra uersatur oratio,
uidere itinera flexusque rerum publicarum, ut cum sciatis quo
quaeque res inclinet, retinere aut ante possitis occurrere. nam 3
rex ille de quo loquor, primum optimi regis caede maculatus
integra mente non erat, et cum metueret ipse poenam sceleris
sui summam, metui se uolebat; deinde uictoriis diuitiisque
subnixus exultabat insolentia, neque suos mores regere poterat
neque suorum libidines. itaque cum maior eius filius Lucretiae **46**
Tricipitini filiae Collatini uxori uim attulisset, mulierque
pudens et nobilis ob illam iniuriam sese ipsa morte multauisset,
tum uir ingenio et uirtute praestans L. Brutus depulit a ciuibus
suis iniustum illud durae seruitutis iugum. qui cum priuatus 2
esset, totam rem publicam sustinuit, primusque in hac ciuitate
docuit in conseruanda ciuium libertate esse priuatum
neminem. quo auctore et principe concitata ciuitas et hac 3
recenti querela Lucretiae patris et propinquorum, et record-
atione superbiae Tarquinii multarumque iniuriarum et ipsius
et filiorum, exulem et regem ipsum et liberos eius et gentem
Tarquiniorum esse iussit.

[26] 'Videtisne igitur ut de rege dominus exstiterit, uniusque **47**

uitio genus rei publicae ex bono in deterrimum conuersum sit?
2 hic est enim dominus populi quem Graeci tyrannum uocant;
nam regem illum uolunt esse qui consulit ut parens populo,
conseruatque eos quibus est praepositus quam optima in condicione uiuendi, sane bonum ut dixi rei publicae genus, sed
tamen inclinatum et quasi pronum ad perniciosissimum
48 statum. simul atque enim se inflexit hic rex in dominatum
iniustiorem, fit continuo tyrannus, quo neque taetrius neque
foedius nec dis hominibusque inuisius animal ullum cogitari
potest; qui quamquam figura est hominis, morum tamen imma-
2 nitate uastissimas uincit beluas. quis enim hunc hominem rite
dixerit, qui sibi cum suis ciuibus, qui denique cum omni
hominum genere nullam iuris communionem, nullam humani-
3 tatis societatem uelit? sed erit hoc de genere nobis alius aptior
dicendi locus, cum res ipsa admonuerit ut in eos dicamus qui
etiam liberata iam ciuitate dominationes appetiuerunt.

49 [27] 'Habetis igitur primum ortum tyranni; nam hoc nomen
Graeci regis iniusti esse uoluerunt; nostri quidem omnes reges
uocitauerunt qui soli in populos perpetuam potestatem habe-
2 rent. itaque et Spurius Cassius et M. Manlius et Spurius
Maelius regnum occupare uoluisse dicti sunt, et modo*

deest folium unum

50 [28] *'<La>cedaemone appellauit, nimis is quidem paucos,
XXVIII, quos penes summam consilii uoluit esse, cum imperii
2 summam rex teneret. ex quo nostri idem illud secuti atque
interpretati, quos senes ille appellauit, nominauerunt senatum,
ut iam Romulum patribus lectis fecisse diximus; tamen excellit
3 atque eminet uis potestas nomenque regium. imperti etiam
populo potestatis aliquid, ut et Lycurgus et Romulus: non
satiaris eum libertate, sed incenderis cupiditate libertatis, cum
4 tantum modo potestatem gustandi feceris. ille quidem semper
impendebit timor, ne rex – quod plerumque euenit – exsistat
5 iniustus. est igitur fragilis ea fortuna populi, quae posita est in
unius ut dixi antea uoluntate uel moribus.

51 [29] 'Quare prima sit haec forma et species et origo tyranni

inuenta nobis in ea re publica quam auspicato Romulus condiderit, non in illa quam, ut perscripsit Plato, sibi ipse Socrates †peripeateto† illo in sermone depinxerit, ut quem ad modum Tarquinius, non nouam potestatem nactus, sed quam habebat usus iniuste, totum genus hoc regiae ciuitatis euerterit; sit huic oppositus alter, bonus et sapiens et peritus utilitatis dignitatisque ciuilis, quasi tutor et procurator rei publicae: sic enim
appelletur quicumque erit rector et gubernator ciuitatis. quem 2
uirum facite ut agnoscatis; iste est enim qui consilio et opera
ciuitatem tueri potest. quod quoniam nomen minus est adhuc 3
tritum sermone nostro, saepiusque genus eius hominis erit in reliqua nobis oratione trac<tandum>*

desunt folia sex

[30] *'<cau>sas requisiuit, ciuitatemque optandam magis **52**
quam sperandam, quam minimam potuit, non quae posset esse,
sed in qua ratio rerum ciuilium perspici posset, effecit. ego 2
autem, si modo consequi potuero, rationibus eisdem quas ille uidit non in umbra et imagine ciuitatis sed in amplissima re publica enitar, ut cuiusque et boni publici et mali causam
tamquam uirgula uidear attingere. iis enim regiis quadraginta 3
annis et ducentis paulo cum interregnis fere amplius praeteritis, pulsoque Tarquinio, tantum odium populum Romanum regalis nominis tenuit, quantum tenuerat post obitum uel
potius excessum Romuli desiderium. itaque ut tum carere rege, 4
sic pulso Tarquinio nomen regis audire non poterat. hic facultatem cum*

desunt folia octo

[31] *'lex illa tota sublata est. hac mente tum nostri maiores **53**
et Collatinum innocentem suspicione cognationis expulerunt, et reliquos Tarquinios offensione nominis, eademque mente P. Valerius et fasces primus demitti iussit, cum dicere in contione coepisset, et aedes suas detulit sub Veliam posteaquam, quod in excelsiore loco Veliae coepisset aedificare eo ipso ubi rex Tullus habitauerat, suspicionem populi sensit moueri; idemque, in quo fuit Publicola maxime, legem ad populum tulit eam quae

centuriatis comitiis prima lata est, ne quis magistratus ciuem
Romanum aduersus prouocationem necaret neue uerberaret.
54 prouocationem autem etiam a regibus fuisse declarant pontificii
libri, significant nostri etiam augurales; itemque ab omni
iudicio poenaque prouocari licere indicant XII tabulae compluribus legibus; et quod proditum memoriae est decemuiros
qui leges scripserint sine prouocatione creatos, satis ostendit
reliquos sine prouocatione magistratus non fuisse; Lucique
Valeri Potiti et M. Horati Barbati, hominum concordiae causa
sapienter popularium, consularis lex sanxit ne qui magistratus
2 sine prouocatione crearetur. neque uero leges Porciae, quae
tres sunt trium Porciorum ut scitis, quicquam praeter sanc-
55 tionem attulerunt noui. itaque Publicola lege illa de prouocatione perlata statim secures de fascibus demi iussit, postridie-
que sibi collegam Sp. Lucretium surrogauit, suosque ad eum
quod erat maior natu lictores transire iussit, instituitque primus
ut singulis consulibus alternis mensibus lictores praeirent, ne
plura insignia essent imperii in libero populo quam in regno
2 fuissent. haud mediocris hic ut ego quidem intellego uir fuit, qui
modica libertate populo data facilius tenuit auctoritatem prin-
3 cipum. neque ego haec nunc sine causa tam uetera uobis et tam
obsoleta decanto, sed illustribus in personis temporibusque
exempla hominum rerumque definio, ad quae reliqua oratio
derigatur mea.

56 [32] 'Tenuit igitur hoc in statu senatus rem publicam temporibus illis, ut in populo libero pauca per populum, pleraque
senatus auctoritate et instituto ac more gererentur, atque uti
consules potestatem haberent tempore dumtaxat annuam,
genere ipso ac iure regiam, quodque erat ad obtinendam
potentiam nobilium uel maximum, uehementer id retinebatur,
populi comitia ne essent rata nisi ea patrum approbauisset
2 auctoritas. atque his ipsis temporibus dictator etiam est institu-
tus decem fere annis post primos consules T. Larcius, nouum-
que id genus imperii uisum est et proximum similitudini regiae.
3 sed tamen omnia summa cum auctoritate a principibus cedente

populo tenebantur, magnaeque res temporibus illis a fortissimis
uiris summo imperio praeditis, dictatoribus atque consulibus,
belli gerebantur.

[33] 'Sed id quod fieri natura rerum ipsa cogebat, ut pluscu- 57
lum sibi iuris populus ascisceret liberatus a regibus, non longo
interuallo, sexto decimo fere anno, Postumo Cominio Sp.
Cassio consulibus consecutum est; in quo defuit fortasse ratio,
sed tamen uincit ipsa rerum publicarum natura saepe
rationem. id enim tenetote quod initio dixi, nisi aequabilis haec 2
in ciuitate compensatio sit et iuris et officii et muneris, ut et
potestatis satis in magistratibus et auctoritatis in principum
consilio et libertatis in populo sit, non posse hunc incommutabilem rei publicae conseruari statum. nam cum esset ex aere 58
alieno commota ciuitas, plebs montem sacrum prius, deinde
Auentinum occupauit. ac ne Lycurgi quidem disciplina tenuit 2
illos in hominibus Graecis frenos: nam etiam Spartae regnante
Theopompo sunt item quinque quos illi ephoros appellant, in
Creta autem decem qui cosmoe uocantur, ut contra consulare
imperium tribuni plebis, sic illi contra uim regiam constituti.

[34] 'Fuerat fortasse aliqua ratio maioribus nostris in illo aere 59
alieno medendi, quae neque Solonem Atheniensem non longis
temporibus ante fugerat, neque post aliquanto nostrum
senatum, cum sunt propter unius libidinem omnia nexa ciuium
liberata nectierque postea desitum, semperque huic oneri, cum
plebes publica calamitate impendiis debilitata deficeret, salutis
omnium causa aliqua subleuatio et medicina quaesita est. quo 2
tum consilio praetermisso causa populo nata est, duobus tribunis plebis per seditionem creatis, ut potentia senatus atque
auctoritas minueretur; quae tamen grauis et magna remanebat,
sapientissimis et fortissimis et armis et consilio ciuitatem tuentibus, quorum auctoritas maxime florebat, quod cum honore
longe antecellerent ceteris, uoluptatibus erant inferiores nec
pecuniis ferme superiores; eoque erat cuiusque gratior in re
publica uirtus, quod in rebus priuatis diligentissime singulos
ciues opera consilio re tuebantur.

60 [35] 'Quo in statu rei publicae Sp. Cassium de occupando
regno molientem, summa apud populum gratia florentem,
quaestor accusauit, eumque ut audistis cum pater in ea culpa
esse comperisse se dixisset, cedente populo morte mactauit.
2 gratamque etiam illam legem quarto circiter et quinquagesimo
anno post primos consules de multa et sacramento Sp. Tarpeius
3 et A. Aternius consules comitiis centuriatis tulerunt. annis
postea XX, ex eo quod L. Papirius P. Pinarius censores multis
dicendis uim armentorum a priuatis in publicum auerterant,
leuis aestumatio pecudum in multa lege C. Iuli P. Papiri
consulum constituta est.

61 [36] 'Sed aliquot ante annis, cum summa esset auctoritas in
senatu populo patiente atque parente, inita ratio est ut et
consules et tribuni plebis magistratu se abdicarent, atque ut
decemuiri maxima potestate sine prouocatione crearentur, qui
2 et summum imperium haberent et leges scriberent. qui cum X
tabulas legum summa aequitate prudentiaque conscripsissent,
in annum posterum decemuiros alios surrogauerunt, quorum
3 non similiter fides nec iustitia laudata. quo tamen e collegio laus
est illa eximia C. Iuli, qui hominem nobilem L. Sestium, cuius
in cubiculo effossum esse se praesente corpus mortuum diceret,
cum ipse potestatem summam haberet quod decemuirum unus
sine prouocatione esset, uades tamen poposcit, quod se legem
illam praeclaram neglecturum negaret, quae de capite ciuis
Romani nisi comitiis centuriatis statui uetaret.

62 [37] 'Tertius est annus decemuiralis consecutus, cum idem
2 essent nec alios subrogare uoluissent. in hoc statu rei publicae,
quem dixi iam saepe non posse esse diuturnum, quod non esset
in omnis ordines ciuitatis aequabilis, erat penes principes tota
res publica, praepositis decemuiris nobilissimis, non oppositis
tribunis plebis, nullis aliis adiunctis magistratibus, non prouo-
63 catione ad populum contra necem et uerbera relicta. ergo
horum ex iniustitia subito exorta est maxima perturbatio et
totius commutatio rei publicae; qui duabus tabulis iniquarum
legum additis, quibus etiam quae diiunctis populis tribui solent

conubia, haec illi ut ne plebei cum patribus essent, inhumanis-
sima lege sanxerunt, quae postea plebei scito Canuleio abrogata
est, libidinose[que] omni imperio et acerbe et auare populo
praefuerunt. nota scilicet illa res et celebrata monumentis pluri- 2
mis litterarum, cum Decimus quidam Verginius uirginem
filiam propter unius ex illis decemuiris intemperiem in foro sua
manu interemisset, ac maerens ad exercitum qui tum erat in
Algido confugisset, milites bellum illud quod erat in manibus
reliquisse, et primum montem sacrum, sicut erat in simili causa
antea factum, deinde Auentinum ar*

desunt folia quattuor

*'<maio>res nostros et probauisse maxime et retinuisse 3
sapientissime iudico.'

LIBER VI

[1] 'Cum in Africam uenissem hoc Manilio consule ad quartam **9**
legionem tribunus ut scitis militum, nihil mihi fuit potius quam
ut Masinissam conuenirem, regem familiae nostrae iustis de
causis amicissimum. ad quem ut ueni, complexus me senex 2
collacrimauit aliquantoque post suspexit ad caelum et "grates"
inquit "tibi ago summe Sol, uobisque reliqui caelites, quod ante
quam ex hac uita migro, conspicio in meo regno et his tectis P.
Cornelium Scipionem, cuius ego nomine ipso recreor: ita[que]
numquam ex animo meo discedit illius optimi atque inuictissimi uiri memoria." deinde ego illum de suo regno, ille me de 3
nostra re publica percontatus est, multisque uerbis ultro citroque habitis ille nobis est consumptus dies.

'Post autem apparatu regio accepti, sermonem in multam **10**
noctem produximus, cum senex nihil nisi de Africano loquer-
etur, omniaque eius non facta solum sed etiam dicta memi-
nisset. deinde ut cubitum discessimus, me et de uia fessum, et 2
qui ad multam noctem uigilassem, artior quam solebat somnus
complexus est. hic mihi – credo equidem ex hoc quod eramus 3
locuti; fit enim fere ut cogitationes sermonesque nostri pariant

aliquid in somno tale, quale de Homero scribit Ennius, de quo
uidelicet saepissime uigilans solebat cogitare et loqui – Africanus se ostendit ea forma quae mihi ex imagine eius quam ex
4 ipso erat notior. quem ubi agnoui, equidem cohorrui; sed ille
"ades" inquit "animo et omitte timorem, Scipio, et quae dicam
trade memoriae.

11 [2] '"Videsne illam urbem, quae parere populo Romano
coacta per me renouat pristina bella nec potest quiescere?"
2 (ostendebat autem Carthaginem de excelso et pleno stellarum,
3 illustri et claro quodam loco.) "ad quam tu oppugnandam
nunc uenis paene miles, hanc hoc biennio consul euertes,
eritque cognomen id tibi per te partum quod habes adhuc a
4 nobis hereditarium. cum autem Carthaginem deleueris,
triumphum egeris censorque fueris, et obieris legatus Aegyptum, Syriam, Asiam, Graeciam, deligere iterum consul absens
5 bellumque maximum conficies, Numantiam exscindes. sed cum
eris curru in Capitolium inuectus, offendes rem publicam consi-
12 liis perturbatam nepotis mei. hic tu, Africane, ostendas oporte-
2 bit patriae lumen animi ingeniique tui consiliique. sed eius
3 temporis ancipitem uideo quasi fatorum uiam. nam cum aetas
tua septenos octiens solis anfractus reditusque conuerterit,
duoque hi numeri, quorum uterque plenus alter altera de causa
habetur, circuitu naturali summam tibi fatalem confecerint, in
te unum atque in tuum nomen se tota conuertet ciuitas: te
senatus, te omnes boni, te socii, te Latini intuebuntur; tu eris
4 unus in quo nitatur ciuitatis salus. ac ne multa: dictator rem
publicam constituas oportet, si impias propinquorum manus
effugeris."'

5 Hic cum exclamauisset Laelius ingemuissentque uehementius ceteri, leniter arridens Scipio 'st! quaeso' inquit 'ne me e
somno excitetis, et parumper audite cetera.'

13 [3] '"Sed quo sis, Africane, alacrior ad tutandam rem publicam, sic habeto: omnibus qui patriam conseruauerint adiuuerint auxerint certum esse in caelo definitum locum, ubi beati
2 aeuo sempiterno fruantur. nihil est enim illi principi deo qui

omnem mundum regit, quod quidem in terris fiat, acceptius
quam concilia coetusque hominum iure sociati, quae ciuitates
appellantur; harum rectores et conseruatores hinc profecti huc
reuertuntur."

'Hic ego etsi eram perterritus non tam mortis metu quam **14**
insidiarum a meis, quaesiui tamen uiueretne ipse et Paullus
pater et alii quos nos exstinctos esse arbitraremur. "immo uero" 2
inquit "hi uiuunt qui e corporum uinclis tamquam e carcere
euolauerunt, uestra uero quae dicitur uita mors est. quin tu 3
aspicis ad te uenientem Paullum patrem?" quem ut uidi, 4
equidem uim lacrimarum profudi, ille autem me complexus
atque osculans flere prohibebat.

'Atque ego ut primum fletu represso loqui posse coepi, **15**
"quaeso," inquam "pater sanctissime atque optume, quoniam
haec est uita, ut Africanum audio dicere, quid moror in terris?
quin huc ad uos uenire propero?"

'"Non est ita" inquit ille. "nisi enim cum deus is, cuius hoc 2
templum est omne quod conspicis, istis te corporis custodiis
liberauerit, huc tibi aditus patere non potest. homines enim 3
sunt hac lege generati, qui tuerentur illum globum quem in hoc
templo medium uides, quae terra dicitur, iisque animus datus
est ex illis sempiternis ignibus quae sidera et stellas uocatis,
quae globosae et rotundae, diuinis animatae mentibus, circos
suos orbesque conficiunt celeritate mirabili. quare et tibi, Publi, 4
et piis omnibus retinendus animus est in custodia corporis nec
iniussu eius, a quo ille est uobis datus, ex hominum uita migrandum est, ne munus humanum assignatum a deo defugisse
uideamini. sed sic, Scipio, ut auus hic tuus, ut ego qui te genui, **16**
iustitiam cole et pietatem, quae cum magna in parentibus et
propinquis, tum in patria maxima est; ea uita uia est in caelum
et in hunc coetum eorum qui iam uixerunt et corpore laxati
illum incolunt locum quem uides" (erat autem is splendidissimo
candore inter flammas circus elucens), "quem uos, ut a Grais
accepistis, orbem lacteum nuncupatis." ex quo omnia mihi 2
contemplanti praeclara cetera et mirabilia uidebantur. erant 3

autem eae stellae quas numquam ex hoc loco uidimus, et eae
magnitudines omnium quas esse numquam suspicati sumus, ex
quibus erat ea minima quae ultima a caelo, citima <a> terris,
4 luce lucebat aliena. stellarum autem globi terrae magnitudinem facile uincebant; iam uero ipsa terra ita mihi parua uisa
est, ut me imperii nostri, quo quasi punctum eius attingimus,
paeniteret.

17 [4] 'Quam cum magis intuerer, "quaeso," inquit Africanus
"quousque humi defixa tua mens erit? nonne aspicis quae in
2 templa ueneris? nouem tibi orbibus uel potius globis conexa
sunt omnia, quorum unus est caelestis, extumus, qui reliquos
omnes complectitur, summus ipse deus arcens et continens
ceteros, in quo sunt infixi illi qui uoluuntur stellarum cursus
sempiterni; cui subiecti sunt septem qui uersantur retro contra-
3 rio motu atque caelum. ex quibus unum globum possidet illa
quam in terris Saturniam nominant; deinde est hominum
generi prosperus et salutaris ille fulgor qui dicitur Iouis; tum
rutilus horribilisque terris quem Martium dicitis; deinde subter
mediam fere regionem Sol obtinet, dux et princeps et moderator luminum reliquorum, mens mundi et temperatio, tanta
4 magnitudine ut cuncta sua luce lustret et compleat. hunc ut
comites consequuntur Veneris alter, alter Mercurii cursus, in
5 infimoque orbe Luna radiis Solis accensa conuertitur. infra
autem iam nihil est nisi mortale et caducum praeter animos
munere deorum hominum generi datos; supra Lunam sunt
6 aeterna omnia. nam ea quae est media et nona, Tellus, neque
mouetur et infima est, et in eam feruntur omnia nutu suo
pondera."

18 [5] 'Quae cum intuerer stupens, ut me recepi, "quid? hic"
inquam "quis est qui complet aures meas tantus et tam dulcis
sonus?"

2 '"Hic est" inquit "ille qui interuallis coniunctus imparibus,
sed tamen pro rata parte ratione distinctis, impulsu et motu
ipsorum orbium efficitur, et acuta cum grauibus temperans
uarios aequabiliter concentus efficit; nec enim silentio tanti

motus incitari possunt, et natura fert ut extrema in altera parte
grauiter, ex altera autem acute sonent. quam ob causam 3
summus ille caeli stellifer cursus, cuius conuersio est concitatior,
acuto et excitato mouetur sono, grauissimo autem hic lunaris
atque infimus; nam terra nona immobilis manens una sede
semper haeret, complexa medium mundi locum. illi autem octo 4
cursus, in quibus eadem uis est duorum, septem efficiunt distinctos interuallis sonos, qui numerus rerum omnium fere nodus
est; quod docti homines neruis imitati atque cantibus aperuer-
unt sibi reditum in hunc locum, sicut alii qui praestantibus
ingeniis in uita humana diuina studia coluerunt. hoc sonitu **19**
oppletae aures hominum obsurduerunt; nec est ullus hebetior
sensus in uobis, sicut ubi Nilus ad illa quae Catadupa nominan-
tur praecipitat ex altissimis montibus, ea gens quae illum locum
accolit propter magnitudinem sonitus sensu audiendi caret. hic 2
uero tantus est totius mundi incitatissima conuersione sonitus,
ut eum aures hominum capere non possint, sicut intueri solem
aduersum nequitis, eiusque radiis acies uestra sensusque
uincitur."

[6] 'Haec ego admirans referebam tamen oculos ad terram **20**
identidem. tum Africanus "sentio" inquit "te sedem etiam nunc 2
hominum ac domum contemplari; quae si tibi parua ut est ita
uidetur, haec caelestia semper spectato, illa humana contemnito. tu enim quam celebritatem sermonis hominum, aut quam 3
expetendam consequi gloriam potes? uides habitari in terra 4
raris et angustis in locis, et in ipsis quasi maculis ubi habitatur
uastas solitudines interiectas, eosque qui incolant terram non
modo interruptos ita esse ut nihil inter ipsos ab aliis ad alios
manare possit, sed partim obliquos, partim transuersos, partim
etiam aduersos stare uobis; a quibus exspectare gloriam certe
nullam potestis.

'"Cernis autem eandem terram quasi quibusdam redimitam **21**
et circumdatam cingulis, e quibus duos maxime inter se diuersos et caeli uerticibus ipsis ex utraque parte subnixos obriguisse
pruina uides, medium autem illum et maximum solis ardore

2 torreri. duo sunt habitabiles, quorum australis ille, in quo qui
insistunt aduersa uobis urgent uestigia, nihil ad uestrum genus;
hic autem alter subiectus aquiloni quem incolitis, cerne quam
3 tenui uos parte contingat. omnis enim terra quae colitur a
uobis, angustata uerticibus, lateribus latior, parua quaedam
insula est circumfusa illo mari quod Atlanticum, quod
magnum, quem Oceanum appellatis in terris, qui tamen tanto
22 nomine quam sit paruus uides. ex his ipsis cultis notisque terris
num aut tuum aut cuiusquam nostrum nomen uel Caucasum
hunc quem cernis transcendere potuit uel illum Gangen trana-
2 tare? quis in reliquis orientis aut obeuntis solis ultimis aut
3 aquilonis austriue partibus tuum nomen audiet? quibus amputatis cernis profecto quantis in angustiis uestra se gloria dilatari
4 uelit. ipsi autem qui de nobis loquuntur, quam loquentur diu?

23 [7] '"Quin etiam si cupiat proles illa futurorum hominum
deinceps laudes unius cuiusque nostrum a patribus acceptas
posteris prodere, tamen propter eluuiones exustionesque terrarum, quas accidere tempore certo necesse est, non modo non
aeternam, sed ne diuturnam quidem gloriam adsequi possu-
2 mus. quid autem interest ab iis qui postea nascentur sermonem
fore de te, cum ab iis nullus fuerit qui ante nati sunt, qui nec
24 pauciores et certe meliores fuerunt uiri; praesertim cum apud
eos ipsos a quibus audiri nomen nostrum potest, nemo unius
2 anni memoriam consequi possit? homines enim populariter
annum tantum modo solis, id est unius astri, reditu metiuntur;
re ipsa autem cum ad idem unde semel profecta sunt cuncta
astra redierint eandemque totius caeli discriptionem longis
interuallis rettulerint, tum ille uere uertens annus appellari
potest: in quo uix dicere audeo quam multa hominum saecla
3 teneantur. namque ut olim deficere sol hominibus exstinguique
uisus est, cum Romuli animus haec ipsa in templa penetrauit,
quandoque ab eadem parte sol eodemque tempore iterum
defecerit, tum signis omnibus ad idem principium stellisque
reuocatis expletum annum habeto; cuius quidem anni nondum
uicesimam partem scito esse conuersam.

'"Quocirca si reditum in hunc locum desperaueris, in quo **25**
omnia sunt magnis et praestantibus uiris, quanti tandem est ista
hominum gloria, quae pertinere uix ad unius anni partem
exiguam potest? igitur alte spectare si uoles atque hanc sedem et 2
aeternam domum contueri neque te sermonibus uulgi dederis
nec in praemiis humanis spem posueris rerum tuarum, suis te
oportet illecebris ipsa uirtus trahat ad uerum decus. quid de te 3
alii loquantur, ipsi uideant, sed loquentur tamen; sermo autem
omnis ille et angustiis cingitur his regionum quas uides nec
umquam de ullo perennis fuit et obruitur hominum interitu et
obliuione posteritatis exstinguitur."

[8] 'Quae cum dixisset, "ego uero," inquam "Africane, **26**
siquidem bene meritis de patria quasi limes ad caeli aditum
patet, quamquam a pueritia uestigiis ingressus patris et tuis
decori uestro non defui, nunc tamen tanto praemio exposito
enitar multo uigilantius."

'Et ille: "tu uero enitere et sic habeto, non esse te mortalem 2
sed corpus hoc; nec enim tu is es quem forma ista declarat, sed
mens cuiusque is est quisque, non ea figura quae digito demonstrari potest. deum te igitur scito esse, siquidem est deus qui 3
uiget, qui sentit, qui meminit, qui prouidet, qui tam regit et
moderatur et mouet id corpus cui praepositus est, quam hunc
mundum ille princeps deus; et ut mundum ex quadam parte
mortalem ipse deus aeternus, sic fragile corpus animus sem-
piternus mouet. nam quod semper mouetur, aeternum est; **27**
quod autem motum adfert alicui quodque ipsum agitatur
aliunde, quando finem habet motus, uiuendi finem habeat
necesse est. solum igitur quod se ipsum mouet, quia numquam 2
deseritur a se, numquam ne moueri quidem desinit; quin etiam
ceteris quae mouentur hic fons, hoc principium est mouendi.
principii autem nulla est origo: nam ex principio oriuntur 3
omnia, ipsum autem nulla ex re alia nasci potest; nec enim esset
id principium quod gigneretur aliunde. quodsi numquam 4
oritur, ne occidit quidem umquam: nam principium exstinc-
tum nec ipsum ab alio renascetur nec ex se aliud creabit,

5 siquidem necesse est a principio oriri omnia. ita fit ut motus principium ex eo sit quod ipsum a se mouetur; id autem nec nasci potest nec mori, uel concidat omne caelum omnisque natura et consistat necesse est, nec uim ullam nanciscatur qua a
28 primo impulsa moueatur. [9] cum pateat igitur aeternum id esse quod a se ipso moueatur, quis est qui hanc naturam animis
2 esse tributam neget? inanimum est enim omne quod pulsu agitatur externo; quod autem est animal, id motu cietur interiore et suo; nam haec est propria natura animi atque uis; quae si est una ex omnibus quae se ipsa moueat, neque nata certe est et
29 aeterna est. hanc tu exerce in optimis rebus! sunt autem optimae curae de salute patriae, quibus agitatus et exercitatus animus uelocius in hanc sedem et domum suam peruolabit; idque ocius faciet, si iam tum cum erit inclusus in corpore, eminebit foras, et ea quae extra erunt contemplans quam
2 maxime se a corpore abstrahet. namque eorum animi qui se corporis uoluptatibus dediderunt earumque se quasi ministros praebuerunt impulsuque libidinum uoluptatibus oboedientium deorum et hominum iura uiolauerunt, corporibus elapsi circum terram ipsam uolutantur nec hunc in locum nisi multis exagitati saeculis reuertuntur."

3 'Ille discessit; ego somno solutus sum.'

COMMENTARY

De re publica 1

Book 1 falls into three parts: the remainder of the preface in C.'s own voice (1–13); a preliminary narrative and conversation, introducing the participants in the dialogue and defining the subject of the work as a whole (14–37); and a discussion of the theory of constitutions (38–69). A brief conclusion (70–1) provides a transition from theory to the historical account of Rome in book 2.

Preface

Seventeen leaves – slightly more than the extant portion of the preface – are lost at the opening of P; the elaborate introduction was far longer than the preface of any other Ciceronian dialogue. The book will have begun with an address to C.'s brother Quintus (cf. 1.13 *mihi tibique*; also *De orat.* 1.1); a reference to their own discussions about public life will have led to the topic of *Rep.* itself. What survives is part of a polemic against the philosophic devaluation of civic responsibility. P begins near the end of a discussion of the role of individual *uirtus* and patriotism in the success of the state (1). From this C. moves to a demonstration that *uirtus* is most suitably employed in public life, itself the manifestation of the highest and most useful form of *uirtus* (2–3). He then rebuts objections to this view: that public life is dangerous (4–8) and unworthy of respectable men (9); and that a philosopher should only take it up in a crisis (10–11). The preface concludes with a reference (presumably reiterating the lost opening) to the value of both political writing and political action, followed by a transition to the dramatic setting of the dialogue itself (12–13). For reconstruction and analysis, cf. Pohlenz 72–7, Meister (1940) 95–101. C.'s sense of the moral and practical necessity of political action was shaped by his own experiences, both his triumph in exposing the Catilinarian conspiracy in 63 and his exile and return in 58–57; the hortatory and protreptic tone of the preface resembles that of *Pro Sestio* of March 56.

1.1 P begins early in the apodosis of a complex sentence, the protasis of which must have been something like 'If they had not preferred virtue to the enticements of *uoluptas* and *otium*'; for supplements cf. Schmidt (1973) 279, Büchner *ad loc.* The fragmentary clause probably referred to the war against Pyrrhus, and Camillus' defeat of the Gauls may have preceded that. The structure of the sentence is elaborate: major elements of the apodosis were articulated by anaphora of *non* (only one now extant) and subdivisions by *nec*; the final section is marked by a tricolon with anaphora of *aut*; and the sentence ends with a double-cretic clausula. C. favours lists of virtuous Romans of old: cf. *Sest.* 143; *Tusc.* 1.89, 110; *Parad.* 1.12; *Sen.* 75; *N.D.* 2.165. This list is chronological: C. Duilius, A. Atilius Calatinus, and L. Caecilius Metellus won battles in the First Punic War; the brothers P. and Cn. Cornelius Scipio (father and uncle of the elder Africanus) were killed in Spain in 211 during the Second Punic War; and Q. Fabius Maximus, M. Claudius Marcellus, and P. Cornelius Scipio Africanus were the greatest heroes of that war. The list ends suitably with Africanus, the adoptive grandfather of Scipio Aemilianus and himself the major speaker of the *Somnium*. **oriens ... restinxissent:** for similar metaphors cf. *Dom.* 144, *Sest.* 82, *Phil.* 13.48. **eneruauisset:** the only other use of the finite vb. (as opposed to *eneruatus* 'effeminate') in C. is *Sen.* 32 *non plane me eneruauit ... senectus*, also meaning 'destroy one's strength'. **contudisset:** cf. 6.1 *qui contuderit eius uim et ecfrenatam illam ferociam.*

1.2 M. ... Catoni: M. Porcius Cato, cos. 195, cens. 184, a dominant political and intellectual figure of the first half of the second century: cf. Astin (1978). In this list he is both the latest person named and the climax (indicated by *uero*), as an instance of lifelong service and as a model of civic virtue. C. frequently cites Cato as a precedent for his own career; he was drawn to him both as a politically successful *nouus homo* (cf. particularly *Verr.* 5.180) and as a public figure who was also an orator and man of letters. For Cato as C.'s spiritual ancestor as a *nouus homo*, cf. Wiseman (1971) 107–10; for a brief discussion of C.'s views of Cato with full bibliography, cf. Powell, ed., *Sen.* pp. 17–19; cf. also 2.1.1n. **ignoto et nouo:** emphasized because Cato's lack of inherited reputation and family tradition would have made a life of *otium* an acceptable alternative to public service. **quo ... exemplari:** abl. of instrument rather than of agent, as *exemplar* is the dominant idea. **in otio delectare:** *otium* (or *otiosus*) occurs 8x in §§1–9, and three more in the introductory conversation at 14. Here (as also §1.2, 5) it is pejorative: 'the easy life', linked at §1.5 with *uoluptas* as an element in C.'s attack on philosophers (Epicureans in particular) for rejecting public life; so also at 8.1 and 9.1. It can also be more positive, as at 7.4, 14.3, 14.5, where it refers to those periods of relaxation from public service which give the statesman an opportunity for reflection and contemplation; for a clear instance of the contrast between good (temporary) and bad (permanent) relaxation, cf. *Brut.* 8 *in portum confugere ... non inertiae neque desidiae, sed oti moderati atque honesti.* This temporary *otium* of holidays, as in 14, is the occasion for the conversations of both *Rep.* and *De orat.*, just as C.'s own enforced political retirement is the occasion for their composition. In these circumstances, *otium* itself merges with the writing and discussion which arise from it (and thus becomes an element in the active life; cf. §2.1n.), and is a positive contribution to the quality of civic life. A third, political meaning of *otium* 'domestic tranquillity' or 'law and order', which appears at §6.2 and 7.4 (also e.g. *Sest.* 5, 15), should also be distinguished. The bibliography (particularly on the phrase *cum dignitate otium* at *Sest.* 98, *De orat.* 1.1, *Fam.* 1.9.21; cf. also *Ag.* 2.9) is large; cf. Kretschmar, Wirszubski (1954), Fuhrmann, André, Wood 193–205. **Tusculi:** Tusculum (some 23 km. SE from Rome) was Cato's place of origin (and the site of one of C.'s favourite villas).

1.3 ut isti putant: Epicureans (such as L. Piso? cf. *Sest.* 23) rather than philosophers in general, as at §2.1, or unnamed Romans who have rejected public life: cf. the Epicurean catchword *uoluptas* at §1.5, 10.1n. **in his undis et tempestatibus:** the metaphor of the storm at sea is part of a larger complex of metaphors, including the ship of state and the voyage of life (or of public policy), all of which C. employs frequently, particularly with reference to his consulate and exile. In *Rep.* 1, cf. 2.1, 3.5, 7.4, 11.1, 45.2, 51.1, 62.1, 63.1. Vivid examples also at *De orat.* 1.2; *Att.* 2.7.4; *Dom.* 24, 137; *Sest.* 46, 73, 98; *Pis.* 20; *Planc.* 94; *Mil.* 5. These metaphors have a long history before C.; brief survey in Nisbet–Hubbard on Hor. *Carm.* 1.14. For a list of metaphors denoting disasters to the *res publica*, cf. Drexler (1957) 279–80. **tranquillitate** continues the nautical metaphor (cf. 11.1 *tranquillo mari*) and modulates back to *otium.*

1.4 quorum singuli: one expects *qui* rather than *quorum*, but for similar uses of the partitive genitive with numbers and expressions of quantity, cf. K–S I 425–6. **<haud> procul:** the two relative clauses must refer to those more recent than Cato, including C.'s contemporaries; Mai's supplement *haud* or Steinacker's *non* is necessary. There is asyndeton between the two main verbs *omitto* and *desino*, as Lehner's punctuation (adopted here) makes clear; for other conjectures or explanations of the text, cf. Hommel (1955b) 353–5 (accepting the transmitted text), Schmidt (1973) 279, Gigon 283–4, and Büchner *ad loc*. For a similar refusal to name the living, cf. *Sest.* 101.

1.5 unum hoc definio 'I make this one assertion.' *definio* 'state' governs the acc. *hoc*, to which the indirect statement which follows is appositive. The usage is relatively uncommon in classical Latin; *definio* followed by an indirect statement is largely found in legal texts (*OLD* s.v. 6). **tantumque amorem:** sc. *uirtutis*. *ad ... defendendam* is a gerundive of purpose with *esse ... datum*, while *datum* formally agrees with *amorem* but applies to both *necessitas* and *amor*, the two together being summarized by *ea uis*. At *Tusc.* 1.33 willingness to labour for the public good is derived from belief in the immortality of the soul rather than from innate *uirtus* and patriotism; in the *Somnium* (cf. 6.25.2), C. avoids drawing that conclusion. **uoluptatis:** normally associated with Epicureans, and therefore generally pejorative in C. *blandior*/*blandus* and *uoluptas* are frequently associated; cf. *Luc.* 139, *Fin.* 1.33, *Tusc.* 4.6 (all of Epicureanism); also *Sen.* 44, *Off.* 2.37; *uoluptas* and *otium* are associated pejoratively at *Sest.* 23 and 139; cf. also *Arch.* 12. For a positive use of *uoluptas*, cf. §3.5.

2 Up to this point, C. has argued that *uirtus* is a natural human characteristic; he now shows that it is to be understood not merely as a mental quality (*ars*), but as something that exists only through being employed in action.

2.1 nisi utare: a pres. general condition, subjunctive because of the indefinite second-person subject. C. prefers the second-person sing. pass. ending in *-ris* only for the pres. indic., that in *-re* for all other tenses; cf. N–W III 204–6. On the style of this sentence, cf. Introduction, pp. 31–2. **etsi ... potest:** the concessive clause *cum* (= 'although') *ea non utare* is subordinated to another, enclosing, concessive clause *etsi ... potest*, which is in turn subordinate to the main clause. *tamen* signposts the construction. **uirtus ... posita est:** so too *Fin.* 5.58 *ergo hoc quidem apparet nos ad agendum esse natos*; *N.D.* 1.110 *uirtus autem actuosa*; *Off.* 1.19 *uirtutis enim laus in actione consistit*. The question whether virtue (ἀρετή) is an abstract or a practical form of knowledge goes back to Plato, but C. conceives it in terms of the Peripatetic debate between Theophrastus' advocacy of the speculative life (βίος θεωρητικός) and Dicaearchus' advocacy of the active life (βίος πρακτικός): see *Att.* 2.12.4, 2.16.3, 7.3.1 (Dicaearchus frr. 25, 27, 28 with Wehrli's commentary), and for the Aristotelian background, see *Pol.* 7.3 and *NE* 1.9 with *Fin.* 2.19 *Aristoteles uirtutis usum cum uitae perfectae prosperitate coniunxit.* C.'s understanding of this issue and its place in the Greek philosophical tradition was influenced by the views of Panaetius and Antiochus of Ascalon: his opinion on the value of theoretical speculation varies somewhat according to his own circumstances (see R. Müller 222–7). *uirtus* for a Roman noble more traditionally means 'the winning of personal pre-eminence and glory by the commission of great deeds in the service of the Roman state' (Earl (1967) 21); here, as throughout *Rep.*, C. alludes to Greek philosophical sources, particularly Plato and Dicaearchus, while simultaneously adapting them to the practical political traditions of Rome. **in usu sui:** the objective genitive of personal pronouns is typically found after verbal nouns. **isti** is contemptuous, and refers here not to Epicureans in particular, but to all school philosophers without practical experience. Both the tone and the praise of the early lawgivers at the expense of philosophers are parallel to Dicaearchus frr. 29–31 W. **in angulis personant:** cf. *De orat.* 1.57 on the relationship between philosophy and oratory: *quibus ego ut his de rebus in angulis consumendi oti causa disserant cum concessero* ... The source of the image is Pl. *Grg.* 485d, ἐν γωνίαι ... ψιθυρίζοντα (see Dodds *ad loc.*), but whereas in Plato Callicles' philosopher is 'whispering' in the corner, C.'s opponents are here speaking loudly. **reapse** = *re ipsa*, contrasted with *oratione*. According to the *grammaticus* in Sen. *Ep.* 108.32 an archaism; used by C. also at *Rep.* 2.66 and 6x elsewhere.

2.2 quod quidem ... dicatur 'at least that may be said decently and honourably': the qualification is important not only as an exclusion of the Epicureans, but also in view of Carneades' attack on the possibility of justice, reproduced by Philus' speech in book 3. Büchner suggests that *recte honesteque* has purely Roman connotations, the former meaning inner righteousness, the latter external reputation; the combination appears also at *Verr.* 3.2, *Parad.* 9, 15, *Fin.* 2.25, *Tusc.* 5.12 (twice), and is used as an equivalent for Greek εὖ at *Tim.* 44. **iis:** the lawgivers of early Greece, notably Solon and Lycurgus; for a less favourable view of the Greek legislators cf. 2.2.1. In this passage C. credits statesmen not only with the establishment of religion (for which cf. *Har.* 19), law, and equity, but with moral and social virtues in general. For the superiority of statesmen to philosophers, cf. 3.5, *De orat.* 1.193–5. **descripta:** the reading of P, retained by Büchner and Bréguet; Ziegler and Krarup follow Halm in printing *discripta*. Confusion between the two is extremely common in all MSS; cf. *TLL* v 1.1354.36–55. By modern convention (and perhaps ancient usage), *discribo* denotes distribution, as in the division of the year into months (Livy 1.19.6), *describo* establishment by definition, as in the case of laws. For *iura describere*, cf. *TLL* v 1.663.15–39; in C., *De orat.* 1.33, 3.76; *Sest.* 91.

2.3 unde enim pietas ... fortitudo: cf. *De orat.* 1.56, a very similar list consisting of topics which philosophers claim as their own, to the exclusion of orators. For an echo of the same context in *De orat.*, cf. §2.1n.: C. adapts his earlier defence of oratory against philosophy to the defence of the active (political) against the contemplative life. The order here moves from religion (*pietas* and *religio*) to the relationships among men (*ius ... aequitas*) to the virtues of individuals (*pudor ... fortitudo*). **hoc ipsum ciuile quod dicitur:** positive law as opposed to the general ethical standards implicit in *ius gentium*; for the relationship between the two cf. *Off.* 3.69. For the phrase cf. *Leg.* 1.14, 17 *hoc ciuile quod vocant*; *hoc ciuile quod dicimus*. **iustitia fides aequitas:** asyndeton of three or more members has an archaic ring; cf. H–S 830. C. avoids asyndeton of only two elements.

2.4 nempe: regularly used by C. to introduce answers to his own rhetorical questions. **disciplinis informata** 'shaped by training'. *disciplinis* here is not 'theory' or 'education', but teaching by example, as at 3.4 and 5.6; cf. Perelli (1971) 390.

3.1 Xenocraten: Xenocrates of Chalcedon, pupil of Plato and head of the Academy from 339/8 to 315/14, teacher of Zeno the founder of Stoicism. C. considered him one of the most important philosophical heirs of Plato: cf. *Ac.* 1.17, *Fin.* 4.79. The saying is reported also by Plutarch; cf. Xenocrates fr. 3 Heinze. The whole passage is an elaboration of the maxim at the beginning of the paragraph, that *uirtus* is embodied through its use, and that its highest use is politics. C. elevates action and concrete accomplishments over mere words, no matter how eloquent.

3.2 ergo ... omnes: either 'that citizen, who compels everyone' (if *ciuis* is nom. sing.) or 'that man, who compels all his fellow-citizens' (if *ciuis* is acc. pl.). For the second interpretation, cf. 52.2 *cum is qui imperat*

... *quas ad res ciues instituit et uocat*, but the word order is very awkward. The first interpretation is preferable: *ciuis* is contrasted with *philosophi* and *doctoribus*, the man of civic action as opposed to men of mere words. In the *post reditum* speeches (cf. *Dom.* 5, 26, 114, 122, 132; *Sest.* 53, 128; *Har.* 58) C. regularly refers to himself as *ciuis* in describing his conduct in the conflict with Clodius, perhaps echoing the letter written on his behalf during his exile by the consul Lentulus, who referred to him as *ciuis* and *seruator rei publicae* (cf. *Pis.* 34 and *Dom.* 85 with Nisbet *ad loc.*). For the double acc. after *cogo* (the person compelled and the action required), cf. K–S I 303. **ipsis est praeferendus doctoribus:** C. alternates between synonyms: *praeferendus* ... *anteponenda* ... *praeferendas* ... *anteponendos*.

3.3 tam exquisita ... anteponenda 'so remarkable as to be preferred'; a consecutive clause.

3.4 quem ad modum: correlative with *sic*. **Ennius:** *Ann.* fr. 590 Sk. C. greatly admired the second-century poet, and quotes him frequently in *Rep.* as in his other philosophical works. The relevance of this quotation is minimal, and the comparison (cities are to villages as statesmen are to philosophers) is scarcely compelling. **uiculis et castellis:** *uiculus* only here in C.; the same combination at Livy 21.33.11. **praesunt ... sint:** the second clause may be considered a clause of characteristic; for the inconcinnity of moods, cf. Pease on *N.D.* 2.44. **longe:** to be taken with *anteponendos*; cf. 2.43.3 *sed haud scio an reliquis simplicibus longe anteponendum.* The hyperbaton is emphatic. **sapientia** (abl. of respect) is polemical: *sapiens* is used below (9–11) in its most usual sense of 'philosopher', but C. here and later in the dialogue (e.g. §13, 2.11.2) equates the practical wisdom of the statesman (usually *prudentia*) with the theoretical knowledge of the philosopher (distinguished at *Off.* 1.153). Cf. also 12.3n.

3.5 et quoniam ... reddere: on the improvement of human happiness and well-being as the goal of politics, cf. Arist. *EN* 1.1–2, 8.9. **rapimur** seems very strong, but cf. e.g. *Sest.* 7. C. is again (cf. §1.5) describing *uirtus* as an instinctive drive. **ad hanc uoluptatem:** emphatic and polemical: C. opposes the pleasure derived from civic responsibility to the self-indulgence of the Epicureans. The reference to *naturae stimulis* may also allude to Epicurean doctrine. **teneamus eum cursum:** the metaphor is nautical (cf. §1.1n.), and the language strongly reminiscent of *Sest.*, e.g. 99 (of the true optimates): ... *ut uigilandum sit iis qui sibi gubernacula patriae depoposcerunt, enitendumque omni scientia ac diligentia ut ... tenere cursum possint et capere oti illum portum et dignitatis.* **receptui canunt:** for the military metaphor cf. *Tusc.* 3.33, *Phil.* 12.9, 13.15. As in §1.1, the switch from one metaphor to another is abrupt.

4–8 C. moves on to refute the idea that the risk of death and the hard work entailed by public life justify refusing to take part. For the immense debt owed by every man to the *patria* cf. fr. 1a Ziegler: *sic, quoniam plura beneficia continet patria, et est antiquior parens quam is qui creauit, maior ei profecto quam parenti debetur gratia.*

4.1 ab iis qui contra disputant: the arguments of the anonymous opponents are set out in a series of third-person pl. verbs and pronouns (*his* 4.2, *putant* and *colligunt* 4.3, *dicunt* 5.2). Only at 6.2 *abstinent* is it made clear that these opponents are in fact admirers of C., and that their argument against political involvement is prompted by C.'s sufferings. **primum:** the expected series is not followed: instead of beginning the next thought with *deinde*, C. begins a new sentence with *adiunguntur.* **<in> re publica:** the bare abl. is difficult, and Schütz's emendation should be accepted. **uel uero etiam:** *uero etiam* is used to emphasize the final term of a series, e.g. *Cat.* 1.12, *Mur.* 45, *Pis.* 66, *Planc.* 43; it is more frequent in the letters than in speeches or philosophical works. Here it is intended to heighten the absurdity of the idea that business is worth greater risks than public service.

4.2 natura ... et senectute: the separation of coordinate pairs of nouns, adjectives, and adverbs is emphatic: in book 1, cf. 6.2 *grauius ... et amantius*; 12.2 *auctoritas ... et gloria*; 32.1 *nec meliores ... nec beatiores*; 32.2 *et melius ... et beatius*; 51.5 *dedecoris ... et insolentis superbiae.* **tempus** 'opportunity'; cf. *OLD* s.v. 9. **reddenda naturae:** for life as a loan from nature, cf. *Tusc.* 1.93, perhaps drawn from Lucr. 3.931–71. For the theme in C., cf. *Sest.* 47 *optandam esse ut uita, quae necessitati debetur, patriae potius donata quam reseruata naturae uideretur*; also *Planc.* 90, *Tusc.* 1.116, *Phil.* 14.31.

4.3 Ingratitude to national leaders was a standard rhetorical theme (*locus* = *locus communis*), particularly applicable (§5.1) to the Athenian democracy; the Roman parallels adduced by C. in §6.1 were probably his own contribution. C. perhaps had in mind the famous attack on 'the Four' – Cimon, Pericles, Miltiades, and Themistocles – at Pl. *Grg.* 515b-517a, in which Socrates argues that the Athenians were right to punish them. On the tradition of Athenian ingratitude and fickleness, see Dodds, ed., *Gorgias* pp. 355–6.

5.1 uolneribus iis: Miltiades was wounded not at Marathon, but on the expedition to Paros; cf. Hdt. 6.136. His death in chains is found in Nep. *Milt.* 7 and later sources. **ex hostium telis ... in ciuium uinclis:** a similar balance in the next example *in Graeciae portus ... in barbariae sinus.* **Themistoclem:** for the exile of Themistocles, see Thuc. 1.135–8 with Gomme *ad loc.* **quam adflixerat:** indic. (rather than subj. in o.o.) as an authorial comment, and true; cf. H–S 547–8.

5.2 nec uero ... exempla deficiunt 'and there is no shortage of examples'; both previous examples are in fact Athenian. For Athenian *leuitas* (contrasted here with Roman *grauitas*), cf. *Sest.* 141, with some of the same examples. **quae nata ... redundasse:** although ascribed to the same anonymous opponents as the previous section (cf. 4.1n.), the parallel between Greece and Rome is characteristic of C. and likely to be his own invention. Nor would anyone but C. himself have compared Cicero to Opimius, Metellus, and the rest – as he does also at, e.g., *Sest.* 130, 140.

6.1 exilium Camilli ... fuga Metelli: six instances of statesmen (two early, four from the late second century) forced to leave Rome, using six different nouns; the seventh and most recent instance (Marius) is distinguished by the superlative *acerbissima*. Camillus was supposedly tried (for *peculatus*? cf. Ogilvie on Livy 5.32.8–9) and exiled in 391 B.C.E.; for sources cf. *MRR* I 93. C. Servilius Ahala, *magister equitum* in 439, killed Sp. Maelius for aiming at tyranny, and was forced into exile by popular hatred; cf. 2.49.2, *MRR* I 56, Cornell 58–61. P. Cornelius Scipio Nasica Serapio, cos. 138, pontifex maximus 141–132, led the riot which culminated in the death of Ti. Gracchus. Sent on an embassy to Asia in 132, he died in Pergamum. P. Popilius Laenas, cos. 132, went into exile during the tribunate of C. Gracchus for his part in the fall of Ti. Gracchus, but was recalled in 120; cf. *Brut.* 128. L. Opimius, cos. 121, was not exiled specifically for his part in the death of C. Gracchus (as C. points out at *Sest.* 140), but for being bribed by Jugurtha. Q. Caecilius Metellus Numidicus, cos. 109, chose exile rather than swear the oath required by Saturninus' agrarian law in 100; sources for these four in Greenidge–Clay 15–16, 78, 68–9, 105–7. Some of these examples are used elsewhere by C.: cf. *Cat.* 1.3 (Ahala,

Opimius), *Red. pop.* 6 (Popilius, Metellus, Marius), *Dom.* 86 (Camillus, Ahala, Popilius, Metellus). **C. Mari clades ... principum caedes:** Marius fled when Sulla marched on Rome in 88. The lacuna after *C. Mari clades* can be filled from *De orat.* 3.8, the list of disasters which L. Crassus, by dying in 91, did not live to see (a passage to which this section is closely related): *non acerbissimam C. Mari fugam, non illam post reditum eius caedem omnium crudelissimam*... . Bréguet (following Ziegler and Pohlenz) suggests *clades <uel crudelissima post reditum eius> principum caedes*, Büchner less probably *clades <uel deinde> principum caedes*. **eorum multorum pestes:** *pestis* 'destruction' or 'death' is most commonly defined in C. by *rei publicae* (e.g. *Dom.* 4, *Har.* 50, *De orat.* 1.3), rarely by genitives that apply to individuals rather than the community (*bonorum*, *Off.* 2.51; *sociorum*, *Prov.*. 13 and *Phil.* 10.12; *ciuis*, *Dom.* 26; also *capitis sui*, *Brut.* 277, *mea*, *Red. sen.* 16 and *Sest.* 44).

6.2 nec uero ... abstinent: for the speakers, cf. 4.1n.: the apparent opponents are revealed as C.'s supporters. If one can believe *De orat.* 3.13, C.'s brother Quintus connected C.'s exile with the previous catastrophes of Roman statesmen; but that too is likely to be C.'s own interpretation.

6.3 sed ... tramittant: the end of the sentence is missing; C. compared the rigours of travel for the sake of education with his own exile. Cf. *Tusc.* 5.107 *iam uero exilium, si rerum naturam, non ignominiam nominis quaerimus, quantum tandem a perpetua peregrinatione differt?* C. made light of the danger of exile even before it happened to him: cf. *Arch.* 14, *Att.* 2.18.1, with Kretschmar 24. *ipsi* must refer to the same (fictional) opponents of political activity who are the subject of the entire paragraph; Gigon's suggestion that Varro is meant is very unlikely. For philosophic travel, cf. also *Fin.* 5.48, 87; the tradition begins as early as Herodotus' account of Solon, 1.29ff. **uisendi causa:** used of tourism also at *Verr.* 4.4. **maria tramittant:** for *transmittere* with the acc., cf. *N.D.* 2.125, *Fin.* 5.87, and the poetic passages collected by Pease on *Aen.* 4.154.

7.1 * saluam esse: C. refers to the last day of his consulate, when the tribune Metellus Nepos prohibited him from delivering a speech describing his accomplishments. The lacuna can be supplemented from *Pis.* 6 *ego cum in contione abiens magistratu dicere a tribuno plebis prohiberer ea quae constitueram, cum mihi is tantummodo ut iurarem permitteret, sine ulla dubitatione iuraui rem publicam atque hanc urbem mea unius opera esse* *saluam*; cf. also *Fam.* 5.2.7, *Dom.* 94. Pohlenz 73 n.3 supplements *si ultimis in terris exul uitam degerem, tamen, cum illius horae memoriam repeterem, qua rem publicam mea unius opera saluam* ... Heck 76–7 places Ziegler fr. 1e (Lactantius 3.16.5) in this lacuna, although it may come from the *Hortensius*; for a survey of opinions, see Pfligersdorffer 69–71 n.93. **compensarem:** cf. *De orat.* 3.14 *summi labores nostri magna compensati gloria mitigantur*. Pohlenz 73 rightly saw this portion of the preface as a sequel to the preface to *De orat.* 3 (cf. esp. 3.13) on the dangers and disasters of public life. The impf. subj. suggests that the missing opening of the sentence contained the protasis of a contrary-to-fact condition, e.g. 'even if I had not been recalled from exile ...'

7.2 quamquam 'and yet' introducing an independent sentence: *OLD* s.v. 3. C. here says essentially the same thing in three different ways. The first two comparisons (*honoris* ... *laboris*, *molestiae* ... *gloriae*) are governed by *habuerunt*; the first is positive and the second negative, and the terms are in chiastic order. The final comparison is more elaborate: *laetitia* comes first in each half followed by another noun with a dependent genitive, but there is a grammatical chiasmus (acc., prep. phrase, prep. phrase, acc.), and the two modified nouns are themselves in chiastic order, *ex desiderio bonorum* ... *improborum dolorem*. *boni* and *improbi* are political as well as moral terms; cf. particularly *Sest.* 138–43 for C.'s views.

7.3 ut dixi: presumably in the lacuna before §6. **qui possem queri** 'how could I complain?' *qui* is the archaic form of the abl., as in 10.3, 11.3. Ziegler punctuates with a question mark after *queri*, but the *cum* clause which follows gives the reason for C.'s lack of grounds for complaint, and hence should be seen as part of the same sentence.

7.4 is = *talis*, as often. **cui** is an addition by the second hand (emended to *qui* by F. C. Wolf); if *cui* is correct, then it stands for *qui, cum mihi (ei)*, but the resulting anacoluthon *cui* ... *dubitauerim* is very harsh. For similar looseness in syntax, compare *N.D.* 1.12 *ex quo exsistit et illud, multa esse probabilia quae, quamquam non perciperentur, tamen quia uisum quendam haberent insignem et illustrem, his sapientis uita regerentur*, with the change from *quae* to *his*. **liceret** governs both *capere* and *subire*. **in quibus ... uixeram:** C. frequently emphasizes the continuity of his literary and philosophical studies, e.g. *Arch.* 1, *De orat.* 1.2, *Fam.* 1.9.23, 15.4.16. **non praecipuam ... condicionem:** for such sentiments in C.'s letters, cf. e.g. *Fam.* 4.15.2, 6.1.1. **grau-**

issimis tempestatibus ... fulminibus ipsis: for the metaphorical language cf. §1.3n.; for *fulmina* compare *Tusc.* 2.66 *fulmina fortunae. fulmina* may allude to the end of the *Prometheus Bound*, portions of which C. translated in *Tusc.* **commune ... otium:** like Cato (§1.2–3), C. is willing to abandon his own *otium* in order to ensure it for his fellow citizens; cf. *Sest.* 138–39 and below, 52.5 *aliis permisso otio suo.*

8 neque enim ... remitteret: C.'s concept of duty to the fatherland is much more active than Plato's, *Cr.* 51c. At *Off.* 1.22 C. cites Pl. *Epist.* 9.358a for the doctrine of our responsibility to country and fellowmen; cf. also *Verr.* 3.161, *Fin.* 2.45. A similar idea is voiced in *Rep.* fr. 1a Ziegler (cf. §4.1n.); cf. also the conclusion of the speech of the Muse Urania to C. in his *De consulatu suo* (fr. 10.78 Courtney) *quod patriae uacat, id studiis nobisque sacrasti.* **alimenta:** Gk. τροφεῖα, repayment for parental support; cf. Pl. *R.* 7.520b. The idea is fairly common, but the metaphorical use of *alimenta* is unusual in Latin (cf. *TLL* 1 1585.15–25), and has no parallel in C.; *quasi* underlines its unfamiliarity. **sed ut ... remitteret:** C. contrasts *sibi ad ... suam* and *nobis in nostrum.* **pigneraretur** 'assert her claim to'; a rare usage, for which this sentence is quoted by Non. 477.32 M.; cf. also *Phil.* 14.32. **tantumque** 'and only so much'; the ellipse is not unusual. **quantum ... posset** 'beyond her own requirements'; *ipsi* (dative) is the indirect object of the compound verb *superesse.*

9–11 The final objection to political activity is that wisdom and virtue are full-time jobs: their followers should not be distracted by occupations both sordid and dangerous. The history of the debate as to whether a philosopher should engage in public life is a long one; it is a major element in books 5–7 of Pl. *R.*, and C. may also owe something indirectly to Arist. *Pol.* 7.2. He certainly knew Peripatetic texts on the relative merits of the βίος πρακτικός and the βίος θεωρητικός; cf. §2.1n., and cf. *Off.* 1.69–73.

9.1 Iam illa perfugia: for transitional *iam* ('furthermore' 'besides') cf. 44.5 and *OLD* s.v. 8. *perfugia* here = 'excuse': cf. e.g. *Cael.* 30 *perfugiis nihil utor aetatis.* **perfruantur:** C. favours compounds in *per-*, particularly in the dialogues and letters, using 163 different adjectives and verbs with this prefix, compared to only nine in Caesar. Such words seem to belong to an urbane conversational style rather than to colloquial language; cf. Powell on *Sen.* 3 and Leeman–Pinkster on *De orat.* 1.1. **comparari ... confligere:** assonance, introducing two parallel phrases of which the second is as usual longer than the first. This clause is echoed by the next sentence, which consists of two balanced phrases introduced by *sapientis* and *liberi*, in which there is also a further balance between *insanos atque indomitos impetus* in the first half and *cum impuris atque immanibus aduersariis* in the second. *comparari* 'to be matched with' (*OLD comparo*[2]); derived from *par* rather than from *parare*.

9.2 accipere habenas: cf. *De orat.* 1.226 ... *cui populus ipse moderandi ac regendi sui potestatem quasi quasdam habenas tradidisset*; the same metaphor at *De orat.* 3.166, *Am.* 45. **liberi:** *libertas* (cf. Wirszubski (1950) 1–3, 6–30; Kohns (1977)) connotes either sovereignty (a free nation) or independent status (not being a slave); here the latter is meant, as the reference to *uerbera* shows. **decertantem:** acc. modifying the unexpressed subject of the infinitives *subire* and *expectare*. For similar instances, cf. 28.4 *despicientem* ... *ducentem*; 45.2 *moderantem* ... *retinentem*. The combination of possessive gen. ('it is not the part of a wise man...'; cf. Woodcock §72 1 (1)) and acc. participle is abrupt, as at 45.2. **contumeliarum uerbera subire:** C. imitates the extravagant language of the philosophers: he nowhere else uses *uerbera* in a metaphorical sense (but cf. *De orat.* 2.222 *aculei contumeliarum*; also Petron. 132.2 *matrona contumeliis uerberata*), and for *uerbera subire*, a poetic usage, cf. Ov. *Am.* 1.13.18, Hor. *S.* 1.3.120f.

9.3 proinde quasi introduces an ironical objection; cf. *Dom.* 31, *Tusc.* 1.86, *Luc.* 109 and elsewhere. The idea that the greatest punishment for withdrawing from public life is being ruled by evil men is drawn from Pl. *R.* 1.347c; compare also the opposite sentiment in *Att.* 2.9.3: *male uehi malo alio gubernante quam tam ingratis uectoribus bene gubernare.* **magno animo praeditis:** for this quality of men active in public life, cf. e.g. *Sest.* 1, 45. **ad rem publicam adeundi** 'entering public life': so also 12.1; cf. *OLD* s.v. *adeo*[1] 10b. **cum ... non queant:** those who have refused to take part in public life are not in a position to help in a crisis even if (*si* = *etsi*) they should want to. **ipsi:** nom. (the good and brave men) rather than dat. (the *res publica*).

10.1 exceptio ... extra quam si 'this limitation ... except when'; this collocation appears elsewhere in C. only at *Inv.* 1.56, 2.172 and *Att.* 6.1.15 (without *si* at *Rep.* 3.34 (Ziegler's emendation) and *Inv.* 2.59). Its use is restricted to the language of law, and in three of the

Ciceronian passages it is explicitly cited from a legal document. For the 'curial style' of the phrase, cf. H–S 595; also *TLL* v 2.2054.15–21. For *exceptio*, cf. Berger 459; Wenger, *RE* vi 1553–4. **tandem:** for the use of *tandem* in questions, cf. *OLD* s.v. 1b. **quod** 'namely that', giving the substance of the restriction; for the usage cf. *OLD* s.v. 2b. For the differing views on the appropriateness of involvement in politics, cf. Seneca, *De otio* 3.2 *duae maximae et in hac re dissident sectae Epicureorum et Stoicorum, sed utraque ad otium diuersa uia mittit. Epicurus ait: 'non accedet ad rem publicam sapiens, nisi si quid interuenerit'; Zenon ait: 'accedet ad rem publicam, nisi si quid impedierit'*; cf. also *Off.* 1.28.

10.3 qui potui: on abl. *qui* (here and 11.3) cf. 7.3n. Modal verbs (possibility, permission, necessity) with the infin. generally appear in the indic. in the apodosis of an unreal condition; cf. Woodcock §200(i). The subj. is also possible, as in the preceding sentence, *quid facere potuissem*; cf. K–S i 173. **equestri loco natus:** it was extremely rare for anyone with no senatorial background to reach the consulate; the two examples of which C. is most conscious are the elder Cato and Marius. Cf. Wiseman (1971) 108–13. **amplissimum:** almost a technical term of status; cf. *OLD* s.v. *amplus* 8.

10.4 opitulandi rei publicae: *opitulor* is an archaism, one of the few in *Rep.* not spoken by one of the characters in the dialogue. Cf. on *reapse* §2.1. The oblique cases of the gerund with an object are relatively uncommon in C.

11.1 doctorum ... didicerint: another attack on the futility of abstract knowledge: the learned men (philosophers) have not learned enough. **tranquillo mari gubernare:** cf. §1.3. For the metaphor of the inexperienced pilot, cf. Pl. *R.* 6.488de and C. *De orat.* 1.174. C. writes of Gabinius at *Sest.* 20 *quis enim clauum tanti imperi tenere et gubernacula rei publicae tractare in maximo cursu ac fluctibus posse arbitraretur hominem...?*

11.2 in eo ... gloriari: except when used absolutely, *glorior* most commonly governs an infinitive. C. occasionally uses it with the abl. alone or governed by *in*, less frequently by *de*. For the constructions of *glorior*, *delector*, *laetor*, etc. see Reid on *Fin.* 1.39, K–S i 396–7. **doctis ... exercitatis:** the contrast (as with oratory in *De orat.*) between abstract learning and practical experience.

11.4 ut uerum esset 'even if it were true', governing both *solere* and *recusare*, and equivalent to a protasis of which the apodosis is *tamen* *arbitrarer*. After refuting the idea that the philosopher will take part in public life only if necessary, C. suggests that, even if that were true, then he should be prepared in case of necessity; *temporibus cogeretur* refers back to *tempus et necessitas coegerit* at 10.1. **descendere:** both 'take part in' in a neutral sense (*OLD* s.v. 4) and 'stoop to' in a pejorative sense (*OLD* s.v. 8). **quibus ... esset** 'which he did not know whether he would need to use at some point.' *uti* emphasizes the importance of practical knowledge.

12.1 plurimis: Moser's emendation *pluribus* (accepted by Ziegler) is unnecessary; cf. *Vat.* 41, *De orat.* 2.296. **his libris:** *Rep.* itself, the proper title of which would be *de re publica libri sex*. Cf. *De orat.* 1.22 *in his libris*. **dubitationem ad rem publicam adeundi:** a major theme of the preface, as it is of the *Pro Sestio*; see introductory note above, and *Sest.* 1, 136.

12.2 quorum summa est auctoritas: C. is probably referring above all to Plato, but also to philosophers in general, particularly the Peripatetics, who wrote extensively on political theory. **functos ... munere:** the function of *Rep.* itself: although C. was not, at the time of writing, taking an active part in public life, the writing of the treatise was in itself a public service.

12.3 omnes paene uideo: the exception was Thales; cf. *De orat.* 3.137. On the importance of the Seven Sages (named by Pl. *Prt.* 343a as Thales, Pittacus, Bias, Solon, Cleobulus, Myson, and Chilon; the list varies in other sources) as practical politicians, compare Dicaearchus frr. 30–1 Wehrli. Dicaearchus (fr. 30) had said that the seven were neither wise men (σοφοί) nor philosophers (φιλόσοφοι), but men of understanding (συνετοί) and lawgivers (νομοθετικοί) – by which he meant that they were not philosophers in a later, technical sense; he admired them as proponents of the βίος πρακτικός. C. follows Dicaearchus' opinions, but does not adopt his polemical terminology; on the question of whether they should be called *sapientes*, cf. *De orat.* 3.56, *Tusc.* 5.7, *Am.* 7.

12.4 A striking conclusion to C.'s argument in favour of political activity, made more emphatic by the chiastic juxtaposition of *deorum numen* and *uirtus... humana*. That humans should try to make themselves like god is a Platonic idea (cf. *Tht.* 176b), modified by the political context in which C. deploys it (cf. Harder 359). The divinity of statesmen is expressed less strongly (immortal glory) at *Sest.* 143, and receives its fullest expression in the *Somnium*; cf. 6.13.2n. **conseruare iam conditas:** for C. himself as *conservator*, cf. *Cat.* 3.1, 15 and frequently in the speeches of 57–56; for a more general description, cf. *Sest.* 138.

13.1 The sentence is problematic, and most editors have agreed that there must be a lacuna after *docendi* in which the main verb is lost; Ziegler suggests *euenit ut*. There are, however, difficulties: (1) both *aliquid ... dignum* and *facultatem* must be taken as objects of *essemus ... consecuti*, but the structure suggests that there ought to be a second verb governing *facultatem*; (2) *auctor* is not a word which C. would use to describe his own expertise; it is used of Plato at 16.2, and generally refers to earlier authors. Mai solved both difficulties by emending *auctores* to *adepti*, but while that clarifies the opening of the sentence it obscures the end by requiring that the main clause begin with *nec uero*, which makes better sense as the beginning of a new sentence. The anacoluthon is harsh, and makes the paragraph into a single, extremely complex, sentence. Buecheler emended the second *essemus* to *esse possumus*, while Büchner accepts the sentence as it stands; the various supplements proposed by others are unconvincing. **idem** 'at the same time'; *OLD* s.v. 8. **studio discendi et docendi:** cf. 11.2 *nec didicisse umquam nec docere*; 2.1.2 *summum uel discendi studium uel docendi*; also *Sest.* 96, *Fin.* 3.66, *Off.* 1.50. **superiores:** Romans, not Greeks. For Greek examples, cf. Arist. *Pol.* 2.21.

13.2 nec uero ... ratio: C. takes refuge behind the claim that the ideas expressed in *Rep.* are not his own; for the fiction, cf. Introduction, pp. 3–6. **unius aetatis ... memoria est:** cf. *De orat.* 1.23 *repetamque ... ea quae quondam accepi in nostrorum hominum eloquentissimorum et omni dignitate principum disputatione esse uersata.* **tibique:** C.'s brother Quintus. **P. Rutilio Rufo:** cf. Introduction, p. 11. Another conversation between C. and Rutilius in Smyrna is recorded at *Br.* 85. **nihil fere:** cf. 25.3n. **omnium <harum> rerum:** some limiting word is necessary, and Ziegler's supplement, given here, is the simplest.

14–37: Introductory conversation

The preliminary conversation begins with Tubero's arrival, and continues until all participants are present (for whom cf. Introduction, pp. 9–12); the gradual introduction of the characters appears to be modelled on Plato's *Protagoras* (which C. had translated), cf. Krarup (1956) 187. The starting-point for discussion is the prodigy of the double sun which had recently been observed (parhelion or 'sun-dogs', a meteorological phenomenon caused by the refraction of sunlight through ice-crystals in the atmosphere; for ancient discussions cf. Pease on *Div.* 1.97). The purpose of introducing this topic is multiple. The double sun was seen as an analogy for the discord in the state (cf. Laelius at 31.3); furthermore, the prodigy was in hindsight considered an omen for what was to happen shortly after the dramatic date of the dialogue, the death of Scipio, the 'second sun' of Rome (cf. *N.D.* 2.14, with Pease *ad loc.*). The astronomical discussion also creates an opportunity to touch on both the importance of scientific knowledge in public affairs and the issue of macrocosm and microcosm (universe and state, society and man) which is of great importance in the dialogue as a whole. And, finally, the astronomy here is balanced by the celestial eschatology which concludes *Rep.* in the *Somnium.* On the role of astronomy in *Rep.*, cf. Ruch.

14.1 hic Paulli filius: Scipio's natural father was L. Aemilius Paullus. *hic* is used to distinguish a younger person from an elder one of the same name; cf. *TLL* VI 2723.15–26. **Tuditano consule et Aquilio:** the consuls of 129. For the word order, cf. *Arch.* 5, *Brut.* 161, 306, 328. **in hortis:** Scipio's *horti* were outside the *pomerium* in the Campus Martius; cf. Richardson 203–4 and *N.D.* 2.11. **Latinis ipsis:** on the first morning of the festival. The *Feriae Latinae* had no fixed date, but took place early in the year, and lasted for three days; cf. Wissowa 125, Scullard 111–15. *De natura deorum* takes place on the same holiday (*N.D.* 1.15), *De oratore* during the *Ludi Romani* (*De orat.* 1.24).

14.2 libenterque uidisset: i.e. *libenter se eum uidisse dixisset.* **tam mane:** a colloquialism; cf. *bene mane*, *Att.* 4.9.2, 14.18.1. There are several Platonic parallels for the early hour (*Cr.* 43a, *Phd.* 59e, *Prt.* 310b). Scipio is in his bedroom and not yet dressed; cf. 18.2. **explicandas:** *explicare* can refer either to the act of unrolling a papyrus volume in order to read it (e.g. *Verr.* 2.106) or, as here and *Brut.* 237, of writing. On Tubero's scholarship, see Introduction, pp. 10–11.

14.3 otiosum: on the importance of *otium*, cf. §1.2n.; cf. also the *otium* described by Crassus in *De orat.* 2.22 (Laelius and Scipio gathering shells). The need for *otium* as a prerequisite for philosophical discourse is a formula of both Ciceronian and Platonic dialogue; for a collection of instances, cf Pease on *N.D.* 2.3. **hoc praesertim motu rei publicae:** for the circumstances, cf. 31.4n.; as in the case of *De orat.*, the dialogue takes place during a political crisis. For the use of *motus*, cf. *Q. fr.* 3.5.2 *maximi motus nostrae ciuitatis.*

14.5 animum ... relaxes: cf. *Div.* 2.100, *Off.* 1.122, *Hort.* fr. 31 M.; *animum remittere* is the more common alternative. **abuti** 'make full use of'; cf. *Fam.* 9.6.5 (to Varro) *quae igitur studia magnorum hominum sententia uacationem habent quandam publici muneris, iis concedente re p. cur non abutamur?*

14.6 Libente me uero: conversational: cf. *De orat.* 2.295 *me uero libente.* **ut ... admoneamur:** probably a final clause rather than a restrictive consecutive clause (which would require a marker such as *ita*). The reference to *doctrinae studia* is appropriate to the learned Tubero. **aliquid aliquando:** in such combinations of *aliquando* with a form of *aliquis* in C., *aliquando* normally follows.

15.1 de isto altero sole: for the phenomenon, cf. 14–37n.

15.3 Panaetium nostrum: Panaetius of Rhodes, in 129 head of the Stoic school in Athens, dedicated several books to Tubero and was also a friend of Scipio; C. refers to the connection at *Mur.* 66, *Fin.* 4.23, *Tusc.* 1.81, *Off.* 1.90, 2.76, *Att.* 9.12.2. Although named here as an expert on astronomy and at 34.2 as having discussed political theory with Polybius and Scipio, his works were probably not major sources of *Rep.*, as was long thought, e.g. by Pohlenz. Although he is cited as an expert on astronomy, he was the only Stoic to reject astrology, divination, the doctrine of *sympatheia*, and the belief in the conflagration of the universe. On his relationship to Scipio, cf. Astin (1967) 296–9.

15.4 aut tractare plane manu: for the language, cf. *N.D.* 1.49 *Epicurus autem, qui res occultas ... non modo uideat animo sed etiam sic tractet ut manu ...* with Pease *ad loc.*

15.5 qui ... deposuerit: causal; cf. 6.10.2 *qui uigilassem.* On Socrates' rejection of physics in general and astronomy in particular, cf. *Tusc.* 5.10 *Socrates ... primus philosophiam deuocauit e caelo et in urbibus collocauit et in domus etiam introduxit et coegit de uita et moribus rebusque bonis et malis quaerere*; cf. also *Acad.* 1.15 with Reid *ad loc.* Socrates' objection to physics is elaborated by Laelius at 32.1.

16.1 Dein: for the form (also at 18.4), cf. *Or.* 154; the abbreviated form is far less common in C. than *deinde*, as is the case with all major classical authors except Sallust (where *deinde* predominates only slightly) and the elder Pliny and Tacitus (in whom *dein* is more frequent).

16.2 multis locis: Tubero clearly alludes to such passages as *R.* 522c-531c, *Phlb.* 55d-57e, *Lg.* 737b-738c in which politics and ethics are combined with mathematics. **Pythagorae more:** the genuine ideas of the sixth-century philosopher were inextricably tangled with the more mystical and numerological elements of Plato's thought; Burkert (1972) is a notable attempt to disentangle them. For C.'s interpretation of Plato as a synthesis of Socrates and Pythagoras, see Burkert (1965) 195, R. Müller 232. C.'s knowledge of Plato's Pythagoreanism may have been drawn from Dicaearchus (cf. fr. 41 Wehrli); for Pythagoreanism in *Rep.* cf. also 2.28–30n., 6.10.3n.

16.3 sunt ista 'quite true'; the phrase refers to what has just been said by an interlocutor or correspondent (= Gk. ἔστι ταῦτα). Cf. *Am.* 6, *Verr.* 4.12, *Att.* 9.5.1, *Q. fr.* 2.14.1. **Platonem ... dedisse:** another version of Plato's travels with a different list of philosophers appears at *Fin.* 5.87; this is the earliest reference to Plato in Egypt: cf. Riginos 64. Archytas, Timaeus, and Philolaus were all Pythagoreans; Archytas is said to have saved Plato's life in 361. For Plato and the Pythagoreans in the West, cf. Burkert (1972) 92–4; for the story of Plato's purchase of Philolaus' books, cf. Riginos 169–74.

16.4 leporem Socraticum: for similar language, cf. *De orat.* 2.270; for his *subtilitas*, cf. *De orat.* 3.60, *Brut.* 31, *Tusc.* 1.55, 3.56. C. does not elsewhere attribute either *grauitas* or *obscuritas* to Pythagoras.

17.1–2 The arrival of the next two guests is told in two parallel sentences, each with a *cum* clause, and repeating *eumque ut salutauit ... eum quoque ut salutauit.* The guests are grouped by age: Philus is Scipio's younger contemporary, and Rutilius is younger than Tubero. The elaborate stylization of manners is as idealized as the conversation itself: one may doubt whether the aristocracy in C.'s own day behaved with such courtesy.

17.2 huius sermonis auctor: cf. 13.2. C. ignores the lack of verisimilitude in reporting a conversation that occurred before his own source for it was present. **propter:** archaic for the classical *prope.*

17.4 sub ipsis Numantiae moenibus: Rutilius served as military tribune under Scipio's command at Numantia in 134–133; cf. Rutilius fr. 13 *HRR*, Appian, *Iber*. 88. Rutilius' autobiography may be C.'s source here.

18 With the scene of Laelius' arrival and the organization of the group, cf. *De orat*. 2.12.

18.2 in porticu: cf. Pl. *Prt*. 314e-315a. **iam aetate quaestorios:** i.e. about 30; when they held the quaestorship is in fact unknown. **coniecit in medium Laelium:** a mark of respect (as was Scipio's going out to greet him), explained (*enim*) in what follows.

18.3 quasi quoddam ius: *quasi*, *quidam*, or both together frequently qualify metaphorical or bold expressions; cf. *OLD* s.v. *quasi* 9, *quidam*[1] 3; for the combination cf. K–S II 455. **ut militiae ... Scipio:** the two clauses are balanced and parallel in order, except that *quod aetate antecedebat* follows the object, perhaps because of the adverb *uicissim*. The precise phrases, however, are varied: *propter ... gloriam* corresponds to the *quod* clause, *ut deum* to *in parentis loco*, and *coleret* to *obseruaret*. Perhaps *ut deum* anticipates the divinization of statesmen in the *Somnium*; for similar language, cf. *De orat*. 1.106, 2.179–80. For the relationship of Scipio and Laelius, cf. also *Am*. 15. **domi** 'in civilian life': locative, contrasting (as is normal) with its polar opposite *militiae*.

18.4 dein: cf. 16.1n. **perpauca:** on C.'s taste for compounds in *per-* (here also *periucundus et pergratus*), cf. 9.1n. **Scipioni ... fuisset:** elliptical; cf. on 14.2 *libenterque uidisset*. **in aprico ... loco:** cf. *Brut*. 24 *tum in pratulo propter Platonis statuam consedimus* and *Att*. 12.6.2.

18.5 uir prudens: an appropriate epithet for the jurisconsult Manilius; cf. Douglas on *Brut*. 23, 98.

19.2 agebatis ... interuenimus: cf. *N.D*. 1.17 *sed ut hic qui interuenit ... ne ignoret quae res agatur, de natura agebamus deorum*.

19.4 Ain uero 'is that so?': expressing surprise and scepticism. C. elsewhere uses *ain tu* or *ain tandem*; *ain uero* is found in comedy. Laelius' tone is ironic, as in 20.3; in this, C.'s characterization of him matches that of Antonius in *De orat*. (cf. also 30.4n., 2.21–2). His comment also serves to turn the conversation to the main topic of the dialogue, the *res publica* itself. **siquidem ... quaerimus** 'seeing that we are asking questions about what is going on in the sky'. The causal use of *siquidem* (giving the reason for a statement) is rare before C.; cf. *OLD* s.v. 3, K–S II 427–8.

19.5 quid fiat domi: the Stoic idea of the *mundus* as the home and *patria* of all men is important in *Rep.*, most clearly in the *Somnium* (6.15, 25), to which the entire discussion of astronomy here serves as a counterpart and introduction. Cf. *N.D.* 2.154 *est enim mundus quasi communis deorum atque hominum domus aut urbs utrorumque* with Pease *ad loc.* (also *Leg.* 1.23, 61; *Fin.* 3.64) and Gigon 217–21.

20.2 integrum 'untouched', 'not yet begun'. **concessero:** the fut. pf. instead of the fut., apparently to stress the fact that the action will take place. It is particularly frequent in comedy, and most commonly employs the verb *uideo* (cf. 2.16.2 *post uidero*); for discussion and examples, see Lebreton 200–2.

20.3 Immo uero introduces an emphatically positive response; cf. 61.4, 6.14.2, and H–S 492. **interdictum aliquod:** the two suns appear to claim possession of the same property (the sky) and hence the interdict *uti possidetis* – an injunction against disturbing possession of a property pending trial – is appropriate. The wording is given by Gaius, *Inst.* 4.160 *uti nunc possidetis, quominus ita possideatis, uim fieri ueto*; cf. Berger 512. The second *ut* 'as' would be followed by the indic. in o.r.

20.4 quid sit suum: the distinction between *suum* and *alienum* is a paramount function of the civil law; cf. *Caec.* 70, *De orat.* 1.173. **P. Mucium:** P. Mucius Scaevola, cos. 133, jurist, and cousin of Quintus Scaevola the participant in the dialogue. On his politics, cf. 31.4n. **consuli:** pres. pass. infin. *consulere* is the normal verb for seeking legal advice; cf. *OLD* s.v. 1c.

21–5 Astronomy and politics. Sections 21–4 are omitted from this edition. Philus' speech (21–2) describes the two celestial spheres of Archimedes taken by M. Marcellus in the siege of Syracuse, together with an account of such spheres which Philus reports having heard from Sulpicius Galus. The text breaks off in the middle of the speech, and of the succeeding six folia only one survives (23), in which (and in 24, the four lines following the lacuna) Scipio describes Galus' explanation to the army in Macedonia of the lunar eclipse of the night of 21 June 168. Where the text printed here resumes, Scipio compares Galus' astronomical explanation to that of Pericles during the Peloponnesian War.

25.1 quiddam is the object of *docuisse.* **obscurato sole:** a partial eclipse of the sun took place at Athens on 3 August 431; cf. Gomme on Thuc. 2.28. Pericles' scientific explanation is referred to also by Plu. *Per.* 35.2. **ab Anaxagora:** C. refers to the pre-Socratic philosopher Anaxagoras as Pericles' teacher also at *De orat.* 3.138, *Brut.* 44, *Orat.* 15 (with a reference to Pl. *Phdr.* 269e). **cum tota ... subiecisset:** the moon is said to pass beneath the sun in coming between the sun and the earth; for similar descriptions of the solar eclipse, cf. *N.D.* 2.103, *Div.* 2.17. **intermenstruo tempore:** at the new moon. The astronomy is correct.

25.2 Thaletem Milesium: C. here ascribes only the explanation of eclipses to the philosopher Thales, while at *Div.* 1.112 he is said to have been able to predict the eclipse of 28 May 585; for discussion and sources, see Pease *ad loc.*

25.3 nostrum ... Ennium: *noster* identifies Ennius as a Roman. The arrangement of Greeks and Romans is deliberate: the Roman Galus leads to Pericles and Anaxagoras, and the Greek Thales to Ennius and Romulus. **qui ut scribit:** the syntax is difficult, and various emendations have been proposed. If the transmitted text is correct, *qui* must be taken as an anaphoric relative equivalent to *et is* and the main verb is *obstitit* in the quotation. **quinquagesimo CCC fere:** an eclipse of the sun took place on 21 June 400, 350 years after the Polybian date for the founding of Rome in 751/0; for discussion of this passage and of the date, cf. Frier 115–17, and for C.'s chronology, cf. on 2.18.2–3. C. frequently uses *fere* with chronological or quantitative expressions; it may reflect genuine uncertainty about the chronology or may be 'a stylistic device to avoid the impression of pedantry' (Skutsch; see next n.). **Nonis Iunis:** Ennius, *Ann.* 153 Sk. Skutsch *ad loc.* points out that the eclipse took place at sunset, so that *luna ... et nox* is in fact accurate.

25.4 in maximis annalibus: the *annales maximi* (cf. 2.28.2n.) did record eclipses; cf. Cato, *Orig.* fr. 77 *HRR*: *non lubet scribere, quod in tabula apud pontificem maximum est, quotiens annona cara, quotiens lunae aut solis lumine caligo aut quid obstiterit.* **Nonis Quinctilibus:** 7 July; cf. D. H. 2.56, Plu. *Rom.* 27. No such eclipse in fact occurred, and the exact year would necessarily depend on the chronology of Romulus' reign; for other putative eclipses connected with Romulus, see Boll, *RE* VI 2352–3. The eclipse at the time of Romulus' death and deification is referred to again at 2.17 and 6.24.3.

26.1 quod paulo ante ... uidebatur: a lacuna must conceal the earlier opinion Africanus has now revised; it may be his rejection of astronomy and physics in 1.15.

26.2–29 Scipio's first speech. When the text resumes, Scipio is discussing the insignificance of man and of human existence. He deals first with glory (26), then with wealth (27) and finally with political power (28), all shown to be unimportant in comparison with the kind of wisdom which frees humans from unnecessary fear and worry. The style is elaborate and is marked by repeated tricola and rhetorical questions. In context, Scipio is arguing that the practical application of scientific knowledge in politics (as in the examples of Pericles and Galus) is relatively unimportant in comparison with a broad sense of man's place in the universe and the detachment from mundane affairs that comes with it. The contradiction between the praise of learning here and the attack on philosophers in §§2–3 is only apparent; Scipio views political activity as a necessary task (27 *imperia consulatusque nostros in necessariis ... rebus*), but one which is placed in its proper perspective by a sense of the value of learning. The speech has close connections with Aristotle, *Protrepticus* fr. 10a Ross = B105 Düring, and with C.'s own later (now fragmentary) *Hortensius*; its themes are taken up again by C. in the preface to book 3 and in the *Somnium*. The role of natural philosophy, particularly astronomy, in establishing a context for *uirtus* appears also at *Fin.* 5.58 from Antiochus, who himself drew on Aristotle's *Protrepticus*; there is a close parallel in content in the praise of *sapientia* delivered by C. at *Leg.* 1.58–62, and in tone and location in the dialogue it is closest to the praise of eloquence delivered by Crassus in *De orat.* 1.30–4. For analysis of the sources and argument of the speech, cf. Perelli (1971).

26.2 The sentence is a deliberative question with one verb (*putet*) and three predicate adjectives (*praeclarum, diuturnum, gloriosum*), each followed by a relative clause modifying the unexpressed indefinite subject. The third (*qui uiderit ...*) is further divided into two indirect questions, of which the first consists of a distinction between *uniuersa* and *ea pars eius quam homines incolant*, and the second is elaborated by modifiers of the subject, *nos*. The balance of the last part of the sentence is deceptive: the clause *quam parua sit terra* corresponds to the participial phrase *quamque nos in exigua parte adfixi* (*quam* modifies *exigua*), while the remainder of the clause (*plurimis ... latissime*) returns to the theme of glory introduced in the opening of the sentence. The exiguousness of the inhabited world is taken up at *Somnium* 6.16, 20–5; cf. also *Hort.* fr. 87 M. *ne in continentibus quidem terris uestrum nomen dilatari potest.* A similar series of rhetorical questions on the lack of concern of the *sapiens* with worldly affairs appears at *Tusc.* 4.37. **uolitare et uagari:** both words usually have in C. a somewhat pejorative sense (except in his poetry); Scipio here is presumably being ironic. There is a possible reminiscence of Ennius' epitaph (fr. 46 Courtney), *uolito uiuus per ora uirum.*

27.1–2 A similar disparagement of material wealth at *Parad.* 1.6–7. Scipio's speech is not strictly Stoic; these are commonplaces of Hellenistic ethics: cf. Bailey on Lucr. 3.971 *uitaque mancipio nulli datur, omnibus usu,* to which C. may be alluding.

27.1 The main clause ends the sentence; it is preceded by the relative clause (*qui ... soleat*), itself preceded by the object of the infinitives within the relative clause. **dominatus** (cf. 59.4, 61.6) normally refers to political power rather than legal title; the technical term (not attested in C.) is *dominium.*

27.2 The sentence consists of three characterizing relative clauses, loosely dependent on *quam est hic fortunatus putandus*. Each (*cui ... sciat, qui ... putet, qui denique ... esset*) contains two pairs of antithetical phrases, ending with the aphorisms ascribed to the elder Africanus by Cato. **non Quiritium ... ciuili nexo:** an extended play on legal language. Roman citizens held property *ex iure Quiritium* (i.e. according to Roman civil law), and *uindicatio* was a method of asserting ownership. *nexum* is properly a form of obligation in early Roman law by which the debtor's person served as surety for a debt (see Berger 595), but C. generally uses it (as did M.' Manilius; cf. Var. *L.* 7.105) for all sales *per aes et libram* (*mancipatio*); cf. *Parad.* 5.35 with Lee's note. **muneris fungendi gratia subeundos:** the idea that public service is obligatory rather than intrinsically desirable (*expetenda*) is found in the preface (esp. §8) and in the *Somnium* (6.13, 15.3–16.1). Public service for profit is condemned at *Off.* 2.77; cf. also Pl. *R.* 1.347a-d. **Cato solitum ... solus esset:** the wording of the aphorism (fr. 127 *HRR*, but assignment to the *Origines* is doubtful) is slightly different at *Off.* 3.1, where C. interprets it to mean that Africanus thought about business even when at leisure; here it means that solitary reflection is as important as public activity. Cf. also Cato fr. 2 *HRR* (= C. *Planc.* 66) *clarorum uirorum atque magnorum non minus otii quam negotii rationem exstare oportere* with Gruen (1992) 60–1.

28.1–3 A series of three parallel rhetorical questions involving comparisons (*quis enim putare ... plus egisse, quis autem non magis solos esse, quis uero diuitiorem*), of which the third is in turn divided into four further comparisons (*diuitiorem, potentiorem, beatiorem, firmiore fortuna*); the series is then followed by another tricolon (*imperium, magistratus, regnum*) with another comparison (*praestantius*).

28.1 plus egisse Dionysium: C. also contrasts the elder Dionysius (tyrant of Syracuse 405–367) with Archimedes (c. 287–212) at *Tusc.* 5.57–67, employing a similar rhetorical question (5.66): *quis est omnium, qui modo cum Musis, id est cum humanitate et cum doctrina, habeat aliquod commercium, qui se non hunc mathematicum malit quam illum tyrannum?* **omnia moliendo** 'by all his machinations'; the pejorative meaning of *molior* also at 31.4 (Moser's emendation) and 2.60.1; also, e.g., at *2 Verr.* 1.40, 133; *Cat.* 1.8, 3.4; *Vat.* 21; *Pis.* 5. **istam ipsam sphaeram:** the celestial sphere was described by Philus in §§21–2 (omitted in this edition). At *Tusc.* 1.62–3, Archimedes' creation of the sphere is compared to the cosmic creation of the Demiurge in Plato's *Timaeus*; cf. *N.D.* 2.88 with Pease *ad loc.* **de qua modo dicebatur:** the position of the clause is awkward: Steinacker moved it to follow *sphaeram*, and Osann deleted it.

28.2 qui in foro ... non habeant: cf. *Att.* 1.18.1 *reperire ex magna turba neminem possumus quocum aut iocari libere aut suspirare familiariter possimus.* For the abl. form in *quicum* cf. 7.3n. **quasi doctissimorum ... se oblectent:** Perelli (1971) 399–400 aptly compares Machiavelli's letter to Vettori: 'When evening comes ... I enter into the ancient courts of ancient men where I am welcomed by them warmly and am nourished by the food that alone is mine ...'

28.3 omni perturbatione animi liberatus: an attribute of the philosophic man, and the subject of book 4 of *Tusc.* Cf. also *Off.* 1.69. **firmiore fortuna:** C. substitutes an abl. of description for the adjs. in the parallel clauses. **uel e naufragio possit efferre:** the anecdote is generally ascribed to Aristippus or to Bias; cf. Otto s.vv. *naufragium* 1, *omnis* 6.

28.4 imperium ... regnum: the first two elements of the tricolon refer back to *imperia consulatusque nostros* at 27.2, while *regnum* refers to Dionysius of Syracuse at 28.1. **despicientem ... uolutare:**

despicientem and *ducentem* modify the unexpressed subject of the infin. *uolutare*; for such constructions, cf. 9.2n. *sapientia* is abl. of comparison. The entire description of the philosophic man is reminiscent of Lucretius 2.7–13.

28.5 appellari ... esse: the contrast between appearance and reality is brought out by the emphatic initial placement of the verbs. **politi propriis humanitatis artibus:** cf. *De orat.* 2.154 *humanitate politiores* of Scipio, Laelius, and Philus. The Isocratean sentiment (cf. *Antid.* 293) is adapted to make *humanitatis artes* refer to philosophical and scientific study rather than rhetorical education; cf. Perelli (1971) 400.

29.1 Platonis illud: the anecdote is normally connected to Aristippus; cf. Riginos 146–7. **perelegans:** cf. 9.1n.

29.2 ut uidisset: a temporal clause in indirect discourse. **exclamauisse ut bono essent animo:** *exclamo* can be followed (like *impero*) by a substantive final clause or (like *dico*) by acc. and infin.; cf. *OLD* s.v. 2b. **consitura** is attested only here. **quam cernebat** has been questioned, but the point is that even though Plato did see cultivated land, it was the evidence of scientific learning that convinced him (*interpretabatur* = 'inferred') of the presence of (truly) human beings.

30–7 The ensuing discussion serves as a transition to the major topic of the work, the nature of the *res publica*. Laelius objects to excessive concentration on scientific and philosophical inquiry, and turns from the question of the practical use of astronomy to the analogy between the phenomenon just observed and the political situation in Rome. The two suns, he argues, are either incomprehensible or irrelevant, but the dissension in the state caused by Tiberius Gracchus is a real, present, and practical question. The topic for discussion should be the *optimus status ciuitatis*, which Scipio, as an experienced statesman familiar with Greek learning, is uniquely qualified to explain.

30.1 non audeo ... dicere: for the construction of *dico* + *ad* 'reply to,' cf. *TLL* v 1.987.68–75. One leaf of P is missing; the point seems to be that such pursuits are acceptable in men of experience such as Scipio, Philus, and Manilius, but are out of place in a young man like Tubero. For the contrast between his single-minded studies and the general learning of Scipio, cf. *De orat.* 3.87.

30.2 Egregie ... Sextus: Ennius, *Ann.* 329 Sk. (cited also at *De orat.*

1.198 and *Tusc.* 1.18), describing the renowned jurisconsult S. Aelius Paetus, cos. 198. The final vowel of *homo* retains its original length. As at 27.2, there is a play on legal language, using *quaerere* and *respondere*: Paetus gave *responsa* to legal questions, but he did not take up scientific research. *cordatus* seems to denote wisdom, *catus* sharpness of mind; cf. Skutsch *ad loc.* **quaerebat ... respondebat:** the indic. is unusual in reporting inferences at second hand (cf. H–S 588), and emphasizes the truth of what is said. **inueniret ... soluerent:** more likely potential than characteristic, but the distinction is artificial. **Gali:** the astronomical learning of C. Sulpicius Galus, cos. 166, was described in the discussion of Archimedes' sphere (21–2, omitted here). The relationship between Paetus and Galus is parallel to that between Laelius and Tubero: the older, more practical man quotes Ennius against the excessive devotion to pure learning of the younger. The discussion is a particular manifestation of the contrast between the contemplative and practical lives; cf. §2.1n. **ille ... Achilles** 'the famous speech of Achilles'.

30.3 Astrologorum ... plagas 'Why do astrologers have to look for signs in the sky? when the Goat or the Scorpion or some other animal rises, no one looks at what is before his feet; they look at the expanse of the sky.' Ennius' *Iphigenia*, *trag.* 185–7 J., presumably adapted from Euripides, *IA* 955f. The metre of the verses is trochaic, two octonarii followed by a septenarius. The text is problematic, and has been much emended; *astrologorum* is taken here as a possessive gen. dependent on *obseruationis*, while *signa* is the object of the verbal element in *obseruationis* (archaic syntax). For discussion, see Jocelyn's commentary; his text and interpretation are followed here.

30.4 atque idem: adversative: despite his rejection of astronomy, he also rejects Zethus' extreme antagonism to learning. **Zethum illum Pacuui:** in Euripides' *Antiope* (on which Pacuvius' *Antiopa* was based), the brothers Zethus and Amphion illustrated respectively the man of action and the man of learning; their debate was used by Callicles in Pl. *Grg.* 485e-486a (cf. Dodds *ad loc.*) to illustrate the childishness of philosophers. Zethus' hostility to philosophy is referred to also at *De orat.* 2.156, where it is also followed by a reference to Ennius' Neoptolemus. **Neoptolemus Ennii:** the full verse (*Andromacha* 95 J.) is quoted by Gel. 5.15.9 (cf. 5.16.5): *philosophandum est paucis; nam omnino haud placet.* C. cites it elsewhere, most significantly at

De orat. 2.156. The parallelism between the two (Zethus followed by Neoptolemus) draws attention to the similarity of the roles of Antonius and Laelius in the two works (cf. 19.4n.): they are the practical and empirical Romans, opposed to the more theoretical philosophizing of Crassus and Scipio; while they do not mind some acquaintance with the less abstruse elements of Greek learning, they object to excessive abstraction, in *De orat.* to dialectic and here to astronomy. The presence of three quotations from Roman adaptations of Greek tragedy in one paragraph implicitly makes the same point about *Rep.* itself: it is not a work of Greek theory, but the adaptation of Greek theory to a specific Roman context. The same point is made more explicitly by Scipio at 36.2.

30.5–6 The idea that philosophy is suitable for children but not for adults is drawn from Callicles' speech, *Grg.* 485cd (cf. also *De orat* 3.58, *Fin.* 1.72). With *liberiora* 'more suitable for a free man' cf. 485c5 ἐλεύθερόν τινα εἶναι; for the social ideal implied, cf. Dodds *ad loc.*

31.2 de Scipione quaesieris: Laelius takes up Tubero's simple *quaero*, and uses the verb 4x in the next two sentences, transferring it from scientific research to political science, and altering *ante pedes* in the quotation from Ennius to *ante oculos.*

31.3 quid enim mihi 'why, may I ask?'; the expostulatory *quid* and the ethic dat. *mihi* (cf. Woodcock §66) establish the tone of Laelius' comments. **L. Paulli nepos:** Tubero was the son of Scipio's sister Aemilia; cf. Introduction, p. 10. Laelius lists Tubero's qualifications for public life. **in hac tam clara re publica natus:** an echo of the funeral oration which Laelius wrote for Q. Fabius Maximus Allobrogicus to deliver over Scipio ... *quod is cum illo animo atque ingenio hac e ciuitate potissimum natus est* (Laelius fr. 22 *ORF*); he imitated it more closely a few years earlier at *Mur.* 75.

31.4 obtrectatores ... P. Mucio: on the political situation of 129, see Introduction, pp. 6–8. P. Licinius Crassus Mucianus, cos. 131, was the father-in-law of C. Gracchus and a member of the agrarian commission set up under Ti. Gracchus' agrarian law; he was elected pontifex maximus after the death of Scipio Nasica in 132 and fell in battle in Asia in 130. Ap. Claudius Pulcher, cos. 143, was a long-standing political rival of Scipio, and was father-in-law of Ti. Gracchus; he too was a member of the agrarian commission, and also died in about 130. Q. Caecilius Metellus Macedonicus, cos. 143, became a political opponent of Scipio sometime in the 130s, but he was not closely attached to the Gracchans, and it is primarily this passage that places him among Scipio's enemies at this time; cf. Astin (1967) 312–15. P. Mucius Scaevola, cos. 133, was closely associated with Ti. Gracchus and succeeded his brother Crassus Mucianus as pontifex maximus in 130. **neque hunc qui unus potest:** Laelius' indignation at the neglect of Scipio is taken up by the prophecy of the *Somnium* (6.12.3–4) that Scipio will re-order the state as dictator, if he survives. **hunc** is the object of *patiuntur.* **sociis et nomine Latino:** *socii* are non-citizen allies, while the Latins (*nomen Latinum*) have partial citizen rights. The reference to their mistreatment by the Gracchans is echoed both in the same passage of the *Somnium* and in the fragmentary conclusion of Laelius' speech on justice at 3.41: ... *Ti. Gracchus, perseuerauit in ciuibus, sociorum nominisque Latini iura neglexit ac foedera.* **triumuiris seditiosissimis:** the commission for land distribution set up by Ti. Gracchus' agrarian law. In 129, the commissioners were C. Gracchus, M. Fulvius Flaccus, and C. Papirius Carbo. **molientibus:** Moser's conjecture is preferable to *mouentibus* in P; cf. 1.28.1n. *locupletibus* was rightly deleted by Mueller: its sense is wrong and the lack of a conjunction is surprising.

32.1–2 Either the second sun is an optical illusion, or what has been seen is a genuine perception. In the latter case there are again two possibilities: either it is beyond our ken or, if it is comprehensible, it is irrelevant to our morals and our happiness. By contrast, the direct value of there being only one Senate and people at Rome is obvious and attainable. Each pair of alternatives in 32.1 is articulated by *aut* ... *aut*; there is also precise correspondence in language between the two parts of the sentence: *modo ne sit molestus* ~ *permolestum*; *aut scire* ... *nihil* ~ *secus esse scimus*; *nec meliores* ... *nec beatiores* ~ *et melius* ... *et beatius.*

32.1 ne metueritis: C. uses the pf. subj. some 45x in prohibitions, as opposed to three times as many exx. of the neg. imper.; he rarely uses the pres. subj.; cf K–S I 189. **sit sane** is jussive; for a similar use cf. 2.51.1. **modo ne** 'only provided that ... not'; cf. *OLD* s.v. *modo* 4. **etiamsi maxime:** for the use of *maxime* to emphasize a condition, cf. H–S 672–3.

32.2 secus 'different', 'not as it should be'; for this quasi-adjectival use, cf. *OLD* s.v. 1c.

33.1 Scaevola, one of the younger members of the group, responds to the address to *adulescentes* in the previous speech; the elder members then approve of Laelius' suggested topic.

33.2 id enim ... munus: i.e. usefulness to the state; Laelius' reference to *artes* and *sapientia* adapts the terminology of Greek learning to the practical uses of Roman life. **uel documentum uel officium:** public service demonstrates the possession of *uirtus* and is a duty of the person who possesses it (cf. §2.1). At *Rab. Post.* 27, C. refers to Rutilius as a *documentum uirtutis.*

33.3 optimum statum ciuitatis: cf. *Q. fr.* 3.5.1, giving the topic of *Rep.* as *de optimo statu ciuitatis et de optimo ciue. status*, here as in 34.2, 70.4, 71.2, 2.2.1 and *Leg.* 1.20, denotes a constitution or form of government. **ad haec ipsa uia peruenturos** 'we will reach the topic of immediate interest (*haec ipsa*) in a methodical fashion'. For *uia* (Gr. ὁδῶι) 'methodically', cf. e.g. *Brut.* 46, *Or.* 10, 116, *N.D.* 2.57 with Pease *ad loc.* The argument is to move from the general consideration of states to ever more specific questions (*alia quaeremus*), leading to a discussion of the immediate crisis.

34.1 admodum approba<uissent>: one leaf of P is missing. A quotation in Diomedes (*GLK* I 365.21–3 *nullum est exemplum cui malimus adsimulare rem publicam*) is usually placed here (cf. Heck 215), but Gigon's suggestion (252–3) that it belongs in one of the lacunae at the conclusion of book 2 is equally probable. For another fragment that may belong here, cf. 46.2n. When P resumes, Laelius is speaking.

34.2 non solum ... rerum ciuilium: Laelius' reasons for asking Scipio to speak – that he has practical political experience as well as knowledge of Greek theory – echo C.'s description of his own qualifications at 13.1. **principem rei publicae** 'one of the leading statesmen'; perhaps an anticipation of the discussion of the *rector*: cf. 45.2n. **cum Panaetio ... Polybio:** on Scipio's friendship with Panaetius and Polybius, cf. Introduction, p. 9. The two here represent the two aspects of *Rep.* itself, the combination of philosophy and Roman history. According to *Leg.* 3.14, Panaetius was one of the few Stoics to deal with political theory, but this passage does not show that C. was following a treatise of Panaetius in *Rep.* **optimum longe:** the reversal of the usual word order is emphatic.

35.2 etenim cum ... consumpserim: an argument *a fortiori* from the comparison of artisan and statesman; a similar comparison (between oratory and acting) is made by Crassus at *De orat.* 1.129–30, and there may also be some reminiscence of the conversation with the young Scipio reported by Polybius 31.23–4. The syntax is complex, and Scipio keeps the focus on his own reactions to the comparison, rather than on the comparison itself: it begins with a causal clause (*cum ... uideam*) which in turn includes two qualifying clauses (*qui quidem excellat*, *nihil aliud ... nisi quo sit ... melior*); *quo sit ... melior* is a final relative clause. The subject of the sentence (*ego*) is followed by another causal clause (*cum ... rei publicae*) and then by the main clause (*non ... quemquam*, the apodosis of a fut. less vivid condition) and the protasis (*si ... consumpserim*). The protasis emphasizes the contrast between Scipio and the artisan through the repeated *minus ... operae* (a frequent form of hyperbaton in Latin), *maxima arte*, *minimis* (sc. *rebus*). **opificem:** cf. *Off.* 1.150 *opificesque omnes in sordida arte uersantur.*

36.1 consultatione: a theoretical question, a topic for debate or discussion; so also at *De orat.* 3.109 and 111 (cf. *Part. or.* 3–4, *Top.* 81–6 and elsewhere). C. lists the Greek philosophers in question (including Plato, Aristotle, Theophrastus, Panaetius, and others) at *Leg.* 3.14. Scipio expresses his usual moderate opinion on the value of Greek learning: neither is he satisfied with what he has read nor does he claim to surpass it.

36.2 neque ut omnino expertem ... quam litteris: cf. Crassus' disclaimer at *De orat.* 1.111: *moderabor ipse, ne ut quidam magister atque artifex, sed quasi unus ex togatorum numero atque ex forensi usu homo mediocris neque omnino rudis uidear ...*; similarly at *Fat.* 4, and probably also in the preface to *Rep.* (cf. fr. 1c Ziegler). The balance between Greek and Roman and between book learning and practical experience is central both to Scipio's character as delineated by C. and to the argument of the dialogue as a whole. **patris diligentia:** Aemilius Paullus had appropriated the library of the kings of Macedon for his children; cf. Astin (1967) 15. **studioque discendi a pueritia incensum:** cf. C.'s self-description at 7.4; similar language also at *De orat.* 1.97.

37.1 idem: cf. 13.1n. **quibus ... fueris** 'what (kind of) studies you have been characterized by'; Moser's addition of *in* (so also Meister (1940) 107) or Maehly's of *deditus* are possible, but unnecessary. Philus' remark is an ironic rejection of Scipio's statement that his education was more through experience than book-learning.

37.2 animum 'enthusiasm', 'zeal' rather than 'mind': cf. *De orat.* 2.212, *Flac.* 61, *OLD* s.v. 8d. Scipio has spoken modestly of his abilities and education, and emphasized his experience and zeal; Philus replies that Scipio has talent, experience, and learning, and that now he is pleased to learn that he also (*quoque*) cares about the science of public affairs. For similar flattery of the main speaker, cf. Scaevola's words to Crassus at *De orat.* 1.105–6. **a Graecis hominibus:** *hominibus* is Orelli's conjecture (cf. also Skutsch (1959) 141 n.2) for *nobis* in P, which makes little sense here (cf. *scripta nobis summi ... homines reliquerunt*, 36.1).

38–69: Scipio's Speech on Constitutions

Aside from the concluding paragraphs (70–1), the rest of book 1 consists of Scipio's discussion (with occasional contributions from Laelius) of the forms of government. The loss of ten leaves of P at various places has made some points obscure, but the structure of the argument is clear; for summary and interpretation, cf. Introduction, pp. 17–22.

38.1 ut potero 'to the best of my ability': like the more frequent *si potero* (or *potuero*), a mark of courteous modesty (also 65.5, 70.4, 70.5; 2.42.3, 52.2); cf. *Att.* 8.4.2. **ea lege ... intellectum prius:** on the importance of beginning with precise definitions (from Pl. *Phdr.* 237bc), cf. *De orat.* 1.209–13, *Or.* 116, *Fin.* 1.29, 2.3–4, *Off.* 1.7. There are three stages: agreement on terms (*ut eius rei ... conueniat*); definition of terms (*explicetur ... nomine*); and finally discussion of substantive issues (*tum ... sermonem*). Understanding of *quid sit* must precede consideration of *quale sit*.

38.3 nec uero ... definiam saepius: Scipio limits his introductory remarks in two respects: he will not bother with anthropological speculations on the remote origins of human society from the family (as e.g. Arist. *Pol.* 1.2 and Plb. 6.6.2), nor will he waste time in overly refined definitions and lists of terms. He emphasizes here, as at the end of his speech (70.1), his position as a Roman statesman rather than a Greek philosopher, addressing others with similar background and experience; a similar disclaimer at *De orat.* 1.23. **de re tam illustri tamque nota:** *illustris* in the sense of 'well-known, familiar'; at the end of this sentence, it is used with the meaning 'clear, lucid'. **reuoluar:** for a similar use, cf. *De orat.* 2.130 *nec quotiens causa dicenda est, totiens ad eius causae seposita argumenta reuolui nos oportet.* The metaphor is from the rolling and unrolling of a papyrus roll. **uerbisque ... definiam saepius** 'give repeated definitions and explanations of each term.' *definiam* is parallel in construction to *reuoluar*, not to *disseram*.

38.4 tamquam magister: cf. *De orat.* 1.111 cited 36.2n. **ut ne qua particula**: *ne quis* frequently follows *ut* in substantive consecutive clauses, e.g. *Verr.* 2.73, 5.7; *De orat.* 2.102; *Am.* 43; *Off.* 1.103: cf. Reid on *Fin.* 1.24. There is a similarly scornful use of *particula* at *De orat.* 2.162.

39.1 Scipio's definition of *res publica* has two parts, first defining the *res publica* in terms of the *populus*, then defining the *populus* itself in both negative (*non omnis ... congregatus*) and positive (*coetus multitudinis ... sociatus*) terms. Although the definition is of great importance both in *Rep.* itself and in subsequent European political theory (on this see particularly Suerbaum (1977)), in context it is not presented as the final word on the subject. In the preceding paragraph Scipio has stated that philosophical precision is not his aim, and this definition is clearly provisional; its terms, particularly *iuris consensus*, are substantially redefined in the course of the dialogue. The sources of the definition are disputed; the first part is probably C.'s own, while the second (and longer) part comes from Peripatetic sources. Panaetius has often been seen as the source (e.g. Pohlenz 82), but there is an important difference between this passage, which makes the formation of states natural, and the Panaetian account in *Off.* 1.11–12, which makes it rational. For recent discussions of all or part of this definition, cf. particularly Cancelli, Werner, Kohns (1974), Suerbaum (1977) 1–37, Wood 123–8; further bibliography in Schmidt (1973) 318–19 and Suerbaum (1978) 74–5. **res publica res populi:** in essence, an etymological definition: *publicus* < *populus* (from Varro, according to a scholiast cited by Mai which no one else has found; cf. also Plaut. *Poen.* 524 *in re populi placida*); C. echoes it repeatedly in *Rep.*: cf. 41.3, 43.2, 48.3; 3.43, 44, 45, 46. The meaning of *res* and the proper translation of *res publica* are difficult: 'commonwealth' emphasizes too much the material aspects of *res*; 'republic' begs the constitutional issues which C. is here careful to leave open; 'public affairs' omits the institutional element. 'Political organization is the organization of the people' is close to the sense of the phrase, but loses the etymological play. Heinze 13 best approximated its scope as 'including all interests of the community of the people' ('alle Interessen der völkischen

Gemeinschaft umfassend'). For a thorough examination of the meanings of *res publica*, cf. Drexler (1957–8). C.'s definition is comparable to Aristotle's description of the *polis* as a κοινωνία πολιτῶν (*Pol.* 3.3), but Aristotle's state is an agglomeration of individual citizens, while C.'s belongs to the *populus* viewed as a single whole; so, most recently, Eder 19 n.11. Perhaps the most significant fact about C.'s definition is its explicit distinction between the *res publica* and the *populus*: while the Roman state was known simply as *populus Romanus*, C. carefully avoids identifying the state (or its constitution – *res publica* may mean both) with the organized people (defined in the second part of the sentence) who make it up. Neither C. nor Romans in general recognized popular sovereignty in its modern form; cf. Wirszubski (1950) 14: 'The notion of res publica ... postulates that the government should be for the people; but it does not necessarily imply the principle of government by the people.' C.'s definition implies no presupposition about the form of the *res publica*, which may include even monarchy (cf. 3.47). Unlike most ancient theorists, moreover, C. does not make ethnic or territorial unity of the *populus* an element in the formation of the state. **non omnis ... congregatus:** cf. Arist. *Pol.* 5.3, 3.6. For the metaphor in *congregatus*, cf. 39.2n. **coetus ... sociatus:** the two elements of C.'s definition of the *populus* must be taken together (cf. also *Off.* 2.9–10 and *Leg.* 1.33 *recteque Socrates exsecrari eum solebat, qui primus utilitatem a iure seiunxisset*), and are (directly or indirectly) Aristotelian. It is agreement on law and shared advantage, rather than imposed law and the advantage of only one group, that differentiates the *populus* from other groups of people. The crucial question raised by this limiting definition of *populus* is whether or not any of the debased forms of government (tyranny, oligarchy, ochlocracy) can be considered a *res publica* at all if both justice and utility are necessary elements of a true *res populi*. There are, in fact, two different answers to this question in *Rep.* In the discussion which follows in book 1 (cf. particularly 43, 45), it is clear that *all* forms of government, good and bad, are *res publicae*. When the subject is resumed at the end of book 3, however (43–6), the definition is refined to require that any true *res publica* exhibit justice. **iuris consensu** 'common idea of what is right' (Poyser) preserves some of the deliberate ambiguity of the phrase. The only exact parallel is in Laelius' quotation of this definition at 3.45, in which *iuris consensus* is the crucial distinction between genuine *res publicae* and their degenerate counterparts; so too at 6.13.2 Africanus uses the phrase *concilia coetusque hominum iure sociati* as the definition of *ciuitates.* It has been taken to mean here the acceptance of shared laws, the recognition of a universal idea of justice, or juridical equality. The last of these is very unlikely given Cicero's anti-democratic views; the second is appropriate to the discussion of natural law in book 3 but would have no context here (for the difference between this passage and 3.45, cf. Pohlenz 95), although it has clear connections with the Greek philosophical tradition (e.g. Arist. *Pol.* 1.2, *SVF* 3.327, 329). What is offered here is a contractual theory of the state, involving the acceptance of the rule of law (and presumably of some means of creating and enforcing it); it implies an equitable (but not equal) distribution of rights and duties: compare the democratic discussion of *ius* and *aequalitas* at 49.2–4. **utilitatis communione:** C. is not offering a utilitarian explanation of the *origin* of society, as was emphasized, for instance, by Epicurus, but simply stating that shared utility is one of the bonds that maintain societies; for *utilitas* cf. *Sest.* 91 *res ad communem utilitatem quas publicas appellamus* (also *Fin.* 3.64).

39.2 prima causa coeundi: the same phrase at 4.3 is explained as *ad illam ciuium beate et honeste uiuendi societatem.* C.'s preference for seeing innate tendencies in man rather than weakness as the primary motive for social organization (so also at *Am.* 19, *Off.* 1.158) aligns him with Aristotle (e.g. *Pol.* 1.2, 3.6) and the Stoics against the utilitarian theories found, for example, in Pl. *R.* 2.369bc and *Prt.* 322ab, in Plb. 6.5.7, and most notably in Epicurus; see Walbank on Polybius *loc. cit.* and Cole (1990) 33–4, 80–96. For detailed analysis of the sentence, cf. Steinmetz, and Kohns (1976). **congregatio:** the metaphor is qualified by *quasi* (cf. 18.3n.), as it more properly refers to animals rather than men; Plb. 6.5.7 uses συναγελάζεσθαι. At *Tusc.* 5.38 C. refers to animals as *partim soliuagas, partim congregatas.* **ne in omnium quidem rerum affluen<tia>*:** for the phrase, cf. *Agr.* 2.95 *ex hac copia atque omnium rerum affluentia*; *Off.* 1.153. One leaf is missing here; Taeger 10 offers a supplement based on *Fin.* 3.65: *affluen<tia uitam in summa solitudine agere uelit>*, and Nonius 321.16 M. supplies one phrase that belongs in the lacuna: *idque ipsa natura non inuitaret solum sed etiam cogeret.* From this, and from the parallels in *Fin.* and in Lactantius 6.10.13–18, it is clear that C.'s point (following, e.g. Arist. *EN* 9.9, Pl.

Lg. 3.678c) is that the urge for community is innate in man. For further discussion, see Heck 91–3. Ziegler's §40 is an extended quotation from Lactantius, most of which either derives from Lucretius or duplicates the extant portion of this paragraph; it (along with the sentence from Nonius cited above) is omitted from this edition. When P resumes, Scipio is stating that not only the desire for community, but justice itself, together with the other virtues and the state itself, exist by nature and not by convention.

41.1 <quae>dam quasi semina: Perelli (1977) 20 supplements the opening of the sentence as: *<nullam hominum gentem reperire possumus, in qua non sint iustitiae quae>dam* . . . The metaphorical use of *semina* is qualified; cf. *Div.* 1.6 with Pease *ad loc. quasi* normally precedes *quidam* as at 1.18.3, 6.21.1; cf. Reid on *Acad.* 1.21.

41.2 sedem . . . constituerunt: from the natural tendency to community, C. moves to the physical creation of the city, and from shelter and defence to the distinctive elements of human society, namely religion and public gatherings. Although this description is cursory, it corresponds to the more detailed description of Romulus' foundation of Rome in book 2. For another Ciceronian account of the origins of society, emphasizing the role of the first leaders in its formation, cf. *Sest.* 91.

41.3 omnis ergo populus . . . ut diuturna sit: a tricolon with anaphora emphasizing the different aspects of society – the *populus*, the *ciuitas*, and the *res publica* itself – in which each noun is followed by an explanatory relative clause, leading finally to the central concerns of the first book, the need for some form of government and the need to assure the continuity of the state. The distinction between *ciuitas* and the other terms is hard to define: although it seems to denote the physical organization of the community, it is in fact used as a virtual synonym elsewhere for both *res publica* (e.g. 33.3, 42.4, 2.52.1–2, 6.13.2) and *populus* (1.49.4); cf. Suerbaum (1977) 18 n.51, 66–70. *consilium* in Scipio's speech is used in two different ways: here, it denotes the leadership and direction necessary for any form of rule – 'executive power' (Suerbaum (1977) 26) or 'deliberative authority' (Krarup (1973) 211) – and it is so applied to the mind at 60.1; elsewhere (e.g. 51.2, 55.3), it is the distinctive attribute of aristocratic government. For *diuturnitas* (or *immortalitas*) as a goal, cf. 2.5.2, 27.4; 3.7, 34, 41.

41.4 C. is not concerned here with universal causes for the formation of all states, but with the practical concerns of particular states. Every state must have some direction (*consilium*) in order to last; and that direction must always be related to the particular reason for which the state came into being. For the use of *referre*, cf. 49.1 *populo ... omnia referente ad incolumitatem et ad libertatem*. The repetition *eam causam ... quae causa* is formal; cf. e.g. *N.D.* 1.90 *forma ... qua forma*, and 2.13n.

42.1 deinde aut uni ... omnibus: C. accepts the three forms of government – by one, by a few, or by the populace at large – traditional in Greek political theory from the fifth century (Pindar, *Pyth.* 2.87–8; Hdt. 3.80–2); cf. Pl. *Plt.* 291cd, 302de, Arist. *Pol.* 3.7, and Plb. 6.3.5 with Walbank's note. The definitions and names in the three following sentences are not in parallel form: the single ruler is named *rex*, the chosen few are named 'the best men', *optimates* (a tendentious term, as is *delecti*, which assumes some mechanism of choice rather than self-selection), but the rule of the multitude is simply called *ciuitas popularis*, for lack of a Latin equivalent to δημοκρατία; hence the parenthetical *sic enim appellant*. In the first two definitions, the parallel phrases *penes unum* and *penes delectos* are used but in the third there is simply *in populo*; in the second and third, the phrase *illa ciuitas* is repeated. For *atque omnibus* equivalent to *id est omnibus*, compare e.g. *Fin.* 1.10, 1.16, *Acad.* 2.36; the phrase *suscipiendum ... omnibus* also at *Planc.* 62.

42.5 'And any of these three types, if it should maintain the bond which originally bound men into a state, would not be perfect nor (in my opinion) the best, but it would be tolerable, and any one might be superior to the rest.' **si teneat ... societate deuinxit:** an amplification of 41.4 *ad eam causam referendum est.* **et aliud alio possit esse praestantius:** potential subj.: in various circumstances, each of the three simple forms might be preferable to another. Most editors add *ut* and make it a consecutive clause, but then the addition of *ita* or *tale* is also desirable.

42.6 aequus ac sapiens: although these adjectives apply grammatically to *rex*, *aequitas* and *sapientia* are in fact defining characteristics of any good government: *aequitas* in maintaining the bond of society, *sapientia* (synonymous with *consilium* as used in 41.3–4) in assuring its continued existence. Except at 1.53.1–2, the distinction between *aequitas* and *aequabilitas* is strictly observed: C. is not a democrat, and believes in a natural system of three orders in society. The rule of the *populus* is thus the least desirable constitution, although, as Scipio grudgingly admits, there can exist a stable democracy so long as *iniquitas* and *cupiditas* are not involved. The favourable example of Rhodian democracy is adduced by Scipio against Mummius in 3.48.

43.1 The brief descriptions of the intrinsic drawbacks of the three constitutional forms are echoed in the more detailed arguments in favour of democracy and aristocracy in 47–53 below. Hommel (1955a) 324 demonstrates the closeness of this paragraph to Aristotelian terminology. **ipsa aequabilitas est iniqua:** for the idea of proportional equality introduced here, cf. Pl. *Lg.* 6.756e–758a; Arist. *EN* 5.3, *Pol.* 3.9; Isocr. *Nic.* 14; also Fantham (1973) 288–90. In C.'s earlier writings, *aequabilitas* refers to juridical equality, but here it apparently means political equality; for a discussion of the term, cf. 53.1–2n., and for a modern adaptation of the sentiment, cf. the Grand Inquisitor: 'When everybody's somebody, then no one's anybody' (W. S. Gilbert, *The Gondoliers*). **cum habeat nullos gradus dignitatis:** the parallel with *cum ... careat* above suggests that Heinrich's emendation of P's *habet* is correct. *gradus dignitatis* ('social distinctions') is repeated at the end of this paragraph; for the various senses in which C. uses the phrase in his speeches, cf. Lepore 261–3. For the definition of *dignitas*, cf. *Inv.* 2.166 *dignitas est alicuius honesta et cultu et honore et uerecundia digna auctoritas.*

43.2 A series of three parallel concessive conditions with anaphora and asyndeton (*si Cyrus ... si Massilienses ... si Athenienses*) gives specific illustrations for the vices of the three constitutions adduced in the first half of the paragraph: the failure of monarchy to seek counsel or share power, the lack of popular liberty in aristocracy, and the lack of *dignitas* in a democracy. **Cyrus ille Perses:** Cyrus the Great (c. 599–530 B.C.E.), described as *amabilis* at 44.3, was an exemplar of the good and just ruler from the time of Herodotus (3.89); Pl. *Lg.* 3.694ab contrasts his good rule with the disasters of his successors. The principal text alluded to here is Xenophon's *Cyropaedia*, which C. reports to have been Scipio's constant reading; cf. *Tusc.* 2.62, *Q. fr.* 1.1.23. **unius nutu ac †modo†:** *qui populos urbisque modo ac uirtute regebant* (*De cons. suo* p. 243 Soubiran = fr. 10.67 Courtney) is not parallel (cf. Courtney *ad loc.*) and *modo* here is corrupt; as C. (at least in *Rep.*) generally uses *ac* and *atque* to connect single words, the corruption is probably limited to *modo*. **Massilienses:** the government of Marseilles was a standard example of a good and stable oligarchy; cf *Flac.* 63, Strabo 4.1.5. **nostri clientes:** not personal clients of Scipio, but a client state of Rome. **quibusdam temporibus**: fifth-century Athenian democracy was a thing of the distant past; cf. *quodam tempore* at 44.4. **sublato Areopago:** the abolition of the power of the aristocratic council of the Areopagus in the fifth century was a standard complaint of conservative theorists; cf. Arist. *Pol.* 2.21, Isoc. *Areopag.* 50–1. **populi scitis:** *populi scitum* (in place of the normal *plebis scitum* for legislation passed by the *concilium plebis*) is also used of the Athenians (who had no *plebs*) at *Opt. gen.* 19; similar uses in a Roman context in *Leg.* For the formal usage of Roman law, cf. the decree of the *pontifices* cited at *Att.* 4.2.3 *si neque populi iussu neque plebis scitu* ... **ornatum suum:** possibly translating Gk. κόσμος 'order'; cf. Hommel (1955a) 325, and for C.'s use of *ornatus* for κόσμος cf. Reid on *Fin.* 1.20, Pease on *N.D.* 2.17, 85. C. frequently uses *ornamentum rei publicae* to refer to outstanding individuals or groups: cf. *Rosc. Am.* 142, *Sul.* 5, *Dom.* 146, *Prov.* 22, *Planc.* 23, *Mil.* 37, *Phil.* 5.39, 11.36.

44.1 non turbatis ... tenentibus: when the three simple constitutions retain their pure form; for *status* cf. 42.6.

44.2 quae genera ... perniciosa alia uitia: not only do the simple forms individually have the intrinsic failings described above, but they are all liable to change into their corrupt equivalents: monarchy to tyranny, aristocracy to oligarchy, democracy to ochlocracy. For these transformations cf. esp. Plb. 6.4.6 with Walbank *ad loc.* **iter ... praeceps ac lubricum:** the metaphor (cf. also *Flac.* 105) is taken up by *procliui cursu ... delabitur* below. **finitimum** 'kindred': cf. *OLD* s.v. 4; for the concept of the 'kindred failing', cf. Arist. *EN* 8.10, Plb. 6.10.7 with Pöschl 22–3, 48 and Cole (1964) 444–5.

44.3 amabili: for *caritas* as an attribute of monarchy, cf. 55.3, 64.1–4. **subest** 'is close by'; cf. 69.5. **ad immutandi animi licentiam** 'in that he can change his character without restriction' (Poyser); for *ad* 'in respect of', cf. *OLD* s.v. (37), K–S I 523. **crudelissimus ille Phalaris**: the sixth-century tyrant of Agrigentum who roasted his opponents in a hollow bronze bull is a paradigm for the oppressive tyrant as early as Pindar, *Pyth.* 1.95. C. reports (*Verr.* 4.73) that Scipio returned the bull, which he had captured in Carthage, to the Agrigentines. **procliui cursu et facile:** the coordination of abl. and adverb is unusual; in all probability either *et* should be deleted or *facile* emended to *facili*.

44.4 triginta <illorum>: the oligarchic rulers of Athens at the end of the Peloponnesian War. Some supplement is necessary, and Moser's is the simplest; cf. *Leg.* 1.42 *triginta illi.* **consensus et factio** 'oligarchic conspiracy'; hendiadys. For *consensus* in a pejorative sense, cf. *Sest.* 86, *Tusc.* 5.46.

44.5 iam Atheniensium ... pesti*: for *iam* cf. 9.1n. One leaf is missing, and the end of the sentence is lost. *ipsi* refers to the Athenians themselves, and Mai tentatively supplemented *pesti<lentem fatentur ...>*. The sense is that the Athenians themselves were later appalled by the excesses of the radical democracy of the fifth century. Büchner's suggestion that Nonius 526.8 M. (fr. 1f Ziegler *nec tantum Carthago habuisset opum sescentos fere annos sine consiliis et disciplina*) belongs here is unconvincing; see Heck 211–12.

45.1 *taeterrimus ... popularis: when the text resumes, C. is describing the instability of the simple constitutions and the numerous possibilities of permutation among them. In this variety of change, C. disagrees with both Plato and Polybius, who posit rigid patterns of degeneration (but cf. *Div.* 2.6 *a Platone didiceram naturales esse quasdam conuersiones rerum publicarum, ut eae tum a principibus tenerentur, tum a populis, aliquando a singulis*). The precise interpretation of the opening words is hindered by one major and one minor textual problem. The minor one is the first word: P reads *teterrimus*, and N. Krarup emended to *deterrimus*, which is not only unnecessary (cf. *taeterrimorum hominum*, 27.1) but begs the important question of what constitution is being described, as *deterrimus* must apply to a tyrant (cf. 65.2, 2.47.1). The major one is in the words *uel factiosa tyrannica illa* in P, which are generally accepted and taken to have a single referent, oligarchic government (e.g. Sabine and Smith, 'a tyrannical government by a party'); but the two adjectives *factiosa tyrannica* would require either a noun or a connective. Mai's conjecture *tyrannis* for *tyrannica* solves one problem, but *tyrannis* should not refer to an oligarchy (which it never does in C.), as it must with the modifier *factiosa*. Another solution is to punctuate between *factiosa* and *tyrannica*, taking *tyrannica illa* as the beginning of a new sequence with asyndeton between the two sets of constitutions; the difficulty with this is that C. uses *factiosus* of individuals only, not of types of government. A third solution, adopted here, is to emend *factiosa* to *factionis* (suggested by E. J. Kenney); for the contrast between *factio* and *optimates* cf. 69.3 *ex rege dominus, ex optimatibus factio, ex populo turba et confusio*. The list has five elements: aristocracy or oligarchy, tyranny or monarchy or democracy. That in turn implies that *taeterrimus* must refer to ochlocracy and not, as is more usual, tyranny. Cf. however, 3.45, where Laelius refers to *tyrannus iste conuentus ... hoc etiam taetrior, quia nihil ista, quae populi speciem et nomen imitatur, immanius belua est.* **efflorescere:** to arise naturally from something; cf. *De orat.* 1.20, 2.319; *Am.* 100. **quasi circuitus:** Plb. 6.9.10 uses the rare word ἀνακύκλωσις to describe the fixed sequence of constitutions which he proposes, and that is presumably C.'s source; Aristotle had earlier (*Pol.* 5.1316a30) rejected Plato's fixed sequence in the *Republic* in part because, if one returns to the first constitution after the last, then it would create a κύκλος. For an earlier use of the image, cf. *Att.* 2.9.1 *minore sonitu quam putaram orbis hic in re publica est conuersus.* C.'s account does not have a fixed cycle, but a virtually infinite set of variations, indicated by his use of the plurals *orbes* and *circuitus* and perhaps by the double pairing *orbes et ... circuitus* and *commutationum et uicissitudinum* (for which cf. *Tusc.* 1.68, 5.69); for the sing. *orbis*, cf. 2.45.1.

45.2 quos cum cognosse ... diuini paene est uiri 'to recognize them takes a wise man; but for someone at the helm of the state, guiding its course and keeping control of it, to foresee them as they approach, takes a great citizen and godlike man': the acc. participles *moderantem* and *retinentem* must be taken as subjects of the infinitives *cognosse* and *prospicere*; for a similar construction, cf. 9.2. This is the first indication of the importance in C.'s theory of the *rector* or *moderator* (here *moderantem*), who stands outside the structure of the mixed constitution but serves somehow to keep it on course; on the *rector*, cf. Introduction, pp. 25–8. For other important passages, cf. 2.45.2, 51, 67–9, 5.9, 6.1; for *prudentia/prouidere*, cf. also *Leg.* 1.60, *Hort.* fr. 33 M. The mark of the good statesman is *prudentia* (the etymological relationship of which to *prouidere* is important in C.'s discussions). The quality of foresight is a traditional attribute of the political leader, from Thucydides (1.138 of Themistocles, 2.60, 65 of Pericles) on. In Arist. *Pol.* 5.8 it is the mark of the πολιτικὸς ἀνήρ to recognize trouble as it arises. **diuini:** not to be taken literally: it is one of C.'s highest terms of praise for moral and intellectual qualities, as at *Q. fr.* 1.1.11,

Red. pop.. 7. The description of the statesman is not germane to the constitutional argument: C. anticipates the subject of the last two books of *Rep.*

45.3 itaque: the logical connection seems to be that because the foresight necessary to maintain a simple constitution is so extraordinary, therefore a constitution which less regularly requires it (cf. 69.4) is preferable. **moderatum et permixtum:** for similar combinations, cf. 69.1 *aequatum et temperatum*; 2.41 *confusa modice*; 2.65 *modice temperatum*; *Leg.* 3.17 *modica et sapiens temperatio.* At 2.42.4 C. distinguishes between *mixta* and *temperata*, giving the first attribute to the constitution of Servius Tullius, the second to the true republican mixed constitution. The idea of the mixed constitution is basically Peripatetic, possibly deriving from Dicaearchus; cf. also Plb. 6.3.7. The emphasis on proportion and equilibrium rather than simple mixture is derived from Pl. *Lg.* 3.694a–98b; cf. Ferrary (1984) 93.

46.1 Hic Laelius: throughout Scipio's speech it is Laelius (as Scipio's closest friend) who asks questions and offers interjections; so also at 54.1, 64.6, 66.3, 68.1, 71.1, as well as the extended dialogue at 55–60. Laelius' interruption serves as a transition from Scipio's brief outline of the theory of constitutions to the more detailed analysis which follows. **ex tribus istis:** referring back to Scipio's brief descriptions at 1.42, 43–5. The question (repeated at 1.54.1) is highly artificial (Scipio has already said that none of the three simple constitutions is satisfactory), but it permits C. to give a vivid portrait of the virtues and defects of each from the point of view of the proponents of democracy and aristocracy. Scipio reports no argument on behalf of monarchy; it is supplied by his own argument in 56–64; cf. also 50n.

46.2 profuerit aliquid ad cog*: not entirely clear. The sense is presumably that the recognition of the best of the simple constitutions will aid in understanding the superiority of the mixed constitution. For the fut. pf., cf. 20.2n. Büchner (1962) 86 places in this lacuna fr. 4 Ziegler (Nonius 276.6 M.) *'cognosce mehercule' inquit 'consuetudinem istam et studium sermonemque'*; Heck 182 suggests that after 1.34.1 is an equally plausible location.

47 When the text resumes after a lacuna of one leaf, Scipio is delivering a justification of democracy (47–50) followed by one of aristocracy (51–3). These views are reported in the third person (e.g. *negant* 48.2, 49.1; *putant* 50.1; *dicunt* 51.3), with occasional uses of the first person for variety or vividness (e.g. *omitto* 47.3). They reflect a tradition of constitutional debate first attested in Herodotus (3.80–2) and continuing as far as Cassius Dio (52.9). The argument for democracy is that liberty only exists under democratic government, and that even in an oligarchic government in which the people have the vote, they have no real power. A democracy is thus (48) the only true *res publica*. Democracy should not be blamed for the failings of ochlocracy; true democracy is in fact the most stable of all constitutions because of shared interest (49). Other forms of government are falsely named (50): there is no difference between monarchy and tyranny from the point of view of the subjects, and aristocrats have simply arrogated to themselves the name *optimates*.

47.1 et talis ... qui illam regit: so too in the contemporary letter to Lentulus, *Fam.* 1.9.12 *erant praeterea haec animaduertenda in ciuitate quae sunt apud Platonem nostrum scripta diuinitus, quales in republica principes essent, tales reliquos solere esse ciues* (presumably drawing on *Lg.* 4.711b; cf. Boyancé (1970) 250–1). A similar point is made by C. at *Leg.* 3.31.

47.2 nulla alia in ciuitate: the form of government is characterized by its distinctive attribute, in the case of democracy *libertas*. Hence without a democracy (the democrat argues) there is no place at all for liberty. **qua ... nihil potest esse dulcius:** cf. *Att.* 15.13.3 *de libertate retinenda, qua certe nihil est dulcius.* **si aequa non est:** for the democrat, *libertas* means political equality (*aequalitas*) rather than equality before the law (*aequitas*); cf. 43 and the aristocratic response in 53. On the two types, cf. Wirszubski (1950) 9–15.

47.3 qui: cf. 7.3n. **in istis ciuitatibus:** moderate oligarchies (like Rome), in which the people vote but are not themselves eligible to hold office; for the same objection to the Sullan constitution cf. Sal. *Hist.* 3.48.26 M., the speech of the tribune Macer.

47.4 magis was rightly deleted by Madvig. **unde** = *a quibus*, cf. *OLD* s.v. 8. Its antecedent is *ipsi.* **sunt enim expertes:** cf. 43.1 *in regnis nimis expertes sunt ceteri communis iuris et consilii.* **uetustatibus:** pl. elsewhere in C. only at *Inv.* 2.168; the only other exx. in *OLD* from Vitruvius.

47.5 ut Rhodi, ut Athenis: Athens is the paradigmatic democratic government, while that of Rhodes seems to have involved a system of rotation in office described in 3.48. The sense is that in truly democratic states all citizens have equal access to office. There is again a lacuna of one leaf.

48.1 *<po>pulo ... succumbentibus: the beginning of the sentence must have contained a neut. pl. noun agreeing with *nata* and referring to the characteristics of oligarchy, e.g. *uitia*. The democrats seem to be blaming the natural weakness or subservience of people for the decay of democracy, and arguing against the idea that democracy is innately corrupt. The sentence is a good illustration of C.'s taste for pairs of synonyms or near-synonyms: *diuitiores opulentioresque*, *fastidio et superbia*, *cedentibus ... et ... succumbentibus*, *ignauis et imbecillis*; cf. also 2.15.1n.

48.2 populi: a generalizing pl. as is *regum ... reges* 48.4. **praestantius, liberius, beatius:** an emphatic asyndeton (cf. §2.3n.), continued by the list of powers of the people in a radical democracy. Scipio's (and C.'s) antidemocratic bias is shown by the placement of *pecuniae* as the climax of the series.

48.4 The historical argument that democracy emerges from monarchy or aristocracy is contradicted by the aristocrats at 52.4 and reversed by Scipio's argument at 58 that monarchy is the original, and therefore the best, form of government. **patrum:** C. here (also in 49.1) slips into specifically Roman terminology. At 2.14 C. explains that the *principes* in the Romulean senate were called *patres propter caritatem*. **in libertatem ... uindicari** 'liberate': a Roman political slogan, used at *Brut.* 212 of Scipio's actions against the Gracchans. See Wirszubski (1950) 103–4 for a collection of examples.

49.1 et uero negant ... repudiari: so too the aristocrats deny responsibility for oligarchies at 51.3–5. For *indomitus* 'uncontrollable' cf. *OLD* s.v. 3. **omnia referente ... ad libertatem suam:** remaining true to its first principles; cf. 41.4. **in qua idem conducat omnibus:** the democratic definition of the state sees it as the aggregate of individual citizens with juridical equality, while the aristocratic (and Ciceronian) definition sees it as an amalgam of classes with different inherent worths and values. The repeated references to *aequitas* and *aequalitas/aequabilitas* (notably at the end of this paragraph) reflect this divergence on definitions; cf. Arist. *Pol.* 3.9. On the ideal community of goals, cf. *Off.* 3.26 *ergo unum debet esse omnibus propositum, ut eadem sit utilitas uniuscuiusque et uniuersorum.* **nulla ... fides est:** Ennius, *Sc.* 320 J., quoted at *Off.* 1.26 with *regni* after *fides*. *regni* should be deleted here: it is either a false repetition of *regnis* in the previous line, or was imported in the wrong place by a copyist who knew *Off.* The expression is proverbial; cf. Otto s.v. *regnum* 1.

49.2 cum lex ... condicio ciuium 'since law is the bond of civic society, and right is equivalent to law, by what right can a society of citizens be held together, when the status of citizens is not the same?' The thought is straightforward, but made difficult by the double meanings of *aequale* (usually 'equal'; here 'equivalent') and *quo iure* (both 'by what idea of justice' and more loosely 'how'). Both this speech and that of the aristocrats involve arguments turning on words used in two senses (cf. 1.51.4–5, and pp. 20–1). For the idea of law expressed here, cf. *Clu.* 53 *hoc* [sc. *lex*] *enim uinculum est huius dignitatis qua fruimur in re publica, hoc fundamentum libertatis, hic fons aequitatis*; for the meaning of *ius ... aequale* cf. Skutsch (1959) 42–3.

50 One leaf of P is missing before this paragraph and two leaves after it, making the reconstruction of the context difficult. Büchner (1962) 25–61 argued that §50 is part of an argument in favour of monarchy; his interpretation was refuted by Kroymann, and Skutsch (1959), but still has adherents: for bibliography cf. Schmidt (1973) 298. The point of view is still that of the democrats: neither monarchy nor aristocracy (*optimates*) deserves the name which its adherents give it; a king is merely a kindly tyrant, and aristocrats are in no sense 'the best'.

50.1 For the language, cf. 48.3 *hanc unam rite rem publicam, id est rem populi, appellari putant.* The earlier passage contains praise of democracy; this one makes the same point by condemning the alternatives: cf. Kroymann 317. **ne appellandas quidem:** cf. *Leg.* 2.13 *nec uero aliam esse ullam legem puto non modo habendam, sed ne appellandam quidem.*

50.2 Iouis optimi nomine: the same argument is levelled against kings by Philus at 3.23 *sunt enim omnes, qui in populum uitae necisque potestatem habent, tyranni, sed se Iouis optimi nomine malunt reges uocari.*

50.3 tam enim ... potest: like the rest of this section, this sentence concerns the proper application of names: '"kindly" can apply to tyrants as well as "cruel" to kings' – in other words, there is no difference between them. Madvig's deletion of *rex* gives a slightly less appropriate meaning: 'A tyrant can be kindly as well as he can be cruel.' *importunitas* is used to describe Tarquinius Superbus at 62.2. **ut hoc ... seruiant** 'so that there is this difference for the citizens, whether they are enslaved to a mild master or a harsh one'; a consecutive clause, in which *hoc* anticipates the double indirect question. For the construction of *interest* with the genitive, cf. K–S I 460–1. **quin seruiant . . . non potest:** cf. the democratic sentiment at 2.43.5 *libertas, quae non in eo est ut iusto utamur domino, sed ut nul<lo>.*

50.4 The logic is somewhat obscure, but the point seems to be that if even Sparta, generally recognized (e.g. by Plato and Polybius) as having the best constitution, had some bad monarchs because of the hereditary principle, then the Spartan kings too should not be given a title (*rex*) that belongs to Jupiter; see Kroymann 321–2. The same criticism of Sparta at 2.24; cf. Arist. *Pol.* 2.9.

50.5 The argument about the false names of forms of government turns from monarchy to aristocracy: by what criterion are *optimates* to be considered *optimi* (as with the monarchists' arrogation of the title of Iuppiter Optimus Maximus), other than their own self-election (*suis comitiis*)?

50.6 qui: cf. 7.3n. **audio: quando*:** the sentence is clearly incomplete: the last two words are supplied by a quotation in Nonius (239.9 M.) which does not include its own lemma, *aemulus*. The point is that oligarchs never use suitable criteria, such as learning or talent, to define 'best', but instead stick to e.g. birth or wealth. For the use of *audio* as an ironic response ('fine') to an imaginary interlocutor, cf. *S. Rosc.* 52, 58; *Tusc.* 2.46.

51–53 After a lacuna of two leaves, the text resumes in a statement of the optimate position (cf. Kroymann 313–14). A ship cannot be governed by a democracy, and even a democracy delegates responsibility. The choice of leaders on the basis of wealth is a mistake, but a true aristocracy is chosen on the basis of *uirtus* and provides the best government. More important (52), an aristocracy provides the ideal form of *consilium* (which is in fact the specific virtue of aristocracy: cf. 55.1), neither the limited judgment of a single ruler nor the folly of the people at large. The *aequabilitas* which democrats praise (53) is both specious and wrong: even extreme democracies choose leaders, and all people do not deserve the same respect.

51.1 The optimates are attacking the use of the lot in democratic governments; cf. 11.1, Xenophon, *Mem.* 1.2.9, also adducing the parallel of the helmsman.

51.2 The praise of a paternalist aristocracy (and gratefully subservient populace) is to be compared with C.'s own arguments in *Sest.*

137; for the democratic rejoinder, cf. 47.2–4. The idea that there are rulers and ruled by nature is Aristotelian: cf. *Pol.* 1.2 (also Pl. *Lg.* 3.690b). Baiter emended *praeessent* to *praeesse*, but the point is that the best in fact rule by nature and the rest are willing subjects, not that the best have a will to power. Creuzer's emendation of *uelint* to *uellent* also avoids the inconcinnity of tenses, but is probably unnecessary. **ciuium:** so Kenney. *ciuitatium*, the reading of the palimpsest, is found in C. only at *Dom.* 75 and *Leg.* 2.9 (*ciuitatum* 74x), and makes little sense: the discussion in this section refers always to a generalized state in the sing., and to the classes of inhabitants in the pl.

51.3 The aristocrats reject responsibility for oligarchy and plutocracy (as the democrats reject responsibility for the degeneration of their chosen form at 48.1) and blame the people for the choice of the wrong leaders. The superiority of *uirtus* over noble birth was part of the ideology of the *nouus homo*: cf. Wiseman (1971) 107–16. **a paucis iudicatur:** Madvig's emendation of *a* for *in* is necessary; *iudicatur* here must mean 'correctly judged'.

51.4 optimatium: dependent on *nomen.* **mordicus tenent** 'cling doggedly to'; for the phrase, cf. *Luc.* 51, *Fin.* 4.78. **eo nomine** 'on that account'; for the usage, cf. *Clu.* 115, *Brut.* 18, and elsewhere. Madvig deleted the phrase; Lenchantin supplemented <*comprehensa*> after *nomine.* C. is making a somewhat forced rhetorical point: the oligarchs cling to the name (*nomen*) of *optimates*, but for that very reason (*eo nomine*) they lack the substance; *re*, not *nomine* is the object of *carent.* The play on *nomen* continues in the next sentence, where it means 'renown' or 'reputation'.

51.5 opes ... superbiae 'wealth devoid of prudence and a method of living and of ruling others is filled with disgrace and inappropriate haughtiness': the syntax is obscured by another strained rhetorical point, the opposition between *uacuae* and *plenae*, which is itself made less clear by the fact that *uacuae* governs the abl. *consilio* and *modo* (the latter governing the gen. gerunds *uiuendi atque ... imperandi*) and *plenae* governs the gen. *dedecoris ... et insolentis superbiae.* For *modo* (= *ratione*), cf. *S. Rosc.* 100 *nullum modum esse hominis occidendi, quo ille non aliquot occiderit*, *TLL* VIII 1264.45–62 (garbled in *OLD* s.v. *modus* 9).

52.1 uirtute uero gubernante rem publicam: the aristocrat sees himself as the personification of *uirtus*, the best men governing by example as well as by precept. So also *Leg.* 3.10 (of the ideal senate) *is* *ordo uitio uacato, ceteris specimen esto* with commentary at 3.30–2; the same requirement at *Rep.* 2.59.2 of the ideal Roman aristocracy. For the abstraction, cf. 3.47 *si enim sapientia est quae gubernet rem publicam* ...

52.2 The rhetorical antitheses continue: *imperat* ~ *seruit*; *nec leges imponit* ~ *sed suam uitam ut legem praefert*; so also below with *unus* ~ *pluribus*, *uniuersi* ~ *nemo*, *ad plures* ~ *ad paucos*. For *praefert* 'hold up, display' cf. *Q. fr.* 1.1.13 *maiora praeferant fasces illi ac secures dignitatis insignia quam potestatis.*

52.3 qui si unus ... posset 'and if he (*is qui imperat*), as one individual, could accomplish everything ...' The only drawback to monarchy in this argument is the lack of adequate capacity and *consilium* in a single person; the similarity of the justifications for monarchy and aristocracy may be one reason for the omission of a speech in favour of monarchy here. Aristocracy is presented as the mean between the rule of one and the rule of all: the one cannot plan well enough, and the multitude cannot agree on what is best. For the greater quantity of judgment in a greater number of people, see Arist. *Pol.* 3.11. **optimum:** neuter.

52.4 A carefully balanced sentence, with the object in the first half and the verb in the second. The first subject consists of a noun followed by a modified genitive, the second of two nouns and an unmodified genitive; the prepositional phrases are in parallel order.

52.5 quibus rem publicam tuentibus ... cogitatione: the paternalism of the argument so incensed Creuzer that he proposed *agitatione* for *cogitatione.* **permisso otio suo ... putet** 'handing over their leisure to be safeguarded by others, who must not give the people reason to think their interests to be neglected by the aristocracy'. The word *otium* is ambiguous (cf. §1.2n.): it may mean the well-earned respite from work of the public figure or simple slothfulness. Cf. esp. 7.4 *meisque propriis periculis parere commune reliquis otium* and *Sest.* 139 *qui autem bonam famam bonorum ... expetunt, aliis otium quaerere debent et uoluptates, non sibi.*

53.1–2 nam aequabilitas ... aequitas iniquissima est: the same criticism of democracy is expressed by Scipio at 43.1. There is some confusion in the variation between *aequabilitas iuris*, *ea ... quae appellatur aequabilitas*, and *aequitas* – perhaps to be attributed to the polemically anti-democratic tone of the passage, which modifies Scipio's earlier phrasing. By employing *aequabilitas iuris* (rather than *aequabilitas* alone), the aristocratic speaker implies that juridical equality and equality of political rights are linked; and it is claimed that since even radical democrats apportion positions of honour unequally, therefore all equality is impossible. This criticism is sharpened by referring to 'so-called equality' as inequitable, and then by making *aequitas* 'fair apportionment' the object of attack. For a slightly different analysis of the passage, cf. Fantham (1973). Later references to *aequabilitas* (69.3; 2.42.1, 43.4, 57.2, 62.2) clearly refer to the proportional equality of the mixed constitution.

54.1 e tribus istis: the three simple constitutional forms. That Scipio has given arguments on behalf of only two of them does not necessitate looking for a lost speech on monarchy (cf. 50n.): Laelius refers back to his own identical formulation at 46.1 and to the generally recognized importance of the three simple forms (so Kroymann 311). More important is whether the brief, and unfortunately damaged, summary of the virtues of monarchy given below makes sense without a preceding full defence of monarchy. It seems probable that it does, and the long speech on monarchy which follows makes it unlikely that there was an earlier one.

54.3 unum ac simplex: *unum* as a choice among the three; *simplex* as one of the pure forms of constitution. The leaf which begins with the words *ac simplex* is missing its lower, outer corner: the ends of seven lines are lost here, and the beginnings of seven lines are missing below. The supplements that are given for a few lines are those of Mai, but the text cannot be fully reconstructed; for an attempt, see Blänsdorf. The first damaged passage contains Scipio's statement of his preference for monarchy among the simple forms. **occurrit nomen ... diligentia:** the argument is summarized at 55.3 by *ita caritate nos capiunt reges*: the virtue of true monarchy is the paternal affection between the best man and his subjects. Blänsdorf's *<et cura uac>uos* is an appealing supplement for the last lacuna; cf. 52.5 *uacuos omni cura et cogitatione.*

55.1 A summary of 52–3. **plusque fore ... quam in uno:** *consilii* is dependent on *plus*; the word order emphasizes the repetition of *plus ... pluribus.* **et eandem tamen aequitatem** 'but the same equity'.

55.2 A summary of the democratic arguments given in 47–50. The opening of the sentence (*ecce ... maxima voce*) characterizes the rudeness and impatience of the mob; cf. the *temeritas* of the people at 52.4.

55.3 ita caritate . . . libertate populi: Scipio ascribes to each form of government its specific virtue. These three attributes (φιλία, φρόνησις, ἐλευθερία – friendship, prudence, freedom) are those given to good government in general by Pl. *Lg.* 3.693bc; Pöschl 18–23 argues that they were distributed among the three forms of simple government in a Peripatetic source used by C.

55.4 Laelius once more forces Scipio to proceed further in the argument. By *quae restant* he means the goal of Scipio's discourse as stated at 33.3, the *optimus status ciuitatis*.

56.1 Imitemur igitur Aratum: *Phaen.* 1 Ἐκ Διὸς ἀρχώμεσθα, 'let us begin from Zeus', translated by C. in his early *Aratea* as *Ab Ioue Musarum primordia*. The *Phaenomena* of Aratus of Soli (c.315–240/39), a hexameter adaptation of the work of the fourth-century astronomer Eudoxus, was immensely popular and was translated into Latin several times after C.'s version. The allusion to Aratus introduces not the invocation one might expect, but an analogy between divine organization and human constitutions.

56.2 Quo Ioue 'what has Jupiter to do with it?' (Sabine and Smith); for the colloquialism cf. 59.2n. Laelius is not imagining a multitude of Jupiters, but expressing his impatience with Scipio's grandiloquence.

56.3 docti indoctique [expoliri] consentiunt: P reads *doctique expoliri*; the second hand added *docti in-* before *doctique* and apparently (in Ziegler's opinion) deleted *expoliri*. Emendation of *expoliri* has been unconvincing; deletion is preferable. **Quid?** 'Well?', as at e.g. 59.4; cf. 58.3 *quid ergo?*, 58.5 *quid supra?*

56.4 ante oculos: Scipio pointedly uses the phrase earlier employed by Laelius (31.2) to turn the discussion to current political affairs. **siue haec . . . cognoscimus:** a dilemma expressed in two parallel conditions: if the monarchic organization of the gods is a political invention of human leaders, we should accept it because it is universally approved; if, on the other hand, the divine order is false and fabulous, then we must accept the judgment of the learned (that there is a single order or principle ruling the universe: this part of the argument is lost in the following lacuna). Scipio does not admit the possibility that the divine order is neither a political invention nor a mere fable, but in fact true. For the argument that monarchy among the gods was invented by human monarchs, cf. Arist. *Pol.* 1.2. **qui nutu, ut ait Homerus:** *Il.* 1.528–30. **et rex et pater:** the

Homeric formula πατὴρ ἀνδρῶν τε θεῶν τε (*Il.* 1.544, etc.) was rendered by Ennius variously as *patrem diuomque hominumque* (592 Sk.), *diuom pater atque hominum rex* (203 Sk.), and *diuomque hominumque pater, rex* (591 Sk.). The presence of *rex* in C. shows that it is Ennius, rather than Homer directly, that Scipio has in mind. **siquidem omnes multos appellari placet:** an ironic understatement: it is not just that there are many witnesses, but that the testimony of humanity is unanimous. **consensisse ... numine:** *consensisse* is an indirect statement dependent on the verb implicit in *auctoritas* and *testes*. Unanimous belief in the superiority of monarchy is an inference from unanimous belief in divine monarchy; cf. Isoc. *Nic.* 26. **didicimus:** Ziegler's *dicimus* is unnecessary: *didicimus* anticipates *doctores* in the following clause. **qui tamquam oculis ... audiendo cognoscimus:** cf. 15.4 (of Panaetius) *qui quae uix coniectura qualia sint possumus suspicari, sic affirmat ut oculis ea cernere uideatur aut tractare plane manu.*

56.5 senserunt omnem hunc mundum mente*: to be completed by *unius regi* or something similar. In the lacuna of two leaves which follows, Scipio presumably summarized philosophical beliefs in a single divine ruler; for a similar doxography (from a hostile Epicurean point of view), cf. *N.D.* 1.25–41. The reference to the mind of a divine ruler (Jupiter) is Stoic in tone, although Coleman 6 sees it as Pythagorean; cf. Sharples 36. In the missing section (57), one quotation from Nonius (85.18 = 289.7 M.), of which Laelius must be the speaker, should probably be located: *quare si placet deduc orationem tuam de eo loco* [variant: *de caelo*] *ad haec citeriora* (cf. Pöschl 28 n.35). The parallel passage at *Leg.* 3.4 suggests that Scipio's argument progressed at Laelius' prompting from philosophers and cosmology to the early history of mankind: *atque ut ad haec citeriora ueniam et notiora nobis: omnes antiquae gentes regibus quondam paruerunt.* The excerpt from Lactantius also printed here by Ziegler does not belong: cf. Heck 95.

58.1 nec ullo modo barbaros: in the preceding lacuna Scipio presumably referred to the early history of kingship, e.g. in Persia or Egypt. **'Istos' inquit 'uolo':** the discussion of the preferability of monarchy is conducted as a Platonic dialogue, with Scipio playing the part of Socrates; 1.56–61, and especially this and the succeeding chapters, present a series of short questions, intended to elicit the proper responses from Laelius. The style of these chapters reflects the conversational manner by colloquialisms, e.g. the use of initial *uero* to assent to a preceding remark; *ualde*; the repeated use of *iste*; the imper. *cedo*; and perhaps the peculiar syntax of Scipio's next speech (cf. 58.2n.). In 56 and 58–64, Scipio begins sentences (or questions) with *quid*, *ergo*, *quid ergo*, or (postpositive) *igitur* 18x; Laelius replies using *uero* 11x (Scipio only once). In these same chapters, C. uses *inquit* to interrupt Laelius' utterances 14x; in Scipio's speeches it is used only 3x. In fact, while *inquit* is used 17x in these chapters, it is used only 13x in the rest of book 1: while it marks Scipio's speeches only 6x in the book, it is used for Laelius 19x (by contrast, in book 2 – where dialogue is relatively unimportant – *inquit* is used 9x, seven of them of Scipio). In part, the purpose of this is practical: *inquit*, even without the name of a speaker, generally indicates a speech by someone other than Scipio; at the same time, however, the authorial interruptions of other speakers tend to diminish their authority in the face of Scipio, whose voice merges with that of the narrator because of the lack of authorial comment. For C.'s consciousness of the effect of *inquit*, cf. *Am.* 3; for analysis of the effect of such interruptions, cf. M. Lambert, *Dickens and the suspended quotation* (New Haven 1981).

58.2 Videsne igitur ... ut sine regibus sit: the syntax of this sentence is difficult, and seems to represent the fusion of two different constructions: *uidesne hanc urbem sine regibus esse* and *uidesne ut haec urbs sine regibus sit*. For the construction *uidere ut* equivalent to an indirect statement, cf. *Sen.* 26 with Powell's note. *quadringentorum annorum* must be taken as a descriptive gen. with *urbem*; numbers and measurements often retain their grammatical case after *plus* or *minus*, and for undeclined *minus* cf. *OLD* s.v. *minus*[1] 2. The chronology is reckoned from 129, the dramatic date of the dialogue, 379 years after the expulsion of the kings in 508 (on C.'s chronology).

58.3 adulta uix: for the application of the life cycle of human beings to the life of a state, cf. 2.3.2, 21.1.

58.4 his annis quadringentis 'within the past four hundred years'. **Et superbus quidem:** Laelius plays on the cognomen of the last king, L. Tarquinius Superbus.

58.5 iustissimus ... rex erat: Ser. Tullius. Romulus had been king for 22 years (according to the chronology followed in book 2) in 729.

58.6 prope senescente iam Graecia: a striking chronological comparison between Greece and Rome (cf. also *Brut.* 39, and 2.17–20 below for a more detailed synchronism between Romulus and his Greek contemporaries), perhaps to be taken as an instance of Laelius' scepticism (cf. 2.21–2n.). Greece was 'old' in the middle of the eighth century only in terms of the Trojan War: it was as long from the traditional date of the destruction of Troy (1184/3 according to Eratosthenes) to the reign of Romulus as it was from the end of the regal period to the dramatic date of *Rep.*

58.7 Cedo, num barbarorum Romulus rex fuit?: *cedo* is imper.: 'come now'. The corrector inserts *Scipio* after *num*, but that must be a gloss: proper names in this position are normally vocatives. **Si ut Graeci dicunt:** the sense is clear despite the syntax. Anacoluthon is often found with such parenthetical phrases; cf. *Leg.* 1.55 *si, ut Aristo Chius dixit, solum bonum esse* ... with H–S 731. **Graios:** C. uses the more elevated *Graius* rather than *Graecus* 4x in the extant portions of *Rep.* (also at 2.9.2, 3.15, 6.16.1); in three of the four, including this one, it is in close proximity to a form of *Graecus* or *Graecia* and is apparently used for variety; the fourth is a highly poetic passage of the *Somnium.*

59.1 argumenta plus quam testes ualent: the unreliability of witnesses in comparison to arguments from probability is a commonplace of ancient forensic rhetoric; in C., cf. esp. *Cael.* 22, and in philosophical argument *N.D.* 1.10 and *Top.* 7.

59.2 Cuius ... sensus?: cf. 56.2 *quo Ioue?*; 61.2 *me? ... quonam modo?* At each stage of the argument Scipio introduces a paradoxical statement to which Laelius replies with an abrupt question.

59.3 Si quando, si forte: the second phrase is a polite (or ironic) correction of the first: Scipio does not assume that Laelius is ever really angry. **uellem:** past potential.

59.4 dominatum animi tui: the metaphorical use of *dominatum* – relatively rare in C. – prepares for the political analogy elaborated in the following sections. In C.'s pre-exile writings, *dominatio* is preferred to *dominatus*, while from 56 the reverse is true.

59.5 sed imitor Archytam: the story is more commonly told of Plato (cf. Riginos 155–6) than of Archytas, but this is the earliest evidence for either form of the anecdote, which C. repeats at *Tusc.* 4.78. **omnia aliter offendisset ac iusserat** 'he found everything in a condition other than he had ordered'. *aliter* in comparisons is followed by *ac* rather than *quam*. For the use of *offendere* 'encounter', cf. 6.11.5 *offendes rem publicam ... perturbatam*; so also *Fam.* 1.9.18,

5.17.2. **a te infelicem:** the interjection *a* is extremely rare in prose, and before C. is generally found in drama. Ziegler's *[in]felicem* is unnecessary, as the imitation by Lactantius (*De ira Dei* 18.4 *miserum te, inquit, quem iam uerberibus necassem, nisi iratus essem*) makes clear.

60.1 iracundiam ... sedari uolebat: the idea that the organization of the mind is political and that the struggle of the passions against the rule of reason is a form of sedition or civil war is based on Pl. *R.* 4.440–4; the use of political metaphors here (*dissidentem, seditionem, consilio, sedari*) is insistent. There is no precise parallel to C.'s use of the psychological analogy as an argument for monarchy, but similar arguments (from Stoic sources) are found at *Tusc.* 2.47–8 and 3.37 below; cf. Solmsen 331 n.17 for further discussion. **adde auaritiam ... libidines:** C. avoids total parallelism within the anaphora: the first and last elements consist of imper. and object, the middle has two imperatives with a single object but two dependent genitives.

60.3 iracundiaeue: the pl. (also at *Q. fr.* 1.1.13, *Tusc.* 3.7, *Fin.* 1.27) is motivated by the preceding *libidines.*

61.1 The question raised by Laelius – and answered in favour of the single ruler by Scipio – is precisely that left open by Plato at the end of *Republic* 4 (445cd): for Plato, the best form of government may be either monarchical or aristocratic (although monarchy is best at *Plt.* 303b). Scipio himself asks a similar rhetorical question at 3.47 *si enim sapientia est quae gubernet rem publicam, quid tandem interest, haec in unone sit an in pluribus*, which he again decides in favour of the one. Laelius here attempts to alter the grounds of decision from *imperium* to *iustitia* – perhaps as a foreshadowing of his role as defender of justice in book 3 – but Scipio ignores the change and continues to deal with the issue of power except for the parenthetical qualification *si modo iusti sint* at 61.6.

61.2 te uti teste: cf. 59.2 *utere igitur argumento . . . sensus tui.*

61.3 in Formiano: Laelius' villa at Formiae is not otherwise known, but both C. himself and Rutilius Rufus had villas there. **interdicere, ut uni dicto audiens esset:** for *interdicere* = *edicere*, cf. *Caec.* 80, 89 (in legal contexts). For *dicto audiens* 'obedient to' followed by the dat. *uni*, cf. *OLD* s.v. *audio* 11c and Ogilvie on Livy 5.3.8.

61.4 Quid domi?: i.e in Rome. There is an implicit contrast between the urban *domus* and the rural estate presided over by a *uilicus.* **Immo uero:** cf. 20.3n.

61.6 Quin: introducing a question, as a polite equivalent to a command; cf. 6.14.3, *OLD* s.v. 1a. **<it>idem:** Ziegler's easy emendation improves the sense; if *idem* is retained it should be taken as neut. acc., and a comma should be inserted after *re publica.* **singulorum dominatus** 'the rule of one man at a time'; the pl. *dominatus* is similar to *Tusc.* 1.108 *singulorum opiniones.* **Adducor, inquit, et propemodum assentior:** *inquit* is Mai's necessary emendation for *igitur* in P; conversely, at 60.2 *probas igitur* the second hand has corrected *inquit* to *igitur.* On the use of these words, cf. 58.1n. There is some merit in Wolff's alteration of *et . . . assentior* to *ut . . . assentiar*, but the paratactic style is appropriate to conversation.

62.1 assentiare: P reads *adsentiar*, and Mai conjectured both *adsentiare* and *adsentiere.* Both are possible, but the potential subj. is closer to the transmitted text. **ut omittam similitudines:** *similitudines* introduces an acc. and infin. construction; the repeated *alteri* picks up *gubernatori* and *medico.* The *praeteritio* here is elaborated at 63.1–2; comparisons to helmsmen and doctors are frequent in Plato (e.g. *R.* 1.332de, 6.489bc), as in C. For the helmsman, cf. also 11.1.

62.2 unius importunitate et superbia Tarquinii: for *importunitas*, cf. 50.3; *superbia* alludes to the cognomen of the last king, as at 58.4. The hyperbaton of *unius . . . Tarquinii* balances that of *nomen . . . regium* immediately following.

62.3 progrediente oratione: 2.53–5, the description of the aftermath of the expulsion of Superbus. The exile referred to is that of Collatinus and the remaining family of Tarquin; *demissi fasces* is the practice of having the lictors lower the *fasces* to the people as a symbol of popular rule; *secessiones* must be a generalizing reference to the first secession of the *plebs* in 494. On the popular excesses resulting from the end of monarchy, see also 2.57–8. C.'s version of the relationship between *patres* and *plebs* in the first years of the Republic contrasts with that of Sallust (*Hist.* 1.11 M., probably derived from Licinius Macer), according to whom the plebeians were badly treated by the patricians except for this period, when the patricians were afraid of an attack by Tarquin and the Etruscans. For *demittere* cf. 2.53; for *exultasse* cf. 2.45.3. **ut in populo essent omnia:** cf. 42.4: *ciuitas popularis . . . in qua in populo sunt omnia.*

63.1–2 In the first sentence, Scipio starts from the political context (*in pace et otio*) and then introduces the similes (*ut in naui ac . . . in morbo leui*); in the second, he begins with the similes and then turns back to the political meaning. The descriptions of sailor and patient are parallel, with slight variations: *ille qui nauigat* ~ *ille aeger*; *cum . . . horrescere* ~ *ingrauescente morbo*. The same vocabulary of disease is used at *Div*. 2.16 and metaphorically of politics at *Cat*. 1.31 *hic morbus, qui est in re publica, uehementius . . . ingrauescet*.

63.2 in pace et domi: the first halves of two polar expressions, *in pace et (in) bello* and *domi militiaeque*, of which the second half of only one is used in the parallel clause below. **appellat, prouocat:** *appellare* is to appeal from one magistrate to another (or to a tribune): cf. *Quinct*. 64, *Verr*. 4.146. *provocare* is to appeal to the popular assembly; cf. 2.53–4. **libido:** cf. 63.1 *lasciuire*.

63.3 grauioribus ... bellis: the pseudo-archaic law at *Leg*. 3.9 gives *duellum grauius* as cause for appointing the *magister populi*.

63.4 For *dico* 'appoint (a magistrate)' cf. *OLD* s.v. 10c. Var. *L*. 6.61 combines the same (false) etymology with *cui dicto audientes omnes essent*; cf. Maltby s.v. C. uses the title *magister populi* at *Leg*. 3.9 (see previous n.); cf. also *Fin*. 3.75. **in nostris libris:** the augural books (for which cf. Linderski 2241–56) are described as *nostri* because both Scipio and Laelius were augurs; for the evidence, cf. *MRR* I 478–9. For the importance of the augurate in *Rep*. cf. 2.16.1n.

63.6 sapienter igitur illi uete<res>: the particular wisdom extolled here is uncertain. In the gap of one leaf before 64, there must have been a transition from the political necessity of undivided *imperium* in a crisis to the affection and loyalty evoked by a good king.

64.1 iusto quidem rege: the emphasis on the necessity for justice, introduced by Laelius in 61, becomes stronger here; thus *iuste paruerunt*, *iustitia regis*, *unius iniustitia* in this paragraph, and similarly in 65. The significance of *iuris consensu* in the definition of the state (39.1) is extended first to imply that the failure of *ius* is the direct cause of the downfall of constitutions, and then in book 3 to show that no organization without *ius* can properly be called a *res publica* at all.

64.1–3 Ennius, *Ann*. 105–9 Sk. C. breaks the quotation into three parts, but it is generally agreed that the verses were consecutive. It seems improbable (cf. Skutsch *ad loc.*) that Ennius called the hearts of the Roman people *dia*, the reading of the corrector in P, especially since *die* is applied to Romulus in the next verse. And while Steinacker's *dura* is the most probable correction, it seems better to ascribe *diu* to C. and leave a gap in the verse. For detailed commentary on these lines, see Skutsch; also Jocelyn 44–5.

64.3 eros: archaic and poetic. **appellabant:** emendation to *appellant* is unnecessary, given the parallel of *existimabant* below. **sed patres:** C. is perhaps thinking of himself; cf. *Sest.* 121 *me, me ille absentem deplorandum putabat, quem Q. Catulus, quem multi alii saepe in senatu patrem patriae nominarant.*

64.5 si regum similitudo permansisset 'if succeeding kings had been like their predecessors'; a very compressed expression.

64.6 studeo ... noscere: the fall of Tarquin and the concomitant end of monarchic government at Rome permits Laelius to turn the discussion to the cycle of constitutions and finally to the mixed constitution itself.

65.1 quod maxime probo: the mixed constitution itself: cf. 45.3, 54.2, 69. **accuratius mihi dicendum:** not in the extant text, but presumably in the lost part of book 6; for *accuratius* cf. 19.1. **minime facile:** for the adverb *facile* with *esse* cf. K–S I 9–10.

65.2 prima et certissima ... mutatio: on the instability of monarchy in particular, cf. 2.43.2 *forma ciuitatis mutabilis maxime*, 2.47–9. **ilico** 'immediately'; most frequently in archaic and archaizing texts; C. uses it 11x (also two archaic quotations and two letters of Caelius). **deterrimum ... optimo:** cf. Arist. *Pol.* 4.2. Cf. 44.2n. **quem si optimates oppresserunt:** C. offers two pairs of alternative progressions of governments, the first grouped by the government overthrown (tyranny replaced by aristocracy or democracy), the second by the overthrowers (ochlocracy replacing monarchy or aristocracy). In the first pair, a bad form is replaced by a good one, in the second a good form by a bad one. **quod ferme euenit:** unlike Plato and Polybius, C. does not envisage a fixed pattern of constitutional succession, but (as at 45.1 and 68.9) recognizes a large set of possible permutations (so also Arist. *Pol.* 5.12). The primary pattern, however, is that of Polybius: from monarchy to tyranny, followed by aristocracy, oligarchy, democracy, and ochlocracy in that order. C. uses the archaic form *ferme* rather than *fere* as at 69.4, 2.10.2, 2.59.2 (cf. Var. *L.* 7.92 *ferme dicitur quod nunc fere*); it is used 10x by C., never in the speeches. **secundarium:** second in order of excellence, according to Scipio, after monarchy.

65.3 est moderatior ... laetatur: perhaps based on Plb. 6.9.4, who states that so long as people survive who remember the evils of oligarchy, 'they regard their present constitution as a blessing, and hold equality and freedom as of the utmost value' (Shuckburgh).

65.4 optimatium sanguinem ... libidini suae: in describing the excesses of mob rule, C.'s language becomes lurid; the manner is continued in his translation from Plato in 66–7. For *sanguinem gustare*, cf. *Phil.* 2.71.

66–7 C.'s version of Pl. *R.* 8.562c-563e1 retains the substance, but changes the form and style considerably. What is in Plato a dialogue between Socrates and Glaucon becomes a monologue, and the rhetoric, with balances and tricola not found in Plato, is clearly Ciceronian. The first sentence elaborates considerably on the metaphor of wine-drinking in Plato (in fact, beyond any other use of it in C.): μεθυσθῆι, for instance, becomes *sitiens hausit*, and πορρωτέρω τοῦ δέοντος ἀκράτου is replaced by the balanced phrasing of *non modice temperatam sed nimis meracam* (for the metaphor of mixed and unmixed wine – applied to marriages between rich and poor – see Pl. *Lg.* 6.773cd). In 67, a dialogue of half a dozen exchanges in Plato is turned into a single sentence by C. (*ergo illa sequuntur ... decedendum sit*). It begins in indirect discourse (*agitari*, *appellari*), but rapidly reverts to finite verbs (*<ef>ferunt*, *mactant*) followed by a series of consecutive clauses in which the ironic tone of Socrates' description of the failings of democracy which lead to tyranny is replaced by Scipio's indignation at the collapse of social distinctions. In some cases, C.'s translation loses Plato's sharpness (e.g. *eos autem qui in magistratu ... differat* for τοὺς δὲ ἄρχοντας μὲν ἀρχομένοις, ἀρχομένους δὲ ἄρχουσιν ὁμοίους 'rulers like ruled, ruled like rulers'), in others he has made antitheses even clearer, as with *ut pater filium metuat, filius patrem neglegat* for πατέρα μὲν ἐθίζεσθαι παιδὶ ὅμοιον γίγνεσθαι καὶ φοβεῖσθαι τοὺς ὑεῖς, ὑὸν δὲ πατρί ... 'the father is accustomed to behave like his child and fear his sons, the son behaves like the father ...' Throughout, he has eliminated concepts that are purely Greek (*peregrinus* replaces both μέτοικος and ξένος, *magister* both διδάσκαλος and παιδαγωγός, *leges* 'laws written and unwritten'), and added Roman overtones: Plato's ἄρχοντας becomes *magistratus et principes*, and ἰδίαι τε καὶ δημοσίαι ἐπαινεῖ τε καὶ τιμᾶι 'both privately and publicly praises and honors' is *efferunt laudibus, mactant honoribus*. For detailed analysis of the passage as a translation, see Poncelet (tendentious in his hostility both to Latin and to C.) and H. Müller 40–5.

66.1 insequitur ... uocat: C. replaces Plato's relatively mild language (κολάζει αἰτιωμένη ὡς μιαρούς τε καὶ ὀλιγαρχικούς 'punishes, accusing them of being foul oligarchs') with two much more emotive parallel tricola.

66.2–3 Although C. has eliminated the dialogue from his version of Plato, he substitutes for it this brief exchange between Scipio and Laelius and one below at 68.1. *nota* in Scipio's statement probably refers to the passage of Plato alone, while *notissima* in Laelius' reply alludes to experience with the circumstances described by Plato and Scipio, in this case the turmoil of contemporary events.

67.1 <ef>ferunt laudibus [et] mactant honoribus: Klotz's emendation of *ferunt* to *ecferunt* (*efferunt* Ziegler) is a necessary change, and the deletion of *et* is an improvement. **plena libertatis esse omnia:** far closer to Plato's phrase at 563c9–d1, πάντα οὕτως μεστὰ ἐλευθερίας γίγνεται, omitted by C. at that point, than to the phrase here, ἐπὶ πᾶν τὸ τῆς ἐλευθερίας ἰέναι 'reach the maximum of liberty' (562e1). **ut et priuata domus omni uacet dominatione:** Ziegler's correction of P's *omnis*, although not printed in his text, is preferable: the following items in the list (*pater, filius, ciuis, magister*) are all generalizing singulars, and *omni* also enhances the etymological paradox (not in Plato) of *domus ... dominatione*. C. may intend a similar play on words with the use of *liberi*, meaning both 'free' and 'children'. His description of the role reversal of young and old (*adulescentes ... graues*) is sharper than Plato's, and imports terms that would be more evocative in Rome (*pondus, ludum, graues*).

67.2 ex quo fit ... decedendum sit: C.'s description of the extreme degeneration of liberty is considerably briefer than Plato's, eliminating both some of the balances (ἐν γυναιξὶ δὲ πρὸς ἄνδρας καὶ ἀνδράσι πρὸς γυναῖκας) and some of the humour: in Plato dogs 'become like their mistresses according to the proverb' and the animals proceed not only ἐλευθέρως 'freely', but σεμνῶς 'proudly'. *eodem iure* also adds a legalistic note not present in Plato.

67.3 haec summa cogitur: τὸ δὲ δὴ κεφάλαιον ... πάντων τούτων ξυνηθροισμένων 'the sum of all these things taken together' in Plato. For the use of *cogo* 'conclude, prove' cf. *TLL* v 1525.20. **plane**

sine ullo domino sint: an attempt to render Plato's emphatic ἵνα δὴ μηδαμῆι μηδεὶς αὐτοῖς ἦι δεσπότης. For the thought, cf. 2.43.5 *libertas, quae non in eo est ut iusto utamur domino, sed ut nul<lo>.*

68.1 prorsus ... ab illo: Laelius' complimentary reply to Scipio's tentative *si modo id exprimere Latine potuero* at 65.5.

68.2 auctorem: Zell's necessary emendation for P's *morem.* The latter would imply that Scipio was now leaving Plato to return to his own argument, but in fact translation from the same passage (563e2–564a8) continues through 68.5, and several more lines are drawn loosely from the same section of the *Republic,* as far as C.'s reference to Pisistratus (68.7). There are, however, more alterations. The purpose of Plato's description of the excesses of democracy was to show the reasons for the origin of tyranny, and he refers back (563e6) to his previous discussion of the collapse of oligarchy into democracy. The context in C. is obviously different, and he rearranged the sentences to fit his own purpose rather more than in 66–7. **ex hac nimia licentia:** C. emphasizes the idea of excess in this passage, using *nimis, nimius* five times while the corresponding section of Plato uses ἄγαν only three times. **ut ex stirpe ... nasci tyrannum:** Plato's phrase here is simply ὅθεν τυραννὶς φύεται, and C. has made the metaphor more explicit, drawing also on *R.* 565d1–2 ὅτανπερ φύηται τύραννος, ἐκ προστατικῆς ῥίζης καὶ οὐκ ἄλλοθεν ἐκβλαστάνει 'whenever a tyrant comes into being, he springs from the root of popular leadership and from no other source'. Both *quadam* and *quasi* are Cicero's additions to qualify the metaphor.

68.6–7 The description of the development of demagogue into tyrant is heavily condensed from *R.* 565c-66d. C.'s *plerumque* replaces ἀεί in Plato, in accordance with C.'s view that there is no one fixed set of constitutional mutations. It is likely that C. had Clodius (described as a tyrant e.g. at *Mil.* 35) in mind; cf. Heinze 154.

68.6 impurus: cf. 9.2 *cum impuris atque immanibus aduersariis.* **consectans proterue:** for *consector* = *persequor* cf. *Inv.* 2.111, *Att.* 2.18.1 and *TLL* IV 385.63–386.2; the adverb *proterue* is not used elsewhere by C. **bene saepe ... meritos:** the placement of the adverbs is odd; cf. *Off.* 2.20 *bene meritorum saepe ciuium expulsiones.* **populo gratificans et aliena et sua:** *gratificari* is not attested before C.; for the construction with dat. and acc., cf. *Off.* 1.42, *Fam.* 1.10. The demagogue gains popular support by his largesse, distributing both his own property (*sua*) and what has been confiscated from others (*aliena*).

68.7 priuato 'in his capacity as a private citizen'; C. is describing the transition from unofficial to official status. **dantur ... continuantur:** the terminology is Roman and fits the circumstances of C.'s own time. He may have Pompey in particular in mind; cf. Meister (1939) 70–1. **ut Athenis Pisistratus:** for the example (not in Plato) cf. Hdt. 1.59.4–6, Arist. *Ath. Pol.* 14.1.

68.8 quos si boni oppresserunt: there is no precedent in either Plato or Polybius for this version of constitutional changes; C. is almost certainly thinking of the fall of Tiberius Gracchus. For the tyrannical nature of the *factio* (which C. more usually calls *boni*), cf. 69.3, 45.1n.

68.9 tamquam pilam: a vivid image, with no obvious ancient parallel (but cf. the modern 'political football'). As above (45.1, 65.2), C. agrees with Arist. *Pol.* 5.12 in denying that there is a fixed order of constitutional change.

69.1 Quod ita cum sit: referring back to the previous argument, particularly to the conclusion of the previous section, that no simple form of constitution can last (*nec diutius umquam tenetur idem rei publicae modus*), which itself refers back to Scipio's initial statement (41.3) that the purpose of any government is *ut diuturna sit*. This is the only occurrence of *quod (quae) ita cum sit (sint)* in C., and it should perhaps be emended to the more usual *quod cum ita sit*. **<ex> tribus primis generibus ... ex tribus primis rerum publicarum modis:** the addition of *ex* (Heinrich) is necessary, as monarchy is itself one of the three primary forms. The second occurrence of *primis* is Zachariae's equally necessary emendation of P's *optimis* (*istis* Meister). The word order of the two clauses is syntactically parallel (predicate, verb, subject), but verbally chiastic (*<ex> tribus primis generibus ... regium, regio ... ex tribus primis ... modis*). **aequatum et temperatum:** cf. 45.3 *moderatum et permixtum* (also at the end of this section *iuncta moderateque permixta*); C. distinguishes between *mixta* and *temperata* at 2.42.4.

69.2 Scipio's formal *sententia*, in a tricolon with anaphora of *esse* and a slightly varied second element: *quiddam, aliud, quasdam*. The conclusion of each phrase is a pair of terms (*praestans et regale*, *impertitum ac tributum*, *iudicio uoluntatique*) with a different connective in each.

69.3 The sentence lists (*primum*, *deinde*) two attributes of the mixed constitution, *aequabilitas* and *firmitudo*, the latter of which is divided into two parts, articulated by repeated *quod*. *firmitudo* is far less common in C. than is *firmitas*, and is found elsewhere only six times, in letters and the early *Inv.* The *quod*-clauses are formally causal, but in fact give reasons why the simple constitutions are not stable rather than reasons why the mixed constitution is. **aequabilitatem quandam [magnam]**: P reads *aequabilitatem magnam*; the corrector added *quandam*; and Nonius cites the sentence without *magnam*.

69.5 The explanation of the stability of the mixed constitution is vague; the general point is that each order is held in place by the other two, and therefore cannot degenerate into its bad equivalent. *conuersio* is normally used in an astronomical context (so at 1.22; cf. 6.12.3n.); with its use here, cf. *Sest.* 99 (*motus conuersionesque*) and *Div.* 2.6, drawing on *Rep.* and on Plato. For the use of *subest*, cf. 44.3.

70–71: Conclusion

69 summarizes the argument in favour of the mixed constitution; at the beginning of 70, Scipio breaks off and reiterates his reluctance to lecture like a professor. Instead, his formal *sententia* on the superiority of the Roman constitution leads into the historical account of its development that occupies most of book 2, and the book concludes with Laelius' statement of Scipio's qualifications – as an experienced statesman, not as a philosopher – to give that account.

70.1 For the reluctance of the Roman statesman to behave like a Greek professor, cf. 36.2, 38.3; for similar modesty and the apology for delivering *praecepta*, cf. *Q. fr.* 1.1.18 *sed nescio quo pacto ad praecipiendi rationem delapsa est oratio mea.* The refusal to be dogmatic and didactic is consonant with C.'s own adherence to the scepticism of the new Academy; cf. Burkert (1965) 184.

70.3 Scipio's formal *sententia* is expressed in a solemn tricolon with anaphora, followed by another tricolon describing the attributes of the Roman constitution, and ending with the role in its preservation of three chronological groups, *maiores*, *patres*, and *nos*; for the transmission of the *res publica* from the *maiores*, cf. *S. Rosc.* 50. The superiority of the Roman constitution is both *nota* and *quaesita* for the participants: their knowledge of the superiority of the Roman system needs to be grounded in political theory to explain why it is superior. That, as Scipio says in what follows, is the topic of his next discourse.

70.4 quam serves both as a proleptic acc. with *qualis sit* and as the subject of *esse*. **expositaque ... de optimo ciuitatis statu:** a reminder of the programme of *Rep.* The second book contains the exposition of the Roman constitution; after that (the abl. abs. is temporal), the further discussion of institutions begins at 2.65, is interrupted by the discussion of justice in book 3, and is resumed in book 4. With *exposita ... ad exemplum* cf. *Phil.* 2.114 *factum ... expositum ad imitandum.*

71.2 Laelius' praise of Scipio's qualifications for the task falls into three rhetorical questions, concerning past (*de maiorum ... institutis*), present (*de optimo statu ciuitatis*), and future (*de consiliis in posterum prouidendis*). The causal *cum* clauses in the first and third questions are parallel, and refer to Scipio's ancestry and to his victories in the wars against Carthage and Numantia in 146 and 133. The middle question is somewhat more difficult: Laelius accepts Scipio's assertion that the Roman constitution is the best, but doubts its present reality. Even in current circumstances, however, Scipio's pre-eminence is generally recognized, however reluctantly: 'in which, if we should get it, certainly no one could be more eminent than you – even if not even now (no one is more eminent).' For the interpretation, cf. Skutsch (1969); Madvig's emendation of *habemus* in P is necessary.

De re publica 2

1–3: Preface

Book 2, like books 4 and 6, has no introduction in C.'s own voice. Instead, Scipio outlines briefly the goals of his account of Roman history: to show the gradual development of Roman institutions to the point of perfection in the early Republic.

1.1 <cupidi>tate audiendi: some thirty rubricated letters have disappeared; Mai's supplement, *< Vt omnis igitur uidit incensos cupidi> tate audiendi*, gives the necessary sense; cf. *De orat.* 3.18 *ibi magna cum audiendi expectatione considitur.* **Catonis hoc senis est:** Cato was considerably older than Scipio, and had been dead for twenty years in 129. The dictum anticipated by *hoc* is not given until §2.1 (*is dicere solebat*); the mild anacoluthon is caused by the elaborate praise of Cato which intervenes (cf. also 1.1.3). The sentence consists of a series of three relative clauses with polyptoton (*quem* ... *cuique* ... *cuius*) followed by a series of laudatory phrases concerning experience, style, and character (*usus* ... *modus* ... *lepos* ... *studium* ... *uita*). Scipio's affection for Cato is probably historical, if overstated: one of Scipio's sisters was married to Cato's son; Scipio probably supported Cato's policies in the Third Punic War; and in 149 Cato singled out Scipio's actions as military tribune for praise expressed in a quotation from Homer (*Od.* 10.495). At *Inv.* 1.5, C. describes Scipio as a *discipulus* of Cato. Cf. Astin (1967) 280–1. **patris utriusque:** Scipio's natural father, L. Aemilius Paullus, and his adoptive father, the son of Scipio Africanus. For *se dedere* in the sense of personal or intellectual devotion, cf. *De orat.* 3.82 *te istis studiis, hominibus, libris intellego deditum.*

1.2 usus rei publicae: cf. 1.37.1. **discendi ... uel docendi:** cf. 1.13.1n. **orationi ... congruens:** perhaps an allusion to Cato's famous definition of the orator as *uir bonus dicendi peritus* (*ad filium* fr. 14 Jordan = Sen. *Controv.* 1 pr. 9, Quintil. 12.1.1).

2.1 is dicere solebat: for resumptive *is* after anacoluthon, cf. 2.4.3 *is igitur ut natus sit.* In context, Cato's observation is presented as an oral comment, but it may come from the first book of Cato's *Origines*. Astin (1978) 225–6 is rightly sceptical of attempts to see this statement as a theoretical basis for Cato's account of early Roman history or as evidence for C.'s dependence on the *Origines* in book 2. **rem publicam** here = 'regime' rather than 'state'. **Minos ... Demetrius:** almost certainly C.'s list, not Cato's. The Cretan Minos and the Spartan Lycurgus are linked as exemplary legislators by Pl. *Lg.* 1.630d, 632d; the Lycurgan constitution in particular was considered the best Greek constitution by Polybius, who compared it and the Carthaginian constitution to that of the Romans (6.48–52; cf. on 2.15.1, 42–43 below). The list of Athenian legislators from the mythical Theseus through the seventh- and sixth-century lawgivers culminates in praises of the Peripatetic philosopher Demetrius of Phalerum who governed Athens at the end of the fourth century under the protection of the Macedonian Cassander, reflecting C.'s admiration for one who was at once philosopher and statesman. **exsanguem iam et iacentem:** the result of defeats at Chaeronea (338) and in the Lamian War (323/2). **sustentasset:** a slight anacoluthon: Demetrius alone is the subject, while the previous lawgivers in the series are subjects of *constituisset.* **nostra autem res**

publica: Scipio/Cato here makes a virtue of the haphazard growth of the Roman constitution, in contrast to the systematic but imperfect work of single lawgivers; Mai on this passage of C. observes: 'Sic fere britanni politici de sua rep. loquuntur.' Polybius likewise praises the result, but does not elevate it above the work of Lycurgus: 'Lycurgus however established his constitution without the discipline of adversity, because he was able to foresee by the light of reason the course which events naturally take and the source from which they come. But though the Romans have arrived at the same result in framing their commonwealth, they have not done so by means of abstract reasoning, but through many struggles and difficulties, and by continually adopting reforms from knowledge gained in disaster. The result has been a constitution like that of Lycurgus, and the best of any existing in my time' (6.10.12–14, tr. Shuckburgh). **non unius ... aetatibus:** the components of the verb (*esset ... constituta*) are distributed between two balanced phrases (*unius ... multorum, una ... aliquot*) comprising abl. of means (*ingenio*) and time (*uita, saeculis et aetatibus*). C. throughout book 2 emphasizes the role of the reason and planning (*ratio, ingenium, consilium, prudentia*) of individual statesmen in the construction of the Roman constitution; in this, he opposes Polybius' ideas of natural growth (κατὰ φύσιν), and of the development of Roman government by reaction to crisis rather than by decision (6.10.14, quoted in previous n.). Cf. on 2.30, 45.2, 57.1.

2.2 nam neque ullum ingenium: the language is emphatic (*ullum, tantum, res nulla, cuncta, in unum, uno tempore, omnia*); *prouidere* is presumably a response to Polybius' προϊδόμενος of Lycurgus in 6.10.12 cited above (cf. also 1.45.2n.). **sine rerum usu et uetustate:** *usus* (cf. *usus rei publicae* of Cato, §1.2) might belong to one man, but *uetustas* implies the experience of many generations (*saeculis et aetatibus* above).

3.1 repetet: similarly *De orat.* 1.1, 4. **originem:** C. alludes to Cato's *Origines*, the first historical work in Latin and presumably a source for book 2 (but cf. §2.1n.).

3.2 et nascentem ... robustam: the gradual growth and maturation of Roman society is repeatedly noted in Scipio's account; cf. 21.1, 30, 33.1; also 1.58.3. For instances of *nascor* used metaphorically cf. Reid on *Luc.* 15. The biological metaphor is drawn from Polybius 6.57.10 (cf. also 30n.), with the important difference that

Polybius views decline as part of the pattern, while C. conceives of the possibility of an immortal state (3.34). **ut apud Platonem Socrates:** C. repeatedly contrasts Scipio's historical reconstruction with Plato's imaginary and impossible *Republic* in book 2: cf. 21–22, 51.1. The charge of invention against Plato is traditional (cf. Lucian, *Ver. Hist.* 2.17), and Plato himself speaks of πλάττειν (*R.* 2.374a, 4.420c, 5.466a); cf. Burkert (1965) 180 n.17. Scipio makes an explicit contrast between Cato and Plato: the Roman statesman and historian and the Greek theoretical philosopher.

4–20: Romulus

Scipio's account of Romulus contains or alludes to most of the standard elements in the story: the abandonment of the twins and the folk-tale stories of the wolf and the defeat of the wicked Amulius, the foundation of the city, the rape of the Sabines and the subsequent sharing of the monarchy with Titus Tatius, the establishment of civic institutions, Romulus' mysterious disappearance, epiphany, and deification. The differences from Livy's familiar narrative (as also from those of D. H. and Plutarch) are, however, striking: there is none of the dramatic element found in Livy's version of the recognition and victory of Romulus or the rape of the Sabines (cf. Ogilvie on Livy 1.3.10–4, 5.3–6.2, 9–13); many familiar parts of the story are told in unadorned language and subordinate clauses. C. deliberately excludes some of the more lurid and disgraceful elements of the story: the rape of Ilia is omitted – indeed, neither Ilia nor Numitor is named – and Remus disappears from the narrative after his infancy. The exposure of the twins is described as a matter of public policy (*ob labefactandi regni timorem* 4.3); the wolf appears demurely as a *siluestris belua* (4.3); the taking of the auspices and the death of Remus are compressed into the single word *auspicato* (5.1); and the rape of the Sabines almost becomes an exercise in matchmaking among noble families (12).

The reason for this approach (true of book 2 as a whole) is that C. eschews the personal and the sensational in favour of constitutional and institutional matters; consequently, he emphasizes particularly Romulus' establishment of the senate and the augurate. His account is carefully structured: he begins with a long section on the importance of Rome's location, drawing on Dicaearchus to contrast the decay of the maritime cities of Greece with the continued success of Rome. To balance this, he concludes the account of Romulus with a detailed examination of chronology (19–20, unfortunately damaged), the point of which is to show that while Greek heroes were deified in a primitive time, Romulus' deification came in a period of reasonably advanced civilization. The point of both sections – between which there is a relatively unadorned account of Romulus' constitutional innovations – is the contrast of Greece and Rome, in favour of the latter. Romulus is repeatedly compared to Lycurgus; there is an implicit reference to Plato's admiration for Sparta in the *Laws*, and in the speech of Laelius which immediately follows the chapters on chronology, C. makes an explicit contrast between Plato and Scipio in which the latter's approach to political theory is seen as distinctly superior.

4.1 habemus 'do we know' so also 33.5. **inquit:** Halm's necessary emendation for *igitur* in P; the same error at 1.61.6. **institutae rei publicae:** for this use of the participle in place of a substantive (*ab urbe condita*), cf. Woodcock §95. The style is solemn and pleonastic: *institutae rei publicae . . . exordium* balances *huius urbis condendae principium*, including four words which are essentially synonymous. **profectum a Romulo:** cf. *Inv.* 1.61 *omnes ab Aristotele . . . profecti.*

4.2 Scipio sees the propagation of the story of Romulus' divine origin as an example of the wisdom of the *maiores* in encouraging service to the state; in Livy, *Praef.* 7, it is accepted because of Romulus' military glory. **famae** is taken up at §4.4 by *a fabulis ad facta.*

4.3 is igitur ut natus sit: the anacoluthon *qui patre Marte natus . . . is* is marked by the resumptive use of *is*; cf. §2.1n. *ut* = 'when'; it is followed by the subj. (as below, *perhibetur ut adoleuerit . . . praestitisse*) as a subordinate clause in o. o. after *dicitur.* This is the only reference to Remus in C.'s account. **ob labefactandi regni timorem:** the emphasis is on rational political calculation, and the story of Amulius' overthrow of Numitor is omitted. C. generally prefers *labefacto* to *labefacio*; cf. Powell on *Sen.* 20, *TLL* VII 2.764.13–22 on the distribution of forms of the two verbs. **quo in loco . . . parerent:** a typical Ciceronian narrative period: a circumstantial *cum* clause with several verbs is followed by a weak main verb (*perhibetur*) governing an infin. (*praestitisse*), itself preceded by a temporal clause and followed by a consecutive clause. The entire narrative of Romulus' early life is told in three sentences, the main verb of each of which is a different passive verb of speaking (*dicitur, perhibetur, fertur*). **siluestris beluae:** the elevated periphrasis evades the problems posed by the ambiguous *lupa* ('wolf' or 'whore'); cf. Livy 1.4.6–7, D. H. 1.84.4, Plu. *Rom.* 4.2–3. For similar language, cf. C.'s own verses on the same subject (fr. 10.42–4 Courtney): *hic siluestris erat Romani nominis altrix,* | *Martia, quae paruos Mauortis semine natos* | *uberibus grauidis uitali rore rigabat*, and Prop. 3.9.51 *eductosque pares siluestri ex ubere reges.* C. always uses *sustentatus* rather than *sustentus*; cf. Powell on *Sen.* 20. **laboreque:** Lebreton 416–17 finds only 42 examples of *-que* appended to short *-e* in C., and notes that when two words one of which ends in *-e* are linked by *-que*, the conjunction is almost always attached to the other. **et corporis uiribus et animi ferocitate:** D. H. 1.79.10 has 'dignity of aspect and elevation of mind' (Cary). Plb. 6.5.7 gives 'physical strength and mental daring' as the outstanding characteristics of a founding monarch; cf. Walbank *ad loc.*

4.4 C.'s omission of the fabulous entails leaving out the rescue of Remus, the recognition scene, and all the dramatic details found in Livy 1.5–6, D. H. 1.79–83, Plu. *Rom.* 7–8. For the order *Longam Albam* compare Livy 1.3.3, *Aen.* 6.766 with Norden's note. **temporibus illis** 'by the standards of the time': C. repeatedly expresses awareness of development and change; cf. esp. 17–18.

5.1 urbem auspicato ... rem publicam 'his first thought is said to have been to found a city after taking the auspices, and to establish a state'. The two actions are different: the creation of the physical city (5–11) is followed by the organization of the government (12–16). The chiastic word order is strange, and on a first reading one is inclined to take *urbem* as the object of both *condere* and *firmare. auspicato* is an impersonal abl. abs. (cf. *TLL* II 1552.16–53; Woodcock §93 n.2); for Romulus' taking of the auspices cf. also *N.D.* 3.5, *Div.* 2.3, *Leg.* 2.13. C. omits the dispute with Remus and the latter's death as unedifying (and irrelevant to his purpose). For the importance of augury to C., cf. 16.1n.

5.2–9.5 A theoretical discussion of the proper location for cities, concentrating on the characteristics of coastal sites, precedes the description of the site of Rome (10–11). According to Aristotle, 'It is a hotly debated question whether connexion with the sea is to the advantage, or the detriment, of a well-ordered state' (*Pol.* 7.6, tr. Barker); C. in this passage definitely draws on one source earlier, and one later, than Aristotle. The general model for C.'s analysis is Pl. *Lg.* 4.704a-705b, the discussion between Clinias and the Athenian about the location of the city. The city is located 80 stades (10 miles) from the sea, too close for the Athenian's ideal state, as it breeds immorality and commercial habits. C.'s debt to this discussion is particularly apparent in §§7–9. For this same passage, however, we have C.'s own statement (*Att.* 6.2.3; see below on 8.2 *Phliasios*) that he copied a section from Dicaearchus' Εἰς Τροφωνίου κατάβασις (fr. 20; cf Wehrli *ad loc.*); like Plato, Dicaearchus objected to the moral dissoluteness arising from maritime commerce. It has been argued (e.g. Heck 25–6) that §§7–9 fit awkwardly in their context and must be taken from Dicaearchus, but that is unlikely. Dicaearchus had said that *all* Peloponnesian states bordered the sea; but C. excepts Phlius. Furthermore, a large part of C.'s account concerns peoples of interest to the Romans: Carthage and Corinth (7), Etruscans and Carthaginians (9). Although he says that he translated Dicaearchus verbatim, C. probably adapted freely the arguments of both Plato and Dicaearchus, took one detail directly from Dicaearchus, and reshaped the whole discussion to fit the context.

5.2 quod 'something which'; neut. **qui diuturnam ... prouidendum:** echoed by *uir excellenti prudentia* and *quae ad spem diuturnitatis conderentur*, 5.3; cf. also 10.2. The agricultural metaphor in *serere* (cf. also 34.1n., *Leg.* 1.20) is chosen to suggest a comparison with long-lived trees, for which the choice of a proper location for planting is essential. It is made more explicit at *Tusc.* 1.31: *ergo arbores seret diligens agricola ...; uir magnus leges instituta rem publicam non seret?*

5.3 The sentence falls into two major clauses *neque enim ... admouit, ... sed ... sensit ac uidit.* The first governs a parenthetical relative clause (*quod ... facillimum*) and an *ut* clause with two verbs (*procederet aut ... conderet*), the second of which in turn governs a parenthetical relative clause (*quem ... deduxit*); it is better to take *ut ... conderet* as a final clause rather than as an explanatory consecutive clause: 'He did not approach the sea – as he could easily have done with the troops at his disposal – in order to proceed against the territory ... or in order to found a city at the Tiber mouth.' **quod ... facillimum** 'which would have been very easy for him': the indic. (rarely in the pf.) rather than the subj. is used in expressions of possibility or obligation; cf. K–S I 171–2, and for the similar use in the apodosis of unreal conditions, cf.

1.10.3n. *illa manu copiisque* is instrumental. **in agrum Rutulorum Aboriginumue:** the Rutuli were centred at Ardea, some 38 km south of Rome near the coast. The Aborigines were allegedly the first inhabitants of Latium; cf. Cato, frr. 5–7 *HRR*, Livy 1.1.5 with Ogilvie *ad loc.* **quem in locum ... deduxit:** cf. 33.3. **ipse** is contrasted with *rex Ancus.* **sed hoc ... uidit:** perhaps directed against Polybius' idea (cf. §2.1n.) that Rome's success was unplanned. **primum quod essent:** the first objection is presented in a subordinate clause as Romulus' own opinion (hence subj.); the second is introduced by *est autem* (7.1) and given as Scipio's observation. **periculis oppositae:** C. uses both *opponere periculo* and *opponere ad periculum* (e.g. *Balb.* 26, *Mur.* 87); in his imitation of this passage in Camillus' speech, Livy writes *expositum ... ad pericula* (5.54.4). On the fear of pirates, cf. Thuc. 1.7. **caecis** 'invisible'; cf. *De orat.* 2.357, *Agr.* 2.36.

6.1 terra continens 'adjacent territory' i.e. of a site surrounded by land; cf. *Hort.* fr. 87 M. (quoted on 1.26.2), *Fam.* 15.2.2, *TLL* IV 710.30–61. **quasi fragore quodam:** *fragor* only here in C. and generally rare in classical prose (cf. *Ad Her.* 4.42 for warning against such coinages); for its use in a highly poetic passage of prose cf. Livy 5.42.4. The series *indiciis et ... fragore ... et sonitu ipso* is in order of increasing specificity. **<ad>esse:** Osann's emendation is necessary. To have to supply *hostem* as a predicate with the transmitted text is harsh, and the point of C.'s argument is that the *arrival* of an enemy by land is immediately obvious. Cf. 16.2 for the same emendation.

6.2 maritimus uero ille: *ille* 'the former', referring back to *urbes maritimae* in 5.3. The dangers present with a naval enemy are in the same order as their absence with a land invasion in the previous sentence: *adesse, qui sit, unde ueniat*; the extra elements are marked as such by *etiam* and *denique.* **qui sit** 'of what sort he is' is slightly different in sense from *quis ... sit* 'who he is' (6.1), but P originally read *quis* rather than *qui*, and C. occasionally has *qui* rather than *quis* before words beginning with *s*-, e.g. *Div. Caec.* 20, *Att.* 3.10.2; cf. Löfstedt II 84 n.1, Fordyce on Catullus 61.46. **pacatus an hostis:** cf. *Sest.* 57 *erat rex, si nondum socius, at non hostis, pacatus, quietus, fretus imperio populi Romani*; also *Pis.* 85.

7–9 The tone of this passage and some of the details are derived from the moral objections to coastal cities voiced by Plato and Dicaearchus; see 5.2–9.5n., 8.1n.

7.2 admiscentur enim: sc. *maritimae urbes.* **sermonibus ac disciplinis:** i.e. *mores*, made up of speech and other acquired behaviour. **aduenticiae:** pejorative; cf. *De orat.* 3.135, cited 29.2n.

7.3 iam 'then'; cf 1.9.1n. **cum manent ... uagantur** 'at the same time as they are present in body, in their minds they are wandering in exile': *cum* is temporal. *exulant et uagantur* is hendiadys.

7.4 labefactatam: cf. §4.3n.; *labefactare* and *peruertere* together also at *Fin.* 3.70. **et Carthaginem et Corinthum:** both destroyed by Rome in 146, the former by Scipio himself; the choice of cities shows that C. is not translating Dicaearchus, as does the preference expressed for agriculture and warfare over trade (for which cf. Cato, *Agr.* pref.). The decadence of Corinth was traditional; C. compares Rome and Carthage several times in the extant portions of *Rep.* (fr. 1f Ziegler; 2.42.1, 4), and the *Somnium* takes place in Africa at the outset of the Third Punic War. **mercandi ... cultum:** the first *et* connects the two gerunds, the second and third link *agrorum* and *armorum.*

8.1 multa ... inuitamenta: cf. *Fin.* 5.17 *prima inuitamenta naturae*; also *Hort.* fr. 80 M. Piracy and trade are the two sources of maritime imports. **desidiosas:** cf. *Ag.* 2.91, *De orat.* 3.88, with *Ad Her.* 4.43 *ut, cum desidiosam artem dicimus, quia desidiosos facit.* C. may have in mind the pleasures of villas on the Campanian coast: the delights of the location are themselves corrupting.

8.2 Phliasios: *Phliuntios* P, following C.'s original text. In May 50 (*Att.* 6.2.3), C. wrote to Atticus from Laodicea, replying in part to Atticus' questions about geography and language in this passage. Atticus had apparently taken issue with the statement that all the Peloponnesian states except Phlius (in the north-eastern corner between Argos and Sicyon) bordered the sea, and C. replied that his source was Dicaearchus: *is multis nominibus ... Graecos in eo reprehendit, quod mare tam secuti sunt, nec ullum in Peloponneso locum excipit. ... itaque istum ego locum totidem uerbis a Dicaearcho transtuli* (for the interpretation, cf. §5.2n.). He then deals with Atticus' linguistic question: *Phliasios autem dici sciebam, et ita fac ut habeas; nos quidem sic habemus, sed primo me* ἀναλογία *deceperat,* Φλιοῦς, Ὀποῦς, Σιποῦς *quod* Ὀπούντιοι, Σιπούντιοι*; sed hoc continuo correximus.* In other words, C. himself had corrected the barbarism *Phliuntios* before Atticus drew his attention to it. The form *Phliasiorum* appears at *Tusc.* 5.8. C. twice later (*Att.* 12.6a.1 (*Or.* 29), 13.44.3 (*Lig.* 33)) attempted to change a previously circulated text; only in the former case was he successful. **Aenianes et Doris et Dolopes:** the Aenianes were a Thessalian people of the upper Spercheios river; the Dolopes lived to their north. Doris is the region south of Mt Oeta.

8.3 quae ... natant: C. plays on the literal meaning of *natare*, 'to swim' – with a possible allusion to the mythical origin of Delos as a floating island – and its figurative meaning 'waver, be uncertain'.

9.2 Graiis: for the form cf. 1.58.7n. **Thracam ... Magnesiam:** added by the corrector in the lower margin. The form *Thracam* (otherwise only in poetry) is supplied by a quotation in Servius on Virg. *Aen.* 12.335 (*Thraciam* p). **unam Magnesiam:** Magnesia on the Maeander, in Caria.

9.3 barbarorum agris quasi attexta quaedam 'some sort of patches sewn on to barbarian territory'. The dat. with *attexo* has no undisputed parallel before the second century; for a possible analogy (with *praetexo*), cf. Ovid, *AA* 1.255 with Kenney, *CQ* 9 (1959) 244f. and Hollis *ad loc.* **praeter Etruscos ... latrocinandi alteri:** a doubly chiastic order: it was as pirates that the Etruscans were renowned, the Carthaginians as merchants.

9.4 C. rounds out the moral criticism of coastal states (with *malorum commutationumque* cf. 7.1 *corruptela ac mutatio morum*) before briefly touching on the commercial advantages pertaining to the same sites. The word order *ante paulo* is not found elsewhere in C., but cf. *Div.* 1.114 *ante multo*; for *perbreuiter* and similar compounds cf. 1.9.1n.

9.5 magna commoditas: defined by a pair of substantive clauses articulated by *et ... et*; the unexpressed antecedent of *quod* is the subject of *possit.* **incolas ... sui:** the change from indefinite second to third person perhaps reflects the looser syntax of conversation.

10–11 C. returns to the site of Rome itself. One paragraph (10) relates the general considerations of the preceding sections to the location of Rome: Romulus' choice of a place with access to, but not on, the sea gave the benefits but not the defects of maritime sites; and by avoiding the moral defects of the coast he opened the possibility – denied to Carthage and Corinth – of lasting power. In the final paragraph (11), C. describes the topography of the site of Rome and its fortifications, with reference not only to Romulus' original foundation but to subsequent developments. The praise of the site of Rome placed by Livy in the mouth of Camillus draws heavily on this passage (5.54.4): *non sine causa di hominesque hunc urbi condendae locum elegerunt – saluberrimos colles, flumen opportunum, quo ex mediterraneis locis fruges deuehantur, quo maritimi commeatus accipiantur, mare uicinum ad commoditates nec expositum nimia propinquitate ad pericula classium externarum, regionem Italiae mediam – ad incrementum urbis natum unice locum.*

10.1 Qui 'how'; cf. 1.7.3n. **perennis amnis ... in ripa:** C.'s glowing description of Rome's access to the sea owes more to panegyric than to fact (so too D. H. 3.44), and exaggerates the navigability of the Tiber. The word order is more suggestive of verse than of prose.

10.2 quo posset ... ex terra: the various advantages of sea and river (cf. also D. H. 3.44.1) are expressed in two balanced pairs of verbs of which *urbs* is the subject. By sea, Rome can both receive imports and dispatch exports (*accipere ... quo egeret, et reddere quo redundaret*); by river it can receive imports both from the sea and from inland (*a mari absorberet, inuectas acciperet ex terra*). P reads *mari absorberet*; any correction is no longer legible. *mari* (printed by Ziegler) has been understood either as pure abl. (Büchner) or dat. (Bréguet); numerous emendations have been proposed, of which the simplest is that given here; cf. *accipere a mari* two lines above. *absorberet* (which has been emended, e.g. to *subueheret*, *arcesseret*, *asportaret*) is odd, but should be allowed to stand: C. uses a similarly aqueous metaphor in *redundaret* two lines earlier. That *inuectas ... ex terra* refers to commerce from upstream is shown by Livy's imitation quoted above on 10–11. **iam tum diuinasse:** cf. 12 *iam tum longe prouidentis*. *diuinare* is an emphatic expression of Romulus' foresight and augural capacities (cf. §5.1, 16–17); it alludes as well to his divine origin and prospective deification (cf. §4.2 *ut genere etiam putaretur, non solum ingenio esse diuino*; 10.1 *diuinius*; 17–20). **sedem aliquando et domum:** C. expands on his initial statement (5.2) that the choice of a site was important for the longevity of a state and connects the site with Rome's imperial power; he similarly extends the geographical horizon of Romulus' choice from Latium to Italy.

11.1 natiua praesidia 'natural defences'; a similar use of *natiuus* at *N.D.* 2.100. **qui non habeat ... cognita?:** the choice of verbs and the present tenses show that Scipio is speaking from his own (or C.'s) observation of the so-called Servian wall, constructed in the fourth century (see Ogilvie on Livy 1.44.3, Richardson 262–3). In the description which follows, C. ascribes the fortifications to the wisdom of successive rulers (*cum Romuli tum etiam reliquorum regum sapientia definitus*) but implicitly ascribes the possibility and planning to the *prudentia* of Romulus himself.

11.2 is ... ut: for *is* equivalent to *talis* (and introducing a consecutive clause), cf. 1.7.4. **ex omni parte ... montibus** 'with high and jagged hills on all sides'; abl. of attendant circumstances. **qui esset ... montem:** the subj. indicates the purpose and planning behind the fortifications, although it could be by attraction. The topography is hard to follow, but C.'s reference to the *agger* and *fossa* (cf. Livy 1.44.3) matches other descriptions of the Servian wall between the Porta Collina and the Porta Esquilina, 'where the Servian wall, instead of following the edge of the hill, was obliged to cross the tableland at the base of the Quirinal, Viminal, and Esquiline' (Platner–Ashby 354, with reference to other sources; cf. also Richardson 262–3). C. is the first to use the name *mons Esquilinus*, which did not become until after the first century C.E. the common appellation for the hills otherwise known as *Esquiliae* (e.g. *N.D.* 3.63; Livy 1.44.3), or *mons Oppius* and *mons Cispius*; cf. Platner–Ashby 202, Richardson 146. **ut ita munita arx:** the *arx* is the northern summit of the Capitoline hill. C. uses *circumcisus* in his ornate description of Enna, *Verr.* 4.107 *ab omni aditu circumcisa atque derecta est*. On access to the Capitoline hill, cf. Richardson 70. **illa tempestate horribili:** the sack of Rome, which took place in 387/6 according to Polybius and C., 390 according to Varro and Livy; cf. Walbank on Plb. 1.6.1, 2.18.6. The use of *tempestate* for *tempore* is solemn, and described as archaic by C. at *De orat.* 3.153; it is used elsewhere by C. only in poetry.

11.3 fontibus abundantem: for the springs cf. Richardson 152–3, 229–32; for the healthfulness of the site, cf. Livy 5.54.4 *saluberrimos colles*. **perflantur** 'have breezes blowing over them'; not elsewhere used by C., but cf. *Div.* 2.40 *perflabilis* (of the Epicurean gods, whose location in the *intermundia* is compared to the location of Romulus' asylum *inter duos lucos*).

12 The settlement of Rome and the rape of the Sabines are told in a single long sentence. Following the retrospective first clause, the first main verb (*constituit*) is followed by an explanatory relative clause (*quam* ... *nominari*), while the second (*secutus est*) is preceded by its object (*consilium*) itself surrounded by two qualifying phrases each containing a gerundive of purpose (*ad firmandam* ... *subagreste*, *ad muniendas* ... *prouidentis*). The actual story of the rape is told in the *cum* clause, itself divided into two parts (*iussit, collocauit*), of which the first contains two relative clauses while the second is extremely simple. The emphasis is on politics rather than drama: the rape is a matter of foreign policy, intended to create attachments between Romans and Sabines (cf. D. H. 2.30.1), and it is coordinate with the founding and naming of the city. **perceleriter:** elsewhere in C. only at *Fam.* 6.12.3; for C.'s use of *per-* compounds, cf. 1.9.1n. **Romam iussit nominari:** the origin of the name of Rome was the subject of considerable antiquarian discussion (a strange set of etymologies in Festus 326–30 L.; more fully Maltby s.v.), but here as elsewhere C. does not digress on such matters. The obvious derivation from Romulus, which C. accepts here, is also found e.g. in Ennius, *Ann.* 77 Sk. and Festus 327.6 L. **et ad firmandam nouam ciuitatem:** cf. §5.1 *firmare* ... *rem publicam. nouam* ... *nouum* is emphatic. **subagreste:** rare; linked with *subrusticum* at *Brut.* 259. C. is here playing on the lack of urbanity (in a social sense) in such a crude plan for founding a city. Compare also §4.3 *in agresti cultu*, used in a literal sense of Romulus. **regni ... prouidentis:** *regni ac populi sui* is a possessive gen. dependent on *opes*; *magni* and *prouidentis* are possessive gen. dependent on *consilium* and contrasting with *subagreste*: 'a crude plan, but one belonging to a great man'. **iam tum:** even at the founding of the city. For *prudentia* cf. on 5.2, 10.2. **Sabinas honesto ortas loco uirgines:** for the phrase, with the same interlocking word order, cf. *Agr.* 1.27 *equestri ortum loco consulem*; cf. also 6.18.4n. C. chooses to emphasize the propriety of the plan: the Sabines come from good families; they are married to the wealthiest Romans. Contrast Livy's account, 1.9.6ff. **anniuersarios:** a technical term for annual rites; cf. *Verr.* 4.84, *Att.* 1.18.3, Livy 22.56.4, Augustus, *Res Gestae* 11. Here it is clearly used predicatively: he founded games which were to be an annual event. **in circo:** the underground altar of Consus was beneath the Circus Maximus, in the valley between the Aventine and Palatine hills; cf. Richardson 100. **Consualibus:** Mai's emendation of *consulibus* in P is certain. According to Fabius Pictor (in Plu. *Rom.* 14.1), the rape took place four months after the founding of the city. In fact the festival of Consus was celebrated in classical times on 21 August (cf. Wissowa 202; Plu. *Rom.* 15.5 incorrectly gives 18 Aug.), exactly four months after the Parilia (21 April), the traditional date for the foundation of Rome. Consus was probably identified with Poseidon Hippios (*Neptunus equestris*, Livy 1.9.6; cf. D. H. 2.31.2–3, Plu. *Rom.* 14.3) because of the horse or mule races at his festival (cf. Ogilvie *ad loc.*); he was originally a god of the granary (from *condere*), but some Romans derived the name from *consilium* (cf. Maltby s.vv. *Consualia*, *Consus*), an etymology to which C. may be alluding here; cf. *subagreste consilium* above.

13 The style of the sentence is formal; there are several technical terms of law or religion, and each half of the sentence is introduced by a resumptive relative (*qua ex causa, quo foedere*); for the formality of *foedus . . . quo foedere* cf. 1.41.4 *ad eam causam . . . quae causa*, 2.14 *curias . . . quas curias*. **proeliique certamen:** the gen. of definition or appositional gen. (cf. Woodcock §72(5)) occurs after *certamen* in C. only in the similar phrase *belli certamen* in a translation from Homer at *Fin.* 5.49. **uarium atque anceps:** the same combination elsewhere in C. only in the ornate language of the letter to Lucceius, *Fam.* 5.12.5. For *anceps* cf. also 6.12.2; it occurs only 20x in C., often in elevated passages. **T. Tatio rege:** Ogilvie (on Livy 1.10.1) rightly calls Tatius 'a mysterious and colourless figure'; his function here is largely to provide an etymology for the name of one of the three tribes and an early instance of shared authority (cf. 14n.). **foedus icit:** a technical term; cf. Livy 1.24.3, 1.32.3; *TLL* VII 1.161.16–27. **matronis:** after the rape the Sabine *uirgines* have become *matronae*. **orantibus:** a possible etymological allusion to their leader, Romulus' wife Hersilia, who was deified as Hora Quirini; cf. Wiseman (1987) 289. **in ciuitatem asciuit:** formal language; cf. 2.33, and Livy 6.40.4, Tac. *Ann.* 11.24. **sacris communicatis** 'by sharing (Roman) religious rituals with them'.

14 The main contribution of this paragraph to Scipio's argument is the value of the Senate in providing *consilium*: C. wishes to emphasize that the constitution was mixed even in the regal period. Subsidiary points of constitutional or antiquarian interest (the tribes and *curiae*) are included parenthetically. The structure of the sentence, using parenthetical relative clauses and anacoluthon with repetition, seems to be an attempt to imitate conversational style; cf. §4.3n., 16.2n., and for the use of parenthesis, cf. H–S 728–9. **interitum ... Tatii:** a bland description of murder, replaced by *eo interfecto* at the end of the sentence. As usual, C. omits the details (Tatius killed by Laurentines after their ambassadors were assaulted by his relatives), for which cf. Livy 1.14.1–3, D. H. 2.51–2, Plu. *Rom.* 23.1–4. **regium consilium:** for the transition from royal council to senate, cf. 15.2n. Other sources give a fixed number for the group based on artificial calculations (cf. Ogilvie on Livy 1.8.7), and no other account associates Tatius with Romulus in the selection. The version of D. H. (2.47) has each of the curiae and tribes pick three senators (99) and Romulus pick one; Tatius was responsible for adding 50 more. The collaboration of Romulus and Tatius in C. emphasizes the importance of consultation (and may vaguely anticipate the consulship): even before there is a senate to provide *consilium*, Romulus has a colleague with whom to work. **qui ... patres:** an important feature of the harmonious state, ascribed in book 1 to Romulus himself (Ennius, quoted 1.64.2); cf. also 1.55.3 *ita caritate nos capiunt reges, consilio optimates, libertate populi.* C. gives no size for this proto-senate, but he probably thought that it was 150; cf. 35.4n. On the meaning of *patres* cf. 23n. **in tribus tres:** C. gives the sources for the tribal names, but he does not give the names themselves until 36.1. The etymologies here – *Rhamnenses* from Romulus, *Titienses* from Titus Tatius, *Luceres* from Lucumo – are traditional, but C. skips the traditional antiquarian problem of the identity of Lucumo (cf. Ogilvie on Livy 1.13.8). That the names are in fact Etruscan was recognized at an early date; cf. Varro, *L.* 5.55, citing the Etruscan tragedian Volnius. The phrase *tribus tres* offers an implicit etymology for *tribus* (Varronian; cf. Maltby s.v.). **curiasque triginta:** the true origin and significance of the *curiae* (< *co-uiria) are obscure; in classical times the *comitia curiata* – the oldest form of electoral assembly – was normally an antiquarian formality employed to ratify adoptions and priestly elections, and was represented by the magistrates' lictors. The *curiae* themselves seem to have been groups of families, although they may have been geographical as well (D. H. 2.7.2–4 in his account includes a distribution of land to the *curiae*). For a full study of the *curiae*, see R. E. A. Palmer, *The archaic community of the Romans* (Cambridge, 1970); for brief accounts, cf. Momigliano (1966) 574–80, *CAH*² VII 2.105. The tradition that they were named after the Sabine women is old (although of the nine surviving names only one, Rapta, has any possible relevance), but there was a problem as to which 30 were the source of curial names. Livy 1.13.7 expresses uncertainty, while C. offers a political interpretation: they were the women responsible for making peace between Romans and Sabines (so too anonymous Roman historians in D. H. 2.47.3–4). He thus once more emphasizes the rewards of civic responsibility. Earlier tradition (represented by Plu. *Rom.* 14.6) recorded that only 30 Sabine women were taken, thus avoiding the problem. **nuncupauit:** a formal word (cf. 6.16.1) chiefly used in legal language, listed by C. (*De orat.* 3.153) among old words which give *dignitas* to style; here the formality is increased by the presence of the cognate *nominibus*. Cf. also *De orat.* 1.245, *N.D.* 2.60. **oratrices:** rare; the fem. only here in C., previously Plautus, *Mil.* 1072. Cf. also 13n. **uiuo:** the hyperbaton emphasizes the opposition *uiuo ... interfecto*. **auctoritate consilioque:** the *auctoritas* of the Senate is a central principle of Ciceronian politics (even though in *Rep.* it is subordinated to the mixed constitution), as it is for Scipio in this dialogue. For other Ciceronian instances, cf. *Dom.* 114, *Pis.* 15, *Sest.* 137, and particularly *Leg.* 2.30 (on the importance of civic religion to the state): *continet enim rem publicam, consilio et auctoritate optimatium semper populum indigere.*

15.1 Quo facto: i.e. by ruling with the advice of the *patres.* **primum:** correlative with *tum*, 16.1. **Lycurgus ... uiderat:** C. later places Lycurgus more than a century earlier than Romulus; cf. 18.3n. In this chapter he minimizes the distance between the two in order to make the comparison more telling. The linking of Romulus and Lycurgus is important for C. (cf. §§2.1, 18–19, 24, 43.1, 50, 58.2), particularly because of Plato's discussion of Lycurgus' mixed constitution in *Lg.* 3.691d-692a; the comparison of the tribunate with the Spartan ephorate at 58.2 is probably based on a Peripatetic interpretation of Plato (cf. Arist. *Pol.* 2.6). The repeated comparisons with Sparta reflect the general admiration in the Peripatetic tradition for the Lycurgan constitution as the best and most durable form of government; the similarity of the Roman and Spartan constitutions is also central to Polybius' account of the mixed constitution (6.10, 48–50). On the traditions of philosophical laconism on which C. drew, cf. Rawson (1969) 61–104. **singulari imperio et potestate regia:** the phrase *imperium singulare* is used of the sole ruler in the democratic criticism of monarchy in 1.50. The two phrases here are basically synonyms, as are *gubernari et regi* and *fultus et munitus*. Amplification is an important element of C.'s style in *Rep.* (cf. 1.48.1n.); here, where it approaches hendiadys, it is intended to emphasize (as is the hyperbaton of *optimi cuiusque ... auctoritas*) the significance of the ideas expressed. The opposition between *imperium* and *potestas* on the one hand and *auctoritas* on the other is basic to C.'s senate-centred theory of the Roman constitution. **optimi cuiusque:** for the conservative significance of this phrase, cf. *Leg.* 3.39, on voting procedure: *habeat sane populus tabellam quasi uindicem libertatis, dummodo haec optimo cuique et grauissimo ciui ostendatur.*

15.2 consilio et quasi senatu: the royal council (cf. 14) was the antecedent of the republican Senate, and *patres* was the designation for both; but (cf. 43.1) the council under a monarchy was not constitutionally equivalent to the Senate, and hence C. uses *quasi* here (but not at 17, 23, 50.2). For the presence of the Senate even under the kings, cf. *Pis.* 23, *Phil.* 3.9; for Romulus' Senate, cf. also D. H. 2.12, compared to Sparta at 2.14.2. **bella ... gessit:** Romulus' reputation as a warrior is not germane to C.'s purpose. For the wars with Veii and Fidenae, cf. Livy 1.14–15. **cum ipse nihil ... reportaret:** cf. the austerity of Numa's religion, 27.1, and of the ideal senate, 59.2.

16.1 id quod retinemus hodie: the augurate had genuine importance throughout the Republic through the ability of the augurs to determine divine approval or disapproval of civic actions and hence their validity; for detailed discussion of their powers, cf. Linderski 2147–225. C. himself was elected to the college of augurs in 53, and was extremely proud of it. **auspiciis:** Livy records (4.4.2) that the augurate was created by Numa, but C. consistently ascribed it to Romulus; cf. *Div.* 1.3 with Pease *ad loc.*

16.2 The institutional creations of the kings are generally told by C. in a relatively bare series of paratactic clauses with coordinate conjunctions: *et ipse ... condidit ... et ... cooptauit ... et habuit ... multaeque dictione ... coercebat.* So also of Numa, 26.2 (*et ... et ... et ... -que*); Tullus, 31.2 (*-que ... -que*); Ancus, 33.3 (*-que ... et ... et*); Tarquinius Priscus, 36.4–5 (*-que ... atque ... -que*). For the parenthetical relative clauses cf. 14n. **qui sibi <ad>essent in auspiciis:** a final clause. Mai's emendation is necessary; for the same correction cf. §6.1. The technical phrase *in auspicio esse* (cf. Wissowa 531 n.7, Linderski 2190–5) is irrelevant, as *auspicio* is always in the sing. **ex singulis tribubus:** the number of augurs was four by 300 B.C.E., when the *lex Ogulnia* increased it to nine (Livy 10.6.6–8; cf. Rotondi 236); Sulla increased the college to fifteen. **et habuit plebem ... discriptam** 'he had the *plebs* divided'; for the usage, rare in C., cf. *OLD* s.v. *habeo* 27. C. is here linking three methods used by Romulus to maintain social order: the augurate stopped undesirable public activity; *clientela* kept the *plebs* in a subordinate role; and the use of financial rather than capital punishment was a sign of wisdom and moderation. For the origins of *clientela*, cf. also D. H. 2.9.2–2.10.4, Plu. *Rom.* 13.2–6. C. rarely uses the word *plebs* in *Rep.*, and he does not use the word *patricius* here, although it is clear (cf. 23) that he derives the distinction between patrician and plebeian from the institution of the *patres*. **quantae ... utilitati** 'how useful'; predicative dat. (cf. Woodcock §68). **post uidero:** in a passage no longer extant. For the use of the fut. pf. instead of the fut., cf. 1.20.2n. **multaeque dictione:** a technical term for the assessment of penalties; cf. Frontinus, *Aqu.* 129 (*lex Quinctia*) *eoque nomine iis ... multae dictio ... esto.* **ouium et boum:** the formal language of law: cf. Pliny, *NH* 18.11 *cautum est ... ne bouem prius quam ouem nominaret qui indiceret multam.* The etymologies are also traditional; cf. Maltby s.vv. *locuples*, *pecunia*.

17 septem et triginta ... annos: the figure is probably Polybian (cf. 27.4), but it is also used by Livy 1.21.6 and D. H. 1.75.1. On the chronology cf. 18.2n. **firmamenta rei publicae:** for *firmare* cf. §5.1, 12; for *firmamenta rei publicae*, cf. *Att.* 1.18.3, *Planc.* 23. The emphasis on the Senate and the auspices as Romulus' most important inventions reflects C.'s own ideas about the bases of political and social stability. **subito sole obscurato:** the eclipse at the death of Romulus also at 1.25.4, 6.24.3; in Livy 1.16.1, D. H. 2.56.2, and Plu. *Rom.* 27.6 there is a sudden storm (an eclipse reported from unnamed sources at D. H. 2.56.6). On the various accounts of his death and deification, cf. 20.3n.

18–19 The deification of Romulus provides the occasion for Scipio to elaborate on the historical arguments in favour of monarchy at 1.58. Here as there, the argument is that even the earliest period of Roman history was contemporary with (and therefore took part in) a high level of culture in Greece. Hence, in this passage, the acceptance of

Romulus' deification indicates a remarkable level of *uirtus* on his part rather than an equivalent level of credulity on that of the Romans. In the larger context of *Rep.*, however, the chronological discussion has several purposes: once again, to link Rome with Sparta, and Romulus with Lycurgus; to establish the antiquity and historicity of Roman legend; and to reveal C. himself as a master of historical scholarship in the Greek manner, just as 21–2 reveal him as a master of political philosophy surpassing the Greeks.

18.1 qui dii ... esse dicuntur: cf. 2.4.2. C. is presumably thinking of the Euhemerist belief (known in Rome through Ennius' *Euhemerus*) that those now worshipped as gods were originally men of great accomplishment, but he is also clearly thinking of the myths of deification of heroes such as Hercules. For C.'s views on men becoming gods, cf. *N.D.* 2.62 *suscepit autem uita hominum consuetudoque communis ut beneficiis excellentes uiros in caelum fama ac uoluntate tollerent*, followed by a list including Hercules, Liber, and Romulus; cf. also *Tusc.* 1.27–8. C. tacitly excludes the Hellenistic practice of deifying eminent individuals ranging from monarchs to philosophers such as Epicurus to Roman magistrates serving in the East; in a hyperbolic passage of *Sest.* (143) he asserts that he considers the heroes of the early Republic to be *in deorum immortalium coetu ac numero*. Phrases used in this sentence are echoed in 19–20: *eximia uirtutis gloria* ~ *uis ingenii atque uirtutis*; *minus eruditis hominum saeculis* ~ *iam doctis hominibus ac temporibus ipsis eruditis*; *fingendi procliuis ... ratio* ~ *ad fingendum uix quicquam esset loci*; *iam inueteratis litteris atque doctrinis* ~ *iam inueterata uita hominum*. **minus his sescentis annis:** cf. 1.58.5. For the construction of *minus* cf. 1.58.2n. **inueteratis litteris:** not, however, in Rome. C. is presumably aware of the speciousness of his own argument; cf. 19.1n. **illo antiquo ... errore sublato:** i.e. credulity, uncritical acceptance of fictions.

18.2 By 'the annals of the Greeks' C. means Polybius, who gave Ol. 7,2 (751/0) as the foundation date of Rome (6.11a.2 = D. H. 1.74.3; see Walbank *ad loc.*) and is said by C. (27.4) to have been his source for early chronology; the same date is given by C.'s other main source for chronology, Cornelius Nepos (fr. 5 Marshall), drawing on Eratosthenes and Apollodorus. Nepos' *Chronica* also established synchronisms between Greek poets and Roman history (cf. frr. 4, 7 Marshall, with Horsfall *ad locc.*) which C. clearly used here and in 20.1–2. The traditional date of 754/3 for the foundation of Rome was established by Varro and Atticus, and was accepted by C. after the Civil War (*Brut.* 72) as later by Livy. For detailed analysis of C.'s chronology in *Rep.*, cf. Fantham (1981). **fabulis:** cf. 19.2; uncivilized peoples accept fairy tales about recent events, while civilized ones only accept them about the distant past.

18.3 The first Olympic victory was traditionally that of Coroebus in 776, but another account, accepted by Aristotle, gave credit for the establishment of the games to Lycurgus and Iphitus of Elea (Plu. *Lyc.* 1.1, cf. Pausanias 5.20.1). Lycurgus' laws, however, were placed in 884 by Eratosthenes and other chronographers – the 108 years referred to here by C. – and the two solutions to this dilemma proposed were either that the first 27 Olympiads were not counted, and thus that Lycurgus had actually founded the games, or that there were two different men named Lycurgus, one the lawgiver of 884, the other the founder of the games in 776. The first solution was apparently accepted by Polybius (unless 6.11a.3 is to be ascribed to Claudius' freedman Polybius rather than the historian); the second by the historian Timaeus (*FGrH* 566 F 127; so also C., *Brut.* 40). If the historian Polybius is the advocate of unrecorded Olympiads between 884 and 776, then C. has here rejected his usual chronological source; see Walbank on Plb. 6.11a.3. **Homerum autem:** Homer's latest possible date is given as 914, which is in agreement with Cornelius Nepos' statement that Homer flourished roughly 160 years before the founding of Rome (Gellius 17.21.3 = fr. 4 Marshall).

19 The complete text of this § is preserved only in the quotation by Augustine, *CD* 22.6.10–16 (Heck 138–9), and there is a lacuna following it. Slightly more than half a leaf of P is lost; from *ante Homerum* to *non numquam* we possess only the first letters of each line; from 20.1 to *immortalitate* only the last letters; *incondite . . . respuit* only in Augustine.

19.1 temporibus ... eruditis: so too of the age of the Twelve Tables at *Tusc.* 4.4; of his own time at *Att.* 12.18.1. One may question the sincerity of C.'s belief in the high culture of the eighth century B.C.E., but it is extremely important for his argument about the planned and rational development of Roman government.

19.2 Cf. 28–9 on the alleged meeting of Numa and Pythagoras. There is no guarantee that the sentence is complete, and a specific object for *respuit* may be lost in the lacuna.

20.1–2 *<Stesichor>us nepos eius: some 5–6 lines of text (less than one page of P) have been lost; in the first lines of this section many letters have been supplemented, largely by Niebuhr, who rightly saw that the purpose of this list of Greek poets (cf. 18.2) was to show that, although living at the same time as the Roman kings, they made no mention of the deification of their contemporaries. C. here seems to be discussing (and denying on chronological grounds) the idea that Stesichorus was Hesiod's grandson; cf. Jacoby on *FGrH* 224 F 337, Fantham (1981) 14. For other synchronisms between Roman kings and Greek poets; cf. *Tusc.* 1.3, Nepos fr. 7 Marshall = Gell. 17.21.8. **cum iam ... cognita** 'at a time when civilization had already been long established and when civilized ways were practiced and known' (Sabine and Smith). For *uita* 'civilized life', cf. *OLD* s.v. 8; the expression is very compressed.

20.3 uis ingenii atque uirtutis: cf. 46.1 *uir ingenio et uirtute praestans L. Brutus.* **Proculo Iulio:** C.'s two references to Proculus Iulius (here and *Leg.* 1.3) show that the legend is earlier than the ascendancy of Julius Caesar (cf. Skutsch on Ennius, *Ann.* 110). According to C. and D. H. 2.63.3, he was a farmer; according to Ovid (*Fasti* 2.499) he was from Alba. D. H. also calls him a descendant of Ascanius, and Plu. *Rom.* 28.1 describes him as an Alban patrician. Livy 1.16.6–7 gives a very poetic version of Proculus' speech, which may derive from Ennius; cf. Ogilvie *ad loc.* and Skutsch 260–1. **impulsu patrum:** the story that Romulus was murdered by the Senate because of tyrannical behaviour is reported also by Livy 1.16.4 (cf. 1.15.7–8), D. H. 2.56.3–4, Ovid, *Fasti* 2.497 and several later sources. This version of the death of Romulus first appears in a speech of one of the consuls attacking Pompey in 67 B.C.E.: 'if he imitates Romulus he will not escape Romulus' end' (Plu. *Pomp.* 25.9). It may derive from the anti-Sullan annalist Licinius Macer; cf. Classen 179, 183–5. *quo ... pellerent* is a relative clause of purpose. **qui nunc Quirinalis uocatur:** C.'s account provides an aetiology for the name of the hill. The identification of Romulus with Quirinus is first attested here and in the similar passage at *Leg.* 1.3; at *N.D.* 2.62 *Romulum, quem quidem eundem esse Quirinum putant*, he seems more tentative (cf. also *Off.* 3.41). Classen 192–9 argued that the identification and the role of Iulius Proculus were invented by Julius Caesar in 54–51, precisely the years when C. was writing *Rep.*; others, more cautiously, believe that the identification is no earlier than the first century. In some form, it is likely to go back to the early third century, when much of the Romulus legend took shape. C. took great pains to avoid anachronism in his dialogues, and had Romulus been identified with Quirinus only in his own lifetime he would not have put it in the mouth of Scipio. For a recent discussion, see Jocelyn 39–46.

21–2: Excursus on Method

After Scipio's account of each king, one of his interlocutors makes a comment to remind the reader that this is, in fact, a dialogue. As Scipio's discussion of Romulus is by far the most important, so too Laelius' comment offers a significant explanation of C.'s historical method in book 2. The approach is explicitly described as new and unknown to the Greeks, exemplifying the virtues and avoiding the weaknesses of Plato on the one hand and the Peripatetics (*reliqui*) on the other. Plato had concentrated on a single state, but a fictitious one; the Peripatetics had catalogued constitutions and political systems, but had not focused on the structural development of any one.

The sceptical tone of Laelius' comment, however, shows that one should be wary of attributing to C. any profound philosophical intent, and it is most unlikely that his goal is the interpretation of Rome in the light of the Platonic Forms (cf. Pöschl 45, Büchner 188). Laelius' description of Scipio's procedure deals first with the weaknesses of Plato which are avoided, then with those of the Peripatetics. Socrates in the *Republic* explicitly makes up everything; Scipio prefers to attribute his own discoveries to others, and to attribute to the *consilium* and *prudentia* of Romulus (and the other kings) what was in fact done *casu aut necessitate*. As opposed to the Peripatetics, Scipio sticks to a single state, *defixa in una re publica*. The comparison with Aristotle and his followers is, in general, valid, but that with Plato is specious: the difference is that Socrates is explicitly inventing a state, while Scipio, with Socratic irony, claims to be giving a historical account while in fact inventing just as much as Socrates. Laelius, in other words, believes that the statecraft of Romulus (particularly the choice of the site of Rome) was fortuitous and really Scipio's creation. The same down-to-earth outlook is expressed by Laelius concerning astronomy at 1.19–20; his role is parallel to that of the practical Antonius in *De orat.* and of Atticus in *Brutus*. On this passage, see now G. Lieberg, *Mnemosyne*) 47 (1994) 12–32.

21.1 ortum ... puberem: the stages of growth, from birth through infancy to maturity; for the biological metaphor, cf. §3.2n.

21.2 nos uero uidemus ~ *Videtisne igitur* 21.1; cf. 1.64.5–6 *sed uides ... uideo uero.* **quae nusquam est in Graecorum libris:** this clearly excludes the possibility that Scipio's account is closely based on the lost *archaeologia* of Polybius book 6.

21.3 princeps ille: Plato, described as *praestantissimus* at *De orat.* 1.217. For *R.* as fiction, cf. §3.2, 51–2; also Plb. 6.47.7–10. **a uita ... a moribus:** cf. *De orat.* 1.224 *nouam quandam finxit in libris ciuitatem; usque eo illa, quae dicenda de iustitia putabat, a uitae consuetudine et a ciuitatum moribus abhorrebant.*

22.1 Although Stoics as well as Peripatetics wrote on political philosophy, C. has the latter in mind, going back to Aristotle's *Politics* (which C. probably had not read) and the various treatises of Theophrastus and Dicaearchus (which he had). Polybius' discussion of constitutional theory in 6.3–10 (itself based largely on Peripatetic theory) is probably also included in Laelius' criticism. The objection to such works is that they dealt with abstract types of constitution or with particular types of situation illustrated by examples from many different states, rather than following the continuous development of a single state; it would appear that C. was unaware of the collection of such histories made by Aristotle, of which *Ath. Pol.* is the only surviving example.

22.2 The first subordinate clause (*ut quae ... fingere*) describes Scipio's improvement of the Platonic model; the sense dictates that the second clause (*et illa ... facta sunt*) be an explanation of the first. Laelius' irony lies in his suggestion that while Plato treats a fictional state as if it were real, Scipio attributes fictional motivations and plans to a historical state. The third clause (*et disputes ... re publica*) must refer to Scipio's improvement on Peripatetic practice: *non uaganti* (i.e. not wandering from state to state) is explained by *defixa in una re publica.* Büchner is wrong to see *uaganti oratione* as a description of Platonic style rather than Peripatetic method; cf. Pöschl 44.

22.3 quasi perfectam rem publicam: *perfectus* is not normally applied to *res publica*, but cf. 1.42.5. Laelius' *quasi* may indicate either that the Republic was not perfected at the fall of the monarchy, or (more in line with Plato) that, being a real state with obvious imperfections, it could never be perfect, even if it became the best possible state.

23–4: Interregnum

The transfer of power to a successor is a crucial issue in the analysis of the *res publica*. C. emphasizes the potential conflict and ultimate cooperation between *patres* and *populus*, pointing out their strengths and weaknesses. The desire of the *patres* for sole power is countered by popular liberty; the *patres* reveal their characteristic *prudentia* in the invention of the *interregnum*, while the collective wisdom of the *populus* is shown in their wise preference (in contrast to the Lycurgan constitution) for elective over hereditary monarchy. The superiority of Roman practical wisdom over Greek complements the preference expressed by Laelius in the preceding paragraph for Scipio's historical account of constitutional theory over Plato's purely theoretical approach.

23 The first part of the sentence consists of a set of nested clauses: the circumstantial *cum ille ... senatus ... temptaret* contains an explanatory relative clause (*qui ... optimatibus*), which in turn contains a further relative clause (*quibus ... liberos*). The verb in the latter is subj. as an expression of Romulus' thoughts, and contains a consecutive clause (*tantum ... ut eos patres uellet nominari*). After this complex introduction, the main clause is emphatically brief and simple: *populus id non tulit*. **ille Romuli senatus:** cf. 15.2n. *optimates* is first used here in *Rep.* of the Roman Senate; compare *optimi cuiusque* at 15.1, and for *optimates* in a more general sense 1.42.3. **patres ... patriciosque:** C. assumes the identification of the hereditary patrician families as the original Romulean Senate; modern scholars have debated the origins of the patriciate and the relationship between *patres* and *conscripti* in the republican Senate. Richard, and Raaflaub 237–43 are useful introductions; R. Mitchell's arguments about the religious basis of the patriciate are unsatisfactory. **regeret sine rege rem publicam:** the first hand reads *gereret*, which is also possible, but the verbal point is clearly deliberate; cf. e.g. *Att.* 7.25 *erat enim ars difficilis recte rem publicam regere*. For the relative rarity of *regere* in this use, cf. Lepore 40–4. **populus id non tulit:** the same desire to rule on the part of the *patres* and resistance by the people, with eventual compromise on the method of choosing and approving a new king, appears in Livy's account (1.17; cf. also D. H. 2.57–58.1). **desiderioque Romuli:** so too *desiderium Romuli*, Livy 1.16.8; both deriving from Ennius, quoted above 1.64.1. **cum prudenter:** for the use of *cum* to connect two independent sentences (*cum inversum*) cf. Woodcock §237. **interregni ineundi:** for the procedure of appointing an *interrex*, cf. Ogilvie on Livy 1.17, 3.8.2; for *ineo* 'to enter a magistracy', *OLD* s.v. 5. **ut quoad certus rex declaratus esset** 'until such time as a specific king should be proclaimed'. *quoad* with the impf. subj. is a temporal form of final clause; cf. Woodcock §224. The *ut*-clause has two verbs (*esset* and *committeretur*); the first of these has two predicates, while the second governs another *ut*-clause which in turn governs a balanced pair of phrases (*ad deponendum imperium tardior* ... *ad obtinendum munitior*). **diuturno rege ... uno** 'with one long-term king'; presumably an abl. of attendant circumstances.

24 id quod fugit ... Lycurgum: an implicit criticism of Polybius' praise (6.10.6) of Lycurgus' foresight in establishing the mixed constitution. **non deligendum ... sed habendum:** the same criticism of Spartan hereditary monarchy is made by the advocate of democracy at 1.50.4. The two royal families of Sparta (Agiad and Eurypontid) claimed descent from Heracles. For Lycurgus in book 2, cf. 15.1n. **qualiscumque is foret:** *foret* (for *futurus esset*) is used elsewhere by C. in prose only at *Att.* 7.21.2, 10.14.3, *Tusc.* 3.38. **qui modo esset:** relative clause of proviso. **nostri illi etiam tum agrestes:** ironic, as C. has gone to some lengths (17–19) to show how advanced civilization was even at the time of Romulus.

25–7: Numa

C.'s brief account of Numa agrees with others (Livy 1.18–21, D. H. 2.59–76, Plu. *Numa*) in emphasizing his establishment of religious institutions and inculcation of peaceful habits. As always, however, C. concentrates on institutions and ignores such stories as Numa's relationship with Egeria.

25.1 praetermissis ... acciuit: similarly Livy 4.3.10 (speech of Canuleius). Numa was proposed by the Senate, and the choice was then ratified by the people in the *comitia curiata*; cf. also Livy 1.17.8–9. The sentence emphasizes the participation of all elements in the community by including *ciues, rex, patres*, and *populus* in the first clause, and the paradoxical results of succession based on qualification rather than heredity by the juxtapositions (*ad regnandum Sabinum hominem,*

Romam Curibus) in the second. Balance is also effected by the rhyme (*asciuit, acciuit*) of the verbs at the ends of the two clauses. **patribus auctoribus:** cf. 56.1 for the need for senatorial ratification of popular votes.

25.2 curiatam legem tulit: the *comitia* had voted to elect him king; Numa proposed a separate law to confer *imperium* on himself (cf. also D. H. 2.60.3). The procedure is repeated by Tullus Hostilius (31.1), Ancus (33.2), Tarquinius Priscus (35.4), and Servius Tullius (38.1). **paulum ... reuocandos:** so also Livy 1.19.2, Plu. *Numa* 8.1–2.

26.1 Agriculture is the pre-eminent form of respectable non-military activity; its proceeds are thus comparable to the military profits of *praeda* and *depopulatio*. For C.'s views of agriculture as an activity at once pleasant, profitable, and socially useful, cf. the encomium put into the mouth of Cato at *Sen.* 51–9, with Powell's commentary. Distribution of land is also attributed to Numa by D. H. 2.62.3–4 and Plu. *Numa* 16.3, but while for C. Numa wished to encourage peacefulness through agriculture, for D. H. it is an attempt to forestall social discontent, and Plutarch mentions both motives; cf. Gabba (1991) 175–7. *uiritim* distribution of land (as opposed to the establishment of colonies) is clearly anachronistic and reflects the procedures of Flaminius (cf. *Brut.* 57, *Sen.* 11) and the Gracchan land commission; it is curious that the anti-Gracchan Scipio should be made to give a precedent for Gracchan practice. **otii et pacis:** *otium* here = 'domestic tranquillity', the internal equivalent to external *pax*. The success of agriculture leads to the love of stability, which permits the development of *iustitia* and *fides*, in turn the best guarantees of agricultural prosperity. **conualescit** 'grow strong' rather than 'recover'. Cf. *Corn.* 1 fr. 51, *Mil.* 25, *Leg.* 3.17, *Att.* 7.3.4. A sing. verb is normal in C. when the subject consists of two abstract nouns; cf. Lebreton 2–6. **perceptioque frugum** 'harvest': *perceptio* in the sense of 'gather' or 'take possession' is a legal term; cf. *OLD* s.v. 1, 2.

26.2 Five religious colleges are named, grouped by their importance in C.'s day rather than in the regal period: the augurs come first – the college of which C. himself was a member – with the *pontifices*; after a sentence on religious legislation come the three colleges of *flamines*, Salii, and Vestals, and a generalizing conclusion. On the historical importance of these bodies, see below; for the paratactic style of such lists, cf. 16.2n. **idemque Pompilius** 'this same Pompilius': the usage is frequent in such lists; cf. *OLD* s.v. *idem* 3. **auspiciis maioribus inuentis:** augural lore ranked the auspices both by the importance of the omen (cf. DS *Aen.* 3.374) and by the office of the magistrate taking the omens (Messalla cited by Gellius 13.15.4); cf. Wissowa 530; as magistrates did not yet exist, the first must be meant here. Romulus had appointed three augurs (16.2). Livy 4.4.2 and D. H. 2.64.4 ascribe the invention of the augurate to Numa, and a college of five augurs is not elsewhere attested; cf. Wissowa 523. **pontifices quinque:** according to Livy 1.20.5, Numa appointed only one *pontifex*, and the stages of expansion of the college are not clear. Livy 10.6.6 records a doubling from four to eight under the *lex Ogulnia* of 300 (cf. 16.2n.), but there had probably been five until then; cf. Wissowa 503 n.4. They were not in charge of most *sacra* until much later; cf. Ogilvie on Livy 1.20.4. On the sphere of responsibility of the *pontifex*, cf. *Leg.* 2.4.7 *de sacris ... de uotis, de feriis et de sepulcris, et si quid eius modi est.* **in monumentis:** not epigraphic monuments, but simply written records; cf. *Dom.* 86 *ut annales populi Romani et monumenta uetustatis loquuntur*, *Sest.* 102 and Frier 115. Numa's legislation is referred to at 5.3 as extant, and as the collection of regal laws known as the *ius Papirianum* may not have been published when C. wrote *Rep.* (cf. Schulz 89) there may have been an independent collection of Numa's laws; cf. Gabba (1967) 161–2. The few fragments ascribed to Numa's religious laws are collected in *FIRA* I 9–14. **ardentes:** cf. 25.2 *bellicis studiis ... incensos.* **flamines Salios uirginesque Vestales:** the three major flaminates (Dialis, Martialis, Quirinalis) are the earliest major priesthoods of Roman religion, responsible for important sacrifices. Cf. Livy 1.20.1 with Ogilvie *ad loc.* and Wissowa 504ff. The Salii, dancing priests of Mars, performed rituals in connection with the campaigning season in March and October. The Vestals were responsible for maintaining the sacred fire in the *Atrium Vestae*; according to D. H. 2.67.1 and Plu. *Numa* 10.1, Numa appointed four of them; D. H. 3.67.2 records an increase to six by Tarquinius Priscus; there were six in historical times. Others (cf. D. H. 2.65) ascribed the appointment of the Vestals to Romulus. Of these three groups, only the Vestals retained any major significance in the late Republic; it was the augurs and *pontifices* who had both religious and political significance.

27.1 diligentiam difficilem: the same principle of complex but inexpensive religion is advanced by C. at *Leg.* 2.25 *quod autem pietatem adhiberi, opes amoueri iubet* [sc. *lex*], *significat probitatem gratam esse deo, sumptum esse removendum.* The frugality of Numa's religious apparatus is mentioned as early as Cassius Hemina (Pliny, *NH* 32.20 = fr. 13 *HRR*), and was something of a commonplace; cf. Persius 2.59–60. The simplicity of religion is ascribed to Romulus by D. H. 2.23.4–5.

27.2 mercatus: the establishment of market-days, *nundinae*, the origin of which was ascribed by others to Romulus or Servius Tullius; cf. Macrob. *Sat.* 1.16.32–4. **ludos ... celebritates:** according to Livy 1.19.7, Numa in his reform of the calendar introduced the concept of *dies fasti* and *nefasti*; presumably C.'s comment is also related to the calendar. *celebritates* in the pl. only here in C., and used as equivalent to *celebrationes.*

27.3 C.'s concluding summary echoes his initial statement of Numa's accomplishments: *bellicis studiis* 25.2 ~ *studiis bellandi* 27.3; *esse reuocandos* 25.2 ~ *reuocauit* 27.3. Similarly *in pace concordiaque* in the following sentence echoes *amorem ... otii et pacis* in 26.1.

27.4 sic ille ... excessit e uita: according to Livy 1.21.6 and D. H. 1.75.2, 2.76.5, he ruled for 43 years. C.'s reference to Polybius' chronology is the only explicit indication of his use of Polybius as a source; see Introduction, pp. 22–4. The complex problems of early Roman chronology are well explained by Walbank on Plb. 6.11a.2. **nostrum:** Polybius' close attachment to Scipio is attested by the historian; cf. esp. 31.23–30. **duabus praeclarissimis ... rebus confirmatis:** parallel to the obituary for Romulus at 17 *haec egregia duo fundamenta rei publicae. praeclarus*, like *utilis*, *aptus*, and similar adjectives, is followed by *ad* + acc. to indicate the purpose or effect; cf. K–S I 315.

28–30: Numa and Pythagoras

The chronological digression at 2.18–20 is paralleled by the detailed discussion of the relative dates of Numa and Pythagoras. Both passages contribute to the recognition of early Rome's innate capacities and high level of culture, uninfluenced at this stage by Greek learning. The idea that Numa was a disciple of Pythagoras is old, possibly originating with Aristoxenus of Tarentum in the late fourth or early third century.

It is firmly rejected by C. on chronological grounds not only here, but also at *De orat.* 2.154 and *Tusc.* 4.2–3; it had also probably been rejected by Ennius (cf. Skutsch's introductory note to *Ann.* book 2), and was later refuted by Livy 1.18.1–3 and D. H. 2.59.1–2. Ovid manages to have it both ways in *Met.* 15. For discussions of some of the ramifications of the legend, see Gabba (1967) 155–63, Gruen (1990) 158–70. The topic may be appropriate to Scipio, as his natural family (the Aemilii) claimed descent from Mamercus the son of Pythagoras; cf. Festus 22.9 L., Plu. *Aem.* 4.

28.1 'uerene' inquit Manilius: a conversational interlude follows each section of Scipio's narrative: thus Laelius at 2.21, 33 (probably), and 37.

28.2 annalium publicorum: the *annales maximi*, the annual records kept by the pontifex maximus and apparently made public by P. Mucius Scaevola who became pontifex maximus in 130 (cf. 1.25.4, *De Orat.* 2.52). Manilius' remark suits the antiquarian and alludes to what may in 129 have been a very recent work of scholarship; but the traditional account and date of the *annales maximi* have been questioned by Frier, and Rawson (1991) 1–15 demonstrated the uncertainty of their contents and the fact that they were not used by historians. It is not clear whether they simply omitted the connection between Numa and Pythagoras, or made no judgment about it; cf. Gabba (1967) 155–6.

28.5 nam quartum iam annum ... aduentum: according to C.'s (Polybian) chronology, Superbus' reign began in Ol. 62,1, 532/1 B.C.E., and Pythagoras arrived in Italy in Ol. 62,4, 529/8. Reconstruction of Polybius' regnal chronology (including a two-year interregnum after the death of Romulus) places Numa's death in 672, 144 years before Pythagoras' arrival.

29.1 qui ... annales: Polybius; cf. 2.27.4.

29.2 quantus ... error: the double exclamation and the final position of *error* are emphatic. **transmarinis:** cf. *De orat.* 3.135 *quid enim M. Catoni praeter hanc politissimam doctrinam transmarinam atque aduenticiam defuit?* For *genuinus* 'natural, innate', cf. *OLD* s.v. 1. In contrast to the earlier annalists (and to D. H. later), C. is careful to distinguish a period of native Roman invention, independent of but comparable to Greek institutions (cf. 15.1 on Lycurgus) from later periods in which Greek influence is explicit and manifest; cf. 34.1.

30 progredientem: for the repeated emphasis on gradual growth and progress, cf. §§2–3, 21.1. **in optimum statum:** cf. 1.34.2. **naturali quodam itinere et cursu:** the use of *quodam* shows that C. uses *naturalis* metaphorically. The biological analogy (teleological development toward the *optimus status*, the mixed constitution) is not the same as in Polybius, who uses φύσις to refer either to the cycle of constitutions (as perhaps at 45.1) or to the natural progress of growth and decay of all governments; cf. Walbank on 6.4.7–9.14. C.'s concept of the 'natural' path of progress, moreover, is based not on inevitable developments, but on the rational contributions of particular kings and statesmen to the creation of the Roman constitution; on the relationship between *ratio* and *natura*, cf. 57.1n. **multa intelleges ... exstitissent:** Roman adaptation and improvement of foreign customs and laws is a commonplace; cf. *Tusc.* 1.1 *meum semper iudicium fuit omnia nostros aut inuenisse per se sapientius quam Graecos aut accepta ab illis fecisse meliora.* **meliora apud nos multo esse facta:** the hyperbaton of *meliora* is emphatic; so too the unnecessarily explicit *ibi ... unde huc translata essent atque ubi primum exstitissent* and the repetitions of *multa ... multo* and *intelleges ... intellegesque.* **non fortuito ... nec tamen aduersante fortuna:** the etymological word-play is deliberate; C.'s belief that neither good nor bad luck played an crucial part in Roman success is an implicit criticism of Polybius' emphasis on τύχη. *consilium* and *disciplina* are named as joint causes of Carthaginian success in fr. 1f Ziegler (quoted 1.44.5n.).

31–2: Tullus Hostilius

C.'s account of Tullus' reign is very brief, made more so by the loss of one leaf after 31. He omits as constitutionally unimportant the war with Alba, the most important event in Livy's and D. H.'s narratives of the reign, leaving only the construction of public buildings and the establishment of fetial law.

31.1 populus ... curiatim: for the procedure, cf. 25.2n.

31.2 fecitque ... constituitque: for the paratactic style, cf. 16.2n. The *comitium* was located between the Forum and the Capitol, and meetings of the *comitia* were held there until 145 B.C.E. The Curia Hostilia (the Senate House) was within the limits of the *comitium*; it was restored by Sulla, and burned down during the funeral of Clodius in

52; cf. Ogilvie on Livy 1.30.2. The two verbs and their objects are in chiastic order: Tullus built the Curia and established the boundaries (*saepsit*) of the *comitium*. **constituitque ... iudicaretur:** *ius fetiale* concerned the laws of war and peace (cf. Watson); it was supervised by the college of 20 *fetiales*. Livy portrays a *fetialis* making a treaty with Alba under Tullus (1.24.4), but ascribes the *ius fetiale* for declaring war to Ancus (1.32.5; cf. Ogilvie *ad locc.*); D. H. 2.72 connects the *fetiales* with Numa. **quod per se ... sanxit:** the rules of war and peace, just in themselves, were given additional protection by the sanctity of religious ritual. **denuntiatum indictumque:** cf. 3.35 *nullum bellum iustum habetur nisi denuntiatum, nisi indictum, nisi de repetitis rebus. denuntiatio* was a formal demand for redress against an aggressor, *indictio* was the ritual declaration of war: cf. Livy 1.32.5–14 with Ogilvie *ad loc.*

31.3 tribuenda quaedam esse populo: another element of the mixed constitution under the monarchy; cf. 24–5 and 1.69.2 *placet ... esse quasdam res seruatas iudicio uoluntatique multitudinis.* **ne insignibus quidem regiis:** according to Macrob. *Sat.* 1.6.7, Tullus instituted the use of lictors, the *sella curulis*, and the *toga picta et praetexta*, after defeating the Etruscans (cf. Pliny, *NH* 9.136); Livy ascribes the lictors and other insignia to Romulus (1.8.2; cf. Ogilvie *ad loc.*).

31.4 Augustine's report (from C.) of Tullus' death by thunderbolt and of the fact that he was not deified (*CD* 3.15=§32) is omitted from this edition. Some reference to an increase in the number of *equites* may be lost in the lacuna of one leaf; cf. 36.3n.

33: Ancus Marcius

The lacuna after §31 conceals the start of one conversational interlude; another ends the section, which devotes only three sentences to Ancus: his accession, his deeds, and his death receive one each. The foundation of Ostia was the only important event associated with his reign.

33.1 For the rapid development of Rome, cf. 21.1; on the *optimus status* see 1.34.2 and 2.30.

33.2 Numae Pompili nepos: the first hereditary element mentioned by C.; cf. Livy 1.32.1, Plu. *Numa* 21.3. D. H. 3.35.2–4 reports a version according to which Ancus' regal descent led him to assassinate Tullus. **a populo:** C. omits (apparently by inadvertence) the *auctoritas patrum* (reported by Livy 1.32.1).

33.3 asciuit eos in ciuitatem: cf. Livy 1.33.1, D. H. 3.37.4; for the phrase cf. 13. **Aventinum et Caelium montem:** according to Livy 1.30.1 and D. H. 3.31.3, the Caelian was added by Tullus and the Albans settled there, but various sources ascribe its addition to every king except Numa and Tarquinius Superbus; cf. Richardson 63. Livy 1.33.2 and D. H. 3.43 agree with C. on Ancus' settlement of the Aventine, but it remained outside the *pomerium* and was the site of the plebeian secessions of the fifth century; cf. 58.1, 63.2, and Ogilvie on Livy 3.31.1. **quosque agros ceperat diuisit:** presumably *uiritim* distribution; cf. 26.1n. **siluas maritimas:** the appropriation of the coastal forest (*silva Maesia*) also in Livy 1.33.9. **ad ostium Tiberis urbem condidit:** the foundation of Ostia is universally attributed to Ancus; cf. Livy 1.33.9 with Ogilvie *ad loc.*, D. H. 3.44.4.

33.5 obscura: the metaphor is taken up by *illustrata* in the next sentence. **ignoramus patrem:** Julius Caesar (cf. Suet. *Julius* 6) boasted descent from Ancus through the noble plebeian family of the Marcii Reges; Laelius' comment may indicate aristocratic condescension.

34–6: Tarquinius Priscus

C.'s account contains the traditional stories about the origin, arrival in Rome, and reign of Tarquinius (known as Priscus 'the elder' to distinguish him from Tarquinius Superbus, his son or grandson; cf. Ogilvie on Livy 1.34.10), as usual concentrating on the establishment of Roman institutions and eschewing the fabulous and miraculous. C. places far greater emphasis than other accounts on Priscus as the source of Greek culture and learning, and none at all on the importance of Etruscan domination of Rome. That is presumably less the result of ignorance or bias than of his concentration on comparisons between Rome and Greece, and particularly between Roman practice and Greek theory, throughout book 2. For a discussion of the evidence about Priscus, see Ogilvie on Livy 1.34, 35–8.

34.1 insitiua quadam disciplina: Saturninus at *Sest.* 101 is termed an *insitiuus Gracchus*; here the point is that Greek learning is grafted on to the sturdy native stock of Roman intelligence. *insitiua* contrasts with *serere* used at §5.1 of natural growth.

34.2 non tenuis quidam ... riuulus 'not some small trickle'. C.

contrasts *tenuis* with *abundantissimus*, *riuulus* with *amnis*. The *disciplinae* and *artes* are not those of high culture but of social organization; so at 36.2 the equestrian organization at Corinth is compared to Priscus' attempted reforms, and at 42–3 there is a final extended comparison between Greek and Roman political organization.

34.3 Demaratum Corinthium: that L. Tarquinius Priscus was the son of the Corinthian Demaratus is recorded as early as Polybius (6.11a.7), and was presumably in Fabius Pictor. Demaratus is sometimes said to have been one of the Bacchiad aristocracy of Corinth, who were overthrown by Cypselus, who ruled for some thirty years beginning in the 650s (D. H. 3.46.3–4, Strabo 5.2.2). C. characterizes him as an aristocrat, unable to endure a tyranny. **cum magna pecunia:** Livy 1.34.2 and Polybius 6.11a.7 emphasize the wealth of the son rather than the father; Tarquin's own wealth may have appeared in the lacuna following 34.5.

34.4 defugit: more decisive than *fugisse* above (*TLL* v 1.375.60 incorrectly takes it as equivalent to *fugit*); for emphatic *de-* cf. e.g. *deuicit* 36.4. **ascitus est ciuis:** Livy 1.34.1, 5 emphasizes the Etruscans' rejection of the family as foreigners as the cause of Priscus' departure for Rome; that does not seem to be an element in C.'s account. The family of the Tarquins is connected to the city of Tarquinii by etymology only; it is more probable that they came from Caere (cf. Ogilvie on Livy 1.60.2). **domicilium et sedes:** C. combines the sing. *domicilium* and pl. *sedes* (itself uncommon in C.) elsewhere only at *Verr.* 2.6.

34.5 The two sons are Lucumo (later L. Tarquinius) and Arruns. It is unclear how much family history was given by C. in the missing leaf: nowhere in the extant text do the names of Lucumo, Arruns, his posthumous son Egerius, or Lucumo's wife Tanaquil appear. The emphasis throughout is on Greek learning and education pertaining to the family's Corinthian origins. For *ad Graecorum disciplinam eru* ... (the precise form is uncertain) cf. 37.5 *ad exquisitissimam consuetudinem Graecorum erudiit*.

35.1 facile in ciuitatem receptus esset: sc. Lucumo; the circumstances of his arrival in Rome are lost in the preceding lacuna. C. presumably omitted the omen of the eagle snatching his cap on the Janiculum (Livy 1.34.8, D. H. 3.47.3–4): *Leg.* 1.4 shows that C. thought the story foolish. His account here is close to that of Polybius

6.11a.7. **propter humanitatem atque doctrinam:** cf. 34 for the emphasis on Greek learning as well as Greek descent. D. H. 3.48.1–3 makes his wealth the important factor. **usque eo ut:** rare in C. after his exile (6 of 24 exx.; there are also 5 exx. in Caelius' letters in *Fam.* 8, none in the rest of *Fam.*): C. may be translating Polybius 6.11a.7 'his intimacy became so close that he lived with Marcius, and assisted him in managing his kingdom' (Shuckburgh).

35.2 For Tarquinius' affability and generosity, cf. Livy 1.34.11 and D. H. 3.48.4. Tarquinius here exhibits the characteristics of a good *patronus*, who distributes financial and legal support to his clients (in this case the citizen body); *comitas* is also ascribed to Servius Tullius at 38.1.

35.3 rex est creatus L. Tarquinius 'he was elected king under the name of L. Tarquinius': *L. Tarquinius* is predicative. The explanatory clause following shows that C. had previously given his name as Lucumo, which is Etruscan rather than Greek; but Osann's emendation of *Graeco* to *Etrusco* should not be accepted, nor should this be seen as an error on C.'s part. His concern, as noted above, is to emphasize Greek influence and minimize Etruscan.

35.4 principio ... minorum: Livy 1.35.6 records the enrolment of the *gentes minores* in the Senate as Priscus' first act, in order to strengthen his own support; in C. no such motive is suggested. Tacitus makes the *gentes minores* the creation of the consul Brutus (*Ann.* 11.25). According to Livy, Romulus had 100, Tullus added more (presumably 100), and Priscus a final 100 (cf. Ogilvie on 1.35.6); D. H. 3.67.1 speaks of Priscus' increasing the number from 200 to 300. C. here speaks of 'doubling', not of adding 100, and his account of Tullus mentions no expansion of the Senate; if the traditional number of 300 at the end of the monarchy is to be retained, then Romulus must have appointed 150 senators – which is in fact a figure given as possible by D. H. 2.47.2 (cf. 14n.). **quos priores sententiam rogabat:** the order of calling the Senate may be C.'s inference from the titles *maiores* and *minores*. No such distinction existed in historical times; cf. *CAH*[2] VII 2.101–2.

36.1–3 C.'s report of Priscus' organization of the *equites* is cursory and somewhat confusing. The custom *qui usque adhuc est retentus* must refer to the system of financing the *equites equo publico* through a tax on widows and orphans on the model of the Corinthians; the refusal of

Attus Navius to permit the use of new names led to the doubling of the *equites* by keeping the original tribal names but adding *primores* and *posteriores* to them (see nn. below). As the text stands, however, the reference to present custom and the explanation of it through the analogy of the Corinthians are separated by the reference to Attus Navius, while the Corinthian analogy in turn separates Navius from the doubling of the numbers of *equites*. Bréguet (following Francken) suggests that *atque etiam ... diligentes* (36.2) be transposed to follow *retentus* (36.1) as a parenthetical interjection. Livy 1.36.2 places the reform of the *equites* after the Sabine War and because of it.

36.1 Titiensium ... nomina: the names of the three Romulean tribes, alluded to at 14, are reported by Livy 1.13.8, 36.2. C. omits the miraculous story of the augur Attus Navius (cf. Livy 1.36.3–6, D. H. 3.71; also *Div.* 1.31–3): Tarquin's testing of his augural ability required him to cut through a whetstone with a razor, which he did.

36.2 The tax on widows and orphans to support the cavalry is not otherwise attested for Corinth; C. here clearly wishes to connect Priscus' reforms with his ancestry. Livy 1.43.9 ascribes this method of financing to Ser. Tullius, and has the tax be on widows only. **publicis ... diligentes:** *TLL* s.v. *diligens* (v 1182.80) takes the gerundives *assignandis et alendis* as dat. ('attentive to the assignment ...'); *OLD* s.v. as abl. ('careful in assigning ...'). At 40.1 *diligens* is followed by the abl., which is more likely here. *tributis* is an abl. of means.

36.3 The two groups of *equites* were formally named *primores* and *posteriores*. The total number in Priscus' organization is disputed: P reads *MACCC*, a minor error for the text given here, *M ac CC* – that is, 1,200. The MSS in the parallel passage of Livy (1.36.7) read either *mille et DCCC* or *mille et CCC*; Ogilvie follows Glareanus in emending to *mille et CC*. Given the distinction between the *equites* and the *sex suffragia* (cf. 39.2n.), it is unlikely that 1,800 is the correct figure here; in any case, although the expansion of the *equites* from the 300 of Romulus to 600 by Tullus Hostilius (Livy 1.30.3) may have been lost in the lacuna after 31, no source attests an enlargement to 900 before Priscus.

36.4 The war with the Aequi is not mentioned by other sources, although the war with the Sabines is (Livy 1.36–7, D. H. 3.55–6, 63–6), after which Priscus is said (Livy 1.38.7, D. H. 3.69.1) to have vowed the Capitoline temple of Jupiter Optimus Maximus. The *ludi* *magni* or *Romani* in honour of Jupiter were traditionally connected to the dedication of this temple, the anniversary of which was celebrated on 13 September; the *ludi*, in the late Republic, took place during the preceding ten days. For a full account, cf. Scullard 183–6. On the completion of the temple by Superbus cf. 44.2. *postea* is Vaucher's necessary emendation for *postquam* in P.

36.5 duodequadraginta ... annos: so also Livy 1.40.1, D. H. 4.1.1.

37–43: Servius Tullius

The loss of leaves of P after chapters 38, 40 (two), and 43 renders C.'s account hard to follow. The first section (37–8) describes Servius' accession; the second (39–40) describes his constitution; the last (42–3) is a general discussion of mixed constitutions, which may have preceded or followed the lost account of his murder and the accession of Tarquinius Superbus. The fragment printed as 41 by modern editors (Nonius 342.39 M.) has been more plausibly located after 2.69 by Büchner (*contra* Heck 191–2). As with the other kings, C. concentrates purely on institutional and constitutional developments, of which the creation of the *comitia centuriata* (39–40) was the most important. Servius' accession and concealment of the death of Priscus, together with his courting of popular approval, marked him in the tradition as taking a large step toward tyranny and personal rule. C.'s account of his reign combines disapproval of his populist tendencies with admiration for the timocratic constitution which he established; for various traditions, see Ogilvie on Livy 1.39–48 and 46–8.

37.1 illud Catonis: cf. §2.1. *nostrae* is Ziegler's plausible addition. Again, a conversational exchange marks the transition from one reign to the next. **in singulos reges** 'with each successive king'; comparable to *in dies* 'from day to day', *OLD* s.v. *in* 5.

37.3 primus iniussu populi: cf. 25.2n. **ex serua Tarquiniensi natum:** Servius' servile origin is an etymological reconstruction from his name. According to Livy 1.39.5, his mother was from Corniculum; for other versions, cf. *RE* s.v. Ocrisia. For his paternity, cf. Ogilvie on Livy 1.39.5.

37.4 non latuit scintilla ingenii: C. rationalizes the prodigy of a halo of fire, as reported in Livy 1.39.1–2; cf. also *Fin.* 5.43 *non sine causa* *eas ... in pueris uirtutum quasi scintillas uidemus, e quibus accendi philosophi ratio debet.* The critical transformation of a legend corresponds both to C.'s general philosophical position and to his historical goals in *Rep.*; for the development of the legend itself, cf. Ogilvie on Livy 1.39.5.

37.5 qui admodum ... liberos 'because his children were quite small at the time'; causal. **ad exquisitissimam consuetudinem Graecorum:** cf. *Brut.* 104 (Gracchus) *semper habuit exquisitos e Graecia magistros* (although there *exquisitos* may be literal 'fetched'); *exquisitus* (cf. 1.3.3) as an adj. appears almost exclusively in C.'s philosophical and rhetorical writings. With Tarquinius Priscus, and even more with Servius, native Roman talent begins to be improved and refined by contact with Greece (cf. 34.2); cf. 42–3 for the explicit comparison of Servius' constitution with those of Carthage and Sparta.

38.1 The circumstances of Servius' rise to power are told in a single, long sentence. The first *cum*-clause (*interisset ... coepisset*) contains an explanatory clause (*quod ... dixisset ... liberauisset ... probauisset*), which in turn contains another circumstantial *cum*-clause (*cum ... diceretur*); the main clause contains a sequence of three verbs culminating in the passage of the formal *lex curiata* making Servius king. **insidiis Anci filiorum:** the story of the plot and its aftermath is told dramatically with circumstantial details derived from Greek history by Livy 1.40–1 (cf. also D. H. 3.72–3); C. eschews the drama and concentrates only on the constitutionally significant fact of Servius' manipulation of legal forms. **non iussu ... ciuium:** C.'s brief account emphasizes the *popularis* elements in Servius: where Livy 1.41.6 has Servius appear with a guard, *primus iniussu populi, uoluntate patrum regnauit* (that is, as the ruler favoured by the Senate), C. emphasizes his courting of the people, and that he ignored the Senate in organizing his own election: *non commisit se patribus.* Both Livy and D. H. place far more emphasis on Servius' conflict with the Senate and courting of the people; Livy (1.46.1) postpones the formal election of Servius to the end of his reign. **obaeratosque pecunia sua liberauisset:** an obvious anachronism, both because coinage did not yet exist and because the problem of debt was traditionally supposed to arise after the fall of the monarchy. Livy 1.46.1 refers to Servius' wooing of the *plebs* through the redistribution of land rather than donations of money – 'a Gracchan touch' (Ogilvie *ad loc.*); D. H. 4.10.1–3 has both. Both *comitas* and largesse are ascribed also to Priscus at 35.2. **iussusque regnare:**

as opposed to his initial assumption of power *iniussu populi*. **legem ... curiatam:** cf. 25.2n.

38.2 Livy 1.42.2–3 and D. H. 4.27 mention a war against Veii and the Etruscans; nothing in C. explains the particular *iniuriae* here. The sentence is incomplete, and one leaf is lost; Mai suggested that the missing passage included a reference to land distribution as well as the start of the account of Servius' constitution.

39–40 The Servian Constitution. The text resumes in the middle of a discussion of Servius' creation of the centuriate assembly. C.'s arithmetic on the distribution of the classes differs substantially from our two fuller (but later) versions, Livy 1.43 and D. H. 4.16–18, and has other problems arising from the fragmentary nature of the text and from C.'s concentration on the timocratic structure of the assembly and its place in the mixed constitution (cf. Nicholls). He omits Servius' replacement of the three kinship tribes of the Romulean state by geographically based divisions (cf. D. H. 4.14); he says virtually nothing about the military purpose of the organization. All three extant accounts of the Servian reforms reflect later revisions of whatever actually happened in the sixth century, when there was only one *classis* which served as the basis of a single hoplite legion. Ogilvie's commentary on Livy 1.43 provides a good introduction to the details of the organization; for historical reconstruction of the constitutional and military developments connected with Servius, cf. Momigliano (1966) 590–8 and *CAH*^{2} VII 2.103–4, 163–5.

39.1 duodeuiginti censu maximo: the eighteen centuries of the *equites*; see 39.2n. on *equitum centuriae*. **equitum magno numero** 'a large number (consisting) of the *equites*': the gen. is defining, not partitive. **in quinque classes:** according to Livy and D. H. there were 80 centuries in the first class, 20 each in the second, third, and fourth, and 30 in the fifth, with successively lower property qualifications and lighter weapons; there were, additionally, centuries of *proletarii* and of *fabri*, musicians, and attendants (on which see 39.2n.). Voting was by centuries rather than by individuals; since there were considerably more members of each century in the lower classes, elections were heavily weighted in favour of the wealthy. The extant text provides a precise figure only for the centuries of *equites*, but C. clearly recognizes 193 centuries, of whom 70 make up the first class. This figure is anachronistic: it represents a class made up of one century apiece of *seniores* and *iuniores* from each of the 35 tribes, the last of which was created only in 241 B.C.E. The understanding of C.'s error depends in large part on the text and interpretation of 39.2; see below. **seniores:** the distinction between *iuniores* (men of military age) and *seniores* was traditionally placed at the age of 46; cf. *Sen.* 60, Plb. 6.19.2, Tubero fr. 4 *HRR* (=Gellius 10.28.1). **ne plurimum ualeant plurimi:** the point is made repeatedly in this paragraph, e.g. 39.2 *nec ualeret nimis*, 40.3. The use of the pres. rather than the impf. subj. here following the pf. *curauit* is the result of the intervening *tenendum est*; see Lebreton 261.

39.2 nunc rationem ... uniuersa: the text of the second hand; the first hand reads: *nunc rationem uidetis esse talem ut equitum certamine cum et suffragiis et prima classis addita centuria quae ad summum usum urbis fabris tignariis est data VIIII centurias – tot enim relicuae sunt – octo solae ...* Sumner's defence of this text (1960) was decisively refuted by Taylor and Staveley. In order to defend C.'s historical accuracy (cf. 39.1n.), it has been suggested that *nunc* is temporal, and that the remainder of the section refers to the constitution in force in 129 rather than the Servian constitution itself. The construction of the sentence, however, makes that impossible, and *nunc* must be adversative: 'If this division were unknown to you, I would explain it; as it is (*nunc*), you see that its logic is such that ...'; see Sumner (1964) 126. But if *nunc* is logical rather than temporal, then C.'s account is either a mistake (so Klebs) or a deliberate falsification (so Mommsen). Livy's comment (1.43.12) on the subsequent changes in the organization and its arithmetic suggests that in his day the history was problematic; see Ogilvie *ad loc.* In constitutional terms, moreover, C.'s account of the Servian reform is as anachronistic as his account of Romulus: the political use of the centuriate assembly was certainly not important before the beginning of the Republic. **equitum centuriae cum sex suffragiis:** according to Festus 452.32 L., the *sex suffragia* ('six votes') were the centuries of *equites* added by Servius to the 1,200 of Tarquinius Priscus; Livy 1.43.8–9, however, is more likely to be right that the *sex suffragia* (which he calls *centuriae*) were those of Priscus and the twelve centuries those added by Servius. See also Ogilvie *ad loc.* and Momigliano (1969) 379–82. **fabris tignariis:** Livy 1.43.3 states that there were two centuries of *fabri* attached to the first class; D. H. 4.17 and 7.57 assigns two to the second class; and it may be the case that C.'s use of the epithet *tignarii* was intended to distinguish them from *fabri aerarii* (ὁπλοποιοί D. H. 4.17, χαλκοτύποι D. H. 7.59). At *Or.* 156, however, C. uses the phrase *centuriam fabrum* from the *censoriae tabulae* to illustrate the archaic gen. pl. ending; this suggests that he knew only a single century. **LXXXVIIII centurias habeat:** the 89 include 18 centuries of *equites*, one of *fabri*, and therefore 70 in the first class. Eight additional centuries are needed to make a majority (97) of the 193 centuries (the same total as given by D. H. 4.18.3). **reliquaque multo maior multitudo:** the number of voters, not the number of centuries. Roman assemblies stopped voting as soon as a majority of the centuries was attained; *suffragiis* here stands for *iure suffragii* (used in 40.3), as at *Agr.* 2.17 and Livy 1.43.10 (cited below); cf. Staveley 303, Nicholls 105. The principal difficulty of this sentence is caused by the change of moods and tenses from *confecta est* to *excluderetur*, leading Skutsch (1959) 140 to add *effecit ut* after *centuriarum*. The parallel sentence in Livy 1.43.10 *sed gradus facti, ut neque exclusus quisquam suffragio uideretur et uis omnis penes primores ciuitatis esse*, suggests that the insertion of *ut* alone will suffice.

40.1 assiduos ... ab aere dando: *assiduus* and *proletarius* are used in the same meanings in fr. 1.4 of the Twelve Tables (cf. Wieacker 304–5) and Varro, *De uita populi Romani* fr. 9 Riposati. The reading of P was wrongly emended by Osann to *ab asse dando* (so also Ziegler, followed by Maltby s.v.): the etymology is that of Aelius Stilo: *is est enim assiduus, ut ait L. Aelius, appellatus ab aere dando* (C. *Topica* 10; the same etymology in Quintil. 5.10.55). For an etymology of *locuples* cf. 16.2. **plus mille quingentos aeris** 'more than 1,500 bronze asses'; the same figure in Gellius 16.10.10; Livy 1.43.7 gives 11,000; D. H. 4.17.2 12,500; Polybius 6.19.2 4,000. Gellius also records a division between *proletarii* and a still lower class of *capite censi* with a division at 375 *asses*. The same origin for the name *proletarii* is recorded in Gellius and elsewhere; cf. Maltby s.v. For the construction of *plus*, cf. 1.58.2n.

40.2 illarum ... centuriarum: this must refer to the 96 centuries of 39.2; there is some peculiarity in that the 96 do not themselves constitute a class or group of classes, but only the residue after eight in the second class have voted (cf. Nicholls 105).

40.4 accensis uelatis ... proletariis: this list must comprise the extra centuries presumably grouped with or below the fifth class.

Although the distribution of the centuries below the *equites*, first class, and *fabri* is uncertain, it is likely that – as in all the other versions – the number of centuries in classes 2–5 was divisible by 10 (i.e. 100 of the 104); this leaves four centuries for the *proletarii* and supernumerary centuries of unarmed attendants (*accensi uelati*; cf. Ogilvie on Livy 1.43.7) and musicians. Hence Mai was probably correct in retaining both the reading of the first hand, *liticinibus*, and the correction of the second, *cornicinibus*, corresponding to the two centuries of *cornicines tubicinesque* in Livy and the σαλπισταί τε καὶ βυκανισταί of D. H. 4.17.3–4 (which are attached to the fourth, rather than the fifth class). *liticen* is extremely rare; Cato fr. 223 *ORF* is the only occurrence before C.

41 Omitted here; see above on 37–43.

42–3 Comparative Constitutions. Two leaves are lost after 40, in which someone must have asked about the relationship between the Servian constitution and the ideal mixed constitution. Scipio's answer serves to clarify one of the major puzzles of book 1, Scipio's preference for monarchy among the simple constitutions and his absolute preference for a mixed constitution. Here it is demonstrated that a monarchy can never be a truly mixed (*temperata*) constitution because a king predominates in any constitution of which he has a part. Much of the language echoes the discussion in book 1; see individual notes below. It is unclear whether the murder of Servius Tullius and the accession of Tarquinius Superbus were described in this lacuna, or in that following 2.43.

42.1 *<quinque et> sexaginta annis antiquior: the subject of the sentence is Carthage, founded in 815/14, 39 years before the first Olympic games of 776, and thus 65 years before Rome (751/0 on the chronology followed by C.); the same figure appears in Velleius 1.6, while Timaeus (D. H. 1.74.1) gave a date one year later. Comparison between Rome and Carthage is evident also in fr. 1f Ziegler *nec tantum Carthago habuisset opum sescentos fere annos sine consiliis et disciplina*; it is employed by C. not merely because of Rome's traditional antagonism and the fact that Scipio was the destroyer of Carthage in 146, but because Carthage and Lycurgan Sparta (and Crete) were traditional examples of successful mixed constitutions; cf. Arist. *Pol.* 2.9–20, and particularly Plb. 6.43–56. Cf. also Cato, fr. 80 *HRR* (Serv. *Aen.* 4.682) *de tribus partibus politiae, populi, optimatium, regiae potestatis, ordinatam fuisse*

Karthaginem. **antiquissimus ille Lycurgus:** the lawgiver of 884 B.C.E.; on the chronology cf. 18.3n. For the need to share power recognized by both Romulus and Lycurgus, cf. 15.1.

42.2 aequabilitas: a characteristic of mixed constitutions, cf. 1.69.3; for the meaning of the term, 1.53.1–2. The phrase *triplex rerum publicarum genus* may reflect Dicaearchus' title *Tripolitikos.*

42.3 sed quod proprium est ... subtilius: P (followed by Ziegler and most editors) reads *proprium sit,* but the indic. is clearly more appropriate in a statement of fact; for the confusion of *est* and *sit* in the manuscripts of C., cf. Madvig on *Fin.* 3.58, Pease on *N.D.* 1.48. It would also be possible to emend *quod* to *quid* and take it as an indirect question in apposition to *id.* For *persequor* 'investigate thoroughly', cf. *De Orat.* 1.98, *Div.* 1.48.

42.4 ita mixta ... nullo fuerint modo: the terminology of book 1 (e.g. *aequatum et temperatum* 1.69.1) is refined to distinguish between constitutions in which the three simple forms all coexist – such as Sparta and Carthage – and the Roman constitution, in which the three simple forms are compounded into something different in kind from any of them. The statement is paradoxical, and is explained in the succeeding section: a constitution in which there is a monarchy (rather than a representation of monarchy through magistrates with *imperium*) is of necessity itself a monarchy, even though elements of other constitutional forms are present. Cf. Arist. *Pol.* 5.4 on states that are balanced but not mixed; Walbank on Plb. 6.10.7.

43.1 Each of the two concessive clauses describing the non-monarchic elements of the constitutions (*quamuis ... senatus, ut sit ... ius*) is followed by parenthetical examples drawn from the earlier account of the monarchic constitution (*ut tum fuit ... Lycurgi legibus, ut fuit apud nostros reges*); cf. the comparison of Romulus' institutions to Lycurgus' at 2.15.1.

43.2 For the ease with which monarchy is corrupted into tyranny, cf. 1.64.5, 65.2, 2.47–50; for the superiority of monarchy over the other simple constitutions, cf. 1.54.2–3, 61.6.

43.3 quoad statum suum retineat: cf. 1.44.1 *suum statum tenentibus.*

43.4 The use of *autem* and the repetition of *unius* show that this sentence describes drawbacks to monarchy: it is precarious, in that one person's power and wisdom are responsible for the well-being of all. For the preservation of *otium*, cf. the aristocratic speech at 1.52.5.

43.5 On the absence of *libertas* under monarchy, cf. 1.43.1, 47, 50.3, 55.2.

44–6: Tarquinius Superbus

The one leaf lost following 43 can not have included a full account of the succession of Tarquinius, but C. in any case omits dramatic episodes such as the murder of Servius Tullius. The actions of Superbus are told very briefly, and although he is characterized as *iniustus dominus* his transformation from king to tyrant is not described until 45. The reason for this brevity is that the actions of Superbus as king are of little constitutional importance, while his tyranny and expulsion are, in that they involve two stages in the cycle of constitutions, from monarchy to tyranny and from tyranny to aristocracy. Far more space is given to the theoretical excursus which follows the expulsion of Superbus (47–52) than to his reign.

Nonius 526.10 M. (*itaque illa praeclara constitutio Romuli cum ducentos annos et XX fere firma mansisset*), which is given by Ziegler at 2.53, probably belongs here (so Grilli); the MS *XX* rather than Mai's conjecture *XXXX* should be accepted. Placed here, and not emended, the period of 220 years refers to the time from the founding of Rome to the degeneration of monarchy into tyranny at the accession of Superbus; placed at 2.53 and emended, it refers to the entire length of the monarchy. That, however, would repeat what is said at 52.3.

44.1 illi ... comitata est: *comitor* with dat. rather than acc. elsewhere in C. only at *Tusc.* 5.68, 100, in the second of which he is translating a Greek construction; cf. *OLD* s.v. 7.

44.2 nam et omne ... deduxit: a paratactic narrative, as with other kings; cf. 16.2n. For the subjugation of the Latins (by a trick in other accounts), cf. Livy 1.50–2, D. H. 4.45–9. **Suessam ... cepit:** for the capture of Suessa Pometia (a Volscian city near the Pomptine marshes), cf. Livy 1.53.2, D. H. 4.50. A similar absolute use of *refertus* is found at *De orat.* 1.161, *Mur.* 20. **uotum patris:** cf. 36.5; for the construction and early history of the temple, cf. Richardson 221–2. The use of the booty from Suessa also in Livy 1.53.3, 55.8;

D. H. 4.59.1. **colonias deduxit:** identified by Livy 1.56.3 and D. H. 4.63.1 as Signia and Circeii. **institutis eorum a quibus ortus erat:** the connection between the Greek origin of the Tarquins and the embassy to Delphi is not made by Livy and D. H., but is C.'s logical conclusion from the facts he has given: before the arrival of Priscus, Rome was culturally independent of the Greeks, and hence an explanation of the Delphic embassy is necessary. For C., the purpose of the embassy is to make an offering; in Livy 1.56.3 it concerns an omen, and in D. H. 4.69.2 it concerns a plague. The story of the embassy is probably false, and C. omits the participation of Brutus and his correct interpretation of the prophecy. **quasi libamenta:** properly of sacrificial offerings, as at *Leg.* 2.29; cf. also Varro, *L.* 6.54 *ex mercibus libamenta porrecta sunt Herculi.*

45.1 Hic ille iam uertetur orbis 'this is the point at which the cycle will turn': for the 'gnomic' future expressing general laws or prescriptions, cf. H–S 310. For the use of *orbis* and *circuitus*, cf. 1.45.1, where the variety of possible permutations is emphasized by the use of the pl. Here C. is referring specifically to the cycle of constitutions as described by Polybius; the metaphor is used with less precise application at *Att.* 2.9.1, 21.2 and *Planc.* 93. For *naturalis*, cf. *Div.* 2.6 *id enim ipsum a Platone philosophiaque didiceram, naturales esse quasdam conuersiones rerum publicarum, ut eae tum a principibus tenerentur tum a populis aliquando a singulis*; at 30 and 57.1 it refers to progress toward the best constitution rather than to the cycle of constitutions.

45.2 caput ciuilis prudentiae 'the fundamental element of public policy'; for the use of *caput*, cf. e.g. *Am.* 45, *De orat.* 2.337. For *ciuilis prudentia*, cf. *Part. or.* 76 *atque illa prudentia in suis rebus domestica, in publicis ciuilis appellari solet*; this quality of statesmanship is described also at 1.45.2. C. perhaps draws on Plb. 6.4.12 'For it is only by seeing distinctly how each of them [the constitutions] is produced that a distinct view can also be obtained of its growth, zenith, and decadence, and the time, circumstance, and place in which each of these may be expected to recur' (tr. Shuckburgh). **itinera flexusque rerum publicarum:** the various changes of constitution; cf. 1.64.6, 2.30. **inclinet:** the metaphor of the balance accords with C.'s non-deterministic approach to constitutional development.

45.3 Two causes are given (*primum ... deinde*) for Superbus' downfall: his fear of punishment for the murder of Servius led him to desire to be feared, and the *insolentia* arising from his victories and wealth led him to allow his own and his family's *insolentia* to go unchecked. **caede maculatus:** C. alludes to the literal spattering of Superbus with the blood of Servius (cf. Livy 1.48.7 of Tullia, *contaminata illa respersaque*); as at 37.4 *scintilla*, he hints at dramatic elements omitted from his own narrative. *maculatus* is also used in a metaphorical sense (cf. also *Har.* 27) of Superbus' moral contamination through the murder of Servius. For *integra mente* 'sane', cf. *Sen.* 72 with Powell's note. **uictoriis diuitiisque subnixus:** for Superbus' enrichment through booty cf. 44.2; for *subnixus* 'encouraged by', cf. *De orat.* 1.246, *OLD* s.v. 3. **exultabat insolentia:** cf. 1.62.3 *Tarquinio exacto mira quadam exultasse populum insolentia libertatis*: the same phrase of the excesses of both tyrant and people. **neque suos ... libidines:** cf. *Fin.* 3.75 *Tarquinius, qui nec se nec suos regere potuit*; both passages turn on the inability of the ruler to rule himself (*regere*; for another play on the word cf. 23).

46.1 Consonant with C.'s emphasis on public affairs, the story of the rape and suicide of Lucretia is told in a pair of *cum*-clauses, and the main clause contains praise of Brutus and a statement of the political effect of his actions (cf. the Sabine women and Verginia, 12, 63.2). More dramatic accounts of these events are found in Livy 1.57–60, D. H. 4.64–85. In early Latin, sentences with correlative *cum* ... *tum* normally have the indic. in both clauses, even when the *cum*-clause (as here) has a causal sense; in C., the subj. is only slightly less frequent than the indic. in causal *cum*-clauses: cf. Lebreton 338–46, K–S II 350–3. **itaque:** the inferential particle draws the conclusion from the two causes of Tarquin's downfall given in the previous sentence. **maior eius filius:** the eldest of three in D. H. 4.55.1, 63.1, 64.2; Livy 1.53.5 and Ovid, *Fasti* 2.691 make him the youngest of three. **uir ingenio et uirtute praestans:** the emphasis on Brutus' *ingenium* alludes to the legend (embodied in his cognomen) that he feigned stupidity; cf. Livy 1.56.7, D. H. 4.68. **depulit ... iugum:** for similar expressions cf. *Cat.* 3.17, *Phil.* 1.6.

46.2 According to Livy 1.59.7 (cf. D. H. 4.71.6) Brutus was *tribunus celerum*; Ogilvie *ad loc.* believes C.'s to be the original version and Livy's a modification in the interest of constitutionalism. C.'s account requires that he be a private citizen, and is motivated by the beliefs expressed in the preface to book 1, that public service is an obligation of all who are capable of undertaking it (cf. 1.7.3 *conseruandorum ciuium causa*, 1.12.4 *ciuitatis . . . conseruare iam conditas*; cf. also Pl. *Prt.* 327a 'no one should be a private citizen in regard to virtue, if the city is to exist'); the placement of *neminem* is emphatic. At *Tusc.* 4.51 C. cites with reference to Scipio Nasica's murder of Ti. Gracchus a Stoic maxim *numquam priuatum esse sapientem*; Nasica is used as an illustration of the responsibility of private citizens in the introduction to the *Somnium*; also *Cat.* 1.3, *Planc.* 88, *Brut.* 212, *Off.* 1.76. **totam rem publicam sustinuit:** for similar expressions, cf. *Flac.* 94, *Dom.* 142, *Sest.* 138.

46.3 quo auctore et principe: the use of *princeps*, in conjunction with the previous sentence, makes Brutus an example of the *rector* or *moderator* who is the subject of the entire work and is described more fully at 51.1. For the collocation, cf. *Fam.* 10.6.3 *deinde te senatui bonisque omnibus auctorem, principem, ducem praebeas*; cf. also *De orat.* 3.63. **et hac recenti . . . esse iussit:** the passage is marked by the polysyndeton of *et*. The sing. *exulem* (agreeing with the nearest noun) is regular; cf. Lebreton 11–13.

47–52: Excursus on tyranny

The long discussion of method after the fall of Superbus matches that after the reign of Romulus; C. links the two by verbal reminiscence (cf. 47.1n.) and by the renewed discussion of Plato's *Republic* (51–2). The excursus falls into three parts: 47–8 on the distinction between *rex* and *tyrannus*; 49–50 (interrupted by the loss of one leaf) on the tendency toward tyranny of any monarchical constitution; and 51–2 on the ideal good citizen who is the opposite of the tyrant, seen in the context of criticism of Plato's imaginary state. This last section is by far the most important and was originally much longer than the other two, but it is severely damaged by the loss of six leaves of P between 51 and 52, and by the further loss of an entire gathering of eight leaves after 52. There is an extensive analysis of this passage by Büchner (1962) 116–47.

47.1 Videtisne . . . uniusque uitio: C. echoes the opening of the excursus on method at 21.1 *uidetisne igitur unius uiri consilio.* For the damage caused by a single individual to the monarchic constitution, cf. 1.62.2, 64.5; 2.43.2. The same theme at 59.1 *propter unius libidinem*; the 'one bad apple' theme may be a defence of the upper classes against plebeian criticism. **ex bono in deterrimum:** monarchy is the best simple constitution, but it is not absolutely the best; the limits of its goodness are explained in the next sentence. Tyranny is described at 1.65.2 as *deterrimum genus et finitimum optimo.*

47.2 hic ... uocant: cf. 1.50.2 (democrats speaking) *cur enim regem appellem ... hominem ... populo oppresso dominantem, non tyrannum potius?* **qui consulit ... condicione uiuendi:** for the qualities of the good king, see 1.54.3, 64.3. For the distinction between king and tyrant, cf. esp. Pl. *Plt.* 301bc. **ut dixi**: referring back to the previous sentence and to 43.2–4, echoed in the final phrases of this sentence.

48.1 fit continuo tyrannus: C.'s point (further elaborated against Plato at 51.1) is that the change from monarchy to tyranny takes place in a single person; so also at 1.44.3, 65.2. **quo neque taetrius ... cogitari potest:** cf. *Verr.* 4.123 *quanto taetrior hic tyrannus Syracusanis fuerit, quam quisquam superiorum.* **morum tamen ... beluas:** so too of the tyrant at *Off.* 3.32 *ista in figura hominis feritas et immanitas beluae*; of the parricide at *S. Rosc.* 63 *esse aliquem humana specie et figura qui ... immanitate bestias uicerit.* The language is reminiscent of Plato's description of the tyrannical man, *R.* 9.574d-575a.

48.2 The phrases in the two halves of the relative clause correspond: *cum suis ciuibus* is answered by *iuris communionem*, *cum omni hominum genere* by *nullam humanitatis societatem.* The two concepts refer back to Scipio's definition of the state at 1.39, where *iuris consensu* is part of the definition of the *populus*, and the origin of society is ascribed to *naturalis quaedam hominum quasi congregatio.* On the separation of the tyrant from human society, cf. also *Am.* 52–3.

48.3 The appropriate place for a discussion of would-be tyrants under the Republic is in the lacuna after 2.63.2, but there may have been further discussion in book 6, in connection with Tiberius Gracchus and Scipio Nasica.

49.1 nam hoc nomen ... haberent: a parenthetical explanation of the difference between the Greek terminology used in 47.2, according to which the tyrant is an unjust, and the king a just, ruler, and Roman usage, in which *rex* is used for anyone with unlimited authority, king or not. *perpetua potestas* is applicable to either good or bad ruler; cf. 43.1.

49.2 On the agrarian proposals and subsequent condemnation of Sp. Cassius (cos. III 486), see 60.1. M. Manlius Capitolinus was executed for treason in 384 (cf. *MRR* I 102), Sp. Maelius was killed by the *magister equitum* Servilius Ahala in 439 (cf. 1.6.1n.). The three are standard examples of radical populism and/or treason, and are grouped by C. at *Dom.* 101, *Phil.* 2.87, 114. The final words of the sentence almost certainly introduce the example of Ti. Gracchus; for Scipio's opinion of him, cf. Introduction, pp. 7–8.

50.1–2 The reference is to the γέροντες, the senate supposedly created by Lycurgus at Sparta; the number is given by Pl. *Lg.* 3.692a, Aristotle (cited by Plu. *Lyc.* 5.7) and others. For Romulus' imitation of Lycurgus, cf. 15.1.

50.2 tamen excellit ... regium: cf. 43.1.

50.3 For Romulus' attention to the people, cf. 16.2; the connection between *potestas* and *libertas* also at 1.43.1. The language here is reminiscent of C.'s translation of Plato at 1.66.1 describing the excessive thirst for liberty of the radical democracy. The vivid imper. *imperti* marks a transition from one unsatisfactory solution to the problem of monarchy to another.

50.5 ut dixi antea: perhaps 43.1–2; otherwise lost.

51.1 C. contrasts for the first time the opposing figures of the tyrant and the good statesman, articulated by two jussive subjunctives (*prima sit haec forma ... sit huic oppositus*; for the construction cf. 1.32.1). As at §3.2 and 21–2, Scipio emphasizes the difference between Plato's imaginary state and the historically grounded constitutional theory developed here. The tyranny of Superbus is described as *prima*, because (as at 48–9) tyranny can – and, in the case of Cassius, Manlius, Maelius, the Decemvirs, and Ti. Gracchus, did (at least in C.'s opinion) – appear later as a corruption of non-monarchic governments as well: C.'s point is that the tyrant is not a different person from the preceding legitimate ruler, but the same person, corrupted. This applies not merely to Superbus, but to the Decemvirs (61–3) and to Ti. Gracchus (cf. 49.2n., 3.41); cf. Büchner (1962) 120–3. **quam auspicato Romulus condiderit:** cf. §5.1n. **†peripeateto† illo in sermone**: the corruption is hopeless, and the reading of the second hand of P is itself the subject of disagreement. *peripeateto* is the reading of the first hand; the correction has been variously read as *peripatetico* or *peri politeias*. Two emendations are attractive: Ziegler's *perpolito*, which has the virtue of supplying a necessary adjective (*illo in sermone* can not stand unmodified as a description of the *Republic*), and of using a form which C. favours (cf. 1.13.1; *De orat.* 1.58, 2.84 and elsewhere); and Poyser's *politico*, a rare word in Latin (elsewhere in C. only *De orat.* 3.109), but one which would supply the background to its only other classical occurrence, Caelius' description of *Rep.* as *politici libri* at *Fam.* 8.1.4. **ut quem ad modum ... euerterit**: a substantive consecutive clause dependent on *sit* ... *inuenta*, combining a general statement about the origins of tyranny (the misuse of existing power) with a particular statement (*quem ad modum Tarquinius* ... *euerterit*) about the origin of Superbus' tyranny (just as Tarquin overturned the monarchy at Rome, so do tyrants in general subvert constitutions through abuse of power). *euerterit* follows both *ut* and *quem ad modum*, and takes its mood from the former. Supplying a verb such as *perspiciatis* (so Büchner (1962) 123 n.9) before *quem ad modum* makes the syntax clearer, but is unnecessary. **sit huic oppositus alter ... gubernator ciuitatis:** the description of the ideal statesman (presumably referring to Brutus) includes three sets of linked terms: he is first given a set of attributes, *bonus et sapiens et peritus utilitatis dignitatisque ciuilis*, which differentiate him from the tyrant, who is scarcely human in his evil (48.1–2), who is insane (45.3), and who is concerned with his own good rather than that of the public (45.3). The second set, *quasi tutor et procurator rei publicae*, offers a designation by which C. wishes this figure to be known (*sic enim appelletur*). It is marked by *quasi* as being metaphorical: *tutor* is a legal term for a guardian, *procurator* the administrator of an estate. C. uses *tutor* to describe the consuls at *Red. sen.* 4, *Red. pop.* 11, *De orat.* 3.3, and both terms at *Off.* 1.85. Both terms may reflect the temporary role, in times of crisis, that C. gives this figure; both suggest the *caritas* and almost parental qualities of the good king in 1.64.3. The final set, *rector et gubernator ciuitatis* offers one unusual and one familiar term for such a position: *regere* is not common (cf. 23n.) while *gubernare* is frequently used by C. to designate not only monarchy, but leadership of the state (cf. on 1.1.3n.). For *rector* cf. the definition of the statesman at *De orat.* 1.211 *sin autem quaereremus quis esset is, qui ad rem publicam moderandam usum et scientiam et studium suum contulisset, definirem hoc modo: qui quibus rebus utilitas rei publicae pareretur* <*et*> *augeretur teneret iisque uteretur, hunc rei publicae rectorem et consilii publici auctorem esse habendum*; C. later used it to mean 'helmsman' at *Div.* 1.24. For *gubernator* cf. the definition of the optimate at *Sest.* 98 *quid est igitur propositum his rei publicae gubernatoribus quod intueri et quo cursum suum* *derigere debeant? id quod est praestantissimum maximeque optabile omnibus sanis et bonis et beatis, cum dignitate otium.* As often, C. combines Roman political terminology with a philosophic model, in this case Plato's βασιλικός or πολιτικὸς ἀνήρ at *Plt.* 268c. C. does not appear to use the word *princeps* in the singular of his ideal citizen, nor does this passage advocate monarchy: the role of the leading citizen can be filled by any one of many qualified and right-minded individuals who happens to be available at the right time, as C. himself was in 63: cf. 1.10.1–3.

51.2 quem uirum facite ut agnoscatis: the responsible citizen must recognize the potential *tutor et procurator* in just the same way that the *tutor* must foresee developments in the state; cf. 1.45.2. For *facite ut* 'make sure to', cf. *OLD* s.v. 16.

51.3 quod quoniam nomen ... sermone nostro: *nomen* here means 'concept' rather than 'name'; cf. Lepore 35. The clause has been interpreted in two different ways: 'since this concept is not yet very familiar in our language' or 'since this concept has not yet been used in our conversation'. Of these the second is almost certainly correct; cf. *Acad.* 2.18 *uisum – iam enim hoc pro phantasia uerbum satis hesterno sermone triuimus.* For the use of *tritus*, cf. also *N.D.* 2.91, *Acad.* 1.27, *Fin.* 3.15, *Off.* 1.33; for the description of the conversation as *sermo*, cf. 1.38.1, 2.33.1, 3.32. There is lexical variation between this and the next clause: *tritum* ~ *trac<tandum>*, *sermone* ~ *oratione*. The *rector* is the subject of the last two books of *Rep.* **genus eius hominis:** the *tutor* is not an individual, but a type occurring frequently in the course of Roman history. The next mentioned after L. Brutus are Valerius Publicola in 53 and L. Valerius Potitus and M. Horatius Barbatus, *hominum concordiae causa sapienter popularium* in 54.1, and there were presumably others in the lost portions of this book, down to and including Scipio himself. The fragment *dictatore L. Quinctio dicto* preserved by Servius on *Geo.* 3.125 refers to the dictatorship of Cincinnatus in 439 and presumably to the killing of Maelius by the *magister equitum* Ahala (cf. 49.2); it was placed by Mai (followed by editors including Ziegler) after 63.2, but Heck 223–4 more plausibly locates it here.

52.1 Various supplements have been proposed, but the loss of the context in the missing six leaves of P makes certainty impossible. This paragraph provides the transition between the discussion of the ideal Platonic statesman (probably in comparison with L. Brutus) that must have occurred in the lacuna, and the resumption of the historical account of the origins of the Roman Republic. The subject of *requisiuit* is Plato. **optandam magis quam sperandam:** cf. 2.21.3 *praeclaram ... sed a uita hominum abhorrentem et a moribus*; for the contrast between *optare* 'desire' and *sperare* 'have hopes of', cf. *De orat.* 1.96, *Fam.* 4.1.2, 5.8.2, *Att.* 8.15a.1, 11.19.1. Plato himself refers to the utopian quality of his state at *R.* 9.592b and *Lg.* 5.736b, 739c. **quam minimam potuit:** size is not a major issue in *R.* itself, but cf. *Lg.* 5.737–8, 740–1.

52.2 Scipio makes the same contrast between his procedures and Plato's as at §3.2, 51.1 (cf. Laelius at 21–2). With *in umbra et imagine*, cf. *Off.* 3.69 *sed nos ueri iuris germanaeque iustitiae solidam et expressam effigiem nullam tenemus, umbra et imaginibus utimur.* The *uirgula* here is not the same as Mercury's *uirgula diuina* at *Off.* 1.158 (or a dowsing rod, as Büchner suggests), but is simply (so Moser) the pointer used by a guide or lecturer.

52.3 iis enim ... praeteritis: from the founding of Rome in 750 to the expulsion of Superbus in 508/7, according to the chronology of C. and Polybius; Walbank (on Plb. 6.11a.2) calculates the total number of regnal years from Romulus to Superbus as 237, with seven additional years of interregnum. C.'s date for the foundation of the Republic is two years later than the standard (Varronian) chronology. **quantum tenuerat ... desiderium:** cf. 1.64.1, 2.23; for the corresponding hatred of Superbus, cf. 1.62.2.

53–63: The Origins of the Republic

An entire gathering of eight leaves is missing between 52 and 53, in which Scipio must have described the foundation of the Republic. Three fragments have been assigned to this lacuna: Nonius 526.10 M., cited above on 2.44–6, almost certainly does not belong here; Augustine, *CD* 5.12 on the decision to have two chief magistrates and call them consuls rather than kings, probably contains material included by C. here, but is not ascribed to him by Augustine (it is bracketed by Ziegler) and is drawn in part from Sallust, *B.C.* 6.7; the third, C.'s reference to Cn. Flavius' publication of the *fasti* in 304 (*Att.* 6.1.8), does belong here. It is generally placed after 63.2, but the context in C.'s letter makes it clear that it came before the account of the

Decemvirate: cf. Heck 23. In this reference to Flavius, as in the reference at 54.1 to the Decemvirate, C. anticipates later constitutional developments. Although the very end of Scipio's account is missing in the lacuna after 63.2, the discussion of the early republican constitution was clearly far less comprehensive than the discussion of the regal period. This may be the result of the sparseness of early accounts of the fifth century in comparison with those of the monarchy (cf. Gabba (1967) 135–9), but it may reflect C.'s deliberate emphasis on the conflict between senatorial domination (an unbalanced aristocratic government) and popular rights within a properly mixed constitution. The missing conclusion of the speech (roughly equivalent in length to 53–6) will have contained the end of the second secession and Scipio's summary of the constitution of the post-Decemviral period as the best form of mixed government.

53 *lex illa tota sublata est: the law must be that permitting the Tarquins to take their possessions into exile, which was repealed upon the discovery of a plot of young nobles to restore Superbus, leading (*hac mente*) to the expulsion of Collatinus and other actions described in the next sentence. For description of all these events as being excessively popular, cf. 1.62.3n. In Livy's account both decisions concerning the *bona regia* are taken by the Senate (2.4.3, 2.5.1), but in Dionysius the first is taken by the *comitia curiata* (5.6.2), the second by the consuls (5.13.2). **hac mente ... offensione nominis:** C. gives in three parallel clauses (*hac mente ... eademque mente ... idemque*) in order of increasing importance the principal effects of popular anti-monarchic agitation: action against the family of the tyrant, against the possibility of future monarchy, and against tyrannical treatment of citizens. The expulsion of the entire *gens Tarquinia* appears at 46.3. L. Tarquinius Collatinus, the husband of Lucretia, was traditionally elected consul together with L. Brutus. In Livy's account (2.2) his voluntary abdication and exile precede the conspiracy; in Dionysius (2.9–12), his leniency towards the conspirators led Brutus to force him to abdicate and leave Rome. Both here and in his later references to Collatinus' departure (*Brut.* 53, *Off.* 3.40), C. describes it as involuntary; further discussion and sources in *MRR* I 1–2 and Ogilvie on Livy 2.2–11. **eademque mente ... sensit moueri:** P. Valerius Publicola (for the cognomen see next n.) is said to have been elected suffect consul succeeding Collatinus (*MRR* I 2); for the lowering of the *fasces* to the people cf. Livy 2.7.7, Plu. *Public.* 10.7. As at 1.62.3, C. uses *demittere* for the more technically correct *submittere* found in Livy's account. The story of Valerius' move from the summit to the foot of the Velia (the north-east spur of the Palatine) is told also by Livy 2.7.6–12 and others; a building site either on or at the foot of the Velia (*Har.* 16 and Asconius on *Pis.* 52 citing Varro and others) is said to have been a public gift to him. Only here is the original site of Valerius' house said to have belonged to Tullus Hostilius; Varro (*De uita pop. Rom.* fr. 7 Riposati) and Solinus 1.22 knew that Tullus' house had been on the Velia, on the site of the later *aedes Penatium.* For topographical discussion, cf. Platner–Ashby 196–7, Richardson 139–40, 289. **in quo fuit Publicola maxime** 'the action in which his concern for the people was most apparent'. Modern conventions of capitalization obscure C.'s etymological play: he interprets the cognomen *Publicola* as a compound noun on the model of *agricola*, *qui populum colit* (on the etymological impossibility of which cf. Ogilvie on Livy 2.8.1), using it simultaneously as a common noun and as the aetiological explanation of the proper name. **quae ... lata est:** C's wording suggests that the *lex Valeria de prouocatione* was the first law passed by the centuriate assembly, not (despite Büchner) that it was merely the first of the laws on *prouocatio* passed by the assembly; cf. Rotondi 190. The only previous laws mentioned – probably including that on the expulsion of the Tarquins – were passed by the *comitia curiata* (see above). **ne quis magistratus ... uerberaret:** the language of law, with *ne quis* (but cf. *ne qui* 54.1) introducing a prohibition. *prouocatio*, the right to appeal from the sentence of a magistrate to the *comitia centuriata*, was seen as the cornerstone of citizens' rights during the Republic; cf Wirszubski (1950) 24–7. The historicity of this law is doubtful (cf. Ogilvie on Livy 2.8); it anticipates two later laws associated with the same family, the *lex Valeria Horatia* of 449 discussed in the next paragraph, and the *lex Valeria* of 300. For details on the legal history in this and the following section, cf. Bleicken, *RE* s.v. *prouocatio*. *aduersus prouocationem* is slightly elliptical: 'in contravention of the right of appeal'.

54 This section is in effect an excursus on the history and extent of the right of *prouocatio*, and consists of four separate points (distinguished here by punctuation which differs from Ziegler's): (*a*) that the right existed before the *lex Valeria* of 509 (508 on C.'s chronology); (*b*) that the Twelve Tables show that the right covered all penalties, not only capital ones; (*c*) that the right of *prouocatio* applied to the rulings of all regular magistracies, as is shown both by the explicit exemption of the Decemvirs from the rule and by the subsequent passage of the *lex Valeria Horatia* of 449; (*d*) that the entire system of *prouocatio* except the penalties for violating it was in existence before the *leges Porciae* (on which see below). The train of thought is obscured by the combination of paratactic syntax (*declarant* . . . *itemque* . . . *indicant* . . . *et* . . . *ostendit* . . . *-que* . . . *sanxit* . . . *neque* . . . *attulerunt*) with a variety of types of argument: the existence of *prouocatio* under the kings is an explicit statement of the pontifical and an implication of the augural books; the range of penalties covered is an inductive argument from a number of statements in the Twelve Tables; and the near-universality of *prouocatio* is an argument *e contrario* from the exception of the Decemvirate. The whole passage is an excellent illustration of C.'s abilities as an antiquarian; cf. Rawson (1991) 64.

54.1 prouocationem autem ... augurales: Livy 1.26.8 shows Horatius appealing to the people by the word *prouoco*, and the existence of *prouocatio* under the kings is one of the details excerpted from *Rep.* by the *philologus* in Seneca, *Epist.* 108.31. On the antiquity of *prouocatio* cf. also *Dom.* 33; for the augural books, cf. 1.63.4n. **itemque ... compluribus legibus:** not found in the extant fragments of the Twelve Tables and not otherwise attested; it is likely that the laws did not establish *prouocatio* in the full sense, but merely placed some limits on magistrates' powers of *coercitio* (cf. Ogilvie on Livy 3.55.3). For the broad extent of *prouocatio*, cf. 1.62.3 *tum prouocationes omnium rerum. iudicium* refers to the court, *poena* to the penalty imposed. **et quod proditum ... non fuisse** 'the tradition that Decemviri ... were installed without *prouocatio* is a sufficient indication': cf. Livy 3.32.6 *placet creari decemuiros sine prouocatione*. C.'s source cannot be determined. **proditum memoriae est:** *memoriaest* in P can legitimately be read as *memoria est* or *memoriae est*. The dat. is far more frequent (cf. 1.16.1, 2.28.1); in the only two (of 26) passages (*Verr.* 1.47, *De orat.* 1.181) where the abl. is printed, the dat. is a variant. **creatos:** the technical term for either the choice (by election or appointment) or the announcement of the choice of a magistrate; cf. 61.1 and *OLD* s.v. 5. **Lucique Valeri ... crearetur:** the consuls of 449 B.C.E.; for the law cf. Ogilvie on Livy 3.55.3, Rotondi 204. **hominum concordiae causa sapienter popularium:** a crucial instance of the role of the individual statesman in preserving the fabric of government: the oligarchic excesses of the Decemviri might have led to excessive democracy (as at 1.62.3 and 2.53) had not limited concessions defused the situation; Publicola himself (55) is another example of such wisdom, which is further illustrated in 56–63 below (see n.). For the propriety of being moderately *popularis*, cf. *Dom.* 77 *a maioribus nostris, qui non ficte et fallaciter populares sed uere et sapienter fuerunt.*

54.2 leges Porciae: this is the only reference to there having been three such laws, although Scipio's *ut scitis* suggests that it was well known. C. elsewhere (*Verr.* 5.163, *Rab. perd.* 8, 12, 13, *Corn.* I fr. 51) names only a single law. For the problem, cf. Rotondi 268–9, *MRR* II 472.

55.1 itaque ... perlata: for the resumptive use of the particle after a digression ('well then'; 'and so'), cf. *OLD* s.v. 3; *illa* here may simply refer back to the initial description of the law in 53, or may be used in its frequent sense of 'that famous'. *perlata* is Moser's necessary emendation of *sublataperta* in P (deleted by the second hand). The distinction between *legem ... tulit eam quae ... prima lata est* in 53 and *lege perlata* here may be between the proposal and the passage of a law (cf. *OLD* s.vv. *fero* 28 and *perfero* 6); the same variation appears in Livy's account of Publicola, 2.8.1–3 *latae deinde leges ... quas cum solus pertulisset.* The temporal and logical sequence of events is reinforced by the subsequent use of the adverbs *statim* and *postridie*: cf. Laughton 104–5. **secures de fascibus ... in regno fuissent:** as with the kings, C.'s list of Publicola's actions is paratactic (*-que ... -que ... -que*); the last element is extended to emphasize the central theme of this section, the differences between monarchy and Republic. D. H. 5.19.3 also ascribes the removal of axes from the *fasces* (but only within the city) to Publicola; Livy 2.8.3 makes the same chronological connection between the passage of the law on *prouocatio* and the election of Sp. Lucretius (to replace Brutus, whose death is not reported by C.), but (2.1.8) he ascribes the alternation of the *fasces* and the reasoning behind it to Brutus rather than Publicola (so also D. H. 5.2.1). **surrogauit:** the technical term for the election of a substitute (here, in place of Brutus); so also 61.2, 62.1. **in libero populo:** cf. 56.1 *in populo libero*; also Livy 2.1.1 *liberi iam hinc populi Romani.*

55.2 Both the litotes of *haud mediocris* (as also the archaizing *haud* itself) and the emphatic personal statement of *ut ego quidem intellego* draw attention to the importance of Publicola as a statesman; his exemplary quality is made explicit by the following sentence. There is a play on the similar meanings of *mediocris* and *modica*: by a small amount of generosity he revealed the largeness of his vision. **tenuit auctoritatem principum** 'he maintained the influence of the *principes*'; cf. *Sen.* 37 *tenebat non modo auctoritatem, sed etiam imperium in suos.*

55.3 obsoleta decanto: cf. *Verr.* 1.56 (of the virtue – and lack of private art collections – of the heroes of old) *uereor ne haec forte cuipiam nimis antiqua et iam obsoleta uideantur.* For a similar use of *obsoletus* in the context of moral decline, cf. *Rep.* 5.2 *quid enim manet ex antiquis moribus, quibus ille dixit rem stare Romanam? quos ita obliuione obsoletos uidemus, ut non modo non colantur, sed iam ignorentur.* For *decanto* 'repeat' or 'rehearse', cf. *De orat.* 2.75 *Graeco aliquo doctore, qui mihi peruulgata praecepta decantet* (also *Fin.* 4.10, *Att.* 13.34.1).

56–63 As indicated in 55.3, the remainder of C.'s account of the formation of the republican constitution consists of *exempla* of provident statesmanship and of its lack. After a paragraph describing the aristocratic state of the early fifth century, C. gives one example of the failure of *ratio* (the first secession, 57–9) followed by three brief illustrations of its use (60) and a final example of its failure (the fall of the Decemvirate, 61–3). It should be recognized that C. does not regard the tribunate of the *plebs* as itself bad, although the fact that secession and sedition were necessary for its institution indicates the failure of senatorial statesmanship; cf. 57.1n.

56.1 Tenuit ... iure regiam: *teneo* 'maintain' is a key word in this passage, from *tenuit* at 55.2 of Publicola through *obtinendam*, *retinebatur*, and *tenebantur* later in this paragraph. The pivotal role of the Senate in the maintenance of stable government is central to C.'s own political theory and to his view of the development of the Roman mixed constitution from monarchy to tyranny to (at this stage) aristocracy (so described too by D. H. 5.1.2). That the potential power of the Senate is excessive is shown by the phrases *potentiam nobilium* and *cedente populo* (cf. below and on 59.2, 60.1); C.'s interpretation of the relationship between Senate and plebeians in the first years of the Republic seems less anti-plebeian than before; cf. 1.62.3n. The effect of senatorial control is described in two parallel consecutive clauses (*ut in populo ... gererentur*, *uti consules ... regiam*), of which the first is divided between the limited role of the people and the predominant role of the Senate (*pauca* ... *pleraque*) and the second describes in two phrases the duration and quality (*tempore* ... *genere*) of consular power, contrasting and emphasizing the significant terms *annuam* and *regiam* at the ends. The two sentences which follow illustrate the manner of senatorial control first over the people and then over the consuls and (on occasion) dictator. **in populo libero** 'though the people were (in principle) free' (for *in* of circumstances cf. *OLD* s.v. 40); contrasted with *pauca per populum*. **auctoritate et instituto ac more:** *institutum* and *mos* are closely linked here, and are as a pair parallel to *auctoritas*. It is striking that C. refers to precedent and custom at the very outset of the Republic. **genere ... regiam:** that the *imperium* of the consuls was regal in nature and inheritance is both central to Roman tradition (cf. *Leg.* 3.8 *regio imperio duo sunto* and passages collected in Wirszubski (1950) 21 n.4) and necessary for the theory of the mixed constitution; cf. Plb. 6.11.12 with Walbank's note and Ogilvie on Livy 2.1.7–2.2. **populi comitia ... auctoritas:** the requirement that popular legislation required subsequent senatorial ratification (ascribed to Romulus by D. H. 2.14.3) was not altered until the *lex Publilia* of 339 B.C.E.; cf. Livy 8.12.15, Rotondi 227. For *auctoritas* 'decree of the Senate', cf. *OLD* s.v. 4, *TLL* II 1225.57–79.

56.2 decem fere annis: Livy 2.18 dates the dictatorship of T. Larcius to 501, while D. H. 5.70.4, 73.1 gives 498, a date with which C.'s 'roughly ten years' seems to agree; for *fere* with numbers cf. 1.25.3n. For the chronological problem, cf. *MRR* I 9–10. **proximum similitudini regiae:** Moser suggested *proximum similitudine regio* (*sc. imperio*). There is no instance in C. of *similitudo* being modified by an adjective rather than a genitive (except for the attraction of demonstratives and relatives, e.g. *ab hac similitudine* for *ab horum s.*, *De orat.* 3.56; cf. K–S I 65, Madvig on *Fin.* 5.42); cf. 1.65 *regum similitudo.*

56.3 omnia ... tenebantur: cf. 61.1 *summa ... auctoritas in senatu, populo patiente atque parente.* The power of the Senate is predominant, and the people give way; cf. 60.1n. and von Fritz 133 n.44. **belli** is locative: 'in war'. The more usual expression is *belli domique* as at 1.38.3.

57.1 The meaning of the sentence is disputed; cf. particularly Perelli (1972), Girardet (1977), Ferrary (1984) 94–7. The meaning of *ratio* is relatively clear (cf. particularly Perelli (1972) 303–8): it refers to the *prudentia* of the statesman by which he can understand, predict, and guide political developments (cf. 1.45.2, 2.45.2); it is repeated below at 59.1, where it is amplified by *consilio.* The meaning of *rerum (publicarum) natura* is more difficult, and is best explained by comparison with 30 and 45.1: there are political and social developments that are in accordance with both human nature and the natural cycle of constitutions (cf. also 1.68), which it is the duty of the statesman to understand and control. The explanation of *uincit . . . rationem* is given by the following sentence (*id enim tenetote* . . .): the aristocratic regime had failed to recognize that the lack of popular liberty described in 56.1 was inadequately balanced (*aequabilis*), and hence that some correction – ultimately, the creation of the tribunate – was both 'natural' and necessary. In particular (58–9), the aristocrats did not anticipate the social crisis caused by debt, as both Solon earlier and other Romans later managed to do. **plusculum . . . iuris:** a judgment expressed more forcefully at 1.62.3, 2.50.3. For *asciscere* 'arrogate to oneself', cf. *OLD* s.v. 4; the patronizing diminutive *plusculum* appears in C. elsewhere only at *De orat.* 2.99, *Fam.* 5.12.3, in the latter of which it is clearly meant to be humorous. **populus:** it may be significant that C. both here and at 59.2 refers to the establishment of the tribunate of the *plebs* as the work of the *populus.* C. uses *plebs* rarely in *Rep.*, preferring to use *populus* as the manifestation of the democratic element of the mixed constitution. At *Corn.* 1 fr. 49 (a text closely related to this portion of *Rep.*), C. says that after the first choice of tribunes by the seceding *plebs*, they were in the next year chosen by the *comitia curiata* (i.e. the *populus*, not the *concilium plebis*); cf. 59.2n. **sexto decimo fere anno:** the qualifying *fere* (cf. 1.25.3n.) reflects gentlemanly aversion to excessive precision rather than uncertainty; at *Corn.* 1 fr. 49 C. gave the same chronology without qualification. The secession of the *plebs* traditionally began in the consulate of Verginius and Veturius (494 B.C.E.); it was ended with the establishment of the tribunate in the following year, in which Cominius and Cassius were consuls. For details, cf. *MRR* 1 13–15. **consecutum est** 'necessarily followed' (cf. *OLD* s.v. 4) is Leopardi's conjecture for *consecutus est* in P.

57.2 tenetote: pl. fut. imper. This solemn ending appears 70x in C., most frequently in the early orations (24 exx. in *Verr.*), and most frequently in the form *scitote*; *tenetote* appears elsewhere only at *Balb.* 17 and 65. It is archaic, and most frequently found in laws and similar texts; cf. N–W III 213–23. **quod initio dixi:** the reference is presumably to the whole discussion of constitutions in book 1, particularly to the conclusion in 1.69; on *aequabilitas* cf. also 2.42.2, 62.2. **incommutabilem:** only here in C.

58.1 ex aere alieno commota ciuitas: for *ex* 'as a result of', cf. *OLD* s.v. 18. C.'s account of the first secession and the establishment of the tribunate is extremely brief, but agrees with that of Livy 2.22–33 (and other ancient versions) in giving an economic cause (debt) and a political solution (the tribunate) for plebeian discontent; for the historical problems, cf. *CAH*² VII 2.212–17. C.'s point is that the state was shaken (*commota*), if not destroyed, and hence that its previous condition was not the ideal described in the previous sentence. **montem sacrum ... occupauit:** the *mons sacer* acquired its name from this secession; cf. *Brut.* 54, *Corn.* 1 fr. 49 *montem illum ... qui hodie mons sacer appellatur*. The site of the two secessions of the *plebs* (see also 63.2n.) was much disputed, and C. appears to have the *plebs* move on both occasions from the *mons sacer* (3 miles away, across the Anio) to the Aventine. For the first secession, both sites are separately attested, the annalist Piso (cited by Livy 2.32.3) naming the Aventine, Festus 422.36 L. and what Livy describes as *frequentior fama* the *mons sacer*; both appear together in Sall. *Hist.* 1.11 M. In *Corn.* 1 fr. 49, C. placed the first secession on the *mons sacer*, the second on the Aventine.

58.2 ac ne Lycurgi ... frenos: C.'s general point is that even the constitutions most admired by Greek theorists underwent modification (and thus that the introduction of the tribunate was not necessarily a bad thing), and that even Greeks could resist authority when necessary. The Cretan and Spartan constitutions were linked by Ephorus (*FGrH* 70 F 33, 148–9) as well as by Pl. *R.* 8.544c and *Lg.* (frequently) and by Arist. *Pol.* 2.10; Polybius makes a point of attacking these accounts of Cretan government as untrue (6.45–47.6; cf. Walbank *ad loc.*). The precise role of the ephorate in the Spartan constitution was disputed: in some versions (e.g. Herod. 1.65.5) it was attributed to Lycurgus himself, although both Pl. *Lg.* 3.692a, and Arist. *Pol.* 5.11 assigned it (as does C.) to Theopompus in the eighth century. Plato uses the word ψάλιον (bridle-bit) to describe the effect of the ephorate on the constitution, and although C. uses *frenos* with an opposite meaning (reining in the people, not the government), it is likely that he had that passage in mind; it is also quoted by Plu. *Lyc.* 7.1. C., like

Plato and Aristotle (*Pol.* 2.6, 9), considers the ephorate a popular element in the constitution (although both (*Lg.* 4.712d, *Pol.* 2.6) were also aware of the tradition which made it a tyrannical element); at *Leg.* 3.16 C. refers more favourably (over the objections of Quintus) to both the ephorate and the tribunate as necessary checks on the power of king and consul. *illos* presumably reflects the fame of Spartan discipline. **nam etiam Spartae ... constituti:** the two parts of the verb *sunt* ... *constituti* are very widely separated, surrounding two pairs of phrases referring first (in closely parallel word order) to the offices in Sparta and Crete, then (in chiastic order) to the analogy between both and the tribunes at Rome. There is no need, with Ziegler, to transpose *quos illi*.

59.1 Fuerat ... medendi: for the indic. cf. §5.3n. *ratio* ... *medendi* refers back to the *ratio* of 57.1, and is taken up after a brief digression by *quo* ... *consilio* in the next sentence. *fortasse* also echoes 57.1, *in quo defuit fortasse ratio* – an indication of C.'s reluctance to criticize the wisdom of the early Senate. **in illo aere alieno:** refers back to *ex aere alieno* in 58.1. The expression is comprehensible, though compressed; Mai suggested *in illo aere alieno medendo.* **quae neque Solonem ... nostrum senatum:** alternative methods of dealing with the problem of debt are given in two examples, one earlier and Greek, one later and Roman. Solon's treatment of debt (the *seisachtheia*) is traditionally dated to 594/3, a full century before the first secession of the *plebs*; an unnamed source (Nepos?) cited by Gellius 17.21.4 made Solon's legislation contemporary with the thirty-third year of Tarquinius Priscus (583), and C. later (*Brut.* 39) reports that Solon was contemporary with the reign of Servius Tullius (577–533). D. H. 5.65.1 has the son of Publicola cite the example of Solon in his recommendations for dealing with the problem of debt: 'the city of Athens ... which not very long before ... had under the guidance of Solon voted a remission of debts to the poor' (tr. Cary). **cum ... desitum:** the *lex Poetelia* of 326 B.C.E. (313 according to Varro, *LL* 7.105; for other sources cf. *MRR* I 146, Rotondi 230–1) abolished debt bondage (*nexum*); according to Livy 8.28, the evil behaviour of L. Papirius, a *faenerator*, was the occasion. For *propter unius libidinem* cf. 47.1n. **nectierque postea desitum:** the archaic pass. infin. in *-ier* is used by C. 25x; this is the only instance which is neither poetry nor the direct quotation of a legal formula. With a pass. infin. the pass.

desitum and *coeptum* (frequently impersonal) are normal rather than *desii* and *coepi*; cf. K–S I 676–7, *OLD* s.v. *desino* 2b. **huic oneri:** Moser's emendation for *huic generi*. **cum plebes ... quaesita est:** the metaphor in *medicina* (used in political contexts elsewhere by C., e.g. *Cat.* 2.17, *Red. pop.* 15, *Red. sen.* 9, *Sest.* 43, 51, 135) is reinforced by *debilitata*, *deficeret*, and *salutis*, all of which can be used with reference to disease and cure. No one action concerning debt is referred to here, rather a whole series of laws and decrees including those cited in 60. *plebes* is rarely used by C., usually in legal contexts; cf. 63.1n.

59.2 duobus tribunis plebis: the original number of tribunes varies in the ancient accounts; C. *Corn.* I fr. 49 has two created on the *mons sacer*, with three more chosen immediately thereafter, and D. H. 6.89.1 has five. For the evidence, cf. *MRR* I 16 n.1; for the election of tribunes, cf. 57.1n. **ut potentia ... minueretur:** *potentia* here (as at 56.1) is clearly negative; at *Corn.* I fr. 49, C. said that the first secession took place *propter nimiam dominationem potentium*. C. (here as in the parallel passage at *Leg.* 3.15–16) clearly views democracy, as represented by the tribunate, as a necessary part of the constitution, but he sees the sedition and secession which brought it into existence as an indication of the failure of *ratio* on the part of the Senate. C's account here suggests that he thought that the excessive debt of the *plebs* unduly limited the *libertas* necessary for a truly balanced constitution, not so much for economic or social reasons but because of the legal restrictions, including debt slavery, incurred by debtors; only if the Senate had acted to restore that liberty in some other fashion could the creation of the tribunate properly have been avoided. According to C.'s account at *De orat.* 2.199, the orator Antonius in his defence of Norbanus had argued that some seditions (including this one) were in the greater interest of justice *etsi omnes molestae semper seditiones fuissent, iustas tamen fuisse non nullas et prope necessarias*. For C.'s views of the tribunate, cf. Perelli (1979). **sapientissimis ... consilio:** chiastic order. **quod cum ... superiores:** the ideal aristocracy excels the populace in dignity, is equal in wealth, and less subject to vice; for the last characteristic, cf. *Sest.* 138 *nam si qui uoluptatibus ducuntur ... missos faciant honores*. Cf. also *Leg.* 3.10 = 28 *is ordo uitio uacato, ceteris specimen esto*. **eoque erat ... tuebantur:** C. makes explicit the link suggested in the previous clause between private virtue and public authority: the aristocrats use their private resources (effort, wisdom, and property) to help individual citizens, and therefore their public leadership is respected.

60.1 Quo in statu rei publicae: the *status* is that of the ideal paternalist aristocracy described in the previous paragraph, in which intelligent action on the part of the nobility avoids the kind of disruption that took place in the two secessions, when aristocratic *ratio* failed. **Sp. Cassium ... mactauit:** first mentioned in 49.2. The nature of Cassius' attempted coup as consul in 486 is unclear; the agrarian legislation reported by Livy 2.41 and other sources is clearly an anachronism, and is not mentioned by C. A host of difficulties surrounds Cassius' trial and execution in 485: C.'s singular *quaestor* is appropriate for the later magistracy, not the archaic judicial *quaestores parricidii*; and they in any case should not have been involved in a case of *perduellio*. The involvement of Cassius' father in his execution is genuine archaic procedure, but Livy 2.41.10–11 offers the quaestors (and assembly) and the father as alternatives (so also D. H. 8.69–79). For the sources, cf. *RE* Cassius (91), *MRR* I 20–2; for discussion, cf. Ogilvie *ad loc.* and Mommsen II 537–43 on the criminal jurisdiction of the quaestor. **molientem:** for the pejorative sense, cf. 1.28.1n. **cedente populo:** C.'s point is that although Cassius was popular (*summa apud populum gratia florentem*), the people gave in to the magistrates and his father, thus avoiding disruption of the state.

60.2–3 The precise significance of the *lex Aternia Tarpeia* of 454, the *lex Iulia Papiria* of 430, and a third not mentioned by C., the *lex Menenia Sestia* of 452, is very unclear, and the evidence is contradictory. The *lex Aternia Tarpeia* and the *lex Menenia Sestia* probably concerned the maximum fine (*multa*) that could be levied by a magistrate (2 sheep and 30 cattle, according to Festus 270.3 L.) without the defendant's having a right of *prouocatio*. The later *lex Iulia Papiria* apparently established a fixed cash equivalence for sheep (10 *asses*) and cattle (100 *asses*) in the assessment of fines. Cf. Rotondi 200–1, 211–12 and *RE* Suppl. VI 544–5 s.v. *Multa*.

60.3 'Twenty years later [430 B.C.E.], because the censors Papirius and Pinarius had transferred many herds from private to public ownership through their assessment of fines, a low evaluation of cattle in the assessment of fines was established by a law of the consuls Julius and Papirius'. **L. Papirius ... auerterant:** these censors are otherwise unknown, as are the details of their action. **C. Iuli P.**

Papiri: Livy 4.30.1 gives the names as L. Iulius and L. Papirius, Diodorus 12.72.1 as L. Iunius and C. Papirius.

61–3 C.'s account of the Decemvirate and the Twelve Tables has the same basic structure as Livy's: the division between the first 'good' Decemvirs of 451 and the second 'evil' board of 450, and between the 'good' ten tables and the 'evil' last two; the story of Julius and Sestius (omitted by D. H.); the attempt on Verginia leading to the second secession of the *plebs* and ultimately (in the lacuna after 63.2) to the restoration of the normal magistracies. The emphases of C.'s account are very different from Livy's: the story of the embassy to Athens is omitted; all drama is left out, including even the name of the wicked Appius Claudius. More important is that C. presents the Decemvirate as the result not of compromise between antagonistic consuls and tribunes, but of the overriding power of the Senate; in this he may be following Polybius (who may not have recognized the existence of the tribunate before 449), for whom the Decemvirate represented the transformation of aristocracy into oligarchy; cf. Taeger 84–5, 143; Ferrary (1984) 90–1. Furthermore, although the fall of the Decemvirate in C.'s account is, as in Livy, the result of one man's lust, it is much more the result of the intrinsic weakness of an unmixed constitution: aristocracy becomes oligarchy when unchecked, and inevitably falls victim to the cycle of constitutions. It may be significant that while Livy considers the appointment of the Decemvirs a *mutatio* of the *forma ciuitatis* (3.33.1–2), C. (63.1) places the *totius commutatio rei publicae* at their fall: for him, the Decemvirate is merely a clearer manifestation of aristocracy in the process of degeneration to oligarchy, while the real change comes with the formal establishment of a mixed constitution by the Valerio-Horatian laws. On the problems of the whole story, cf. Ogilvie on Livy 3.33–42 and von Ungern-Sternberg; for the ancient sources, cf. *MRR* I 45–9.

61.1 Sed aliquot ante annis: the preceding paragraph is a digression on the good (paternalist) aspects of aristocratic government; here, C. goes back to take up the historical account from the establishment of the tribunate in 59.2. **qui et summum ... scriberent:** C. makes no mention (nor does Diodorus 12.26) of the prior embassy to collect Greek laws, specifically the laws of Solon (which C. had mentioned in 59.1). The embassy is found in no source earlier than C., although Pliny, *NH* 34.21 reports the existence of a statue of their interpreter, and C. himself at *Leg.* 2.59, 64 describes funeral regulations in the Twelve Tables as coming from the laws of Solon. Greek influence on the form and content of the laws is strong, and while the story of the embassy may not be true, it is not entirely implausible; cf. Wieacker 330–53.

61.3 Livy 3.33.9–10 tells the same story, but places far more emphasis on the horror of the crime and has the body brought into the Forum. C. naturally emphasizes the legal aspects: the main clause and principal relative clause (*laus est ... C. Iuli, qui ... L. Sestium ... uades ... poposcit*) stress the importance of proper procedure; the corpse appears only in o. o. within a subordinate clause, and the bulk of the sentence (*cum ipse ... esset, quod se legem ... uetaret*) concerns the right of *prouocatio*, the central legal issue in the fall of the Decemvirate. **quo tamen e collegio:** the first set of Decemvirs, not the second. **diceret:** verbs of saying and thinking are frequently attracted into the subj. in subordinate clauses in C. and Caesar; cf. K–S II 200–1. **cum ipse ... esset:** although as a magistrate not subject to *prouocatio* he could have punished Sestius on his own, he chose to allow him a public trial. **L. Sestium ... uades tamen poposcit** 'he demanded sureties from L. Sestius'; *uades* (*OLD* s.v. *uas*[1]) are guarantors (subject to a fixed penalty) for the presence of a defendant at trial. For *poscere* with two acc. objects, cf. *OLD* s.v. 2. **legem illam praeclaram:** presumably the *lex Valeria* on *prouocatio* described in 53. **quae de capite ... uetaret:** cf. *Sest.* 73 *de capite ... ne iudicari quidem posse nisi comitiis centuriatis*. This is in fact a part of the Twelve Tables themselves (9.1–2).

62.2 in hoc statu rei publicae: oligarchic government, here merely an instance of any of the simple (and thus corruptible) constitutions. **quem ... diuturnum:** cf. 1.44.2, 68–9; 2.57.2. For duration as one of the goals of any government, cf. 1.41.3. For *aequabilitas*, cf. 57.1n. **praepositis decemuiris nobilissimis:** their *nobilitas* is emphasized in order to bring out the aristocratic nature of their government; conversely, that in the previous year Julius prosecuted Sestius, himself a noble, shows the virtue of the preceding Decemvirs. **contra necem et uerbera:** cf. 53, the first Valerian law *ne quis magistratus ciuem Romanum aduersus prouocationem necaret neue uerberaret*.

63.1 commutatio rei publicae: cf. 1.45.1, 65.1. **duabus tabulis ... additis:** Livy does not report the tradition that Tables 11 and 12 had unjust laws, and the only law of the Twelve Tables that is regularly so described is the one named by Cicero, forbidding intermarriage between patricians and plebeians. The injustice of the last Tables is inferred from the character of the second board of Decemvirs and the one known law. **quae diiunctis ... conubia:** cf. Livy 4.3.4 (Canuleius) *conubium petimus, quod finitimis externisque dari solet.* **ut ne:** for *ut ne* after verbs of decision, commanding, agreeing, etc. cf. K–S II 222; it is solemn and archaic (cf. L–H 762). **plebei cum patribus:** the first hand reads *plebi et patribus*, the second *plebei cum patribus*; the latter is the more common construction (cf. Livy 4.4.5 *ne conubium patribus cum plebe esset*), and in context the archaic form of the dat. (which can also be gen., as below), although used only twice elsewhere by C., seems more likely; in the next line *plebei scito* (cf. *Dom.* 44) of the first hand is preferable to *plebiscito* of the corrector. For the form, cf. N–W I 575. **plebei scito Canuleio:** Canuleius was tribune in 445; a dramatic account of his speech and the legislation in Livy 4.1.1–6.4. **libidinose[que]:** as transmitted, both *sanxerunt* and *praefuerunt* are in the relative clause introduced by *quibus*, and there is no main verb. It seems preferable to delete *-que* with Moser than *quibus* with Zachariae. **omni imperio:** abl. ('in all their governmental acts' Keyes) rather than a dat. object parallel to *populo* ('(they) overrode the authority of every magistrate' (Sabine and Smith)). There is no clear parallel to this phrase in C.

63.2 nota scilicet ... litterarum: a clear indication (if one is necessary) both that C. was well read (*plurimis*) in earlier Roman historiography and that dramatic treatments of the story of Verginia already existed. The story is told more fully in Livy 3.44–9; for its development, cf. Ogilvie *ad loc.* In D. S. 12.24 the story is very brief, and told without names. Here the first (anecdotal) part of the tale is told in a subordinate clause (*cum ... confugisset*), and the main action (the second secession of the *plebs*) is in o. o. following a verb implied in *nota ... res et celebrata.* For *monumentis* cf. 26.2. **Decimus quidam Verginius:** elsewhere (Livy 3.44.2, D. H. 11.28, Ascon. 77 C., and C.'s own reference to the story at *Fin.* 2.66) his *praenomen* is given as Lucius; the manuscripts at Livy 3.54.11 give Aulus. For the use of *quidam* to introduce a previously unmentioned person, cf. *OLD* s.v. 1c. **propter unius ... intemperiem:** at *Fin.* 2.66 C. names Appius Claudius; in *Corn.* 1, according to Ascon. 77 C., no proper names were given. Here the emphasis is on the fact that the behaviour of a single member of the oligarchy (whose identity is irrelevant) can overthrow the whole government; Wiseman (1979) 107 suggests that the evil Decemvir was not given a name until the early 40s, possibly by Valerius Antias. *intemperies* 'outrageous behaviour' appears also at *Att.* 4.6.3; *intemperantia* is far more common in C. **ad exercitum ... in Algido:** the *mons Algidus* is 'the dramatic and commanding pass by which the *Via Latina* passes through and out of the Alban crater' (Ogilvie on Livy 3.2.6), and the site of many battles between the Romans and the Volsci and (as on this occasion) the Aequi. **quod erat in manibus:** for *in manibus esse/habere* 'to be engaged on', cf. *OLD* s.v. *manus* 13a. **primum montem sacrum ... Auentinum:** as in the first secession; cf. 58.1. According to Livy (3.50–2) they moved from the Aventine to the *mons sacer*. Mai's supplement, *ar*<*matos insedisse* ... > gives the required sense: that the plebeians were armed is an important element of the tradition. In the lacuna of four leaves which follows, Scipio presumably recounted the end of the secession, the restoration of consulate and tribunate, and the passage of the Valerio-Horatian laws, particularly the law on *prouocatio*. Like Polybius in the 'archaeology' of book 6, C. ends his account of constitutional development with the restoration of legitimate government after the fall of the Decemvirate (Cato too may have ended book 1 of the *Origines* at this point; cf. Ferrary (1984) 89); from that time on until the Second Punic War, the constitution was essentially stable, although it continued to improve (cf. Walbank on Plb. 6.11.1). Two fragments are assigned by Ziegler to this lacuna: the story of the scribe Cn. Flavius more properly belongs in the lacuna after 52, and the phrase *dictatore L. Quinctio dicto* probably belongs in the lacuna after 51 (cf. *ad locc.*).

63.3 The conclusion of Scipio's speech recalls his solemn *sententia* on the excellence of the Roman constitution in 1.70.3.

Little remains of the end of the book. In the following paragraph, Tubero objects that Scipio has given an encomium of the Roman *res publica* rather than an explanation of how (*qua disciplina quibus moribus aut legibus*) the *res publica* can be preserved; after postponing the discussion of that topic (to be taken up in book 4), Scipio then (65–6) defends his account as an answer to Laelius' question about the best constitution. P breaks off as he introduces a discussion of government based on the analogy of nature, perhaps (so Ferrary (1984) 97–8) using the analogy of the universe and the Platonic Demiurge. For discussion of the (largely lost) books 3–5, cf. Introduction, pp. 16–17, 24–5: book 3 contained the debate between Philus and Laelius on the possibility of just government, followed by Scipio's redefinition of the *res publica*; book 4 contrasted Roman education and social institutions with those of Pl. *R.*; and book 5 discussed the education and nature of the true statesman.

De re publica 6

The *Somnium Scipionis* is the only substantial extant portion of the second half of *Rep.* (for its preservation, cf. Introduction, p. 34); it concludes the sixth and final book of *Rep.*, the subject of which was the behaviour of the statesman in times of crisis. Both in its placement within *Rep.* and in its eschatological concerns, the *Somnium* clearly echoes the Myth of Er which concludes Plato's *Republic*; but there are important differences (cf. Introduction, p. 15). Er's tale is deliberately fantastic and set in a far-off land; Scipio's is the report of his own dream, which had taken place twenty years earlier, in which the souls of his own father and grandfather had appeared. In its structure and argument, the *Somnium* is closely tied to the life of Scipio, and through him to the social and political emphases of *Rep.* as a whole. The prophecy which opens the dream deals with Scipio's own destiny; then, in order to encourage his grandson to virtuous political action, Africanus introduces the subject of the afterlife, which in turn leads to discussion of the immortality of the soul which begins (14–16) and ends (26–9) the eschatological portion of the dream. Within that framework, C. describes first the organization of the cosmos (17–19) and then the limitations of earthly glory (20–4); his summary of the relevance of all this to individual actions (25) leads back to the final proof of the immortality of the soul. All this is very different from Er's tale; but as the Myth of Er returns to the eschatological issues raised by Cephalus in the very opening of the *Republic*, so the *Somnium* recapitulates and reinforces the protreptic themes of the preface and introductory conversation of book 1.

C. himself had criticized Plato's *Republic* for its lack of political realism, and others had criticized the Myth of Er specifically for its improbability; perhaps as a result, C. makes a considerable effort to lend verisimilitude to the *Somnium*. The *Somnium* requires no suspension of disbelief: although a vision of the afterlife can rarely expect to appeal to the reader's own experience, it is a realistic narrative. Thus at 6.10.3 Scipio explains the dream as the product of his waking thoughts and places it in the tradition of literary dreams as well as prophetic ones; when his hearers groan, Scipio's joke ironically undercuts the solemnity of the dream. In introducing the *Somnium*, moreover, Scipio almost certainly referred to Colotes' criticisms of Plato (cf. Introduction, p. 14 n. 35); he may have suggested that the realism of his own account reinforced its claims to veracity. Clearly, that claim is bolstered by the contents of the dream itself: there are no whorls and spindles here, but precise information about the earth and the universe, derived not only from Plato, but from Aristotle, the Platonist Heraclides of Pontus, the Stoics, and the Hellenistic scientific poets Eratosthenes and Alexander of Ephesus (for particular debts, see individual notes below). Finally, the fact that the soul of Africanus translates closely a passage of Plato's *Phaedrus* as the proof of its own immortality shows that the dream is the product more of reason than of revelation; but by undercutting the supernatural quality of the *Somnium*, C. increases the verisimilitude of *Rep.* as a whole. We are left knowing that the dream incorporates a great statesman's deepest beliefs; whether its source was the *princeps deus* or his own mind makes little difference.

9–10 The context of the dream is sketched rapidly: Scipio's arrival in Africa, his reception by Masinissa, and their conversation take only a few lines. The factual context is balanced by the literary ancestry of the dream, descending from Ennius.

9.1 Cum in Africam ... militum: the dramatic date is 149, the first year of the Third Punic War, when Scipio served as military tribune of the fourth legion. **hoc Manilio consule:** temporal abl. abs. Sigonius' emendation *M.' Manilio consuli* is generally printed, but *hoc* (in A alone; other MSS have *a* or *Anicio*) and the abl. *consule* (in all MSS) are preferable: Manilius is present, listening to Scipio's account, and *hoc* is deictic. The *praenomen* would only be appropriate when the *Somnium* was read as an independent text; cf. Montanari Caldini. **potius** 'more important'; the substantive clause which follows is comparable to that following verbs of taking care, planning, etc.; cf.

K–S II 213–14. **Masinissam:** the old king of Numidia, who died not long after the date of the *Somnium* (when he was about 90), had opportunely transferred his allegiance from Carthage to Rome and Africanus in 206. At the end of the Second Punic War he was rewarded with an enlarged kingdom, and remained steadfastly loyal to Rome for the rest of his life; cf. Livy 28.16.12 *constantissima ad ultimam senectam fides*. Scipio's only known meeting with Masinissa was in the winter of 151/0, when he went on an embassy to get elephants for the Celtiberian War (cf. Astin (1967) 271–2); his other known visit to Numidia was after the king had died; cf. Evrard-Gillis 217–18. **iustis de causis** 'for good reason'; causal *de* is limited in classical Latin prose to a few expressions; cf. 10.2 *de uia* and K–S I 497–8, *OLD* s.v. 14.

9.2 grates ... caelites: the language of the prayer is suitably solemn and archaic: *grates* is most commonly found in prayer (cf. *OLD* s.v.); for *caelites* cf. Enn. *Sc.* 171, 270 J., Plaut. *Rud.* 2, Catul. 61.190. *summe Sol* appears in Medea's prayer in Ennius 234 J. Masinissa addresses the sun less because of Numidian solar religion than because of the importance of the sun in *Rep.* (e.g. the prodigy of the double sun at 1.15.1) and particularly in the *Somnium*; cf. 17.3n. The form of the prayer ('Sun and all the other gods') is traditional. **ex hac uita migro:** cf. 15.4n. Masinissa assumes the eschatology of the *Somnium*, that the soul is immortal and death merely a transfer from this world to the next. **et his tectis:** the use of *tectum* for *domus* is poetic, as is the use of the pl. for the sing. **cuius ... recreor:** even though Masinissa's friend Africanus is long dead, the presence of *a* P. Cornelius Scipio in his palace is itself restorative. **inuictissimi:** elsewhere in C. only *Pis.* 34 of Pompey.

9.3 deinde ego ... percontatus est: the parallelism of the phrases accords with *uerbis ultro citroque habitis* in the following clause. A conversation on political affairs during the day precedes the more personal conversation at dinner, reflecting the balance between *negotium* and *otium* that shapes C.'s dialogue; cf. *De orat.* 1.26 and Harder 378 n.79. **percontatus:** for C.'s use of such compounds, cf. 1.9.1n. **uerbis ... habitis:** elsewhere in C. of oratory; cf. *Inv.* 2.140, *De orat.* 2.196, 316. **ille ... est consumptus dies:** the placement of *dies* at the end of the paragraph (with the hyperbaton of *ille ... dies*) is emphatic, and leads into the description of the night (and dream) which follow.

10.1 apparatu: used of great (sometimes regal) opulence; cf. *Sest.* 77, *Rab. Post.* 6, *Or.* 83, *Tusc.* 5.62, *Off.* 1.25. **in multam noctem** 'until late at night'; cf. *ad multam noctem* 10.3 and *Sen.* 46.

10.2 cubitum 'to bed'; acc. of the supine. **de uia fessum:** for causal *de*, cf. 9.1n. *fessus* is a more elevated word than *lassus*, which C. rarely uses; for the distinction between them, cf. B. Axelson, *Unpoetische Wörter* (Lund 1949) 29–30. **qui ... uigilassem:** causal. **artior ... complexus est:** the image of the embrace or binding of sleep is common: cf. e.g. Ennius, *Ann.* 2 Sk., Lucr. 4.453. The *Somnium* ends with the corresponding phrase *somno solutus sum* (29.3). Deep sleep is associated with prophetic dreams (cf. *Div.* 1.59), but the lateness of the hour is probably not meant to allude to the idea (cf. Hor. *Serm.* 1.10.33) that dreams after midnight are true.

10.3 The learned and awkward parenthesis postponing the appearance of Africanus derives from C.'s desire to offer a rationalistic and realistic context for his eschatology. It also gives a literary pedigree for the dream itself, comparing it explicitly to the famous vision in book 1 of Ennius' *Annales* (cited also *Luc.* 2.51) in which the apparition of Homer appeared to explain in Pythagorean terms how Ennius was in fact a reincarnation of Homer himself (cf. Skutsch on *Ann.* 1 ii–x), and implicitly connecting the *Somnium* to the tradition of visions stretching from Hesiod to Callimachus to Ennius. Lucr. 1.124–5 also referred to Ennius' dream, and it is likely that C. has that passage in mind as well. **fit enim fere** 'it is generally the case'; for the colloquial expression, cf. *Inv.* 2.14. For the idea that our waking thoughts influence subsequent dreams, cf. *Div.* 1.45, 2.128; Lucr. 4.962–70. **cogitationes sermonesque nostri** is taken up by *cogitare et loqui* at the end of the parenthesis. **ex imagine eius:** the mask of Africanus would have been among the images of notable ancestors in Scipio's atrium. Scipio was only two years old when Africanus died in 183, and could scarcely have remembered the man himself.

10.4 ades ... animo 'stay calm' as in *Mil.* 4, responding to *cohorrui* (a normal reaction to supernatural apparitions), rather than 'pay attention' as in *Sull.* 33, *Phil.* 8.30.

11.1–12.4 Africanus' prophecy falls into two parts. The summary of Scipio's career from 149 to 132 – events prior to the dramatic date of *Rep.* – is rapid and precise (11.3–4) in the manner of a formal *elogium*, perhaps reminiscent of the famous epitaphs on the tomb of the Scipiones (*ILLRP* 309–17), which C. knew. The remainder (11.5–12.4), as it concerns what has not yet happened, is vague and ominous, and the astronomical language used to describe Scipio's age in 12.3 anticipates the description of the cosmos in 16–19.

11.1 per me: stronger than *a me* in emphasizing Africanus' decisive role in the Second Punic War; so also *per te*, 11.3. **nec potest quiescere:** cf. Livy 30.44.8 (Hannibal) *nulla magna ciuitas diu quiescere potest*. Africanus speaks from a distinctly Roman perspective; Carthage made serious efforts to avoid the Third Punic War.

11.2 Scipio's aside give the first indication, still quite vague, that the location of the dream is different from that of the dreamer. The celestial perspective gradually recedes from, and then approaches, the earth (so Powell): here, details of the earth can be seen; at 16.1 they are observing (and perhaps are on) the Milky Way; in 17–18 they see the entire cosmos, and in 21–2 they again observe terrestrial geography. **excelso ... claro:** the first pair of adjectives describes the physical location, the second its celestial brightness.

11.3 ad quam: correlative with *hanc* in the next clause. **paene miles:** the military tribunate was Scipio's first command; from the point of view of anyone but Africanus it is scarcely the same as being a common soldier, but the phrase contrasts nicely with *consul*. **hoc ... euertes:** in fact longer: Scipio was consul in 147, but destroyed Carthage as proconsul in 146 (cf. *OLD* s.v. *consul* 1b). **eritque ... hereditarium:** the clauses are carefully balanced: *id* ~ *quod*; *erit ... tibi ... partum* ~ *habes ... hereditarium*; *per te* ~ *a nobis*. **cognomen:** Africanus.

11.4 The next fourteen years of Scipio's career are summarized briefly and formally. Scipio was censor in 142, and in the subsequent three years served as a *legatus* with L. Caecilius Metellus Calvus and Sp. Mummius (a participant in *Rep.*) from Rome to the major states of the East (cf. 3.48); he was elected consul again for 134 and concluded the Numantine War in Spain in the following year. **deligere:** for the second-person ending (here fut.), cf. 1.2.1n. **absens:** there is no other evidence for this detail, and C. may have invented it to emphasize the exceptional nature of Scipio's career; cf. Evrard-Gillis 220–1. **exscindes** 'destroy utterly'; of Numantia also at *Off.* 1.76.

11.5 sed ... inuectus = *triumphum egeris*. Scipio's second triumph took place in 132. **offendes** 'find'; cf. 1.59.7n. The language of the prophecy is deliberately vague, for dramatic effect as well as for verisimilitude. **nepotis mei:** Tiberius Gracchus, the son of Africanus' daughter Cornelia. For the situation in 129, cf. 1.31.4 with n., and Introduction, pp. 6–8.

12.1 lumen: the metaphor (cf. 2.69 *splendore animi*) corresponds to the description at 17.3 of the sun as the ruler of a state; throughout the *Somnium*, cosmic order and human government are linked.

12.2 ancipitem ... fatorum uiam 'the two-fold path of fate'; C. alludes to the choice of Hercules in Prodicus' tale (Xen. *Mem.* 2.1.21–33; cf. also 25.2n.) between the paths of virtue and vice; he may also wish to evoke Achilles' choice between a brief life of glory and long anonymity and possibly the Pythagorean Y, the symbol for the choice of lives. In this case, however, there is no choice: whether Scipio lives or dies is up to fate, not Scipio. *quasi* qualifies the metaphor of the road. **uideo:** typical language of prophetic foresight; cf. Virg. *Aen.* 6.87 *cerno*.

12.3 aetas tua ... conuertet ciuitas 'when your life has turned through fifty-six revolutions ... the state will turn to you': *conuerto* is the regular term for the revolution of planets around the earth; cf. 17.4, 18.3, 24.3 and *OLD* s.v. *conuersio* 1a, *conuerto* 1. It is also used by C. to describe political revolutions; cf. 1.69.5n. **septenos ... reditusque:** fifty-six years: Scipio was born in 185. *anfractus* alone could refer to the annual return of the sun (cf. *Leg.* 2.19, in one of C.'s archaizing laws); 'turn and return' describes the annual course of the sun from winter to summer solstice and back: cf. the use of *accedo* and *recedo* with the same meaning at *N.D.* 2.49, 103. **duoque hi numeri ... habetur:** numerological mysticism is principally associated with Pythagoreanism, but is prominent also in Plato; Macrobius devotes considerable space and ingenuity to explaining the perfection of these two numbers, clearly chosen by C. because Scipio was in fact 56. Seven is traditionally a mystical number, and the climacteric (in ancient theory, a critical turning-point) at age 63 was 7 x 9 years; eight is the first number other than 1 expressing the cube of a positive integer; both are important in the account of the music of the spheres at 18.4. For a brief account of number symbolism, cf. Burkert (1972) 466–76. **plenus** 'complete'; equivalent to Gk. τέλειος which, in addition to its technical meaning 'perfect' in the Euclidean sense of a number that is the sum of its divisors (e.g. 6 and 28), had a wider range of symbolic meanings; cf. Burkert (1972) 431–5. **in tuum nomen:** cf. Masinissa's reference to his name, 9.2. **te senatus ... intuebuntur:** Scipio's prospective role in Rome corresponds to that of the sun in the universe; cf. 17.3 and 12.1n. The repetition of the second-person pronoun is reminiscent of the style of prayer, and *intueor* (cf. 17.1, 18.1, 19.2) also suggests reverence and admiration. The list of those looking to Scipio reflects both C.'s own political theory and the particular circumstances of 129. The *consensus omnium bonorum* was a key element in C.'s plans for the preservation of Roman society in the 50s (cf. e.g. *Har.* 45, *Fam.* 1.9.13, 5.2.8). At the same time, the *equites* on whom C. relied in his own actions are omitted to reflect the circumstances of the Gracchan period, before the *equites* acquired political importance, while the *socii* and Latins are included because Ti. Gracchus' agrarian legislation had worked to their disadvantage: the same grouping appears also at *Am.* 12. The unjust treatment of these groups by Gracchus was the culmination of Laelius' speech on justice at 3.41; cf. also 1.31.4. On Gracchus' law and its effect, see Introduction, pp. 6–8.

12.4 ne multa 'to make a long story short'; a colloquialism found elsewhere 12x in C., most frequently in *Verr.* and *Att.* **dictator ... oportet:** Sulla had taken the title of *dictator rei publicae constituendae*, and C. anachronistically introduces a phrase that gained constitutional significance only in his own lifetime; Nicolet argues that there was a real possibililty of Scipio's becoming dictator, but Evrard-Gillis 222 n.21 is rightly sceptical. The precision of this prophecy has, in the absence of most of the second half of *Rep.*, caused considerable speculation about C.'s purpose here – an allusion to Pompey's sole consulship in 52, advocacy of dictatorship as the only way to solve the constitutional problems of Rome in the 50s, or even the indirect offer of himself as prospective dictator. The dictatorship had long been obsolete at the time of the Gracchan crisis; its function was to some degree taken over by the authority conferred on the consuls by the *senatus consultum ultimum.* C. uses it here, despite the anachronism, not to advocate its resurrection in his own day, but as a specific instance of the need for a single person of authority at moments of great crisis. The fact that Scipio did not live to do anything of the sort makes it possible for C. to have Africanus give such a prophecy and simultaneously removes from it any political significance for Scipio or for C. himself.

si . . . effugeris: the manner of Scipio's death was obscure at the time, although Cicero seems to have believed – as did many of Scipio's contemporaries – that he had been murdered by the Gracchans; cf. Introduction, p. 8.

12.5 The only break in Scipio's narrative of the dream. The irony of Scipio's joke only serves to heighten the seriousness of what follows. **parumper** (cf. 1.12.2) is Bouhier's certain conjecture for MS *parum rebus*. **st! quaeso:** colloquial; cf. 12.4 *ne multa*, 15.1 *quaeso*.

13 The concluding section of Africanus' first speech provides a transition from prophecy to eschatology. In order to encourage Scipio to serve his country despite the risks, Africanus describes the rewards of the statesman in the afterlife; in so doing, he introduces two major themes of the *Somnium*: the immortality of the soul and the relationship between human society and the divine order of the universe.

13.1 Sed . . . alacrior: Africanus' speech continues as if there had been no interruption. For the exhortation, cf. Virg. *Aen.* 6.718 *quo magis Italia mecum laetere reperta.* **sic habeto** 'know this for certain'; so also 26.2. The use of the fut. imper. is solemn and formal (cf. 2.57.2n.): it appears in the *Somnium* at 20.2, 24.3, 26.2, all significant junctures in the argument. **omnibus . . . fruantur:** for the immortality of the statesman, cf. *Sest.* 143. Plato too (cf. *Phd.* 82a, *Smp.* 209a) gave just statesmen privileges in the afterlife, but he ranked them lower than philosophers. C.'s eschatology throughout the *Somnium* is based on Plato, but the emphases are changed to reflect both the importance of the active life and the centrality of just government in *Rep.* **conseruauerint adiuuerint auxerint:** for the solemnity of the tricolon with asyndeton cf. 1.2.3n. **certum . . . locum** 'an assured place has been marked out'; *esse . . . definitum* is an infin. (for *definio* cf. 2.11.2n.). **beati** 'in blessedness'; proleptic.

13.2 C. here combines two leading ideas of *Rep.*, the divine qualities of statesmanship (cf. 1.12.4) and the conception of the true state as the embodiment of justice (cf. 1.39.1 and 3.45), and links them in turn to the divine order of the universe which both explains and justifies proper political action. A crucial step in this argument – Laelius' defence of natural justice (3.33–41) – is very fragmentary and omitted from this edition; for a reconstruction, cf. Ferrary (1974). **illi principi deo:** so also 26.3. The hegemony of a single, ruling god suits Scipio's analogical argument in favour of monarchy at 1.56.5, and is derived from Platonic and Stoic cosmology. The use of *principi* reinforces the analogy between cosmic and political organization which was applied to natural and human law by Laelius in book 3. The god can be identified either with the outer sphere of the cosmos (17.2) or with the sun (17.3); cf. 17.3n. **quod ... fiat:** a similar clause at 1.2.2. **coetusque ... sociati:** C. echoes the definition of the *populus* at 1.39.1, *coetus multitudinis iuris consensu et utilitatis communione sociatus.* **hinc profecti huc reuertuntur:** C. here goes beyond the promise of a heavenly reward introduced in the previous sentence to assert both the immortality of the soul and its close ties to the celestial order. Both ideas are Platonic (and are explained more fully below: see on 14–16, 26), but C. does not accept Plato's concomitant beliefs in metempsychosis and anamnesis: each soul, for C., has one earthly existence and – if deserving – a permanent heavenly reward for actions in that one life.

14.1 Despite the fact that Scipio is less afraid of death than of betrayal, his question – which elicits the first detailed explanation of the soul – concerns not his own fate but the nature of the after-life. **a meis:** source; cf. *ab iis ... sermonem fore*, 23.2; *meis* refers to the same people as *propinquorum*, 12.4. **ipse:** Africanus. **Paullus pater:** Scipio's natural father, L. Aemilius Paullus.

14.2 immo uero: cf. 1.20.3n. **hi uiuunt ... mors est:** the complementary ideas of the body as a prison (or tomb) and of human life as in fact death are derived from Plato; cf. *Phd.* 67d, *Phdr.* 250c, *Grg.* 492e–493a, *Cra.* 400bc, passages in which these ideas are attributed to Pythagorean sources (but for 'Pythagorean' in this context cf Burkert (1972) 78 n.157, 248 nn.47–48); also [Plato], *Ax.* 365e. At *Scaur.* 4, C. wrongly attributed the statement in *Phd.* to Plato himself; cf. also *Tusc.* 1.74–75, *Sen.* 77, 81 with Powell *ad locc.*, and below on 15.2, 4. The discussions of the soul and the afterlife at *Tusc.* 1.71–5 and *Sen.* 77–84 are closely parallel to, and in parts based on, this section of the *Somnium.* **e corporum uinclis:** Platonic (cf. *Ti.* 44b, 81d); so also *Tusc.* 1.75, *Sen.* 81, *Am.* 14 (referring to this passage). **euolauerunt:** so *Am.* 14; cf. *De orat.* 2.22, *rus ex urbe tamquam e uinclis euolare.* **quae dicitur** 'so-called'; C. in the *Somnium* repeatedly draws attention to the difference between human language or perception and the underlying reality; cf. 15.3n.

14.3 quin: cf. 1.61.6n. Scipio turns from the general to the specific, and the appearance of Paullus is a demonstration of the truth of what he has been saying. **uim lacrimarum profudi** 'I burst into a flood of tears'; for *uis* 'quantity' cf. *OLD* s.v. 8b. **me complexus:** in a dream, unlike a waking encounter with someone dead (e.g. Virg. *Aen.* 6.700–2), an embrace is possible.

15.2–4 The discussion of suicide (cf. also *Scaur.* 4, *Tusc.* 1.74, *Sen.* 73) is similar to (and partly based on) Plato, *Phd.* 61d-62c, where the prohibition is attributed to Philolaus the Pythagorean; cf. Powell on *Sen.* 73.

15.2 nisi ... cum 'except when'; 'until': many MSS and some editors omit *cum*, but it is a common construction (cf. K–S II 416–17) and may suggest legal language; cf. *Verr.* 2.146, *Prov.* 17. **templum:** C. emphasizes the sacredness of the universe as a whole, seen as the precinct of the god who rules it (so also 17.1; also at 3.14 and *Leg.* 2.26 of the Persians' belief that enclosing gods in temples was sacrilegious). There are also overtones of *templum* 'region', as a technical term for an area marked off for taking the auspices; cf. *OLD* s.v. 1, 4a, and cf. also 24.3 and the repeated use of *contemplor* (cf. 16.2, 20.2, 29.1 and Pease on *N.D.* 2.37). For the various meanings of *templum* cf. Jocelyn on Enn. *Sc.* 88, 171 and Linderski 2256–89. **custodiis** 'prison'; cf. 14.2 *e corporum uinclis*. C. is adapting the phrase ἔν τινι φρουρᾶι from *Phd.* 62b; but cf. 15.4n.

15.3 hac lege: cf. *Tusc.* 3.59, *ea lege nos esse natos.* **qui tuerentur:** a final relative clause. *tueor* here clearly = 'protect' rather than 'observe', as its object is the earth rather than the universe. The context (cf. 13.1–2, 16.1) gives the guardianship of earth an explicitly political meaning, and the argument significantly strengthens C.'s initial statement (1.3.5) that political activity is natural, by making it not merely natural but divinely ordained. In the parallel passage at *Sen.* 77 (which is less political), C. (following Plato, *R.* 6.500bc, *Ti.* 47bc) links protection of the earth with contemplation of the heavens: *ut essent qui terras tuerentur quique caelestium ordinem contemplantes imitarentur eum.* That connection is implicit both in Scipio's first speech (1.26.2) and later in the *Somnium* (25.2). Cf. Pease on *N.D.* 2.37, Powell on *Sen.* 77. **illum globum quem ... uides:** C. accepts the Platonic structure (cf. *Phd.* 108e, *R.* 616d–617b, *Ti.* 33b–38e) of a spherical earth at the centre of a spherical universe. This brief description is elaborated in 17–18; cf. *ad loc.* **dicitur:** as in 14.2 (cf. *uocatis* in this

§; also 17.3), C. is at pains to emphasize the limitations of human perspective and knowledge. **iisque animus ... ignibus:** an expansion of 13.2 *hinc profecti huc reuertuntur*. The idea of astral immortality is probably taken (directly or indirectly) from Plato, *Ti.* 41d–42b; for the development of the concept, cf. Burkert (1972) 357–68. **sidera et stellas** 'constellations and stars'. **globosae et rotundae:** *globosus* is, according to C. himself (*Tim.* 17; cf. *N.D.* 2.47), a translation of the Greek σφαιροειδής (Pl. *Ti.* 33b); for Plato, the sphere was the most perfect of solid figures as the circle was of plane figures. *rotundae* may express the circular form as it would be seen by a distant observer, but may (as is the case with *circos ... orbesque* below) be no more than a gloss on the less familiar term. According to 17.2 the stars are embedded in the outer sphere of the cosmos; the apparent attribution to them here of three-dimensional shape and independent motion is surprising. **diuinis animatae mentibus** cf. Pl. *Ti.* 40b; for other believers in the divinity of the stars, cf. Pease on *N.D.* 1.27. **circos ... orbesque:** cf. *N.D.* 2.44, *orbem circumque*. *circus* is less common in C. than *circulus* (the reading of a number of MSS here); but cf. 16.1 and Pease on *N.D.* 2.47.

15.4 Publi: Scipio's father addresses him by his *praenomen*, a mark of affection; in the next sentence he returns to the formality of the *cognomen*. **in custodia corporis:** cf. 15.2 *corporis custodiis*. *Phd.* 62b ἔν τινι φρουρᾶι, which lies behind C.'s expression, means 'under guard', but it has also been taken to mean 'on guard', and it has been suggested that C. here has both meanings in mind. *corporis*, however, rules that out: we are here not to guard the body, but are imprisoned by it while guarding the earth. **nec iniussu eius:** cf. *Tusc.* 1.74, *Sen.* 73. C. is almost certainly combining the prohibition of suicide in the *Phaedo* with the prohibition against leaving one's (metaphorical) post at *Ap.* 28d. **migrandum:** cf. 9.2. At *Tusc.* 1.98 C. translates ἀποδημῆσαι (*Ap.* 40e, of dying) as *migrationem*: death is not an end, but merely emigration to a better place. **munus humanum:** cf. *Sen.* 77, *Hort.* fr. 97 M. **defugisse:** cf. 2.34.4n.

16.1 auus hic tuus: Africanus. For deictic *hic*, cf. 9.1n. **iustitiam ... pietatem:** for the close connection of the two, cf. *N.D.* 2.153 with Pease *ad loc.* **in parentibus** 'in respect of one's parents'; cf. *OLD* s.v. 41a, 42. **tum in patria maxima est:** C. returns to a theme which he enunciated in the preface; cf. fr. 1a (cited on 1.4.1), 1.8. The complete absence of the usual prime recipients of *pietas*, the gods, is surprising, but may be because both the individual and, in a sense, the state are themselves divinized in C.'s theory. **hunc coetum:** cf. 13.2 (also 1.39.1) where the same word is used for political organizations on earth. **qui iam uixerunt** 'whose life is over'. The pf. of *uiuo* and *sum* is a common euphemism for death; cf. Virg. *Aen.* 4.653 *uixi et quem dederat cursum fortuna peregi.* **corpore laxati:** freed from *corporum uincla* (14.2); a translation of ἐκλυομένην ... ἐκ τοῦ σώματος, *Phd.* 67d. **illum ... locum ... nuncupatis:** the Milky Way as the abode of the souls of the dead is not Platonic, but is almost certainly drawn from the eschatological vision of Empedotimus written by Heraclides Ponticus; cf. frr. 96–7 Wehrli with Gottschalk 100–5, 149–54. C. does not make clear where in the cosmos he places the Milky Way; Heraclides located it between the moon and the sun (on the order of the spheres, cf. 17.3–4n.), but C.'s identification of souls with stars suggests that he views it as part of the outer sphere of the cosmos. **splendidissimo ... elucens:** cf. *Aratea* 248–9 *uidisti magnum candentem serpere circum, | Lacteus hic nimio fulgens candore notatur.* **ut a Grais accepistis:** i.e. γαλάκτιος κύκλος, γαλαξίας. For *Graius*, cf. 1.58.7n.; here its poeticism is reinforced by *nuncupatis* (cf. 2.14n.). For the emphasis on human names, cf. 15.3n.

16.2 ex: more likely to be temporal (cf. *OLD* s.v. 9) than local, as Scipio is not on the Milky Way. **mihi contemplanti:** for C.'s use of the dat. participle with a verb of reciprocal meaning (cf. *De Orat.* 1.1, 3.1) cf. Laughton 37–8; for *contemplor* (also at 20.2, 29.1), cf. 15.3n. **cetera:** although not expressed until 16.4, *ipsa terra* (rather than the Milky Way) must be the term contrasting with *cetera*. As the next sentence shows, Scipio views everything in the cosmos in comparison with what he has seen from the earth.

16.3 The threefold *eae ... eae ... ea* draws attention emphatically to the falseness of earthly impressions (cf. 15.3n.): there are more and larger celestial bodies than we could ever realize, and that which is largest to us (the moon) is in fact the smallest. **quas numquam ... uidimus:** invisible from the earth, or from Rome; Arist. *Cael.* 2.9 points out the difference in the visibility of stars between Egypt and Europe. **ultima a caelo, citima <a> terris:** the moon. J. F. Gronovius' addition seems called for by the parallelism of construction. On the order of the celestial bodies cf. 17.3–4. That the moon had no light of its own had long been known; for a list of authorities, cf. Pease on *N.D.* 2.103. *citimus* is rare; in C. only at *Tim.* 25.

16.4 iam uero ... paeniteret: cf. 1.26.2. This clause marks the transition from discussion of the immortality of the soul and the prospect of an afterlife to their negative corollary, the insignificance of human power and glory. Only at the end (6.26) does C. return to the nature of the soul and the afterlife. There is an apparent contradiction between the emphasis on the insignificance of the earth in the central section of the *Somnium* and the eschatological importance of public service on earth in the opening and closing sections (cf. Harder 357), but in fact the two arguments reinforce one another: human life is insignificant *sub specie aeternitatis*, but the earth is still the centre of the cosmos and its protection is assigned to human souls by god. One's actions here are not important because of their success or fame on earth, but because they prepare for eternity. **quo ... attingimus** 'through which we come into contact with only a tiny spot of it'. From the Hellenistic period on, it was normal to describe the earth as a στιγμή or σημεῖον in comparison with the universe (cf. *punctum* at *Tusc.* 1.40; Sen. *N.Q.* 1 pr. 8); to describe the Roman Empire as a *punctum* of earth has no classical parallel, and hence C. qualifies it with *quasi*.

17.1 Quam cum magis intuerer: echoed at 18.1. Scipio continues to look at the earth, but it is necessary, not only for him in his celestial vision but for all humans, to contemplate the heavens in order to act rightly on earth; cf. 25.2. The contemplation of the heavens in the large sense advocated in the *Somnium* serves as a coda to the themes of astronomy in book 1 and of divine and human law in book 3, and the description of the spheres which follows immediately looks back to the mechanical imitation of the heavens created by Archimedes and described in book 1. The order and beauty of the universe are used (among other examples) as an analogy for oratory at *De orat.* 3.178 and described in detail as part of the Stoic argument for the divinity of the universe at *N.D.* 2.49–56. **templa:** cf. 15.2n.

17.2–6 C. sets out briefly and succinctly his understanding of the structure of the universe, which is loosely based on the description of the spindle of Necessity in the Myth of Er (*R.* 10.616c–617b) and on the astronomy of *Ti.* 38c–39d, but owes much both to later Hellenistic astronomy (probably Eudoxus and Archimedes) and – as is the case with the description of the earth in 20–4 – to poetic descriptions of the cosmos and the world. C.'s universe consists of nine concentric spheres, of which the outermost contains the fixed stars and is itself the god ruling the universe; then come, in descending order, Saturn, Jupiter, Mars, the sun, Venus, Mercury, and the moon; the inmost sphere is the earth itself, fixed and unmoving in the centre of the universe. Except for the order of the spheres (see below), this is standard Hellenistic astronomy: the sphere of the fixed stars revolves rapidly from east to west, and pulls the planetary spheres (including the sun and moon) with it, thus creating the diurnal changes (night and day) which heliocentric cosmology explains by the rotation of the earth; but at the same time, the planetary spheres revolve from west to east (*retro contrario motu atque caelum*, 17.2), causing the slower westward progression of the sun and planets through the Zodiac. In astronomical terms, C.'s account is seriously oversimplified: he does not, for instance, mention the ecliptic; his description of the relationship of the orbits of Mercury and Venus to that of the sun is excessively vague; and he does not acknowledge the complications of planetary motion which Plato himself is said to have set as a problem for his pupils (on Plato's astronomy – its strengths and its limitations – cf. Vlastos 23–65; for a more detailed analysis of the relationship between Plato's and other systems, cf. Burkert (1972) 299–337).

The most significant difference in physical astronomy (on the music of the spheres, cf. 18n.) between C.'s universe and that of both Plato and most Hellenistic authorities lies in the order of the spheres (on which cf. Boyancé (1936) 59–65). Plato, Eudoxus, and Eratosthenes placed the sphere of the sun between that of the moon and those of Mercury and Venus; the order is described as 'Egyptian' by Macrobius. In Archimedes, the late Hellenistic poet Alexander of Ephesus, and C. himself, however, the spheres are in the 'Chaldaean' order, according to which the sun's sphere is between Venus and Mars. C. knew Alexander's poem (cf. *Att.* 2.22.7), and Archimedes' celestial orrery – which presumably displayed his preferred order of the spheres – is discussed by C. at 1.22 with great admiration; in all probability, it was Alexander's poem which he found most useful, as his sequence of topics (celestial structure – music of the spheres – zones of the earth) is the one followed in the *Somnium* (it is also found in Eratosthenes' *Hermes*, but the order of the spheres is different). From the point of view of the argument of the *Somnium* and of *Rep.* as a whole, however, the main reason for adopting the order of the spheres given here is that it places the sun in the middle as the guide and leader of the celestial order and an analogy for the statesman on earth.

17.2: tibi 'as you see': ethic dat. **orbibus uel potius globis:** the revolutions of the planets appear to be circles, *orbes*, but in fact they are spheres, *globi*, in which the planets are fixed. **unus est caelestis ... cursus sempiterni:** the identification of the outer sphere of the cosmos with the supreme divinity is Stoic (cf. *Luc.* 2.126, *N.D.* 1.36, 37 with Pease *ad loc.*); Plato and Aristotle posited a higher, extracosmic god. Whether or not the fixed stars were attached to the outer sphere or had their own was a matter of disagreement among the Stoics: here, C. follows Cleanthes in connecting the two, while Chrysippus and Posidonius apparently thought that they were separate; cf. Boyancé (1936) 68–70 and *N.D.* 2.54–5 with Pease *ad loc.* **caelestis:** for *caelum* = *aether* (the outer heaven), cf. *N.D.* 2.41, 91, 101. **arcens et continens ceteros** 'bounding and containing the others (sc. spheres)': the same terminology for the relationship of the stomach to its contents at *N.D.* 2.136. **infixi:** C.'s regular term (= Gk. ἐμπεπηγότες); cf. *Tusc.* 1.62, 5.69, *Tim.* 36, *N.D.* 1.34 with Pease *ad loc.* and on 2.54. **stellarum cursus:** cf. 18.3 *stellifer cursus*; and of the orbits of the planets, 17.4, 18.4. Although all the fixed stars are part of the single motion of the *caelum*, they have different circular orbits. **septem ... caelum** 'which move backward with a motion opposite to that of the heavens'; cf. 17.2–6n. C. is probably drawing on Pl. *Ti.* 36cd; cf. also *N.D.* 2.49 with Pease *ad loc.* At 1.22, in describing Archimedes' orrery, C. speaks of *solis et lunae ... et earum quinque stellarum quae errantes et quasi uagae nominarentur* (= Gk. πλανήτης), but here he avoids the technical term and the problems of whether the sun and moon are properly 'planets' and whether 'wandering' is a suitable description for regular celestial motion; cf. Vlastos 32, 99–102.

17.3 quam ... nominant: on the unreliability of human names and understanding, cf. 15.3n.; also *dicitur*, *dicitis* in this §. **illa:** sc. *stella.* **Saturniam:** the planet is associated with the god, but is not yet identified with him: cf. Pease on *N.D.* 2.52; on the names of the planets cf. Cumont. The use of the possessive adj. rather than the gen. *Saturni* is archaic; cf. Löfstedt I 107–24. In this sentence, C. alternates between the two types. **prosperus et salutaris:** Jupiter's name was derived from *iuuare*; cf. *N.D.* 2.64 *appellamus a iuuando Iouem*, with

Pease *ad loc.* and Maltby s.v. *Iuppiter.* **fulgor:** the poetic periphrasis for *stella* may also reflect the name Phaethon given to the planet Jupiter: cf. [Arist.] *Mu.* 2, Pease on *N.D.* 2.52. **rutilus:** Mars is ὑπέρυθρον in Pl. *R.* 10.617a and named Πυρόεις at [Arist.] *Mu.* 2 and *N.D.* 2.53. **horribilis:** because of the god Mars' association with war. **subter:** adverbial. **mediam fere regionem:** on the position of the sun in Cicero's cosmography, cf. 17.2–6n.; at *N.D.* 2.119 C. (following a Stoic source) gives the Platonic order of the planets. *fere* may refer (cf. Macrob. 1.19.15–17) to the fact that the outer planets and stars were thought to be further from the sun than the sun from the earth, or may simply be C.'s usual qualification with expressions of quantity; cf. 1.25.3n. **dux ... temperatio:** the political language used here is not unique: at *N.D.* 2.49 C. refers to *sol, qui astrorum tenet principatum*, at *N.D.* 2.92 he calls the sun *princeps*, and at *T.D.* 1.68 he speaks of *eorumque omnium* [day and night, seasons, climate] *moderatorem et ducem solem.* C. at this point abandons the identification of the divinity with the sphere of the fixed stars accepted by most Stoics and follows the view of Cleanthes, who identified the ruling principle, the ἡγεμονικόν, with the sun: cf. *Luc.* 2.126, *SVF* I 499, and Boyancé (1936) 78–104. C.'s language links his astronomy to *Rep.* as a whole: the sun's role in the universe is analogous to that of the *rector rei publicae* in the state; in particular, *temperatio* reflects the balance of the ideal government: cf. 1.45.3n. Furthermore, the sun's leadership in the world is active as well as analogous: the prodigy of the two suns and the eclipse at the death of Romulus show cosmic concern with the governance of Rome. **cuncta ... compleat:** cf. *N.D.* 2.49, 92; the use of *lustro* is poetic and solemn.

17.4 ut comites consequuntur: *ut* is adverbial. C. is again vague (as indeed is Pl. *R.* 10.617b, *Ti.* 38d) concerning a major problem of geocentric astronomy, the orbits and relative positions of Mercury and Venus. At *N.D.* 2.54, Venus is placed closer to the earth than is Mercury (as in Plato), while here the order of names suggests that C. adopts the reverse order; from a heliocentric point of view that is right, but geocentrically it is impossible to determine which is 'correct': cf. Burkert (1972) 300. The problem arises from the fact that Mercury, Venus, and the sun are 'isodromous' – they all circle the Zodiac in approximately one year, and neither Mercury nor Venus is ever far from the sun. Hence, although most astronomers considered that the two revolved around the earth, Pl. *Ti.* 38d says that they revolve in the opposite direction from the sun, and Heraclides Ponticus (cf. Gottschalk 69–83) makes their orbits epicycles centred on the sun. C.'s use of *comites* to describe their relationship to the sun reinforces the political language of the previous §. **radiis Solis accensa:** cf. 16.3n.

17.5 nihil ... caducum: the idea of the mortality of the sublunary sphere is apparently pre-Socratic, and is common in later Platonism; for sources cf. Pease on *N.D.* 2.56. **praeter animos ... datos:** cf. 15.3.

17.6 nutu suo: etymologically 'nod'; hence 'inclination' and here 'gravity'; cf. *OLD* s.v. 4.

18 The idea of the music of the spheres was ascribed in antiquity to the Pythagoreans, but the mathematical explanations of celestial harmony show that it presupposes the complex astronomical systems of the *Timaeus* or of Plato's contemporary Eudoxus. Here (cf. 18.4), as in many other accounts, the music is related to the strings of the lyre; so, for instance, in the cosmological poems of Eratosthenes and of Alexander of Ephesus (which C. knew: cf. 17.2–6n.). C.'s source was clearly not Plato: at *R.* 10.617b the music is the singing of the Sirens mounted on the various spheres, and at *Ti.* 37b the movement of the world-soul is expressly said to be silent. The topic is both obscure and complex, and C. seems quite deliberately to have avoided going into details which would interfere with the grandeur of his description: his goal is to demonstrate that the harmony of the universe corresponds to, and inspires, both literal and metaphorical harmony on earth. For a list of ancient discussions of the music of the spheres, cf. Pease on *N.D.* 3.27; the most important pre-Ciceronian account is Arist. *Cael.* 2.9. There are useful modern discussions of the history of the idea in Burkert (1972) 350–7 and of C.'s account in Boyancé (1936) 104–15.

18.1 Quae cum intuerer: cf. 17.1. **quid ... quis:** the text is variously printed and punctuated; Ziegler's first edition is followed here.

18.2 Hic ... efficit 'This is the sound that is caused by the action and motion of the spheres themselves. Its harmony is based on uneven intervals, but the inequality of the intervals is proportional and based on reason, and by blending high notes with low itself causes balanced music.' Africanus begins with a general statement, the details of which are explained in the next two sentences. Each planet produces a single note, the pitch of which is directly related to the speed with which it circles the earth, which in turn – although C. does not say so explicitly – is proportional to its distance from the earth. The intervals between the planets, and thus between the notes they produce, are different (*interuallis ... imparibus*), but the combined effect is harmonious (*coniunctus* reflects the technical term of Greek music συνημμένος 'harmonic'), because the intervals are in proper proportions to one another (*pro rata parte ... distinctis*). The sense is clear, but the text is difficult: Macrobius reads *disiunctus* rather than *coniunctus*, and some MSS read *pro rata partium ratione*. **ratione:** the universe is ordered by right reason (*recta ratio*, 3.33), and the harmony of the spheres is a manifestation of that reason. The expression of divine reason through number and proportion is based on the *Timaeus* (on harmony and reason cf. 47de) rather than on observation; the actual physical intervals between the planets, even as they were calculated in the Hellenistic age, do not produce ratios corresponding to the musical scale. **et acuta cum grauibus temperans** 'blending high notes with low'. Both *temperans* (cf. 17.3n.) and *aequabiliter* (cf. 1.43.1n.) have clear political implications. At 2.69 Scipio compares the concord of the well-ordered state to musical harmony: *ex summis et infimis et mediis interiectis ordinibus ut sonis moderata ratione ciuitas consensu dissimillimorum concinit; et quae harmonia a musicis dicitur in cantu, ea est in ciuitate concordia.* **nec enim silentio:** a similar mechanical explanation of the music is ascribed by Aristotle (*Cael.* 2.9) to the Pythagoreans.

18.3 C. understands the relative speed of the spheres in terms of their daily revolutions around the earth: the fixed stars, being furthest away, must traverse the greatest distance in 24 hours, while the moon, being closest, has the shortest distance to travel. In this, C. agrees with Arist. *Cael.* 2.9; cf. also [Arist.] *Mu.* 6. Other accounts take progression through the Zodiac as the basis for determining relative speed, and therefore reverse the order given by C. **stellifer:** only here in C. Compounds of this form (object + verb, usually *fero* or *gero*) are archaic and generally limited to poetry.

18.4 illi autem ... sonos: Burkert (1972) 353 rightly calls C.'s combination of eight spheres and seven notes 'a patchwork compromise'. The earth does not move, and therefore produces no note; the eight spheres produce seven different notes, but Cicero does not make clear which two produce the same note, and two different solutions have been advanced. Macrob. *Comm.* 2.4.9 believed that Mercury and Venus (cf. 17.4n.) shared one note, but it has rightly been objected that if their closeness to the sun gives them the same speed, then the sun too should produce the same note. Boyancé (1936) 111–12 suggested that the moon and the fixed stars produce the same note an octave apart. This has the advantage of explaining *uis* (a translation of δύναμις, which is used to describe the octave), but as *sonus* must mean 'note', his interpretation requires taking *septem* as abl. agreeing with *interuallis*, 'they produce distinct notes at seven intervals'. Though the interlocking word order is unusual and misleading, this interpretation agrees with the accounts of Plato (*R.* 10.617b) and Eratosthenes (*SH* 397A), and on balance is preferable; for another example of interlocking word order, cf. 2.12 *honesto ortas loco uirgines.* **qui numerus ... nodus est:** cf. 12.3n. The two numbers reproduce those of Africanus' prophecy to Scipio. **docti homines ... cantibus:** *cantus* is the music made by the strings (*neruis*) of the lyre, frequently adduced (cf. Burkert (1972) 351) as the model for, or copy of, the music of the spheres. In particular, C. appears to be following (as in the order of the planets) the cosmological poem of Alexander of Ephesus (*SH* 21; cf. the Latin version of Varro Atacinus, fr. 15 Courtney), in which Hermes apparently made the lyre in imitation of the sound of the universe. The idea that music purifies the soul is Pythagorean; but its importance here is that it is the only recognition in the *Somnium* that anyone other than a public figure could acquire entry to heaven. The admission of musicians (presumably Orpheus and Amphion are meant) and other cultural figures to Elysium (or the Milky Way) is found in Virg. *Aen.* 6.663 *qui uitam excoluere per artes* and in the anonymous Orphic catabasis of P. Bologna 4; cf. Zetzel (1989) 266.n.13. **diuina studia:** the phrase is found elsewhere only at *Sen.* 24, where it refers to poetry and philosophy. Cf. also *Tusc.* 1.72 *in corporibus humanis uitam imitati deorum.*

19.1 hoc sonitu ... obsurduerunt: in *Cael.* 2.9, Aristotle reports the Pythagorean explanation of our deafness to the music of the spheres, that it is so constant that we are unaware of it. **ubi Nilus ... praecipitat:** presumably the second or great cataract of the Nile at Wadi Halfa; for the deafness of the inhabitants, cf. Seneca, *N.Q.* 4.2.5. *Catadupa* is from Greek καταδουπεῖν, to fall with a heavy sound. C.'s analogy is imperfect: humans do not hear the music of the spheres (but can hear other sounds) because our ears are filled with it at all times, but the people of the Catadupa hear nothing at all because they are deafened by the noise.

19.2 incitatissima: cf. *incitari*, 18.2; *concitatior*, 18.3. **capere** 'take in'; cf. *OLD* s.v. 29. **sicut ... nequitis:** the closing simile of the discussion of the music of the spheres turns back from sound to sight, and in particular to the sun, both the ruling sphere of the universe and the image of the true statesman. C. may well have in mind Plato's use of the sun as the image of the Good, which the inhabitants of the cave are unable to look upon: cf. *R.* 7.515e–516b. For the image of looking at the sun, cf. also *Phd.* 99d, adapted by C. at *Tusc.* 1.73. **acies ... sensusque** 'the sense of sight'; hendiadys.

20.1 As if to demonstrate the truth of the previous sentence, Scipio once again (cf. 17.1) turns away from the heavens to look at the earth, thus giving Africanus the occasion to minimize the importance of human fame and achievements because of the physical and chronological limitations of human existence. **admirans:** concessive, as shown by *tamen*: despite his wonder at the universe, Scipio cannot help looking down repeatedly (*identidem*) at the earth.

20.2 sedem ... ac domum: the same phrase of Rome as the seat of empire, 2.10.2; of the true celestial home at 25.2, 29.1. There is perhaps a reminiscence of Philus' argument (1.19.5) that the universe is our *domus*. **contemplari**: cf. 16.2n. **si tibi ... ita uidetur** cf. 16.4 *ipsa terra ita mihi parua uisa est*; the reference to the diminutive size of the earth serves first to introduce the grandeur of the heavens, and here to introduce a more detailed description of the earth itself. *ut est* emphasizes the difference between normal human perspective and the true divine perspective (cf. 15.3n.); that they now coincide is an indication of Scipio's growing understanding of the universe. **haec ... contemnito:** Africanus' solemn injunction (for the fut. imper. cf. 13.1n.) has both a particular and a general meaning. In the immediate context, Scipio is being admonished to pay attention to his grandfather's instruction and to observe the heavens which have just been described. At the same time, however, it is the dominant advice of the *Somnium* as a whole (elaborated at 25.2, 29.2), an admonition to be concerned with eternal rather than ephemeral concerns, with the divine rather than the human. Although such exhortations (cf. *Luc.* 127; Arist. *Protrept.* frr. 10a, 11 Ross = B105, 18–19 Düring) generally entail rejection of earthly involvement, that is not the case here (or in the parallel passage in Scipio's first speech, 1.26): throughout the *Somnium* political participation is a necessary preparation for the eternal happiness of the soul; what is to be scorned is the idea that the earthly glory which attends public life is valuable in itself.

20.3 quam celebritatem ... gloriam potes: cf. *Tusc.* 1.109 *nihil habet in se gloria cur expetatur. expetendam* as well as *consequi potes* should be taken with both *celebritatem* and *gloriam*, and provides an important qualification: what fame or glory that is worth seeking can you achieve? This serves to introduce a cosmological argument against excessive concern with human glory: not only is the earth itself tiny – and therefore of negligible importance – in comparison with the cosmos, but the portion of it which Scipio's name can reach is small, and the earth itself is limited not only physically but chronologically by periodic destructions of the world. The relative smallness and unimportance of the world was apparently a commonplace of Hellenistic tracts on despising glory; C. himself may have been responsible for the combination of this with the detailed description of the earth itself.

20.4 habitari 'people live': for the use, cf. *OLD* s.v. 3. **raris et angustis:** the adjectives anticipate the description of the earth which follows: *angustus* because the two habitable zones are narrow in comparison with the size of the earth, *rarus* because there are only four regions on the entire globe that are inhabited. **maculis** 'blotches' is scornful; the equivalent σπίλοι in [Arist.] *Mu.* 3, also describes the inhabited portions of the earth. **manare** 'spread', 'become known'; cf. *OLD* s.v. 6. **partim obliquos ... aduersos:** as with the descriptions of the music of the spheres (cf. 18.2n.), a general statement precedes the details. In the geography which follows, the earth is divided into five zones, of which the two temperate and habitable zones are separated by an impassable equatorial band of heat (21.1–2); it is also divided by oceans in such a way as to split the temperate zones themselves (21.3). The world of Rome may be described as the north-eastern quadrant of the globe; the people who are *obliqui* live at the same longitude, but southern latitude; the *transuersi* are at the same latitude, but western longitude; the *aduersi* (*antipodes*; cf. *Luc.* 123 with Reid *ad loc.*) are directly through the centre of the globe, at southern latitude and western longitude. Since they are all permanently separated from Rome, it is impossible for the report of any Roman deed however glorious – the position of *nullam* is emphatic – to reach them.

21.1 eandem terram 'this same earth'; cf. *OLD* s.v. *idem* 3. **quasi quibusdam ... cingulis:** the division of the earth into five zones – frigid at either pole, hot at the equator, and temperate in two bands between the equator and the poles – is as old as Parmenides (Strabo 2.2.2), and is found, for instance, in Arist. *Mete.* 2.5; among the texts which Cicero is most likely to have used, it appears in Eratosthenes' *Hermes* (fr. 16 Powell) and probably in the *Cosmographia* of Alexander of Ephesus (cf. the translation of Varro Atacinus, fr. 17 Courtney). *cinguli* 'belts' (masc. only here) translates the Greek ζῶναι (cf. Eratosthenes 16.3; in Latin Varro, *Men.* fr. 92.2 Buecheler, Varro Atac. 17.1, Virg. *Geo.* 1.233). Elsewhere (*N.D.* 1.24, *Tusc.* 1.45) C. is less precise and uses *regiones*; Arist. *Mete.* 2.5 had used τμήματα and ἐκτμήματα, 'slices'. *redimitam*, used by C. elsewhere of garlands (4.5; *Cat.* 2.10, *Pro Gallio* fr.1), is glossed by the virtually synonymous *circumdatam*. **maxime inter se diuersos** 'most distant from one another'. **caeli uerticibus ... subnixos** 'resting on the opposing poles of the sky': the poles of the earth lie on the axis of the universe itself, and hence the polar regions can be said to lean on it; cf. [Arist.] *Mu.* 2. *subnixos* is poetic; cf. on *subiectus aquiloni*, 21.2. **obriguisse pruina:** cf. *N.D.* 1.24 *pars obriguerit niue pruinaque*.

21.2 australis ille: the southern temperate zone (cf. *Tusc.* 1.68), which in fact includes the *obliqui* as well as the *aduersi*. **aduersa ... uestigia:** cf. *Luc.* 123 *qui aduersis uestigiis stent contra nostra uestigia, quos antipodes uocatis*. The word ἀντίπους (which C. is paraphrasing here) appears with this meaning in Pl. *Ti.* 63a; cf. also Eratosthenes, fr. 16.19 Powell. **urgent** 'press' is poetic; cf. *OLD* s.v. 1. **nihil:** sc. *pertinent*; a frequent ellipse. **subiectus aquiloni** 'exposed to the north wind' is poetic; at *Tusc.* 1.68 C. uses a quotation from Accius' *Philocteta* to describe the northern zone: *sub axe posita ad stellas septem, unde horrifer | Aquilonis stridor gelidos molitur niues*; cf. also Virg. *Geo.* 3.381 *septem subiecta trioni*.

21.3 quae colitur a uobis: a translation of Gk. οἰκουμένη 'the inhabited world' (including the three continents Europe, Africa, and Asia), for which there is no Latin equivalent. **angustata ... latior** 'narrow at the ends, wider from side to side'; Eratosthenes (cf. Strabo 2.5.14, 11.11.7; Macrob., *Comm.* 2.9.8) compared the shape of the οἰκουμένη to a Greek *chlamys*, wider at the base than at the top; Arist. *Mete.* 2.5 compared it to a drum. C.'s pl. *uerticibus* is puzzling, as it suggests a diamond shape. **insula:** for the known world as an island, cf. *N.D.* 2.165 (earlier sources cited by Pease *ad loc.*); also presumably Alexander of Ephesus: cf. Varro Atac. fr. 16 Courtney. **quod Atlanticum ... Oceanum:** the body of water surrounding the world was traditionally called Ocean, but Plb. 16.29.6 and [Arist.] *Mu.* 3 give it both names. **quem Oceanum:** the relative is attracted into the gender of its predicate noun. **qui ... uides:** the antecedent of *qui* is *Oceanum*, but *paruus* is contrasted in sense with *magnum*. For *paruus* (and the contrast between name and reality) cf. 20.2n.

22.1 cultis: cf. *colitur* 21.3. **uel Caucasum ... Gangen tranatare:** the furthest points of Roman knowledge to the north east and south east; the choice of verbs matches the nature of the geographical features. **quem cernis** (cf. *uides* 20.4, *cernis* 21.1) draws attention to Scipio's location above the earth. They are now closer to earth than in 17–19.

22.2 reliquis: because the two places specifically named are in the east. **orientis ... partibus:** the traditional description of the world in terms of the four points of the compass; two are named from the path of the sun, two from the winds blowing from those directions (cf *aquilonis*, 21.2). *partibus* governs all four.

22.3 quibus amputatis: even within the quarter of the globe in which Scipio lives, the extremes in all directions are beyond the reach of Roman glory; what remains is small indeed. **dilatari:** cf. *Hort.* fr. 87 M. (quoted 1.26.2n.).

22.4 Africanus turns from the extent of glory to the people who will provide it, and thus to the chronological limitations described in the next paragraph. The discussion of the limits of glory was echoed by C. in the *Hortensius* (cf. previous n., and on 24.2, 3) and by Boethius in *Cons.* 2.7; cf. Boyancé (1936) 148–51. The unusual word order *quam loquentur diu* gives a double-cretic clausula.

23.1 proles: singled out as a poetic archaism by C. at *De orat.* 3.153; it is used in an etymology at 2.40.1, but elsewhere by C. only in the *Aratea* (quoted at *N.D.* 2.159) and in a pseudo-archaic law at *Leg.* 3.7. **deinceps** 'from one to the next' 'in succession'; cf. 1.58.5. **a patribus acceptas posteris prodere:** the due transmission of knowledge from one generation to another – although its limits are acknowledged here – is one of the major topics of *Rep.* and the situation of its dramatic setting. For other exx. of *posteris prodere*, cf. *Mil.* 83, *Leg.* 3.4, *Sen.* 25, *Off.* 2.63, and Caelius, *Fam.* 8.3.3. **propter eluuiones exustionesque terrarum:** C. draws on Pl. *Ti.* 22c (cf. *Lg.* 3.677a on floods; also Plb. 6.5.5), referring to destructions of humans by fire and flood; at *Ti.* 23ab Plato implies that these destructions occur at regular intervals. According to Censorinus 18.11, Aristotle saw the recurring floods and fires as the winter and summer of the great year (cf. 24.2n.), and C. may have that in mind. It is unlikely that he is referring to the Stoic theory that the end of the great year was marked by a conflagration (ἐκπύρωσις) in which the universe was destroyed (references in Pease on *N.D.* 2.119): C.'s universe is eternal, and these periodic disasters terminate periods of human history alone. *exustio* occurs only here in C.; for the same combination of fire and flood, cf. *Div.* 1.111. **non modo non ... quidem:** the second *non* is omitted by at least one manuscript, and was deleted by Gruter, but C. tends to retain it in all cases where there is a strong opposition between the contrasted terms; cf. Hommel (1955b) 356–7. **ne diuturnam quidem** echoes *quam loquentur diu*, 22.4.

23.2–24.1 The argument is somewhat compressed. Even if those who come after you (before the next fire or flood) speak of you, that is a relatively small amount of glory, since those who preceded you certainly did not know of you. Furthermore, the glory which you can achieve within these narrow temporal and geographical limits lasts, in cosmic terms, less than a single year. Hence human glory is truly evanescent. The argument that those who precede us cannot have heard of us is distinctly frigid; it is similar to the argument against the fear of death (Lucr. 3.831–42; cf. *Tusc.* 1.91) that just as the pain of previous generations does not affect us so too whatever happens after death will not affect us; cf. also the 'mirror' argument at Lucr. 3.972–7.

23.2 qui nec pauciores ... uiri: the dead are greater in number than the living; cf. *OLD* s.v. *plures* 2b. *meliores* presumably refers to the common Roman belief in continuous decline from a more glorious past, stated emphatically by C. at *Rep.* 5.1–2; cf. e.g. Lucr. 3.1026, Hor. *Carm.* 3.6.46–8.

24.1 praesertim cum: the connection is very abrupt, and the clause explains not the immediately preceding clause but the general argument about the brevity of glory. **nomen nostrum** the name shared by Africanus and Scipio.

24.2 re ipsa autem cum: so Macrob.; the MSS of the *Somnium* read *cum autem. re ipsa* is necessary for the contrast with *homines*; it is one more example of the difference between human perception and truth. **cum ad idem ... astra redierint:** the 'perfect year' in which all eight celestial spheres return to the same position they originally held is described by Pl. *Ti.* 39d (translated by C. *Tim.* 33), and it was variously calculated and explained by Hellenistic cosmologists. In *Hort.* fr. 35 M. the *magnus annus* is defined as 12,954 solar years; cf. also *Fin.* 2.102, *N.D.* 2.51–2 (with Pease *ad loc.*). **eandemque totius caeli discriptionem** 'the same disposition of the heavens'; Mueller's emendation of MS *descriptionem* is necessary; for the frequent confusion of the two, cf. 1.2.2n. **uere:** opposed to *populariter.* **uertens annus:** an astronomical year; cf. *OLD* s.v. *uerto* 1c. The phrase is particularly appropriate because C. is explicitly concerned with the revolutions of the spheres. **hominum saecla:** reference to generations is appropriate in the light of C.'s previous (23.1) discussion of the transmission of memory from fathers to sons. On the brevity of human life cf. also *Tusc.* 1.94.

24.3 The third (1.25.4, 2.17) mention in the extant text of *Rep.* of the eclipse at the death of Romulus (cf. *Hort.* fr. 54 M., also in connection with the *magnus annus*). Here the death of Romulus is made the marker of the beginning of a celestial year, a remarkable equation of Roman and cosmic affairs (cf. Ruch 166–8). The language is solemn: *templa* is used in its augural sense (cf. 15.2n.); *quandoque* for *quandocumque* is archaic (see next n.); the fullness of *eadem . . . eodem* and *signis omnibus . . . stellisque* is impressive; and the fut. imper. *habeto . . . scito* mark the importance of the moment. **quandoque** 'whenever'; a rare and archaic usage, found only here in C. Cf. H–S 608. **nondum uicesimam partem:** from the death of Romulus (716) to the dramatic date of the *Somnium* (149) is 567 years, hence on this calculation the *magnus annus* must be somewhat longer than 11,340 years; this matches the figure given in *Hort.* **conuersam:** astronomical language; for *conuerto* cf. 12.3n.

25.1 Quocirca: frequently used to introduce the conclusion of a philosophical argument (e.g. *Fin.* 1.68, 5.52; *N.D.* 2.30, 116), but also in the perorations of *Dom.* (144) and *Deiot.* (43). Both uses are appropriate here. **si ... desperaueris** 'if you should lose hope': the protasis of a fut. less vivid condition, of which the apodosis is the question *quanti ... est ista ... gloria?* The argument is somewhat abbreviated: if you think it impossible to attain heaven (and therefore aim at merely human glory), remember that human glory is not a worthwhile goal. This leaves only the alternative of virtuous action for its own sake, the conclusion reached in the next sentence. *despero* regularly takes a direct object; cf. *OLD* s.v. 1. **in ... uiris** 'in which great and outstanding men have all things'; dat. of possession. **quanti ... gloria:** both *tandem* ('may I ask'; cf. *OLD* s.v. 1) and *ista* are contemptuous.

25.2 Scipio fills out the advice given at 20.2, *haec caelestia semper spectato, illa humana contemnito.* The logic of the argument is obscured by Ziegler's punctuation; Powell is followed here with slight modification. The sentence is a fut. more vivid condition, of which the protasis has three verbs: *uoles* (fut.) governs the infinitives *spectare* and *contueri*, and is parallel to the two negative clauses *neque ... dederis* and *nec ... posueris* (both fut. pf.); the apodosis is *oportet ... ipsa uirtus trahat.* If the two negative clauses are taken as prohibitions with pf. subj., the structure is somewhat disconnected. **igitur:** initial *igitur* is common in archaic Latin, but rare in C.: other than in letters to Atticus and Tiro, it is apparently used only, as here, to introduce the conclusion of an argument; cf. Madvig on *Fin.* 1.61. **spectare ... contueri:** *spectare* echoes 20.2; *contueri* involves philosophical contemplation as much as observation; cf. 15.3n. Cf. *Tusc.* 1.82 *uideo te alte spectare et uelle in caelum migrare.* **hanc sedem et aeternam domum** so also 29.1. Both *hanc* and *aeternam* are emphatic, and draw attention to the contrast with 20.2 *sedem ... hominum ac domum.* **sermonibus uulgi ... praemiis humanis:** Africanus echoes and makes more emphatic the language of 20.2 *celebritatem sermonis hominum* and *gloriam.* **illecebris** 'allurements': the application to virtue of a word almost invariably attached to vice (in the other 13 exx. of its use by C.) is emphatic and extraordinary. For Africanus (and in the true perspective of eternity) it is virtue that is attractive and seductive. C. clearly looks back to the preface of *Rep.*, where *uirtus* is said (1.1.5) to overcome *omnia blandimenta uoluptatis otique.* It is possible that C. also has in mind the choice of Hercules (Xen. *Mem.* 2.1.21–33) between Virtue and Pleasure; but in this case there is (or ought to be) no contest. **ipsa uirtus trahat ad uerum decus:** *uirtus* appears only here in the *Somnium* proper, although the true rewards of *diuina uirtus* served as the introduction to Scipio's narrative of his dream (quoted above, Introduction n.39). C. here brings to its conclusion one of the major themes of *Rep.*, the relationship of *uirtus* and glory. In the preface, *uirtus* consists in political action, and human glory seems to have some (if not paramount) worth. At 3.40, Laelius argued that the intrinsic rewards of virtue are its own recompense. Here it is made clear that the active life of true virtue is right action in conformity with divine and eternal standards; its rewards are not earthly glory, but *uerum decus*. The development of the concept of *uirtus* in *Rep.* is parallel to (and necessarily involved in) the development of the concepts of *res publica* and *ius*: from the Preface, to Laelius' speech in book 3, to the *Somnium* all are extended from merely human concepts and creations to transcendent and eternal truths.

25.3 ipsi uideant: C. uses the pf. more often than the pres. in this phrase; cf. e.g. *De orat.* 1.246, *Tusc.* 5.34, 120. **sed loquentur tamen:** the sentence must include both praise and blame: people will speak of you (for good or ill) whatever you do; but their comments are (*sub specie aeternitatis*) irrelevant. **sermo ... exstinguitur:** Africanus summarizes the geographical and temporal limitations on human reputation expounded in 21–4. **umquam de ullo:** emphatic. **obruitur ... exstinguitur:** the word order of the two clauses is reversed: verb, gen., noun, noun, gen., verb.

26.1 bene meritis: cf. 2.4.2, *bene meritis de rebus communibus.* **limes:** a poetic synonym for *uia*, as at 16.1, and found only here in C.; cf. *OLD.* s.v. 3. **uestigiis:** dat.; cf. *OLD* s.v. 5c. C. may have in mind Lucr. 5.55 *cuius ego ingressus uestigia.* **decori uestro:** cf. 25.2. C. extends the traditional Roman idea that one should imitate one's ancestors' (earthly) accomplishments to encompass the divine glory that is the true goal. **praemio:** cf. 25.2 *praemiis humanis.*

26.2–28.2 Just as Scipio's reference to the path to heaven echoes the opening part of the eschatology of the *Somnium*, so Africanus' reply turns back to his own initial statement that the home of the soul is in the stars and offers a detailed proof of the immortality of the soul, in three parts. He first demonstrates (26.2) that the true identity of a human is the mind or soul, not the body; he then argues (26.3) from the analogy with the cosmos that the soul is divine; and finally (27–8) he proves, starting from the mention of motion in 26.3, that the soul is immortal. The last proof is a very close translation of Pl. *Phdr.* 245c5–246a2.

26.2 tu uero enitere: imperative. Africanus repeats Scipio's *enitar*; *uero* adds emphasis. **sic habeto:** cf. 13.1n. **non esse te mortalem ... is est quisque:** C.'s emphatic statement of the distinction between mortal body and immortal soul, and of the identification of the person with the soul rather than the body (or the combined soul and body) is Platonic (cf. esp. *Phd.* 115c–e, *Lg.* 12.959ab), and was further elaborated in the Platonic tradition. C. here is almost certainly drawing on [Pl.] *Alc. I* 128e–133c, and perhaps also on [Pl.] *Ax.* 365e. The change from the Platonic ψυχή to *mens* may also reflect the later Platonic tradition. For discussion of C.'s sources, cf. Boyancé (1936) 121–4, (1970) 268 and Ferrary (1974) 757–9. For the identification of the person with the soul, cf. also *Tusc.* 1.52. **mens cuiusque is est quisque:** the resumptive use of *is* without any intervening phrase is archaic, and rare in classical Latin; cf. H–S 187, *OLD* s.v. B6b. The gender of *is* is assimilated to that of *quisque.* **digito demonstrari:** the phrase refers not only to the material nature of the body, but to the concern for earthly fame: cf. e.g. Hor. *Carm.* 4.3.22 *quod monstror digito praetereuntium*; Persius 1.28 *at pulchrum est digito monstrari et dicier 'hic est'.*

26.3 The divinity of the soul is implicit in Africanus' earlier statements: if souls come from (and return to) the stars, and the stars are a part of the divine outer sphere of the cosmos, then the soul itself must be divine. The further development from 'the soul is divine' to 'the soul is (a) god' is justified by the analogical argument given here: if the soul rules the body in the same way that *ille princeps deus* rules the universe, then the soul is the god in the human machine (cf. the similar argument at *Tusc.* 1.56–70). There is some ambiguity in the cosmic identity of the supreme god, as at 17.2–3; on balance, it seems more likely that C. means the sun rather than the outer sphere. In the parallel passage at *Tusc.* 1.65, C. is more circumspect in his language: *animus ... ut ego dico, diuinus est, ut Euripides dicere audet, deus* (fr. 1018 N²). Both forms of expression have Platonic antecedents, at *Ti.* 41a (θεῖον) and *Lg.* 10.899b (θεούς); C. refers to the ideas of divinity in both dialogues at *N.D.* 1.30. **siquidem:** for the causal use cf. 1.19.4n. **qui uiget ... qui prouidet:** cf. *Tusc.* 1.65 *quae autem diuina? uigere, sapere, inuenire, meminisse*; 1.66 (quoting the lost *Consolatio*) *ita, quidquid est illud quod sentit, quod sapit, quod uiuit, quod uiget, caeleste et diuinum ob eamque rem aeternum sit necesse est.* **regit et moderatur:** analogous to the sun at 17.3, *dux et princeps et moderator.* **mouet ... mouet:** the repeated verb provides the transition to C.'s final argument for the immortality of the soul, as something which is the source of its own motion and is therefore eternal.

27–8 C.'s translation of *Phdr.* 245c5–246a2 is extremely precise and accurate. For the most part, his equivalents for Plato's terminology are consistent: ἀθάνατος is always *aeternus*; ἀρχή is *principium*; κινεῖν is *mouere*; γίγνεσθαι is generally translated by *oriri* or *nasci*. In a few places (see commentary) he is unable to maintain this consistency, or to match Plato's verbal twists; and he is regularly compelled to substitute relative clauses for Plato's frequent neuter participles. C. clearly thought highly of his own translation, as he quotes it from *Rep.* at *Tusc.* 1.53–4 (a condensed version also at *Sen.* 78). The versions in *Tusc.* and in the *Somnium* differ slightly, and Ziegler argued that the one in *Tusc.* (which agrees in several details with Macrobius' quotations) was C.'s final revision, while the text in the *Somnium* itself reflects an earlier draft. The evidence is neither sufficient nor consistent enough to permit such a conclusion, and readings from both versions are printed both by Ziegler and here.

27.1 semper mouetur: C. agrees with the medieval MSS of Plato, which read ἀεικίνητον; P. Oxy. 1017 gives the much better reading αὐτοκίνητον, 'self-moved'. **quod autem ... agitatur aliunde:** τὸ δ' ἄλλο κινοῦν καὶ ὑπ' ἄλλου κινούμενον. For the parallelism between active and passive participles in Plato, C. substitutes parallel relative clauses. **quando** 'when' is rare in classical prose; cf. *OLD* s.v. 2. **finem ... finem:** C. substitutes chiasmus for Plato's parallel word order: παῦλαν ἔχον κινήσεως, παῦλαν ἔχει ζωῆς.

27.2 quod se ipsum mouet: the reading of *Tusc.* and Macrobius, preferable to *sese mouet* in most MSS as a translation of τὸ αὑτὸ κινοῦν. **hic fons, hoc principium est mouendi:** τοῦτο πηγὴ καὶ ἀρχὴ κινήσεως. As with the repeated relative in the previous sentence, C. uses anaphora absent in Plato.

27.3 nam ex principio ... nasci potest: ἐξ ἀρχῆς γὰρ ἀνάγκη πᾶν τὸ γιγνόμενον γίγνεσθαι, αὐτὴν δὲ μηδ' ἐξ ἑνός. C.'s clauses are more balanced than Plato's, and for the repeated use of γίγνομαι he substitutes *oriuntur ... nasci.* **nec enim ... aliunde:** εἰ γὰρ ἔκ του ἀρχὴ γίγνοιτο, οὐκ ἂν ἀρχὴ (C.'s text; ἔτι ἀρχὴ Buttmann) γίγνοιτο. C. does not try to reproduce the concision and word-play of Plato's language; hence the repeated γίγνοιτο becomes *esset* ... *gigneretur*.

27.4 oritur ... occidit: as C. has used *origo* and *oriuntur* to translate ἀγένητον and γίγνεσθαι, he uses *oritur* in translating ἀγένητον here; consequently, he substitutes *occidit* (and the metaphor of rising and setting) for Plato's ἀδιάφθορον (and the vocabulary of creation and destruction).

27.5 motus: genitive. **uel concidat ... necesse est:** C. uses two alliterative verbs (*concidat* ... *consistat*) to translate Plato's alliterative participle and infinitive, συμπεσοῦσαν στῆναι, also employing a chiastic order absent in the Greek. C.'s *natura* translates the MS γένεσιν rather than Philoponus' γῆν εἰς ἓν printed by Burnet. **impulsa moueatur:** κινηθέντα γενήσεται: the various meanings of γίγνομαι again cause a variation in C.'s terminology.

28.1 quod a se ipso moueatur: the reading of the MSS of the *Somnium*, printed here, is closer to the Greek τοῦ ὑφ' ἑαυτοῦ κινουμένου than *se ipsum moueat* in *Tusc.* printed by Ziegler. **esse tributam:** sc. *a deo*. There is no equivalent in Plato, who merely refers to ψυχῆς οὐσίαν.

28.2 inanimum ... animal: ἄψυχον ... ἔμψυχον. **natura ... atque uis:** φύσεως; for the same phrase, cf. *Tusc.* 1.66. **neque nata ... et aeterna:** ἀγένητόν τε καὶ ἀθάνατον. C. consistently translates ἀθάνατος by *aeternus*, and hence loses Plato's assonance. Similarly, *orior* will not do here (as before) for -γεν-, and *neque nata* is somewhat weaker than the Greek. **certe:** ἐξ ἀνάγκης.

29 Having proved that the soul is immortal and divine, Africanus returns in his conclusion to summarize its proper uses in public service. Here alone C. gives some indication that an alternative fate awaits those who do not act properly in their lives; but unlike Plato in the *Republic*, C. is not interested in the judgment of souls, but only in the rewards that await good ones.

29.1 in optimis rebus: specified by what follows, which serves as the conclusion not only to the dream, but to *Rep.* as a whole. **agitatus et exercitatus:** *exercitatus* picks up *exerce* in the previous sentence; *agitatus* suggests that the active motion of the soul on earth – motion being the evidence for immortality and divinity – will make it move to the firmament more rapidly after death. **hanc sedem et**

domum suam: cf. 25.2n. **idque ocius ... abstrahet:** the idea of acting in life so as to prepare for a happy posthumous existence is largely drawn from the *Phaedo*; cf. esp. 66b–67d. In a fragment of book 2 (Nonius 373.30 M.; assigned to 3.11 by Ziegler following Mai, but cf. Heck 119–20) the same goal is ascribed to justice: *iustitia foras spectat et proiecta tota est atque eminet*. Cf. also *Tusc.* 1.75, *Hort.* fr. 97 M. **contemplans:** cf. 16.2n.

29.2 qui se ... praebuerunt: cf. *Phd.* 81bc. The emphatic repetition of *uoluptatibus* looks back to the attack on Epicurean hedonism in the preface to book 1; in keeping with the enlarged context of the *Somnium*, however, the penalties for enslavement to pleasure are not merely political disaster, but the loss of eternal bliss. **deorum ... iura uiolauerunt:** C.'s final allusion to the links between divine and human justice. **corporibus elapsi ... reuertuntur:** cf. *Phd.* 81d, *Phdr.* 248e (where the period of exile is 10,000 years). **circum terram ipsam:** beneath the orbit of the moon; cf. 17.5. **ego somno solutus sum:** cf. 10.2 *artior ... somnus complexus est*. Although the *Somnium* was the conclusion of *Rep.*, there was probably at least one further paragraph in which the participants separated; cf. Pl. *R.* 10.621b–d, *De orat.* 3.228–30.

WORKS CITED BY SHORT TITLE

Editions of De re publica

The following editions (and commentaries and translations) are cited by the editor's name alone; for a fuller list of editions in languages other than English, cf. Schmidt (1973) 266–71.

Bréguet, E. (1980). *Cicéron, la république.* Paris (text, translation, and notes).

Büchner, K. (1984). *M. Tullius Cicero, de re publica.* Heidelberg (commentary).

Keyes, C. W. (1928). *Cicero: de re publica and de legibus.* London and New York (text and translation).

Krarup, P. (1967). *M. Tulli Ciceronis de re publica librorum sex quae supersunt.* Florence (text).

Mai, A. (1822). *M. Tulli Ciceronis de re publica quae supersunt.* Rome and Stuttgart (text and commentary).

Moser, G. H. (1826). *M. Tulli Ciceronis de re publica quae supersunt.* Frankfurt (text and commentary).

Powell, J. G. F. (1991). *Cicero: on friendship and the dream of Scipio.* Warminster (text, translation, and commentary).

Poyser, G. H. (1948). *Selections from Cicero, de re publica.* Cambridge (excerpts and commentary).

Ronconi, A. (1966). *Cicerone: somnium Scipionis.* 2nd edn Florence (text and commentary).

Sabine, G. H. and Smith, S. B. (1929). *Marcus Tullius Cicero: on the commonwealth.* Columbus (translation).

Ziegler, C. (1969). *M. Tullius Cicero: de re publica.* 7th edn Leipzig (text).

Books and articles

Standard commentaries on other texts are cited by the name of the commentator (e.g. 'Pease on *N.D.* 1.44') and are omitted from this list.

Albrecht, M. von. (1989). *Masters of Roman prose*, trans. Neil Adkin. Leeds.

Alexander, M. C. (1990). *Trials in the late Roman Republic*. Toronto.

André, J.-M. (1966). *L'Otium dans la vie morale et intellectuelle romaine*. Paris.

Astin, A. E. (1967). *Scipio Aemilianus*. Oxford.

(1978). *Cato the Censor*. Oxford.

Badian, E. (1956). 'Q. Mucius Scaevola and the province of Asia', *Athenaeum* 34: 104–23.

(1964). *Studies in Greek and Roman history*. Oxford.

(1971). 'Three fragments', in *Pro munere grates: studies presented to H. L. Gonin* 1–6. Pretoria.

(1972). 'Tiberius Gracchus and the beginning of the Roman revolution', *ANRW* I 1: 668–732.

Barker-Benfield, B. C. (1983). 'Macrobius', in (ed.) L. D. Reynolds, *Texts and transmission* 222–35. Oxford.

Barnes, J. (1989). 'Antiochus of Ascalon', in (edd.) J. Barnes and M. Griffin, *Philosophia togata* 51–96. Oxford.

Bauman, R. (1983). *Lawyers in Roman republican politics*. Munich.

Behr, C. A. (1974). 'A new fragment of Cicero's *De republica*', *A.J.Ph.* 95: 141–9.

Berger, A. (1953). *Encyclopedic dictionary of Roman law*. Philadelphia.

Bernstein, A. (1978). *Tiberius Sempronius Gracchus*. Ithaca.

Blänsdorf, J. (1961). 'Cicero, de re publica I 54–55', *R.C.C.M.* 3: 167–76.

Boyancé, P. (1936). *Etudes sur le Songe de Scipion*. Limoges.

(1970). *Etudes sur l'humanisme cicéronien*. Brussels.

Bréguet, E. (1964). 'Les archaïsmes dans le *De re publica* de Cicéron', in *Hommages à Jean Bayet* (Collection Latomus 70) 122–31. Brussels.

Büchner, K. (1962). *Studien zur römischen Literatur II: Cicero*. Wiesbaden.

Burkert, W. L. (1965). 'Cicero als Platoniker und Skeptiker', *Gymnasium* 72: 175–200.

(1972). *Lore and science in ancient Pythagoreanism*, transl. Edwin L. Minar, Jr. Cambridge, Mass.

Cancelli, F. (1972). '"Iuris consensu" nella definizione ciceroniana di "res publica"', *R.C.C.M.* 14: 247–67.

Clark, A. C. (1918). *The descent of manuscripts*. Oxford.

Classen, J. (1962). 'Romulus in der römischen Republik', *Philologus* 106: 174–203.

Cole, T. (1964). 'The sources and composition of Polybius VI', *Historia* 13: 440–86.

(1990). *Democritus and the sources of Greek anthropology.* 2nd edn Atlanta.

Coleman, R. (1964). 'The dream of Cicero', *P.C.Ph.S.* 190: 1–14.

Cornell, T. (1986). 'The value of the literary tradition concerning archaic Rome', in (ed.) K. Raaflaub, *Social struggles in archaic Rome.* 52–76. Berkeley and Los Angeles.

Cumont, F. (1935). 'Les noms des planètes et l'astrolatrie chez les grecs', *A.C.* 4: 5–43.

Drexler, H. (1957, 1958). 'Res publica', *Maia* 9: 247–81, 10: 3–37.

Earl, D. C. (1963). *Tiberius Gracchus: a study in politics.* Brussels.

(1967). *The moral and political tradition of Rome.* Ithaca.

Eder, W. (1990). 'Der Bürger und sein Staat – der Staat und seine Bürger', in (ed.) W. Eder, *Staat und Staatlichkeit in der frühen römischen Republik* 12–32. Stuttgart.

Evrard-Gillis, J. (1977). 'Historicité et composition littéraire dans le *Somnium Scipionis*: quelques observations', *Ancient Society* 8: 217–22.

Fantham, E. (1972). *Comparative studies in republican Latin imagery.* Toronto.

(1973). '*Aequabilitas* in Cicero's political theory, and the Greek tradition of proportional justice', *C.Q.* 23: 285–90.

(1981). 'The synchronistic chapter of Gellius (*NA* 17.21) and some aspects of Roman chronology and cultural history between 60 and 50 B.C.', *L.C.M.* 6.1: 7–17.

Ferrary, J.-L. (1974). 'Le discours de Laelius dans le troisième livre du *de re publica* de Cicéron', *M.E.F.R.A.* 86: 745–71.

(1977). 'Le discours de Philus (Cicéron, *de re publica*, III, 8–31) et la philosophie de Carnéade', *R.E.L.* 55: 128–56.

(1984). 'L'Archéologie du *de re publica* (2, 2, 4–37, 63): Cicéron entre Polybe et Platon', *J.R.S.* 74: 87–98.

Frede, D. (1989). 'Constitution and citizenship: Peripatetic influence on Cicero's political conceptions in the *De re publica*', in (ed.) W. W. Fortenbaugh and P. Steinmetz, *Cicero's knowledge of the Peripatos* (Rutgers University Studies in Classical Humanities 4) 77–100. New Brunswick.

Frier, B. W. (1979). *Libri annales pontificum maximorum: the origins of the annalistic tradition* (Papers and Monographs of the American Academy in Rome 27). Rome.

Fritz, K. von. (1954). The theory of the mixed constitution in antiquity. New York.

Fuhrmann, M. (1960). 'Cum dignitate otium', *Gymnasium* 67: 481–500.

Gabba, E. (1967). 'Considerazioni sulla tradizione letteraria sulle origini della Repubblica', in *Les origines de la république romaine* (Entretiens sur l'antiquité classique 13) 133–69. Vandoeuvres.

(1991). *Dionysius and the history of archaic Rome.* Berkeley and Los Angeles.

Gelzer, M. (1969). *Cicero: ein biographischer Versuch.* Wiesbaden.

Gigon, O. (1977). *Die antike Philosophie als Maßstab und Realität.* Zurich.

Girardet, K. (1977). 'Ciceros Urteil über die Enstehung des Tribunates als Institution der römischen Verfassung', in *Bonner Festgabe J. Straub* (Bonn 1977) 179–200.

(1983). *Die Ordnung der Welt.* Wiesbaden.

Gottschalk, H. B. (1980). *Heraclides of Pontus.* Oxford.

Greenidge, A. and Clay, A. (1960). *Sources for Roman history 133–70 B.C.* 2nd edn revised by E. W. Gray. Oxford.

Grilli, A. (1958). 'Cicero de rep. 2.53 (= Nonio 526, 10 L.)', *Parola del passato* 13: 131–4.

Gruen, E. (1990). *Studies in Greek culture and Roman policy.* Leiden.

(1992). *Culture and national identity in Republican Rome.* Ithaca.

Habinek, T. (1985). *The colometry of Latin prose.* Berkeley and Los Angeles.

Hagendahl, H. (1967). *Augustine and the Latin classics.* Göteborg.

Harder, R. (1960). *Kleine Schriften,* ed. W. Marg. Munich.

Heck, E. (1966). *Die Bezeugung von Ciceros Schrift De re publica.* Hildesheim.

Heinze, R. (1960). *Vom Geist des Römertums.* 3rd edn Darmstadt.

Hirzel, R. (1895). *Der Dialog.* 2 vols. Leipzig.

Hommel, H. (1955a). 'Cicero und der Peripatos', *Gymnasium* 62: 319–34.

(1955b). 'Zum Text von Cicero, De re publica', *Gymnasium* 62: 353–9.

How, W. W. (1930). 'Cicero's ideal in his *De re publica*', *J.R.S.* 20: 24–42.

Jocelyn, H. D. (1989). 'Romulus and the *di genitales* (Ennius, *Annales* 110–111 Skutsch)', in (ed.) J. Diggle, J. B. Hall, and H. D. Jocelyn, *Studies in Latin literature and its tradition in honour of C. O. Brink* 39–65. Cambridge.

Kohns, H. (1974).'Consensus iuris – communio utilitatis', *Gymnasium* 81: 485–98.

(1976). 'Prima causa coeundi', *Gymnasium* 83: 209–14.

(1977). 'Libertas populi und libertas ciuium in Ciceros Schrift De re publica', in *Bonner Festgabe J. Straub* 201–11. Bonn.

Krarup, P. (1956). *Rector rei publicae*. Copenhagen. [In Danish; cited from English summary pp. 175–206]

(1963). 'The Corrector of the codex of Cicero's *De re publica* and the quotations in Nonius', *C. & M.* 24: 76–9.

(1973). 'Scipio Aemilianus as a defender of kingship', *Classica et mediaevalia Francisco Blatt septuagenario dedicata* 209–23. Copenhagen.

Kretschmar, M. (1938). *Otium, studia litterarum, Philosophie, und* βίος θεωρητικός *im Leben und Denken Ciceros*. Leipzig.

Kroymann, J. (1958). 'Die Stellung des Königtums im I. Buch von Ciceros Staat', *H.S.C.P.* 63: 309–32.

Laughton, E. (1964). *The participle in Cicero*. Oxford.

Laurand, L. (1936–8). *Etudes sur le style des discours de Cicéron*. 4th edn Paris.

Lebreton, J. (1965). *Etudes sur la langue et la grammaire de Cicéron*. Hildesheim; rpt. of Paris 1901.

Lepore, E. (1954). *Il princeps ciceroniano e gli ideali politici della tarda reppublica*. Naples.

Linderski, J. (1986). 'The augural law', *ANRW* II 16.3: 2146–2312.

Löfstedt, E. (1956). *Syntactica*. 2 vols. 2nd edn Lund.

Long, A. A. (1974). *Hellenistic philosophy*. New York.

Maltby, R. (1991). *A lexicon of ancient Latin etymologies*. Leeds.

Meister, R. (1939). 'Der Staatslenker in Ciceros De re publica', *W.S.* 57: 57–112.

(1940). 'Zur Rekonstruktion und Textgestaltung von Ciceros De re publica I', *W.S.* 58: 95–112.

Mitchell, R. (1990). *Patricians and plebeians*. Ithaca and London.

Mitchell, T. (1991). *Cicero: the senior statesman*. New Haven and London.

Momigliano, A. D. (1966). *Terzo contributo alla storia degli studi classici e del mondo antico*. Rome.

(1969). *Quarto contributo alla storia degli studi classici e del mondo antico*. Rome.

Mommsen. T. (1887). *Römisches Staatsrecht*. 3rd edn Leipzig.

Montanari Caldini, R. (1984). '*Cum in Africam uenissem hoc Manilio consule* (Cic., Rep. 6, 9)', *Prometheus* 10: 224–40.

Müller, H. (1964). *Ciceros Prosabersetzungen*. Marburg.

Müller, R. (1968). 'Bíos θεωρητικός bei Antiochos von Askalon und Cicero', *Helikon* 8: 222–37.

Nicholls, J. J. (1964). 'Cicero *de re publica* 2.39–40 and the centuriate assembly', *C.P.* 59: 102–5.

Nicolet, C. (1964). 'Le *de republica* (VI, 12) et la dictature de Scipion', *R.E.L.* 42: 212–30.

Otto, A. (1890). *Die Sprichwörter und sprichwörtlichen Redensarten der Römer*. Leipzig.

Perelli, L. (1971). 'L'Elogio della vita filosofica in *de re publica*, I, 26–29', *Bollettino di studi latini* 7: 389–401.

(1972). '*Natura* e *ratio* nel II libro del *de re publica* ciceroniano', *R.F.I.C.* 100: 295–311.

(1977). *Il de republica e il pensiero politico di Cicerone*. Turin.

(1979).'Note sul tribunato della plebe nella riflessione ciceroniana', *Quaderni di storia* 5: 285–303.

Pfligersdorffer, G. (1969). *Politik und Muße*. Munich.

Platner, S. and Ashby, T. (1929). *A topographical dictionary of ancient Rome*. London.

Pohlenz, M. (1931). 'Cicero De re publica als Kunstwerk', *Festschrift R. Reitzenstein* 70–105. Leipzig and Berlin (rpt. *Kleine Schriften* (Hildesheim 1965) 374–409).

Poncelet, R. (1947). 'Cicéron traducteur de Platon', *R.E.L.* 25: 178–96.

Pöschl, V. (1936). *Römischer Staat und griechisches Staatsdenken bei Cicero*. Berlin.

Raaflaub, K. (1986). 'From protection and defence to offense and participation: stages in the conflict of the orders', in (ed.) K. Raaflaub, *Social struggles in archaic Rome* 198–243. Berkeley and Los Angeles.

Rawson, E. (1969). *The Spartan tradition in European thought*. Oxford.

(1975). *Cicero: a portrait*. London.

(1991). *Roman culture and society*. Oxford.

Reitzenstein, R. (1924). 'Zu Cicero De re publica', *Hermes* 59: 357–62.

Richard, J.-C. (1986). 'Patricians and plebeians: the origin of a social dichotomy', in (ed.) K. Raaflaub, *Social struggles in archaic Rome* 105–29. Berkeley and Los Angeles.

Richardson, Jr., L. (1992). *A new topographical dictionary of ancient Rome.* Baltimore.

Riginos, A. S. (1976). *Platonica: the anecdotes concerning the life and writings of Plato* (Columbia Studies in the Classical Tradition 3). Leiden.

Rotondi, G. (1966). *Leges publicae populi romani.* Hildesheim.

Ruch, M. (1948). 'La composition du *de republica*', *R.E.L.* 26: 157–71.

Schmidt, P. L. (1969). *Die Abfassungszeit von Ciceros Schrift über die Gesetze.* Rome.

(1973). 'Cicero "De re publica": Die Forschung der letzten fünf Dezennien', *ANRW* I 4: 262–333.

Schulz, F. (1946). *A history of Roman legal science.* Oxford.

Schütrumpf, E. (1988). 'Platonic elements in the structure of Cicero *De oratore* book 1', *Rhetorica* 6: 237–58.

Scullard, H. H. (1981). *Festivals and ceremonies of the Roman republic.* London.

Sharples, R. W. (1986). 'Cicero's *Republic* and Greek political theory', *Polis* 5.2: 30–50.

Skutsch, O. (1959). 'Kleinigkeiten zu Ciceros "Staat"', *Philologus* 103: 140–4.

(1969). 'Cic. rep. 1,71', *Gymnasium* 76: 357.

Solmsen, F. (1933). 'Die Theorie der Staatsformen bei Cicero de re publ. I', *Philologus* 88: 326–41 (rpt. *Kleine Schriften* (Hildesheim 1968) 380–95.

Staveley, E. S. (1962). 'Cicero and the comitia centuriata', *Historia* 11: 299–314.

Steinmetz, F. (1969). 'Staatengründung – aus Schwäche oder natürlichem Geselligkeitsdrang?', *Palingenesia* 4: 181–99.

Stockton, D. (1979). *The Gracchi.* Oxford.

Suerbaum W. (1977). *Vom antiken zum frühmittelalterlichen Staatsbegriff.* 3rd edn Münster.

(1978). 'Studienbibliographie zu Ciceros De re publica', *Gymnasium* 85: 59–88.

Sumner, G. V. (1960). 'Cicero on the *comitia centuriata: de re publica*, II, 22, 39–40', *A.J.P.* 81: 136–56.

(1964). 'Cicero and the *comitia centuriata*', *Historia* 13: 125–8.

(1973). *The orators in Cicero's* Brutus*: prosopography and chronology.* Toronto.

Taeger, F. (1922). *Die Archaeologie des Polybios*. Stuttgart.

Taylor, L. R. (1961). 'The corrector of the codex of Cicero's *de republica*', *A.J.P.* 82: 337–45.

Ungern-Sternberg, J. von, (1986). 'The formation of the "annalistic tradition": the example of the Decemvirate', in (ed.) K. Raaflaub, *Social struggles in archaic Rome* 77–104. Berkeley and Los Angeles.

Vlastos, G. (1975). *Plato's universe*. Seattle.

Walbank, F. (1972). *Polybius*. Berkeley and Los Angeles.

Watson, A. (1993). *International law in archaic Rome: war and religion*. Baltimore.

Werner, R. (1973). 'Über Herkunft und Bedeutung von Ciceros Staatsdefinition', *Chiron* 3: 163–78.

Wieacker, F. (1967). 'Die XII Tafeln in ihrem Jahrhundert', in *Les origines de la république romaine* (Entretiens sur l'antiquité classique 13) 291–358. Vandoeuvres.

Wilkinson, L. P. (1963). *Golden Latin artistry*. Cambridge.

Wirszubski, C. (1950). *Libertas as a political idea at Rome during the late republic and early principate*. Cambridge.

(1954). 'Cicero's *cum dignitate otium*: a reconsideration', *J.R.S.* 44: 1–13.

Wiseman, T. P. (1971). *New men in the Roman senate 139 B.C.–14 A.D.* Oxford.

(1979). *Clio's cosmetics*. Leicester.

(1987). *Roman studies*. Liverpool.

Wissowa, G. (1912). *Religion und Kultus der Römer*. 2nd edn Munich.

Wood, N. (1988). *Cicero's social and political thought*. Berkeley and Los Angeles.

Woodcock E. C. (1960). *A new Latin syntax*. Cambridge, Mass.

Zetzel, J. E. G. (1972). 'Cicero and the Scipionic circle', *H.S.C.P.* 76: 173–9.

(1989). '*Romane memento*: justice and judgment in *Aeneid* 6', *T.A.P.A.* 119: 263–84.

(1994). 'Looking backward: past and present in the late Roman Republic'. *Pegasus: The Journal of the Exeter University Classics Society* 37: 20–32.

Zoll, G. (1962). *Cicero Platonis aemulus*. Zurich.

INDEXES

(References are to lemmata in the Commentary; the names of the speakers in the dialogue are not included.)

1 Latin words

2 General

Printed in the United Kingdom
by Lightning Source UK Ltd.
92890